Inflation-indexed Securities

Wiley Finance Series

Inflation-Indexed Securities: Bonds, Swaps and Other Derivatives, 2nd Edition
Mark Deacon, Andrew Derry and Dariush Mirfendereski
European Fixed Income Markets: Money, Bond and Interest Rates
Jonathan Batten, Thomas Fetherston and Peter Szilagyi (Editors)
Global Securitisation and CDOs
John Deacon
Applied Quantitative Methods for Trading and Investment
Christian L. Dunis, Jason Laws and Patrick Naïm (Editors)
Country Risk Assessment: A Guide to Global Investment Strategy
Michel Henry Bouchet, Ephraim Clark and Bertrand Groslambert
Credit Derivatives Pricing Models: Models, Pricing and Implementation
Philipp J. Schönbucher
Hedge Funds: A Resource for Investors
Simone Borla
A Foreign Exchange Primer
Shani Shamah
The Simple Rules: Revisiting the Art of Financial Risk Management
Erik Banks
Option Theory
Peter James
Risk-adjusted Lending Conditions
Werner Rosenberger
Measuring Market Risk
Kevin Dowd
An Introduction to Market Risk Management
Kevin Dowd
Behavioural Finance
James Montier
Asset Management: Equities Demystified
Shanta Acharya
An Introduction to Capital Markets: Products, Strategies, Participants
Andrew M. Chisholm
Hedge Funds: Myths and Limits
François-Serge Lhabitant
The Manager's Concise Guide to Risk
Jihad S. Nader
Securities Operations: A Guide to Trade and Position Management
Michael Simmons
Modeling, Measuring and Hedging Operational Risk
Marcelo Cruz
Monte Carlo Methods in Finance
Peter Jäckel
Building and Using Dynamic Interest Rate Models
Ken Kortanek and Vladimir Medvedev
Structured Equity Derivatives: The Definitive Guide to Exotic Options and Structured Notes
Harry Kat
Advanced Modelling in Finance Using Excel and VBA
Mary Jackson and Mike Staunton
Operational Risk: Measurement and Modelling
Jack King
Interest Rate Modelling
Jessica James and Nick Webber

Inflation-indexed Securities

Bonds, Swaps and Other Derivatives
Second Edition

Mark Deacon

Andrew Derry

and

Dariush Mirfendereski

John Wiley & Sons, Ltd

Published 2004 John Wiley & Sons Ltd, The Atrium, Southern Gate, Chichester,
West Sussex PO19 8SQ, England

Telephone (+44) 1243 779777

Email (for orders and customer service enquiries): cs-books@wiley.co.uk
Visit our Home Page on www.wileyeurope.com or www.wiley.com

Reprinted July 2004

Other Wiley Editorial Offices

John Wiley & Sons Inc., 111 River Street, Hoboken, NJ 07030, USA

Jossey-Bass, 989 Market Street, San Francisco, CA 94103-1741, USA

Wiley-VCH Verlag GmbH, Boschstr. 12, D-69469 Weinheim, Germany

John Wiley & Sons Australia Ltd, 33 Park Road, Milton, Queensland 4064, Australia

John Wiley & Sons (Asia) Pte Ltd, 2 Clementi Loop #02-01, Jin Xing Distripark, Singapore 129809

John Wiley & Sons Canada Ltd, 22 Worcester Road, Etobicoke, Ontario, Canada M9W 1L1

Wiley also publishes its books in a variety of electronic formats. Some content that appears in print may not be available in electronic books.

Library of Congress Cataloging-in-Publication Data

Deacon, Mark.
Inflation-indexed securities : bonds, swaps and other derivatives /
Mark Deacon, Andrew Derry, and Dariush Mirfendereski. — 2nd ed.
p. cm.—(Wiley finance series)
Previously published: London: Prentice Hall Europe, 1998.
Includes bibliographical references and index.
ISBN 0-470-86812-0 (cloth : alk. paper)
1. Bonds. 2. Government securities. 3. Bond market. 4. Indexation (Economics) 5. Inflation (Finance) I. Derry, Andrew. II. Mirfendereski, Dariush. III. Title. IV. Series.
HG4651.D4 2004
332.63′2044—dc22 2003021827

British Library Cataloguing in Publication Data

A catalogue record for this book is available from the British Library

ISBN 0-470-86812-0

Typeset in 10/12pt Times by Originator, Gt Yarmouth, Norfolk
Printed and bound in Great Britain by Antony Rowe Ltd, Chippenham, Wiltshire
This book is printed on acid-free paper responsibly manufactured from sustainable forestry in which at least two trees are planted for each one used for paper production.

Contents

Exhibits

Figures

Tables

About the Authors

Mark Deacon has worked as a quantitative analyst at the UK Debt Management Office (DMO) in London since April 1998, having formerly worked at the Bank of England, in both the Quantitative Financial Economics Group and the Gilt-Edged & Money Markets Division.

The research carried out by Andrew Derry and Mark on the use of indexed and nominal bond prices to derive estimates of inflation expectations formed the basis of the 1994 book *Estimating and Interpreting the Yield Curve* (which they co-authored with three others). Mark and Andrew worked together again on the first edition of *Inflation-indexed Securities*, which was published in 1998. In addition, Mark wrote a chapter on the UK index-linked gilt market in the *Handbook of Inflation Indexed Bonds* and a chapter on government bond markets that appears in *Investment Banking: Theory and Practice*.

He was instrumental in organising the Bank of England's 1995 conference aimed at developing the UK indexed bond market, and in 2001 led the DMO's consultation exercise on index-linked gilt redesign. He has given numerous international lectures and presentations on the development of global indexed bond markets.

Mark has an MSc and a BSc in Mathematics from Warwick University and has also studied at the London School of Economics. In 1998 he was awarded Chartered Mathematician status and in 2001 joined the Editorial Board of the *Journal of Bond Trading and Management*.

Andrew Derry works for JWM Partners, a hedge fund manager specialising in "relative value" fixed-income investment strategies. He is based in London and is part of the team responsible for the funds' European fixed income investments, with particular responsibility for managing positions in the UK and other non-EMU countries, a role he has performed since the company's formation in 1999.

Prior to joining JWM Partners, from 1994 to 1999 Andrew worked for LTCM in London and Tokyo where he was involved in a number of the firm's activities including research, the financing of the funds' European and Asian positions and the management of their fixed income strategies in non-Japan Asia. Previously, from 1991 to 1994 he worked as an analyst in the Quantitative Financial Economics Group at the Bank of England.

Andrew has a BSc in Economics with Computing and Statistics from the University of Bath and an MSc in Applied Statistics and Operational Research from Birkbeck College, University of London.

Dariush Mirfendereski is the head of inflation-indexed bonds and derivatives trading for UK/Europe at UBS in London with additional responsibility for USCPI derivatives. Prior to joining UBS in 2004, Dariush was the senior inflation derivatives trader at Barclays Capital where he traded the product from 1998.

From 1996 to 1998, Dariush was a structurer in insurance derivatives and also worked on the exotic interest rate derivatives trading desk at Barclays.

From 1993 to 1996, Dariush worked in San Francisco at EQECAT, a risk consultancy specializing in catastrophe risk assessment for insurance and reinsurance companies, where he was responsible for the modelling of the risk-simulation and insurance pricing models.

Dariush has over a dozen conference papers and journal publications in the fields of micro-electro mechanical engineering, catastrophe insurance loss modelling, option pricing, and inflation derivatives dating from 1991 to present. More recently, he has also been an invited speaker/panelist at conferences organised by the Bond Market Association of America (New York 2003, London 2004), Futures and Options World (London 2003), and at the Global Derivatives and Risk Management Conference series (Madrid 2004).

Dariush obtained his BSc and MSc degrees from UCL and Imperial College London and subsequently a PhD in engineering at the University of California at Berkeley.

Foreword by Sir Edward George

I am delighted to provide the foreword to the second edition of this book. Work on the first edition, published in 1998, began while the authors were at the Bank of England, and it quickly became established as one of the most authoritative guides to the index-linked securities markets worldwide. This new edition contains much new material, reflecting the further development of the markets globally, with the decisions by the US (1997) and French (1998) governments to issue index-linked stocks, the growth of private sector issuance and the emergence of inflation-indexed derivatives markets.

My own involvement with index-linked debt goes back more than 20 years to the debates preceding the decision to first issue index-linked gilts in 1981. This was an extraordinary experiment for the rather conservative gilt-edged market of the time. The minimum lending rate was 12% and long gilt yields more than 14%. Not surprisingly, therefore, the main motivation for the UK authorities was that this might be a new way of issuing debt at a lower cost. The first £1 billion 2% Index-linked Treasury 1996 was indeed issued at par on 27 March 1981. It was a step into the unknown, with only New Zealand issuing similar instruments at the time. There was considerable uncertainty about how to price the bonds. I recall that one academic economist suggested issuing zero coupon, irredeemable index-linked gilts, which would have been an even better deal for the UK taxpayer! More seriously, some argued that "indexation of everything" might follow, perhaps weakening resistance to inflation within the population or even making it impossible to issue conventional gilts. Others were concerned that overseas purchases might put upward pressure on the exchange rate, and the UK authorities did in fact initially confine holders to UK pension funds and life insurers.

Over time it became clear that index-linked gilts had been a great success. Today they are a firmly established part of the UK Government's debt portfolio, comprising some 27% of gilts outstanding by market value. They have proven good value for the issuer, with market-derived inflation expectations consistently overestimating future UK inflation outturns during the 1980s and 1990s, perhaps because an inflation risk premium was being paid on conventional bonds. And the existence of government bonds offering real returns has also enabled investors to reduce risks, particularly savings institutions like pension funds seeking to hedge future liabilities linked to real variables, such as earnings.

Another great benefit is the information about expected real interest rates and inflation, which can be derived from comparing index-linked and conventional bond yield curves. This was hardly in the minds of UK policy makers in 1981, but has become steadily more significant over time: for example, it was a reason cited by the US authorities for beginning to issue Treasury Inflation-Indexed Securities in 1997. In the UK, it depended on the development of analytical techniques (including work by two of the authors of this book) and the freeing up in 1982 of the market to all investors, which allowed proper arbitrage between the two types of instrument. The UK Monetary Policy Committee has, from its beginning in 1997, made extensive use of such estimates of expected future inflation and real interest rates in its assessments of the prospects for GDP growth and inflation. Interpretation requires a degree of skill because from time to time there can be distortions in both markets, but having market-based estimates is an invaluable complement to other indicators, such as surveys.

More generally, market-based estimates of real interest rates and inflation are useful in a wide range of contexts: for example, for firms and government when evaluating expected returns on new investment projects against the cost of capital and for investors when assessing expected returns on other assets, such as equities. Although it is impossible to know, this information may well have led to a better allocation of capital in the economy.

The success of index-linked securities markets is demonstrated by their adoption by an increasing number of government issuers worldwide, including Australia, Canada, France, Sweden and the USA; together with growing private sector issuance and the developing inflation-indexed derivatives markets. I welcome the second edition of this book as a helpful and thorough reference source for all interested in these markets.

May 2003
Sir Edward George
Governor of the Bank of England

Preface to the Second Edition

The concept of inflation indexation is not a new idea, but is in fact an aspect of finance that has been understood for several hundred years. As long ago as the early 18th century contracts existed that sought to protect lenders from changes in the prices of goods, and the issuance of inflation-indexed debt by governments and corporations is a proposal that has won the support of many eminent economists since then.

At a theoretical level, the attraction of such financial instruments is clear: in the final analysis, savers should be concerned only with the *real* purchasing power of their savings. The fact that securities and other savings arrangements have historically been transacted and quoted on a nominal basis serves only to provide a potential source of "money illusion". If individuals can be certain that deferred consumption is equivalent to more consumption, that in itself should provide a powerful incentive to save. The parallel argument for corporations is also valid: to the extent that the future *real* value of their capital is increased, so too is their incentive to refrain from immediate investment.

The preponderance of nominal investment and savings vehicles through history has clouded this clarity. However, the experiences of the Western economies in the second half of the 20th century, not to mention those of many South American countries and (perhaps most spectacularly) pre-war Germany, to name but a few, have changed the world's view about the impact of nominal price instability in the real economy. A number of governments around the world have experimented with the indexation of their debt, the motivation of many being to bring credibility to their macroeconomic policies and therefore stability to their currencies. The introduction of index-linked gilts by the UK authorities in 1981 marked one of the earliest attempts by a Western government to issue such securities, at a time when the UK itself was recovering from the effects of a period of historically high inflation. Shortly afterward a number of other industrialised countries followed suit, with Australia, Canada and Sweden all having issued index-linked bonds by the mid-1990s.

When the first edition of this book was published in early 1998 it still appeared that the benefits offered by the product were outweighed by practical difficulties in their design, implementation and sponsorship as well as by general investor apathy. In spite of some limited success in each of the countries where the securities had been issued, it was not until the index-linked bond programmes of the US and French governments (launched in 1997 and 1998, respectively) had become established that the shift from niche market to mainstream investment product began. In 2000 the US TIIS (Treasury

Inflation-Indexed Securities) market overtook that of the UK to become the largest government inflation-linked bond market by capitalisation, and the following year the French Government began to issue its OAT€*i* bonds linked to the Euro-zone Harmonised Index of Consumer Prices (HICP) excluding tobacco. Around the same time the market for inflation-linked derivatives also began to evolve, from practically nothing in 1998 to a multi-billion dollar market today.

This series of developments has led to the point where, in mid-2003, there exists a liquid, truly global market in inflation-indexed securities and derivatives. This second edition of *Inflation-indexed Securities* looks to both update and expand the material of the original. There are two major additions: first, the descriptions of the markets are updated – in particular those of the French and US government inflation-indexed bond markets. Information has been collated from over 25 central banks and debt management offices worldwide to ensure that the coverage is as comprehensive and up to date as possible. Second, there are two new chapters to cover inflation-indexed derivative contracts in some detail. Taken together with material from the first edition – including thorough reference sections detailing the cash flow and yield formulae used in all the major bond markets – this book is intended to form an important reference for those already familiar with the subject as well as for academics and bond market practitioners approaching the subject for the first time.

Acknowledgements

There are a number of people without whom this book would never have been written and many more whose assistance, enthusiasm and support have been invaluable. All responsibility for any errors or omissions do of course remain our own.

We would like to offer a special thanks to Sir Edward George for generously agreeing to write the foreword for this book and to Paul Tucker and David Rule at the Bank of England for helping to arrange this.

Additional, highly valued support for this project came from two prominent analysts of global inflation-indexed bond markets – Mark Capleton at Morgan Stanley and Andrew Roberts at Merrill Lynch – who kindly agreed to review the draft manuscript for us.

We also owe a deep debt of gratitude to Gurminder Bhachu and Hamish Watson from the UK Debt Management Office for providing us with detailed comments on both the content and presentation of the material in this book.

Numerous others assisted us in the production of this book, but we would particularly like to thank David Hockey, James Knight, Lauren Sharman and Theo Thomas for their help. At Wileys we would like to offer our thanks to Samantha Whittaker, Patricia Morrison, Carole Millett, Sam Hartley, Peter Baker and Paula Soutinho for their support and patience. We are also grateful to Wileys for giving us permission to develop some ideas from *Estimating and Interpreting the Yield Curve* (Anderson *et al.*, 1996) and in particular to reproduce a section that appears in this book as Appendix 2.2.

In addition, we would like to express our gratitude to all those that provided material for the second edition of this book including Gerald Dodgson (Australian Office of Financial Management), Armando Pinell Siles (Central Bank of Bolivia), Rubens Sardenberg (National Treasury, Brazil), Anderson Caputo Delfino Silva (National Treasury, Brazil), Aline Dieguez Barreiro de Meneses Silva (National Treasury, Brazil), Danielle Ayres Delduque (National Treasury, Brazil), David Bolder (formerly of the Bank of Canada), Pablo Cruzat Arteaga (Ministry of Finance, Chile), Carlos Eduardo León Rincón (Ministry of Finance and Public Credit, Republic of Colombia), Jiří Franta (Ministry of Finance, Czech Republic), Lars Risbjerg Johannesen (National Bank of Denmark), Peter Nyberg (Ministry of Finance, Finland), Olivier Cuny (Agence France Trésor), Sébastien Moynot (Agence France Trésor), François Naudin (Agence France Trésor), Charoulla Dreni (Ministry of Finance, Greece), Jóna Ísaksdóttir (National Debt Management Agency, Republic of Iceland), Sigurður Árni Kjartansson

(National Debt Management Agency, Republic of Iceland), Jón Óskar Sólnes (Kaupthing Bank, Republic of Iceland), Gaby Fiszman (Bank of Israel), Dr Edward Offenbacher (Bank of Israel), Davide Iacovoni (Ministry of Economics and Finance, Italy), Batyrbek Alzhanov (National Bank of Kazakhstan), Mariana Campos (Investor Relations Office, Ministry of Finance and Public Credit, Mexico), Andrew Turner (New Zealand Debt Management Office), Luis Delgado (Central Reserve Bank of Peru), Agnieszka Grąt (National Bank of Poland), Johan Schoeman (National Treasury, Republic of South Africa), Phakamani Hadebe (National Treasury, Republic of South Africa), Phumzile Maseko (National Treasury, Republic of South Africa), Mark Greenwood (Rand Merchant Bank, Republic of South Africa), Anders Holmlund (Swedish National Debt Office), Joy Sundberg (Swedish National Debt Office), Thomas Wigren (Swedish National Debt Office), Magnus Andersson (Swedish National Debt Office), Ayse Nihal Aslan (Central Bank of the Republic of Turkey), Joe Ganley (Bank of England), John Williams (Barclays Capital, UK), David Pottinton (CSFB, UK), Graham Stock (JP Morgan, UK), Bob Day (National Savings & Investments, UK), Christine Ludwick (US Treasury), Jeff Huther (US Treasury), Kim Treat (US Treasury), Will Lloyd (Bridgewater Associates, USA), Pu Shen (Federal Reserve Bank of Kansas City) and Brian Sack (Board of Governors of the Federal Reserve System, USA).

Mark would also like to offer a special thanks to his family and friends for the support and encouragement that they have given him while writing this book – in particular, his parents Ann and Colin, and John and Hilda, as well as David Ainsworth, Elizabeth Pohl, Eric Edmond, Jenny Boyle, Mark Ambrose, Pam Henness, Paul Doran, Robert Knight, Sarah Ellis and Steve Whiting.

Andrew would like to thank all his colleagues at JWM Partners for the help they have provided over many years and all their encouragement during the preparation of this book. In addition he would like to offer his gratitude for the seemingly unending patience and support of his family, particularly Clare, Luke and Natasha, over the past six months.

Dariush would also like to offer a special thanks to his family and friends for the support, encouragement and understanding that they have given him while writing this book. Additionally, Dariush would like to thank Richard Gladwin for important contributions to his understanding of the practical pricing and hedging of inflation-linked derivatives over the past five years. He would also like to thank Oliver Cooke for fruitful discussions regarding inflation options, some of which are incorporated in this book. Thanks also go to the numerous individuals who have had direct and indirect input over the past five years into the evolution of ideas related to the pricing and hedging of inflation-linked financial products and into the understanding of client exposures and hedging requirements – in particular (and in alphabetical order) Dariush would like to thank: Karan Bhagat, Mark Capleton, Fred Cleary, Paul Coleman, Ksenia Craig, Edward de Waal, Stephen Dodds, Julie Finch, Sorayah Kazziha, Riccardo Rebonato, Mike Sherring and Sean Violante. Finally, Dariush wishes to express deep debt and gratitude to David Newton who, until his untimely death earlier this year, was for him the most important contributor of ideas and insights regarding the global trading of index-linked bonds.

Disclaimer

The editorial content provided herein is entirely the responsibility of the authors. Barclays Bank PLC, the UK Debt Management Office, JWM Partners (UK), Ltd. and their respective affiliates, officers, directors, partners and employees take no responsibility whatsoever for any information or opinion contained herein or omitted herefrom, nor do they accept any liability whatsoever for any direct or consequential loss arising from any use of this publication or its contents. The securities and instruments described herein may involve a high degree of risk and may not be suitable for all investors. Investors should consult any independent advisor they believe necessary to evaluate any issuer, security or instrument discussed in this publication.

Abbreviations

AFT	*Agence France Trésor*
AI	Accrued Interest
ARIMA	Auto Regressive Integrated Moving Average
ÁKK	Hungarian Debt Management Agency
BARRA	A type of Argentine government indexed bond
BCI	Building Cost Index (Iceland)
BCPs	*Bonos Banco Central en Pesos* (Chile)
BCUs	*Bonos Banco Central en Unidad de Fomento* (Chile)
BESA	Bond Exchange of South Africa
BLS	Bureau of Labor Statistics (USA)
BMA	Bond Market Association (USA)
BRISA	*Brisa-Auto Estradas de Portugal*
BTANs	Bons du Trésor à taux fixe et à intérêts annuels (France)
BTFs	Bons du Trésor à taux fixe et à intérêts précomptés (France)
BTN	Treasury indexed bond (Brazil)
BTP	*Buoni Poliennali del Tesoro* (Italy)
BZW	Barclays de Zoete Wedd
CADES	*Caisse d'Amortissement de la Dette Sociale* (France)
CBOT	Chicago Board of Trade
CD	Certificate of Deposit
CDC	*Caisse des Dépôts et Consignations* (France)
CDS	Canadian Depository for Securities
CFB	Credit Foncier Bond (Australia)
CGS	Commonwealth Government Securities (Australia)
CIB	Capital Indexed Bond
CIR	Cox, Ingersoll and Ross
CLI	Cost of Living Index (Iceland)
CME	Chicago Mercantile Exchange
CNA	*Caisse Nationale des Autoroutes* (France)
COFIDE	*Corporación Financiera de Desarrollo* (Peru)
COI	A type of Polish indexed bond
CPI	Consumer Price Index
CPI-U	Consumer Price Index for All Urban Consumers (USA)

CPI-W	Consumer Price Index for Urban Wage Earners and Clerical Workers (USA)
CPI-X	Consumer Price Index Housing Subindex
CSA	Credit Support Annex
CSO	Customer Service Outlet (Poland)
CTI	Credit Terms Index (Iceland)
CTRs	*Certificato del Tesoro Reali* (Italy)
DANE	Departamento Administrativo Nacional de Estadísticas (Colombia)
DB	Defined Benefit
DMO	Debt Management Office (New Zealand or UK)
EBRD	European Bank for Reconstruction and Development
ECB	European Central Bank
ECI	Employment Cost Index (USA)
EG	Earnings-linked Gilts (UK)
EIB	European Investment Bank
ERM	Exchange Rate Mechanism
EURIBOR	Euro Inter Bank Offer Rate
Euro-HICP	Euro-zone Harmonised Index of Consumer Prices
FRN	Floating Rate Note
FRS-17	Financial Reporting Standard No. 17
FSA	An insurance company
GBP	Sterling
GEMMA	Gilt-edged Market Makers Association
GGB	Greek Government Bond
HFA	Housing Finance Agency (Iceland)
HICP	Harmonised Index of Consumer Prices
HJM	Heath, Jarrow and Morton
HPR	Holding Period Return
I-Bond	Inflation-indexed Savings Bond (USA)
IAB	Indexed Annuity Bond
IASB	Inflation-Adjusted Savings Bond (New Zealand) International Accounting Standards Board
IBRD	International Bank for Reconstruction and Development
ICF	Investment Credit Fund (Iceland)
IFR	International Financing Review
IG	Index-linked Gilt (UK)
IGN	Deposit Guarantee Board (Sweden)
IGP-M	Index of General Market Prices (Brazil)
IIB	Interest Indexed Bond
IITS	Inflation-Indexed Treasury Securities (Kazakhstan)
IL	Inflation-linked
ILNZGS	Index Linked New Zealand Government Stock
ILS	Inflation-linked Swap
INE	Instituto Nacional de Estadísticas (Chile)
INSEE	French National Institute of Statistics and Economic Studies
IPCA	Consumer Price Index (Brazil)
IRS	Interest Rate Swap

ISDA	International Swaps and Derivatives Association
ISIN	International Securities Identification Number
IZCB	Indexed Zero-Coupon Bond
JGB	Japanese Government Bond
KAF	Swedish Nuclear Waste Fund
KfW	Kreditanstalt für Wiederaufbau
LIBOR	London Inter Bank Offer Rate
LIFFE	London International Financial Futures and Options Exchange
LPI	Limited Price Indexation (UK)
LS	LIBOR Spread
MFR	Minimum Funding Requirement (UK)
MTN	Medium-Term Notes
MUICP	Monetary Union Index of Consumer Prices
NCPI	National Consumer Price Index (Mexico)
NDMA	National Debt Management Agency (Iceland)
NDP	Nominal Dirty Price
NDPB	Non-Departmental Public Body (UK)
NHS	National Health Service (UK)
NIB	Nordic Investment Bank
NTN	National Treasury Note (Brazil)
OATs	*Obligations assimilables du Trésor* (France)
ODPM	Office of the Deputy Prime Minister (UK)
ORTN	Readjustable National Treasury Obligations (Brazil)
OTC	Over The Counter
OTN	National Treasury Obligation (Brazil)
PDBCs	*Pagarés Descontables del Banco Central* (Chile)
PFI	Private Finance Initiative (UK)
PPM	Premium Pension Authority (Sweden)
PPP	Purchasing Power Parity
PRBCs	*Pagarés Reajustables del Banco Central* (Chile)
PRCs	*Pagarés Reajustables Pago Cupones* (Chile)
REAL	Real yield securities (USA)
RFF	*Réseau Ferré de France*
RMB	Rand Merchant Bank (South Africa)
RPI	Retail Prices Index (UK)
RPIX	Retail Prices Index excluding mortgage interest (UK)
RPIY	Retail Prices Index excluding mortgage interest and direct taxes (UK)
RRB	Real Return Bond (Canada)
RRSP	Registered Retirement Savings Plan (Canada)
RS	Real Spread
RSA	Republic of South Africa
SAFA	South Australian Government Financing Authority
SAIL	South African Inflation-Linked
SBIL	State Bonds Index-Linked (Greece)
SCMB	Standard Corporate and Merchant Bank (South Africa)
SDE	Stochastic Differential Equation
SDR	Special Drawing Right from the IMF

SEB	*Skandinaviska Enskilda Banken* (Sweden)
SNDO	Swedish National Debt Office
SPV	Special Purpose Vehicle
STRIPS	Separate Trading of Registered Interest and Principal of Securities
SVT	Selected primary dealers (France)
TCTA	Trans-Caledon Tunnel Authority (South Africa)
TCV	Treasury Corporation of Victoria (Australia)
TEC 10	Taux de l'Échéance Constante à 10 ans (France)
TES-IPC	Treasury Notes-Index of Consumer Prices (Colombia)
TIB	Treasury Indexed Bond
TIIB	Treasury Inflation-Indexed Bond (USA)
TIIN	Treasury Inflation-Indexed Note (USA)
TIIS	Treasury Inflation-Indexed Security (USA)
TIPS	Treasury Inflation-Protection Security (USA)
TTIPS	Trans-Texas Inflation Protector (USA)
UDI	*Unidad de Inversión* (Mexico)
UF	*Unidad de Fomento* (Chile)
UFV	*Unidad de Fomento de Vivienda* (Bolivia)
UPAC	*Unidad de Poder Adquisitivo Constante* (Colombia)
UVR	Real Value Unit (Chile)
VAVIS	A type of Argentine government indexed bond
VNAs	*Valores Nacionales Ajustables* (Argentina)
WI	When Issued
	Wage Index (Iceland)
WPI	Wholesale Price Index

1 What Are Inflation-indexed Securities and Derivatives?

Many securities have cash flows linked to an index of some kind, in order to protect both investors and issuers from the economic consequences of fluctuations in prices of goods reflected by that index. In general, an *indexed security* can be linked to any index, such as a basket of currencies or a combination of interest rates. This book focuses on one particular class of such instruments – collectively known as *inflation-indexed securities* – which has grown rapidly over the last few years.

As their name would suggest, inflation-indexed securities are designed to help protect borrowers and investors alike from changes in the general level of prices in the real economy. They therefore provide at least some degree of purchasing power certainty for a bondholder and similarly a constant *real* or *inflation-adjusted* cost of finance for a borrower. However, as often seems to be the case with financial innovation, markets for index-linked bonds around the world have developed somewhat independently. This has resulted in a variety of instruments with each having its own idiosyncrasies, despite the fact that all were designed with broadly the same objective.

This book sets out to explore why such bonds are of interest to investors and issuers alike, the various forms they can take (and why such design features are chosen) and how information from their market prices can be useful to a wide range of practitioners including policy makers and academics. It also reviews in detail not only the international markets for the securities themselves but also the markets for inflation-indexed *derivatives* which have grown rapidly in recent years as the underlying bond markets have become more established. As the bond and derivatives markets have grown so they have become more intertwined, making it ever more difficult to analyse the two independently of one another.

1.1 A HISTORICAL PERSPECTIVE

Though indexation has become increasingly popular in the last two decades, its roots can be traced back at least as far as the 18th century. In 1707 Bishop William Fleetwood produced an in-depth study into the erosion of the purchasing power of money,[1] detailing the administration of a fellowship established around 1450 whose membership was restricted to those with an annual income of less than £5. Having examined changes in the prices of corn, meat, drink and cloth between 1450 and 1700, Fleetwood found that there had been a sixfold increase. He therefore concluded that

[1] See Fisher (1922) for a more detailed discussion.

an individual with a nominal annual income of £6 in 1707 should be admitted to the fellowship since his real income was less than £5 when measured against 1450 prices.

The indexation of financial instruments dates back to at least 1742, when the State of Massachusetts first issued bills of public credit linked to the cost of silver on the London Exchange.[2] However, this first experiment had an unfortunate outcome for the issuer: as the price of silver appreciated more rapidly than the general price level during the 1740s the real burden of the debt increased and the State sustained significant economic losses. As a result, its Parliament passed a law in 1747 that decreed that a broader group of commodities be used should any future debt be indexed. The State's next attempt to issue indexed debt came in 1780 with the issuance of *Depreciation Notes* (Figure 1.1) to soldiers in lieu of wages during the American Revolution. These notes had the following terms that perhaps constitute the first attempt to define a basket of goods and the associated price index:

> *Both Principal and Interest to be paid in the then current Money of said State, in a greater or less Sum, according as Five Bushels of Corn, Sixty-eight Pounds and four-seventh Parts of a Pound of Beef, Ten Pounds of Sheeps Wool, and Sixteen Pounds of Sole Leather shall then cost more or less than One Hundred and Thirty Pounds current Money, at the then current Prices of said Articles.*

After the war, intense public discontent over various perceived economic injustices led to the remaining debt being converted into non-indexed form. Even though only a limited range of commodities were specified to be used in the Depreciation Notes' indexation formula, these were clearly index-linked bonds in the sense we know them today.[3]

This issuance of Depreciation Notes by the State of Massachusetts predates the works of the economists traditionally credited with developing the concept of indexation. Perhaps the first of these was Sir George Shuckburgh Evelyn who, in his 1798 article "An account of some endeavours to ascertain a standard of weight and measure", attempted to construct an index to represent the general level of prices. Inspired by Evelyn, Joseph Lowe advocated the widespread use of indexation[4] in his 1822 book *The Present State of England in Regard to Agriculture and Finance*. The topic was again raised in 1833 by G. Poulett Scrope who, in his *Principles of Political Economy*, discussed the construction of an index number from the weighted average price of a range of commodities. Scrope argued that indexation would reduce business risk resulting from unforeseen changes in nominal prices.

Since then, a long line of distinguished economists have been proponents of the indexation of debt. In 1875 W. Stanley Jevons drew attention to the variability in the price of gold and suggested that the gold standard be replaced by a price index. Jevons thought that indexation could offer a myriad of benefits: it would guarantee the value of fixed incomes, discourage speculation, reduce business risk, lessen social tension brought on by inflation and reduce the magnitude of business fluctuations. Jevons even went as far as to suggest that the use of indexed debt in private contracts might

[2] A more detailed account of the Massachusetts issues appears in Fisher (1913).

[3] For more information on indexed bonds in early America see Shiller (2003).

[4] In addition to advocating indexation of financial contracts, Lowe also proposed that wage contracts and land-rent agreements be similarly linked to the price level.

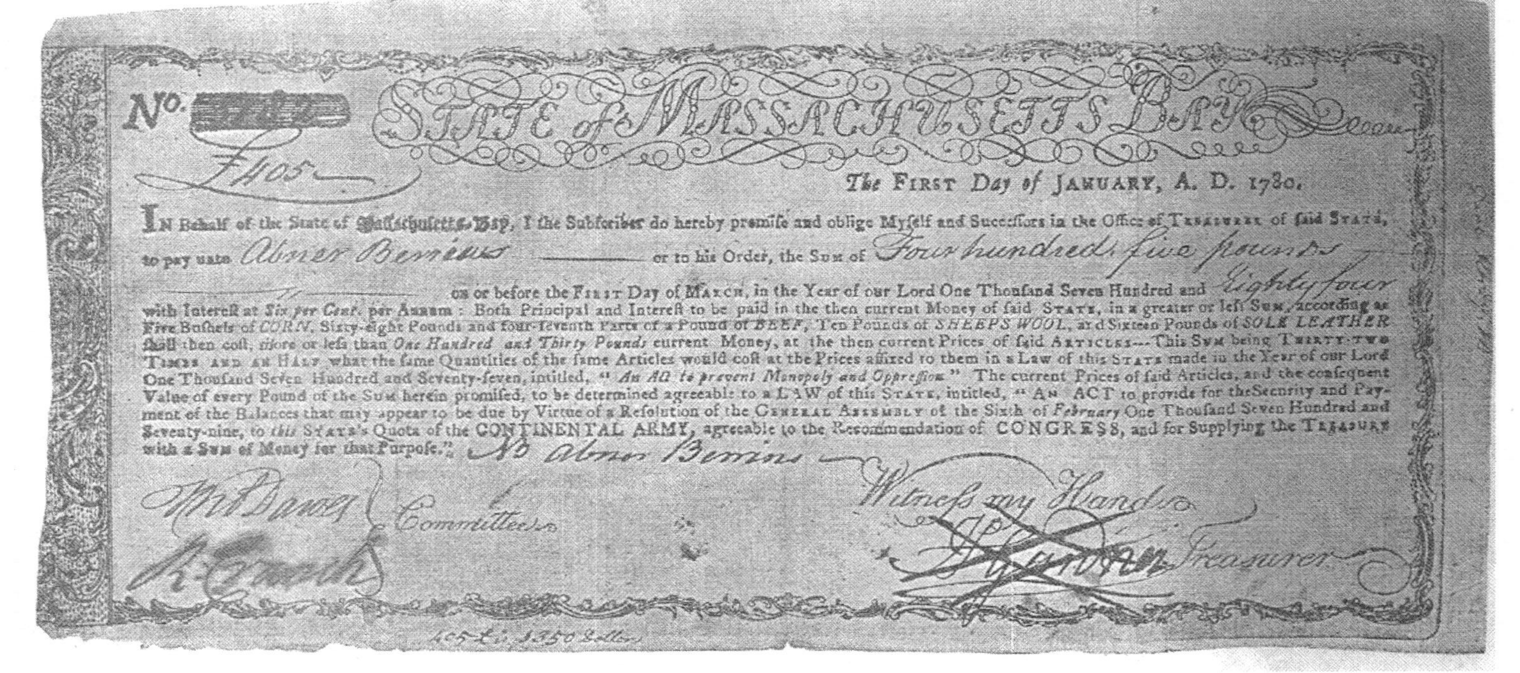

No.

STATE of MASSACHUSETTS BAY

£405

The FIRST DAY of JANUARY, A. D. 1780.

IN Behalf of the State of Massachusetts-Bay, I the Subscriber do hereby promise and oblige Myself and Successors in the Office of TREASURER of said STATE, to pay unto Abner Bemis ——— or to his Order, the Sum of Four hundred & five pounds ——— on or before the FIRST Day of MARCH, in the Year of our Lord One Thousand Seven Hundred and Eighty four with Interest at *Six per Cent.* per Annum: Both Principal and Interest to be paid in the then current Money of said STATE, in a greater or less SUM, according as Five Bushels of *CORN*, Sixty-eight Pounds and four-seventh Parts of a Pound of *BEEF*, Ten Pounds of *SHEEPS WOOL*, and Sixteen Pounds of *SOLE LEATHER* shall then cost, more or less than *One Hundred and Thirty Pounds* current Money, at the then current Prices of said ARTICLES—This SUM being THIRTY-TWO TIMES AND AN HALF what the same Quantities of the same Articles would cost at the Prices affixed to them in a Law of this STATE made in the Year of our Lord One Thousand Seven Hundred and Seventy-seven, intitled, "*An Act to prevent Monopoly and Oppression.*" The current Prices of said Articles, and the consequent Value of every Pound of the SUM herein promised, to be determined agreeable to a LAW of this STATE, intitled, "AN ACT to provide for the Security and Payment of the Balances that may appear to be due by Virtue of a Resolution of the GENERAL ASSEMBLY of the Sixth of *February* One Thousand Seven Hundred and Seventy-nine, to *this* STATE's Quota of the CONTINENTAL ARMY, agreeable to the Recommendation of CONGRESS, and for Supplying the TREASURY with a SUM of Money for that Purpose."

Committee

Witness my Hand

Treasurer

405 £ = 1350 Dolls

Figure 1.1 Facsimile of a soldier's Depreciation Note of 1780.
Reproduced from Fisher (1913)

be made compulsory. The only problem that he could envisage with this concept was the definition of the index itself.

In 1886 Alfred Marshall proposed a plan with the intention of drawing greater attention to the concept of indexation. Marshall's plan involved the passage of a law to permit, though not require, its use in contracts for deferred payments. Irving Fisher believed that, if Marshall's plan could be widely adopted, it would protect both debtors and creditors from the adverse effects of inflation: "the ideal is that neither debtor nor creditor should be worse off from having been deceived by unforeseen changes."[5] Fisher did, however, recognise that there were problems with indexation, including the administrative burden of having to calculate adjusted nominal values. Nonetheless, he continued to advocate the concept and was involved with several early efforts to index wages and financial instruments.[6]

John Maynard Keynes was also a strong supporter of the idea. As early as 1924 he proposed to the Royal Commission on National Debt and Taxation that the British government issue index-linked bonds. Besides offering investors the opportunity to protect their purchasing power, Keynes argued that the government might also be able to save on its interest costs since risk-averse investors might be prepared to pay a premium for such bonds. More recent support for indexation has come from Richard Musgrave, Milton Friedman and Robert Barro.

Despite the support of such eminent economists it was only really during the second half of the 20th century that indexed debt came to prominence in financial markets, following periods of high and volatile inflation in a number of economies. As part of their price stabilisation programmes after the Second World War, for example, both France and Finland issued indexed debt. These programmes were discontinued on devaluation of the respective currencies, reflecting concerns that higher import prices coupled with the widespread indexation of debt would create further inflationary pressures. During the 1950s and 1960s several countries experiencing hyperinflation – such as Argentina, Brazil and Mexico[7] – issued such securities as a means of maintaining the acceptability of long-term debt contracts.

More recently, however, indexed bonds have typically been issued by governments with a different set of motives. Those countries that have embarked on index-linked issuance since the early 1980s have generally been those with a commitment to low inflation already established and so have looked to indexed debt for cost savings and to enhance the credibility of their monetary policies.[8] Recent issuers include the UK (1981), Australia (1985), Canada (1991), Sweden (1994), the USA (1997), France (1998), Greece (2003) and Italy (2003). Table 1.1 demonstrates just how global the market for public-sector indexed debt has become.

1.2 HOW INDEXED BONDS WORK

An indexed bond is one whose cash flows are linked to movements in a specific price index, with the aim of providing investors with a means to protect the real value of their

[5] See Fisher (1922).
[6] See Fisher (1918) and Jud (1978).
[7] Campbell and Shiller (1996) provide an interesting table that illustrates the inflation rate for each country with indexed bonds, at the point in time such debt was first issued.
[8] That is, to demonstrate a commitment to low inflation.

Table 1.1 Countries in which indexed public sector bonds have been issued[1]

Country	Issue date	Index used
Argentina	1972–1989	Non-agricultural wholesale prices
Australia	1983–2003	Consumer prices
	1991	Average weekly earnings
Austria	1953	Electricity prices
	2003–	European consumer prices
		US consumer prices
Bolivia	2002–	Consumer prices
Brazil	1964–1990	Wholesale prices
	1991–	General prices
	2002–	Consumer prices
Canada	1991–	Consumer prices
Chile	1966–	Consumer prices
Colombia	1967	Wholesale prices
	1995–	Consumer prices
Czech Republic	1997	Consumer prices
Denmark	1982–	Consumer prices
Finland	1945–1967	Wholesale prices
France	1952, 1973	Gold price
	1956	Level of industrial production
	1956	Average value of French securities
	1957	Price of equities
	1998–	Domestic consumer prices
	2001–	European consumer prices
Germany	2002, 2003	European consumer prices
Greece	1997	Consumer prices
	2003–	European consumer prices
Hungary	1995–1999	Consumer prices
Iceland	1955	Consumer prices
	1964–1980	Cost of building index
	1980–1994	Credit terms index
	1995–	Consumer prices
India	1997	Wholesale prices
Ireland	1983–1985	Consumer prices
Israel	1955–	Consumer prices
Italy	1983	Deflator of GDP at factor cost
	2003–	European consumer prices
Kazakhstan	1999–	Consumer prices
Mexico	1989–	Consumer prices
New Zealand	1977–1984	Consumer prices
	1995–1999	Consumer prices
Norway	1982	Consumer prices
Peru	1999–	Consumer prices
Poland	1992–	Consumer prices
South Africa	2000–	Consumer prices
Sweden	1952	Consumer prices
	1994–	Consumer prices
Turkey	1994–1997	Wholesale prices
	1997–	Consumer prices
UK	1975–	Consumer prices[2]
	1981–	Consumer prices[3]
USA	1742, 1780	Commodity prices
	1997–	Consumer prices

[1] In addition to government bonds Table 1.1 also includes issues by public corporations, semi-government authorities and those that carry a government guarantee. The table is intended to provide a flavour of the global nature of the inflation-indexed bond market and is by no means exhaustive.
[2] National Savings certificates. These are non-marketable retail savings instruments.
[3] Gilt-edged securities (marketable government bonds).

savings. The bonds are usually indexed to a broad measure of prices, typically a domestic Consumer Price Index (CPI), but other "inflation" indices (such as wholesale prices, average earnings and the GDP deflator) have been used. Although they take a variety of forms the *capital-indexed* structure has become the most widely utilised, with all income and principal payments adjusted for inflation.

The value inherent in an indexed bond is often decomposed into two fundamental factors: a real rate of return, plus the compensation for the erosion of purchasing power arising from inflation.[9] At the time of purchase the *real* return to maturity on an indexed bond is "certain" – to the extent that the price index captures relevant price moves in the real economy – while its *nominal* (or cash) return is uncertain since this will depend on the realised future path of the price index. When purchasing a nominal (or conventional) bond the reverse is the case – in this instance it is the *nominal* return to maturity that is certain, while the eventual *real* return will of course depend on the extent to which realised inflation erodes the real value of the fixed nominal cash payments.[10]

A simple example is useful at this stage to clarify these concepts: suppose that an investor is faced with the choice between two instruments with the same maturity: a conventional bond yielding a nominal 5% and an index-linked bond offering a real yield of 3%. The market's valuations of these two bonds would imply that inflation is expected to be of the order of 2% per annum over their lifetime.[11] If the rate of inflation actually turns out to be higher at, say, 4% on average, then at maturity the indexed bond will have generated a 3% real return (precisely as expected) whereas the conventional bond's 5% nominal return will have been eroded such that its *ex post* real yield is only 1%. Of course, the reverse could occur instead: should inflation turn out to be lower on average than had been expected at, say, 1%, then the conventional bond's real return would turn out to be 4%, while that on the indexed bond would still have been 3%. This simple example demonstrates the key attribute of index-linked bonds: that they offer *real value certainty* when held to maturity.

However, although indexed bonds are designed with the explicit aim of providing investors with a certain real return (and the issuer a known real debt service burden), in practice they cannot offer *complete* real value certainty. One fundamental reason is that any given price index provides only an approximation to any individual investor's particular consumption basket. Except in the highly unlikely event that the investor wishes to consume the *precise* weighted collection of goods and services specified by the price index, there will be a degree of uncertainty surrounding exactly what will be affordable with the proceeds of the bond at maturity. The choice of price index is one of the key decisions facing those designing indexed bonds and is discussed in depth in the next chapter.

A second and more practical issue arises from the fact that a price index series, however relevant, cannot in general be published continuously and instantaneously. There is always a lag between the relevant time period for which an index value is

[9] For the time being we ignore other factors that should be considered in a full analysis, such as the value of *convexity*, *risk* and *liquidity premia*. These are treated in some detail later in the book, particularly in Chapter 5.

[10] Strictly speaking, these statements are true only for zero-coupon bonds, since for coupon-bearing instruments investors also face *reinvestment* risk – the risk that they will not be able to reinvest future coupon payments at the redemption yield at purchase.

[11] Again, this analysis ignores convexity effects as well as risk and liquidity premia for ease of exposition. The expected inflation rate required to equalise the nominal returns between an index-linked bond and a conventional bond of the same maturity is referred to as the *break-even inflation rate* – a concept that is discussed further in Chapter 5.

computed and the date on which that number is published, due to the amount of time required to compile, check and publish the data. The length of this publication lag is of course much less important for index-linked bonds issued in countries with stable inflation than for those issued where the price index is highly variable. In reality, indexation lags can vary from just a few days to over a year. Chapter 2 describes how different issuers have tackled this problem and how it is possible to minimise the length of indexation lag when designing indexed securities.

There is a third reason why inflation-indexed bonds may not deliver real value certainty – tax. Even if it were possible to design a "perfectly" indexed bond with cash flows adjusted by inflation right up to the moment they are paid (i.e., with no indexation lag), the various tax regimes in existence tend to cause *post-tax* real returns to remain uncertain even if *pre-tax* real yields are known. Even the uncertainty surrounding whether or not a particular set of tax rules will remain in existence throughout the lifetime of a bond is enough to introduce such uncertainty. So, the prevalent tax regime provides a third factor that needs to be considered when choosing a structure for index-linked securities, a further topic discussed in Chapter 2.

However, despite such imperfections in their design, it is important to realise that indexed bonds do still offer a high degree of protection against unexpected inflation, particularly when compared with conventional bonds. Holders of long-term nominal securities will suffer an erosion of purchasing power when inflation exceeds expectations. During periods of high and volatile inflation this can be disastrous; but even during periods of relatively stable prices, low but persistent inflation can substantially affect the real return on long-term investments. As Chapter 3 discusses, with cash flows that adjust in line with inflation, indexed bonds should appeal to investors with a preference for stable and predictable real income.

1.3 THE ROLE OF DERIVATIVES

As the global market for index-linked bonds has become more established over the past few years, the parallel market for *inflation derivatives* has evolved so rapidly that, by mid-2003, turnover in some markets has become a significant proportion of that in the underlying bond markets.[12] Although the two markets sometimes appear distinct – indeed, some investors are not able to access derivative markets at all – they are inseparable, since prices in one market will depend on and influence those in the other.

As is the case with all derivatives, inflation derivatives are designed to help "plug the gaps" in the market for the underlying securities. In general, derivative contracts are designed to meet more precisely a particular investor's or issuer's demands. For example, consider the situation in the Euro-zone where – as of mid-2003 – liquid inflation-linked bond markets are limited to those based on one of just two inflation indices: a domestic French inflation index or a pan-European index.[13] This is all very well for French investors, for whom protection against unexpected changes in domestic French inflation would seem to be a valuable characteristic. However, what about

[12] For example, in the largest index-linked derivatives market (for contracts linked to Euro-zone HICP excluding tobacco) turnover is estimated to be 25% of that of the corresponding OAT€*i* bonds.

[13] The first government indexed-bonds in the Euro-zone were brought by the French government and indexed to French CPI excluding tobacco. More recently the French, Greek and Italian governments have issued bonds indexed to the Euro-zone Harmonised Index of Consumer Prices (HICP) excluding tobacco. See Chapters 6 and 7 for more detail.

investors from other countries within EMU? Receiving cash flows linked to the price index of another country – albeit one with the same currency – would seem suboptimal to say the least. Cash flows linked to a pan-European index should serve better, although in the long run, if inflation within each of the member states converges as economic theory might suggest, this might be less of an issue. But there is clearly a risk that the "long run" may be beyond the investor's horizon and that realised cash flows linked to a pan-European CPI do not adequately match the inflation experienced by the investor in their home country.

This is an example of where the derivatives market can play an important part, by developing contracts to meet the investor's precise need. In the above example, assume the investor wants to buy an asset linked to Spanish inflation. A local Spanish financial institution may issue such a bond, with cash flows linked to a domestic CPI measure, to meet this demand. If an instrument existed that was linked to the Spanish CPI (the most obvious example being an index-linked bond issued by the Spanish government), then the financial institution could buy that instrument as a "hedge" for its own bond. In the absence of such an instrument, the institution could buy either a French or Euro-zone indexed bond and thus run the risk itself that the price indices differ (often referred to as *inflation basis risk*), or write a derivative contract with another institution – which would usually be a contract to "swap" a series of French (or Euro-zone) inflation-indexed payments for a series linked to domestic Spanish inflation. This would enable the Spanish bank to perfectly match its liabilities with a combination of the non-Spanish government bond and the swap contract.

But who would want to be on the other side of this contract, responsible for paying Spanish inflation and receiving French inflation? Initially, such positions were more typically taken by "proprietary" risk takers in investment banks, or by hedge funds, who would take the view that the expected payout from the derivative contract compensated them adequately for underwriting the risk of an adverse outcome. However, market participants with a more natural demand for such a swap can often be found: for example, consider a French company with a Spanish subsidiary that generates a series of cash flows that are expected to grow broadly in line with Spanish inflation – perhaps a utility company or a property company earning rental income. Such a company might not want to take the risk that Spanish inflation differs materially from that experienced in France and so could "swap" its expected future Spanish inflation-indexed cash flows for a series linked to the French CPI.

Of course, the above example is oversimplified in order to give a flavour for how derivatives can be used to meet investor or issuer demands that cannot be perfectly accommodated by existing bond markets. In reality, contracts can be written to hedge a multitude of risks: to match the timing and frequency of cash flows, index matching (as in the above example), maturity matching and so on. The list of possibilities is endless, although market "standards" have begun to appear for some of the more popular structures. The evolution of the inflation-linked derivative market is described in Chapters 8 and 9, along with examples of some of the more commonly used derivative contracts that serve to highlight the linkages back to the underlying bond markets.

Whether or not an investor or issuer can directly access the derivatives markets, their interaction with index-linked bond markets and the valuable information they provide should not be ignored. The two markets complement one another and both look set to grow rapidly together in the future.

2
Security Design

Inflation-indexed bonds can take many different forms. This chapter considers the key choices and constraints that face their designers: the choice of index, the cash flow structure of the bond, the application of the index to the cash flows and the impact of tax regulations. In addition, the final section briefly examines different methods for issuing indexed bonds which, although not directly linked to the design of the instruments or indeed relevant only to index-linked bonds, is of keen interest to debt managers. Wherever possible, specific attributes are illustrated by means of examples from index-linked bond markets.

2.1 CHOICE OF PRICE INDEX

Although the Consumer Price Index (CPI) has become by far the most common measure used to index bond cash flows, many others have also been employed. These include indices for wholesale prices, export prices, average earnings and the GDP deflator.[1] The main factors that influence this choice are set out below.

2.1.1 Index matching

Borrowers and lenders who utilise the capital markets are often seeking to match assets against similar liabilities, and so a good choice of index would be one that meets the hedging requirements of both parties. In practice, however, it is unlikely that the needs of borrower and lender will precisely coincide – indeed, different issuers are likely to have different requirements, and of course the same is likely to be true of investors. For instance, a government issuer may prefer to employ a broad-based index, such as the GDP deflator, as this is likely to provide the best correlation with its revenues and expenses. On the other hand, other issuers may prefer to sell bonds linked to more specific indices – in the 1950s, for example, electrical utilities in both Austria and France issued bonds tied to the price of electricity to ensure that their interest payments fluctuated with their revenues.

Similarly, while retail investors may prefer securities indexed to consumer prices, pension funds are likely to have a preference for earnings-indexed bonds to offset the component of their future liabilities that is largely linked to wage inflation. Indeed, in the UK the Wilson Report of 1980 recommended that index-linked gilts – which were initially to be aimed exclusively at pension funds – should be tied to average earnings. However, deficiencies with the average earnings index led the authorities to opt instead

[1] Indexed bonds have also been linked to (among other things) the market value of equities, the gold price, the level of industrial production, as well, of course, to different exchange rates.

Table 2.1 Cumulative growth for different measures of US inflation

Time period	CPI-U (%)	CPI-W (%)	GDP deflator (%)	Average hourly earnings (%)	Total ECI (%)
1970–1995	305	296	260	267	n/a
1985–1995	46	45	40	38	51
1970–1979	87	87	81	91	n/a
1980–1989	50	48	49	45	n/a
1990–1995	20	20	18	18	23

Data source: US Department of Commerce, Bureau of Labor Statistics.
CPI-U = Consumer Price Index for All Urban Consumers; CPI-W = Consumer Price Index for Urban Wage Earners and Clerical Workers; ECI = Employment Cost Index.

for the Retail Prices Index (RPI).[2] Bootle (1991) suggests that, while this is unlikely to have constituted a serious detraction for pension funds, it does make index-linked gilts less than ideal instruments for them. Since the growth of average earnings in the UK has typically been two to three percentage points higher per year than that of retail prices, one would expect real coupons on bonds linked to earnings to be significantly lower than those on comparable RPI-indexed bonds. The idea of introducing Earnings-linked Gilts (EGs) was again mooted in 1995 at a conference organised by the Bank of England to discuss ways in which the index-linked gilt market might be improved.[3] However, it was felt that to introduce EGs alongside RPI-indexed bonds could have segmented the market and reduced liquidity.

When consulting on the issue in 1996, the Department of the US Treasury (1996a) suggested four possible price indices to use for its inflation-indexed notes: the non-seasonally adjusted CPI for All Urban Consumers (CPI-U), the Core CPI (CPI-U, excluding food and energy), the Employment Cost Index (ECI) and the GDP deflator. Of these, the CPI-U index was chosen because it was felt to be the most widely understood of the four. The Treasury opted to use a non-seasonally adjusted measure of the CPI in order to avoid the periodic revisions that are likely to affect a seasonally adjusted series. Both Dudley *et al.* (1996) and Basta *et al.* (1996) emphasise the cumulative difference that the choice of index can make to cash flows. As in the UK, wage increases have typically outpaced consumer price inflation in the USA. For instance, over the period from 1985 to 1995 cumulative inflation as measured by the total Employment Cost Index[4] was five percentage points higher than that measured by CPI-U. The cumulative difference between CPI-U inflation and average hourly earnings over the same period was even greater, with cumulative CPI-U inflation higher by eight percentage points. Table 2.1 shows the cumulative growth rates of several different US indices between 1970 and 1995.

Investors using indexed bonds to hedge against liabilities that are linked to inflation will be exposed to the *basis risk* characterised by the difference between the measure used to index the bond's cash flows and that most closely associated with their liabilities. Clearly, the larger this basis risk the smaller the risk reduction benefits from

[2] The reasons for this decision are discussed later in the chapter.
[3] See Bank of England (1996, p. 84). The Bank was UK debt manager at the time.
[4] The ECI is often used as a proxy for pension plan liabilities as it is usually regarded to be the best measure of the inflation rate of employment compensation.

holding inflation-indexed bonds. This problem of index mismatch is often cited as a reason for the relatively low volume of indexed bonds issued by the private sector.

2.1.2 Index reliability and integrity

Index bias

Publication of the Boskin Report in the USA in 1996 focused attention on the measurement bias that can be inherent in price indices. Professor Boskin and his team were appointed in 1995 by the Senate Finance Committee, with the principal objective to ascertain whether or not the CPI overstated the real rate of increase in the cost of living for consumers. Their conclusion was that the CPI did indeed overstate inflation, by about 1.1 percentage points annually.[5] If, as in this case, the chosen index is biased upward, then indexed bonds will pay a higher inflation adjustment than is necessary to hedge against "true" consumer price inflation. However, as Shen (1995) points out, this need not be a problem for index-linked bonds since their prices should rise to reflect this increase in value, provided that the biases are known and reasonably stable.

Index definition changes and data revisions

It is desirable that the chosen index should not be subject to regular revision and that clear rules exist to describe the impact on bondholders should a revision occur. Ideally, indexed bond prospectuses should provide full details of how revisions, rebasings and other changes to the index will be dealt with. The importance of such clauses was highlighted in 1979 by the case of the French government's *Rentes Giscard* bond, which had payments linked to an index that was abolished several years before the bond was redeemed.[6] More recently, ahead of the launch of its CPI indexed bonds in 1998, the French Trésor debated whether they would best be indexed to domestic or Euro-zone inflation. At that time the Euro-zone Harmonised Index of Consumer Prices (Euro-HICP) was relatively new, its composition was still changing and there were fears that it might be subject to revision. These factors were almost certainly behind the Trésor's decision to instead index its first CPI-linked bonds to the well-established French domestic price index. However, following the introduction of the euro in 1999 the Euro-HICP gained increased recognition, and in 2001 the Trésor began issuing Euro-HICP bonds alongside the existing series.

The issue of revisions to the price index used for inflation-linked bonds arose in South Africa in May 2003 when a fund manager questioned an assumption used to compute the rental component of the housing sub-index of the CPI. He claimed that the CPIX inflation rate could be overstating inflation by up to 2%, and as a result of the ensuing investigation by Stats SA (the South African statistical office) the CPI was duly revised. The terms and conditions for the Treasury's indexed bonds stipulate that the base CPI levels would also be adjusted and thereby the impact of the revision on the bonds would be removed, if the change to the indexation method was deemed to be "fundamental". However, after due consideration, the National Treasury announced that it considered the change to be "technical" as opposed to fundamental,[7] with the

[5] A summary of the Boskin Report appears in Basta *et al.* (1996, p. 8).
[6] This issue is discussed in more detail in Chapter 6.
[7] See Republic of South Africa National Treasury (2003).

implication that the base CPI levels for each bond remained unchanged. This episode resulted in an immediate valuation loss to the indexed government bond market, estimated by Myburgh (2003) to be as high as R726.8mn.

In the UK, all index-linked gilts have a prospectus clause that sets out the consequences of a change in either the coverage or the basic calculation of the RPI.[8] For bonds issued before March 1982, a fundamental change in the RPI that is determined to be materially detrimental to index-linked gilt holders would trigger the clause, and the Treasury would be obliged to offer holders the opportunity of early redemption at (inflation-adjusted) par. The corresponding clause for bonds issued between March 1982 and January 2002 is slightly different in that it allows for the possibility of switching to a substitute price index without triggering the early redemption clauses, so long as the index change also does not result in material detriment to the holders. In 2002 the UK Debt Management Office (DMO) announced its intention to bring the indexation clause into line with the approach used in most other major markets.[9] Instead of making provision for the early redemption of bonds affected by an index change, the new clause places the onus on the government to seek advice from an independent institution with regard to a satisfactory replacement index – a change that, in the view of the DMO, reduces the potential impact on the index-linked gilt market of any change in the construction of the RPI.

The importance of using a stable index was demonstrated in the USA. Publication of the Boskin Report in December 1996 – a month before the US Treasury was scheduled to hold its first inflation-indexed note auction – caused much uncertainty in the market. Investors and traders alike were concerned that CPI-U might at some stage undergo downward adjustment or that a new and more representative measure of consumer inflation might be introduced. There was speculation that investors would charge an index risk premium of up to 30 basis points to reflect such a level of uncertainty. As a result the Treasury decided to postpone the auction by three weeks, in order to clarify the rights enjoyed by indexed note investors should the index be changed. The details of such contingencies were set out in the documentation accompanying the sale of its indexed securities:[10] in the event that the applicable CPI is discontinued, *fundamentally* altered in a manner materially adverse to the interests of investors or altered by law in a similarly detrimental manner, the Bureau of Labor Statistics (BLS) will substitute an appropriate index. However, from the outset the Treasury made it clear that if the Boskin recommendations (or any subsequent study) resulted either in methodological changes in the calculation of the CPI-U or in changes to its coverage, then these would constitute "technical" rather than "fundamental" changes. In practice there have been several technical changes of this kind, and one estimate[11] from 2002 puts the resulting cumulative reduction in the annual inflation rate at around 0.65%.[12]

In addition to describing how revisions, rebasings and other changes to the index will be dealt with, a bond's prospectus should also provide details as to contingencies in the event that publication of any given index value is delayed. For instance, if the CPI-U

[8] See UK Debt Management Office (2001d).
[9] See UK Debt Management Office (2002a).
[10] See, for example, Department of the (US) Treasury (1997a).
[11] See Barclays Capital (2002b).
[12] Wynne and Rodriguez-Palenzuela (2002) summarise the current state of knowledge about the potential for measurement bias or error in the Euro-HICP. Based on the evidence reviewed they conclude that "at this point in time there is very little scientific basis for putting a point or even an interval estimate on the likely magnitude of the overall bias in the HICP."

for a particular month is not reported by the last day of the following month, then the US Treasury will announce an index number based on the latest available 12-month change in the CPI. So, if the CPI for month M is not reported in time, the Treasury calculates a substitute index number using the following formula:

$$\mathrm{CPI}_M = \mathrm{CPI}_{M\text{-}1} \times \left(\frac{\mathrm{CPI}_{M\text{-}1}}{\mathrm{CPI}_{M\text{-}13}} \right)^{1/12}$$

If it proves necessary to employ a substitute index number, then the Treasury will use it for all subsequent calculations that rely on that month's index number. They do not replace it with the actual CPI when it is finally published.

The use of such substitute index numbers is certainly not desirable, as short-term distortions can arise should estimates turn out to be significantly different from the true figures that are eventually published. One reason why such discrepancies can occur is due to the seasonality of price indices – the presence of seasonal factors means that the growth in a price index between months M-13 and M-1 might be very different from that between months M-12 and M. Just such a situation occurred in the Canadian RRB (Real Return Bond) market in 1998, when the late release of the January 1998 CPI number forced the authorities to publish a substitute index value.[13] As prescribed, the authorities applied the year-on-year inflation rate for the period from December 1996 to December 1997 as a proxy for the growth in the index from January 1997 to January 1998, and thereby computed the substitute index number for January 1998 – which resulted in a value that represented a 0.1% monthly increase from December. However, in Canada the inflation rate typically runs above average in both January and February, and the formula to compute the substitute number clearly takes no account of such seasonality. In this instance the official CPI value for January 1998 (when eventually published) showed a 0.6% monthly increase, representing a significant difference between the official and substitute index values. In such instances the impact is not usually hugely detrimental (except when bonds change hands during such an episode) since the index "catches up" with the correct level the following month, and the accrued interest calculation convention works to compensate investors in full with only one month's delay. However, such occurrences do little to help the transparency of the market and can cause a degree of confusion, particularly if a substitute index value is used to set the nominal value of a cash flow, when, more importantly it could also result in a cash loss or gain to bond holders.

Index integrity

To help ensure that indexed bonds are viewed as reliable investments, it is important that the index itself is published by a body known to be independent of the issuer. This is not normally a problem for corporate issuers, but may be for governments if the agency that publishes price indices and that responsible for government debt issuance are both public sector bodies. In this case it is clearly desirable that the two entities be demonstrably independent. Although the possibility of straightforward manipulation may seem remote, there are a number of more subtle but perfectly legitimate means by which a government might achieve a similar result. In his review of the Swedish

[13] See Barclays Capital (1998b, pp. 7–9).

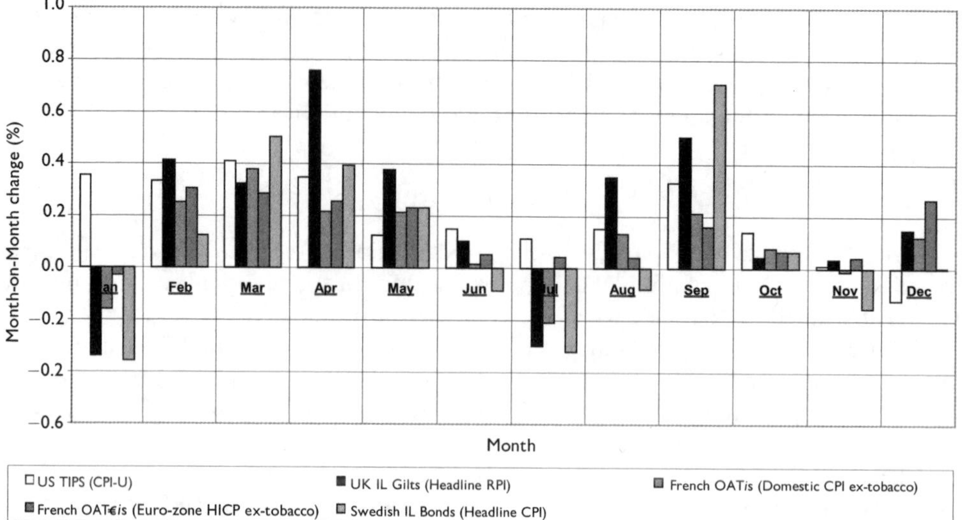

Figure 2.1 Seasonality of monthly changes in consumer price indices (average monthly change from 1996 to 2002)
TIPS = Treasury Inflation-Protection Securities; CPI-U = Consumer Price Index for All Urban Consumers; IL = Index-linked; OATs = Obligations assimilables du Trésor; HICP = Harmonised Index of Consumer Prices. Data source: Bloomberg

index-linked bond market, Persson (1997) notes that the inclusion of indirect taxes in the composition of the CPI makes it a less than ideal index in this regard as these tax rates are set directly by the government. An unscrupulous finance minister might be tempted to shift the fiscal burden from sales taxes to income tax prior to an indexed bond's redemption date, solely to induce a fall in the CPI and thereby reduce the government's borrowing costs. In general price indices net of indirect taxes are not well established, so Persson suggests that a government wanting to gain credibility is best served by building the credibility of existing measures rather than resorting to the use of net indices. Furthermore, this aim could be facilitated by structuring the debt portfolio such that indexed cash flows are spread evenly through time, as opposed to liabilities being concentrated in the form of just one or two large zero-coupon indexed bonds (the situation in Sweden at the time that Persson wrote his paper).

In the UK the use of the RPI as a price index for gilts has been criticised by some because it includes the cost of mortgage interest payments.[14] Since the majority of home loans are variable rate mortgages, the UK monetary authorities can have a more direct impact on household finances than perhaps is the case elsewhere. Before the Bank of England was granted operational independence to set interest rates in May 1997, the Chancellor of the Exchequer[15] was ultimately responsible both for managing the national debt and for the operation of monetary policy. While this situation remained the case, the risk existed that a chancellor who faced large redemptions of index-linked bonds might be tempted to hold down interest rates and thus dampen the level of the RPI. Of course, there is no suggestion that anything of this nature occurred at any point

[14] See Hetzel (1992, p. 17).
[15] The UK's Finance Minister.

in the past, but the separation of responsibilities represented by the granting of the Bank's independence all but ensures that such an event cannot occur in the future and thereby adds to the integrity of the RPI as an index for inflation-linked government bonds.

It is also important that index numbers are disseminated as widely and as quickly as possible on publication. If news of the latest inflation figure is slow to circulate or even leaked prematurely, market prices may be slow to reflect the new information and obviously those first in receipt of the news may be able to exploit the information unfairly. Huberman and Schwert (1985) provide some evidence that bond markets have in fact been reasonably efficient at incorporating inflation data into current prices. They suggest that in the Israeli indexed bond market, bond prices reflect 85% of new information about inflation immediately it becomes available, while the remaining 15% is usually incorporated by the end of the following business day.

Index seasonality

Consumer behaviour can exhibit seasonal features: in many industrialised countries consumer spending peaks in the run-up to Christmas, which in turn is often followed by a period of price discounting in January; the demand for energy and warm clothing tends to be higher in the cold winter months than in the summer, and so on. To the extent that such behaviour causes prices to fluctuate this should in turn be reflected by seasonal movements in the consumer price indices. Government behaviour can also influence these cycles – should indirect taxes always be adjusted at the same time each year, then another seasonal pattern in the index will exist.

Seasonality *per se* in a consumer price index is not a flaw in so far as it faithfully reflects economic reality – after all, seasons are a fact of life. However, its existence can complicate the analysis of inflation-linked bond prices. There are significant advantages in a well-established index being employed, as discussed above, but such indices often exhibit seasonal patterns. One potential solution is to use a seasonally adjusted price index, but in general such series may be less well understood than their unadjusted counterparts. In any case, most seasonal adjustment procedures require back month revisions – a feature that in itself can cause problems when determining indexed bond cash flows. For these reasons most issuers have opted to use an unadjusted but better established index. Figure 2.1 illustrates the seasonality in the indices used in some of the largest index-linked government bond markets.

The choice of a seasonal price index creates two further issues: the expected nominal size of future cash flows will be impacted by their timing with respect to the seasonal pattern, and yields quoted using standard market conventions will also be impacted. From an issuer's perspective it is perhaps the former that is the most relevant, since the choice of coupon cycle can materially impact the size of their coupon and redemption payments. For example, in a country that regularly experiences consumer price discounting in "January sales", consider the choice between issuing a bond whose annual payments are reset according to the level of the CPI in December and one whose cash flows use the CPI from one month later. To the extent that the January price discounting is not offset by other factors, the expected monthly inflation rate each January is likely to be below the average for the year. Other things being equal, efficient markets should correctly recognise the difference in expected nominal cash flows, with the result that the quoted real yield on the December-cycle bond is lower than that on the January-cycle bond. Issuers have taken different approaches to confront this issue: in the UK, for example, the government appears to have deliberately avoided issuing index-linked gilts whose cash flows are set by months whose RPI numbers have shown a strong seasonal influence.[16] In contrast, the Swedish government has issued bonds whose final cash flows are on 1 December and whose "index factor"[17] is therefore set by the CPI number for the previous September – a high point in the historical seasonal pattern displayed by the series, as illustrated by Figure 2.1.

Of course, in principle, markets will recognise such seasonality and price bonds accordingly. However, this process is somewhat complicated by the yield formulae conventionally used in the larger markets, each of which has built in an assumption of constant future inflation, and so the resulting yields are computed in such a way that any seasonality in the price index is disguised.[18] All else being equal, the use of such conventions implies that quoted yields will fluctuate throughout the year on the basis of any seasonal pattern in the CPI. Viewed from a different angle, if the quoted yield on an index-linked bond remains constant throughout the year, then the returns it generates will vary from month to month, unlike the constant returns generated by a conventional bond under the same conditions. This idiosyncrasy is therefore one that demands consideration by investors and issuers alike, not least because the patterns are usually somewhat predictable.

2.1.3 Other practical considerations

It is clearly important that the index chosen is widely understood, published on a frequent basis and in as timely a manner as possible. The lack of interest in the Italian CTR (Certificato del Tesoro Reali) bond issued in 1983 is widely put down to the selection of a statistic, the deflator of GDP at factor cost, which failed to meet any of these criteria: its properties were not well understood, it was published only annually and with a one year lag. However, in most major markets today, indexed bonds are tied to well-known indices whose publication occurs within a month of the relevant date. Indeed, some bonds use interpolation methods to help to reduce the impact of publication lags on investors. These issues are discussed in more detail later in this chapter (Section 2.3).

Of the *government* bonds currently being issued all are linked to a version of the consumer price index except those in Brazil, where bonds indexed to both consumer prices and "general" prices[19] exist. The reasons behind the popularity of the CPI are clear: typically it is widely disseminated, well understood, broadly based, rarely revised and issued on a regular and timely basis with a short lag. By way of example, Rutterford (1983) illustrates this thinking in the UK by listing likely reasons why the RPI was chosen for index-linked gilts, as opposed to either the index of average earn-

[16] As Figure 2.1 illustrates, January, April and July exhibit the largest absolute seasonal factors for the UK's RPI series. Since index-linked gilts pay semi-annual coupons and are indexed with an eight-month lag, coupons on the March–September and June–December cycles would be impacted most by this seasonality. There are currently no linkers on these coupon cycles.
[17] See Section 2.3.
[18] This observation applies both to the formula developed for the Canadian RRB market and adopted in most of the other major markets, as well as to the yield formula unique to the UK (with its explicit inflation assumption). See Chapter 5 for a general discussion of real redemption yields and Chapter 6 for details of the formulae used to compute yields in each of the major markets.
[19] The general prices index is a weighted average of the consumer, wholesale and construction price indices.

ings or the GDP deflator (the two main contenders considered by the UK government before the bonds' design was finalised):

1. Whereas the average earnings index and the GDP deflator were at the time available only annually and published with substantial lags, the RPI was published on a monthly basis and with a maximum lag of two months.
2. Both the GDP deflator and the average earnings index were subject to revision, unlike the RPI.
3. The RPI was the index most likely to protect most savers against their particular inflation risk.
4. The RPI had already been used for index linking of state pensions.

2.2 CASH FLOW STRUCTURE

Inflation-indexed bonds are all designed to protect investors against the erosion of principal and interest payments due to inflation, but they can take a variety of forms despite all being constructed to serve the same general purpose. In addition to the two most common forms – the *capital indexed* bond and the *interest indexed* bond – this section also examines three other designs that have been implemented: *current pay*, *indexed annuity* and *indexed zero-coupon* bonds.

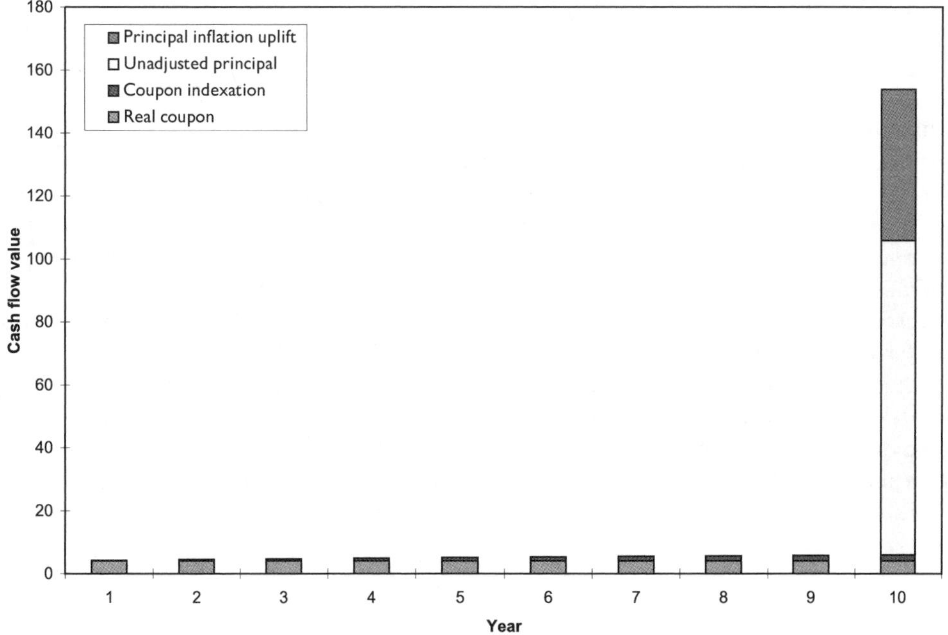

Figure 2.2 Capital Indexed Bond (CIB) cash flow structure

2.2.1 Capital Indexed Bond (CIB)

CIBs have a fixed real coupon rate and a nominal principal value that rises with inflation. Periodic coupon payments are calculated as the real coupon rate times the inflation-adjusted principal, and the inflation-adjusted principal itself is repaid at maturity. CIBs are the most widespread form of index-linked bonds by far and have been issued by the governments of Australia, Canada, France, Italy, New Zealand, South Africa, Sweden, the UK and the USA. Figure 2.2 and Table 2.2 illustrate the cash flow profile of a 4% annual coupon 10-year CIB under a hypothetical inflationary path.[20]

Table 2.2 Capital Indexed Bond (CIB) example: cash flow details

Year	Real coupon (1)	Inflation rate (2)	Compounded inflation (3)	Coupon indexation (4) = (5) − (1)	Coupon payment (5) = (1) × (3)	Redemption payment (6) = 100 × (3)
1	4.00	6.00	1.0600	0.24	4.24	
2	4.00	5.50	1.1183	0.47	4.47	
3	4.00	5.00	1.1742	0.70	4.70	
4	4.00	5.00	1.2329	0.93	4.93	
5	4.00	4.00	1.2822	1.13	5.13	
6	4.00	3.50	1.3271	1.31	5.31	
7	4.00	3.00	1.3669	1.47	5.47	
8	4.00	3.00	1.4079	1.63	5.63	
9	4.00	2.50	1.4431	1.77	5.77	
10	4.00	2.50	1.4792	1.92	5.92	147.92

2.2.2 Interest Indexed Bond (IIB)

IIBs pay a fixed coupon plus an indexation of the fixed principal every period. The principal repayment at maturity is *not* adjusted (i.e., the nominal principal is repaid at par, as for a conventional bond). All the inflation adjustment comes through the coupons, which are calculated simply by adding the periodic inflation rate to the coupon rate of the bond. As such, IIBs are often said to pay a margin over inflation and are best viewed as a form of inflation-protected floating rate bond. The Australian government issued several IIBs in the 1980s, but these proved much less popular than the CIBs (issued in parallel), and as a result sales of new IIBs ceased in 1988.

An important distinction between the CIB and IIB structures is that only the former provides for the preservation of future cash flows in terms of purchasing power at the issue date, thereby providing the better inflation protection. Figure 2.3 and Table 2.3 illustrate the cash flow profile of a 4% annual coupon 10-year IIB under a hypothetical inflationary path.

[20] For simplicity this example as well as others in the following sections assume perfect indexation (i.e., that there is no indexation lag).

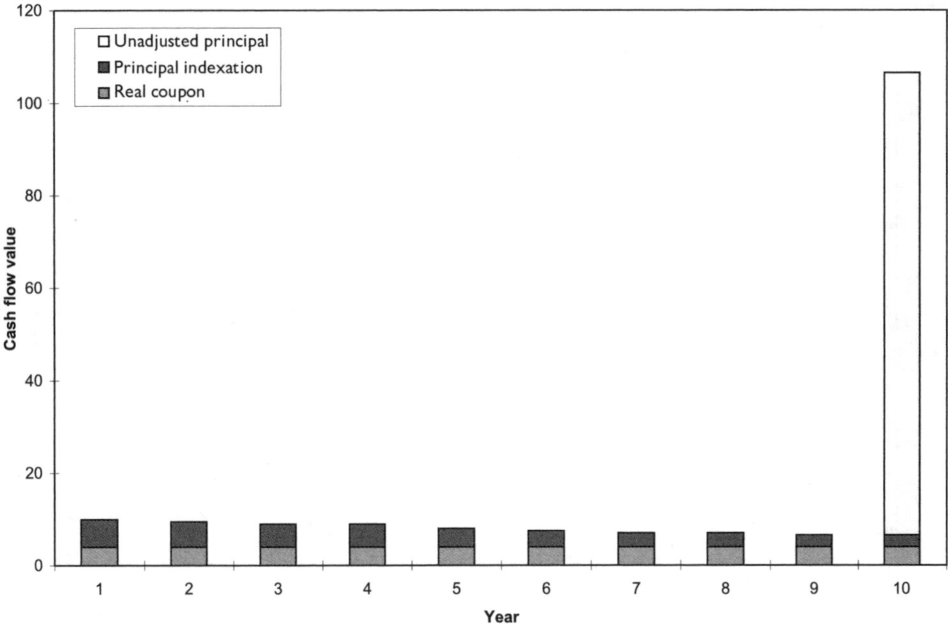

Figure 2.3 Interest Indexed Bond (IIB) cash flow structure

Table 2.3 Interest Indexed Bond (IIB) example: cash flow details

Year	Real coupon (1)	Inflation rate (2)	Principal indexation (3) = (2)	Coupon payment (4) = (1) + (3)	Redemption payment (5)
1	4.00	6.00	6.00	10.00	
2	4.00	5.50	5.50	9.50	
3	4.00	5.00	5.00	9.00	
4	4.00	5.00	5.00	9.00	
5	4.00	4.00	4.00	8.00	
6	4.00	3.50	3.50	7.50	
7	4.00	3.00	3.00	7.00	
8	4.00	3.00	3.00	7.00	
9	4.00	2.50	2.50	6.50	
10	4.00	2.50	2.50	6.50	100.00

2.2.3 Current Pay Bond (CPB)

CPBs are very similar to IIBs. Like IIBs, the principal repayment at maturity is not adjusted for inflation. However, while IIBs pay a *fixed* coupon with an indexation of the fixed principal every period, CPBs pay both an *inflation-adjusted* coupon as well as an indexation of the fixed principal. Like IIBs, CPBs are a type of inflation-protected

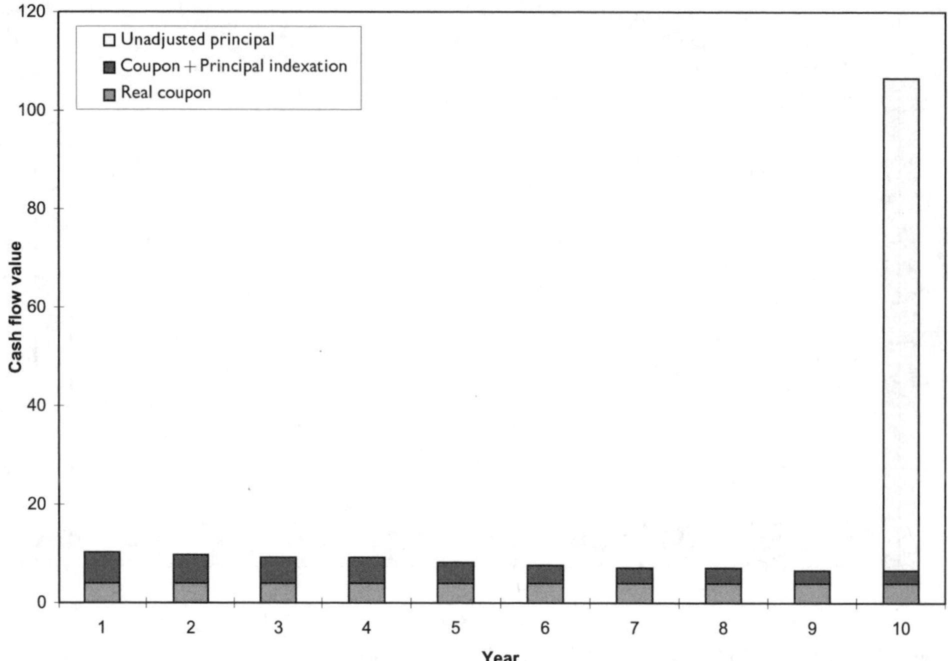

Figure 2.4 Current Pay Bond (CPB) cash flow structure

floating rate bond. When the US Treasury consulted the market on the introduction of indexed bonds it considered the current pay format, but opted instead to issue CIBs.[21] Turkey issued CPBs between March 1997 and June 1999.[22] Figure 2.4 and Table 2.4 illustrate the cash flow profile of a 4% annual coupon 10-year CPB under a hypothetical inflationary path.

Table 2.4 Current Pay Bond (CPB) example: cash flow details

Year	Real coupon (1)	Inflation rate (2)	Coupon indexation (3)	Principal indexation (4)	"Coupon" payment (5) = (1) + (3) + (4)	Redemption payment (6)
1	4.00	6.00	0.24	6.00	10.24	
2	4.00	5.50	0.22	5.50	9.72	
3	4.00	5.00	0.20	5.00	9.20	
4	4.00	5.00	0.20	5.00	9.20	
5	4.00	4.00	0.16	4.00	8.16	
6	4.00	3.50	0.14	3.50	7.64	
7	4.00	3.00	0.12	3.00	7.12	
8	4.00	3.00	0.12	3.00	7.12	
9	4.00	2.50	0.10	2.50	6.60	
10	4.00	2.50	0.10	2.50	6.60	100.00

[21] Abuhoff and Malik (1996) compare these two designs in more detail. Although several US index-linked corporate and municipal issues have been described in some newspaper reports as current pay bonds they are in fact interest indexed bonds.
[22] The Turkish authorities still have the ability to issue small quantities of indexed bonds directly to investors (see Chapter 7).

2.2.4 Indexed Annuity Bond (IAB)

IABs consist of a fixed annuity payment and a variable element to compensate for inflation. Several public corporations in Australia have issued IABs. Figure 2.5 and Table 2.5 illustrate the cash flow profile of an annual coupon 10-year IAB under a hypothetical inflationary path and a 4% real interest rate assumption.

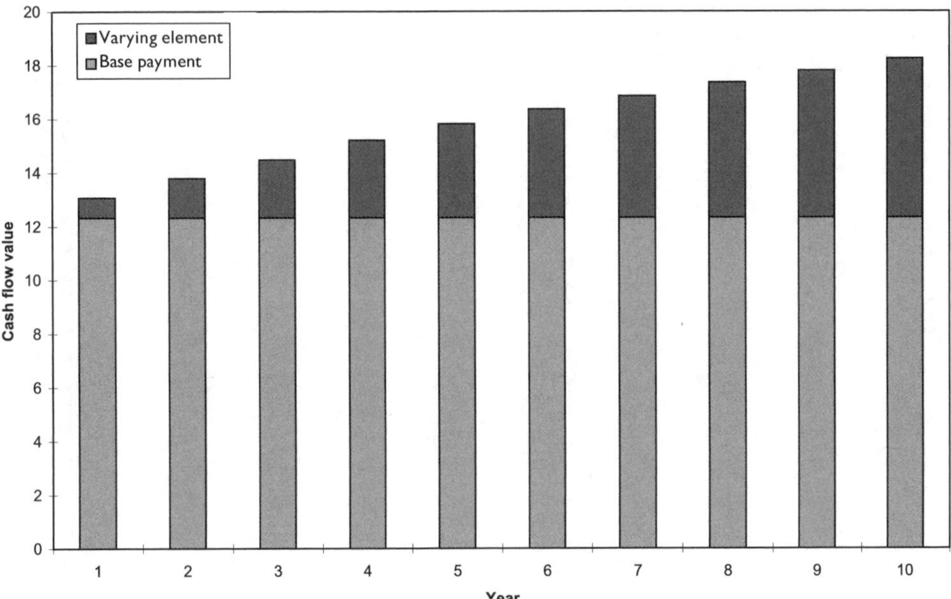

Figure 2.5 Indexed Annuity Bond (IAB) cash flow structure

Table 2.5 Indexed Annuity Bond (IAB) example: cash flow details*

Year	Base payment (1)	Inflation rate (2)	Compounded inflation (3)	Varying element (4) = (1) × [(3) − 1]	Total cash flow (5) = (1) + (4)
1	12.33	6.00	1.0600	0.74	13.07
2	12.33	5.50	1.1183	1.46	13.79
3	12.33	5.00	1.1742	2.15	14.48
4	12.33	5.00	1.2329	2.87	15.20
5	12.33	4.00	1.2822	3.48	15.81
6	12.33	3.50	1.3271	4.03	16.36
7	12.33	3.00	1.3669	4.52	16.85
8	12.33	3.00	1.4079	5.03	17.36
9	12.33	2.50	1.4431	5.46	17.79
10	12.33	2.50	1.4792	5.91	18.24

* Appendix 2.1 explains how the value of the base payment is determined.

2.2.5 Indexed Zero-Coupon Bond (IZCB)

IZCBs consist of a single payment of inflation-adjusted principal on redemption. As the name suggests, no coupon interest is paid. IZCBs have been issued in Iceland, Poland and Sweden. Figure 2.6 and Table 2.6 illustrate the cash flow profile of a 10-year IZCB under a hypothetical inflationary path.

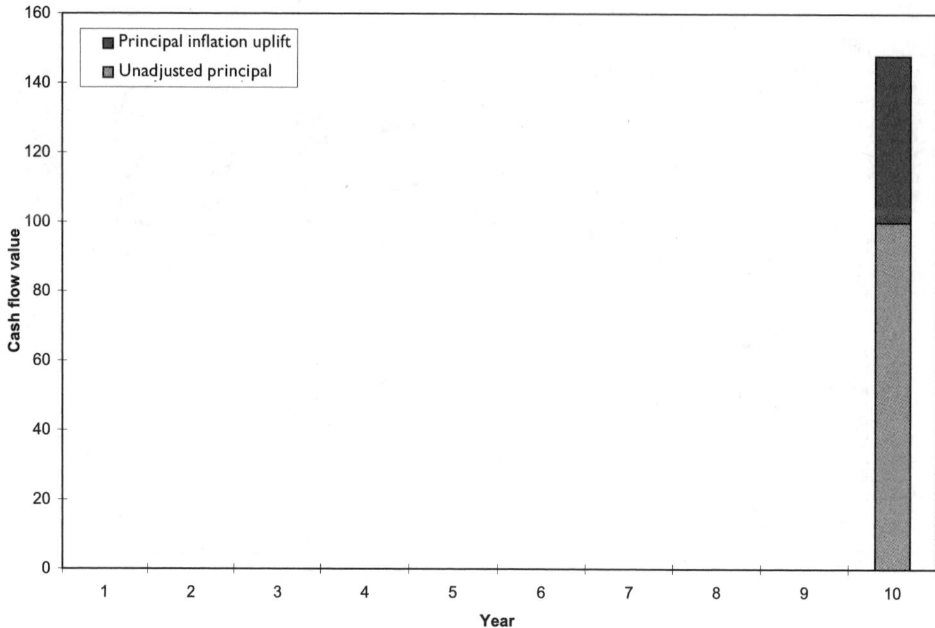

Figure 2.6 Indexed Zero-Coupon Bond (IZCB) cash flow structure

Table 2.6 Indexed Zero-Coupon Bond (IZCB) example: cash flow details

Year	Real coupon (1)	Inflation rate (2)	Compounded inflation (3)	Redemption payment (4) = 100 × (3)
1	0.00	6.00	1.0600	
2	0.00	5.50	1.1183	
3	0.00	5.00	1.1742	
4	0.00	5.00	1.2329	
5	0.00	4.00	1.2822	
6	0.00	3.50	1.3271	
7	0.00	3.00	1.3669	
8	0.00	3.00	1.4079	
9	0.00	2.50	1.4431	
10	0.00	2.50	1.4792	147.92

2.2.6 Other types of indexed bonds

In addition to the five major types of indexed bond described above, variations on these designs have been employed in several countries. For instance, as well as issuing straight IZCBs, both the Icelandic and Polish governments have issued indexed bonds that accumulate interest until redemption. Like zero-coupon bonds these instruments only pay a single cash flow consisting of interest and principal components. In practical terms this means that these bonds can trade at a premium to par, unlike pure zero-coupon bonds which will always trade at a discount to par. In the case of the Icelandic bonds both components are adjusted for inflation, whereas for the Polish instruments only the principal was inflation-adjusted. Both types of bond are discussed in more detail in Chapter 7.

2.2.7 Cash flows of the different structures

Table 2.7 illustrates algebraically the cash flow structures of the different types of indexed bonds discussed above. Again, the formulae are based on an assumption that the bonds pay annual coupons and that there is no lag in indexation.

Table 2.7 Indexed bond cash flow structures

Type of indexed bond	Interest payments	Final payment*
Capital Indexed Bond	$r \times \frac{P_t}{P_0}$	$100 \times \frac{P_{\text{mat}}}{P_0} + r \times \frac{P_{\text{mat}}}{P_0}$
Interest Indexed Bond	$r + 100 \times \left(\frac{P_t}{P_{t-1}} - 1\right)$	$100 \times \frac{P_{\text{mat}}}{P_{\text{mat}-1}} + r$
Current Pay Bond	$r \times \frac{P_t}{P_{t-1}} + 100 \times \left(\frac{P_t}{P_{t-1}} - 1\right)$	$100 \times \frac{P_{\text{mat}}}{P_{\text{mat}-1}} + r \times \frac{P_{\text{mat}}}{P_{\text{mat}-1}}$
Indexed Annuity Bond	$B \times \frac{P_t}{P_0}$	$B \times \frac{P_{\text{mat}}}{P_0}$
Indexed Zero-Coupon Bond	–	$100 \times \frac{P_{\text{mat}}}{P_0}$
Icelandic Indexed Bond	–	$100 \times \frac{P_{\text{mat}}}{P_0} \times \left(1 + \frac{r}{100}\right)^{\text{mat}}$
Polish IR Bond**	–	$100 + 100 \times \left(\left(\frac{P_{\text{mat}}}{P_0} - 1\right) + \frac{r}{100}\right)$

where: r = annual real coupon rate (%)
P_0 = value of the price index when the bond is issued
P_t = value of the price index at time t
P_{mat} = value of the price index at maturity
$P_{\text{mat}-1}$ = value of the price index on the penultimate interest payment date
B = base annuity payment.

* This consists of the redemption payment and, where applicable, the final interest payment.
** This formula is in fact a slight simplification. The annual CPI growth factor for these bonds was actually computed as the product of the 12 monthly growth factors. See Chapter 7 for more details.

2.2.8 Factors that influence the choice of security design

When deciding which cash flow structure to adopt for its indexed bonds, an issuer must consider both the potential investor demand for competing designs as well as its own requirements. Factors that are likely to be important to both issuers and investors include the duration, reinvestment risk and tax treatment of the bonds.

The *duration* of a bond is the average time to each of its cash flows weighted by present value and provides a measure of the interest rate risk of a bond – the higher a bond's duration, the more its price will fluctuate with moves in interest rates. For any given maturity, of the main structures discussed earlier zero-coupon bonds will have the longest duration and annuities the shortest, with CIBs having a higher duration than IIBs. In general, indexed bonds will have longer duration than conventional bonds of a comparable cash flow structure[23] and so are likely to be popular with investors who have long-duration liabilities to hedge.

In Sweden the longest IZCB had a duration of 20 years when first issued,[24] while the duration of the longest conventional bond at the time was between seven and eight years. There has been some speculation that this lack of substitutability between the two asset classes was at least partially responsible for the poor initial demand for Swedish indexed bonds, which in turn led to suggestions that their issuance be limited to those of similar duration to existing conventional bonds. However, as Persson (1997) notes, intuition might suggest the opposite view: "the major welfare gains (and maybe the major cost savings) are to be made by spanning the space as widely as possible, that is, by issuing instruments for which *no* good substitutes exist."

Like conventional bonds, indexed bonds are subject to *reinvestment risk*, because the rate at which future cash flows can be reinvested is unknown when the bond is purchased, and so the true real yield that will be attained by holding a bond to maturity is unknown at the time of purchase. Clearly, those bonds with a higher proportion of the return in the form of periodic coupon payments are most exposed to this form of risk. So, of the structures considered, indexed annuities have the highest exposure, followed by IIBs and then CIBs. IZCBs are not subject to reinvestment risk, simply because there are no coupon payments to reinvest. Table 2.8 helps to illustrate how the reinvestment risk can differ for the two most common designs, CIBs and IIBs, by comparing the realised real returns of a 10-year CIB with those of a 10-year IIB for different coupon reinvestment rates.[25]

Tax regimes in many countries tend to favour the interest indexed design over the capital indexed or zero-coupon structures, because the inflation uplift component of an indexed bond's nominal redemption payment is usually treated as current income for tax purposes. Applying such a system to CIBs or IZCBs results in tax on the inflation uplift being levied on an annual basis, even though the uplift itself is not paid out until maturity. Taxing *phantom* income in this way presents CIB investors with the risk that they face potentially negative post-tax cash flows in the event of high inflation, while for investors in IZCBs negative annual post-tax cash flows are certain in the years prior to

[23] This is because the nominal cash flows generated by an index-linked bond grow over time, if inflation is positive. Chapter 5 examines how the duration of an indexed bond differs from that of a nominal bond.

[24] Measured with respect to real yields.

[25] These returns are computed on the assumption that the bonds are held to redemption and that there is no lag in indexation. Both bonds have a real coupon rate of 3.375% and inflation is assumed to be constant at a rate of 3% for the IIB calculations.

Table 2.8 Real return of Capital and Interest Indexed Bonds as a function of the real reinvestment rate

Real reinvestment rate (%)	Real return to maturity (%)	
	Capital Indexed Bond	Interest Indexed Bond
0.000	2.930	2.560
2.000	3.190	3.010
3.375	3.375	3.340
5.000	3.620	3.750
7.000	3.940	4.290

Reproduced from Prout *et al.* (1997) by permission of Bankers Trust.

redemption. The effects that different tax regimes can have on indexed bonds are considered in greater detail later in this chapter.

Since pension funds are typically large holders of indexed bonds it may seem odd that CIBs, rather than indexed zeros, are the predominant inflation-indexed product,[26] but there are several reasons why this might be the case. First, in most markets the authorities' decision to begin issuing indexed bonds was itself seen as a bold step – to depart from the established bond format at the same time, by issuing zeros, might have been considered too risky. For governments the issuance of IZCBs or non-indexed bonds can also convey an unfortunate policy signal – because they backload interest payments they can be used to produce a short-term saving in a government's borrowing requirement. In any case, in some indexed bond markets the authorities have granted market practitioners the right to strip indexed bonds, making zero-coupon issuance largely irrelevant. *Stripping*[27] is a means by which market intermediaries can separate a bond into its individual cash flows. The right to strip indexed bonds provides the market with the option to create IZCBs without the issuer taking on any of the risks associated with their direct issuance, and a liquid strips market enables a complete zero-coupon curve to be constructed (i.e., zero-coupon bonds at regular and frequent maturities along the yield curve). To replicate this by sales of zero-coupon bonds would be a major logistical exercise,[28] although it would give authorities the flexibility to target the maturities where demand is greatest and would probably also provide more liquidity than the equivalent strips market as each zero-coupon bond, particularly at longer maturities, would be significantly larger.

Many government bond markets already have the general market infrastructure in place that enables participants to strip conventional bonds, but among the larger issuers only Canada, New Zealand and the USA[29] permit the stripping of indexed bonds. While bonds in Canada and the USA can be stripped into separate indexed cash flows, a less conventional approach exists in New Zealand where indexed bonds are

[26] By purchasing a series of IZCBs, a pension fund would be able to construct indexed annuities or deferred payment bonds that more closely match their liabilities than would a combination of CIBs. In theory, IZCBs should also enable a shorter indexation lag to be used than is possible for indexed bonds with periodic coupon payments.
[27] STRIPS is an acronym for Separate Trading of Registered Interest and Principal of Securities.
[28] For example, consider the hypothetical case in which a government wishes to establish a zero-coupon index-linked bond market with the longest maturity issue at 30 years. The alternative to issuing a single, strippable 30-year bond would be to issue 30 independent zero-coupon bonds (or 60 if coupons are paid semi-annually).
[29] In addition, the authorities in France and South Africa have announced their intentions to permit the stripping of their indexed bonds at some point in the future.

eligible to be stripped into three components: the unadjusted principal, the principal uplift and the set of adjusted coupon payments. To date, this facility has not proved particularly popular in any of these markets,[30] primarily due to the perceived illiquidity of individual coupon strips. This is more of an issue for indexed strips than conventional strips since the former typically have lower coupons (resulting in smaller coupon strips) and because of the complexity of making coupon strips from different indexed bonds *fungible* with one another.[31] Details of the method used by the US Treasury to create fungible coupon strips from its inflation-indexed securities can be found in Grieves and Sunner (1999).

The properties of CIBs and IIBs are considered further by Munnell and Grolnic (1986) and Prout *et al.* (1997), while those of CIBs and CPBs are discussed in detail by Abuhoff and Malik (1996).

2.3 APPLICATION OF THE INDEX TO THE CASH FLOWS

2.3.1 The problem of the indexation lag

One of the most important characteristics of inflation-indexed bonds is that they provide a high degree of real value certainty. In order to ensure *complete* real value certainty, all cash flows would have to be adjusted for inflation right up to the moment at which they are paid. However, in practice, unavoidable lags between actual movements in the price index and the corresponding adjustments to cash flows distort the "inflation-proofing" properties of indexed bonds. As a result there is a period at the end of a bond's life when there is no inflation protection at all,[32] counterbalanced by a period of equal length before it is issued for which inflation compensation is paid. In general the inflation rate in these two periods will not be the same, and consequently the real return on an indexed bond will not be fully invariant to inflation – the longer the lag, the poorer the instrument's inflation proofing.

For instance, consider the simple case of an IZCB. As Figure 2.7 shows,[33] if the bond were perfectly indexed its nominal redemption value would be $100(P_{\text{maturity}}/P_{\text{issue}})$, whereas with a six-month lag it would be $100(P_{\text{maturity}-1}/P_{\text{issue}-1})$. Clearly, there is no guarantee that $(P_{\text{maturity}}/P_{\text{issue}})$ and $(P_{\text{maturity}-1}/P_{\text{issue}-1})$ will be equal.

The shorter a bond's residual maturity, the more the indexation lag becomes relevant, since the proportion of its remaining life for which it is effectively a nominal security increases as the security ages. For instance, a UK index-linked gilt with two years to maturity exposes investors to inflation risk over the eight-month period that represents the final one-third of its remaining life. Such indexation lags are of most concern when inflation is volatile.

[30] See Chapters 6 and 7 for further discussion of individual markets.

[31] In this context, coupons from different bonds payable on the same date are said to be "fungible" if they are perfectly substitutable with one another.

[32] This period is eight months in the case of UK index-linked gilts but shorter in most other markets.

[33] This example assumes that time is measured in six-month periods.

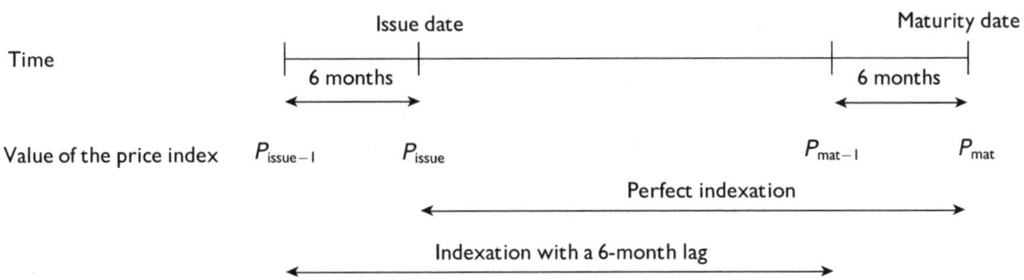

Figure 2.7 Cash flow impact of the indexation lag

2.3.2 Why indexation lags are necessary

There are two reasons why cash flows must be indexed to inflation with a lag. First, it takes time to compile and publish price indices. In most countries the CPI for a given month is typically published in the middle of the following month and so at best could be applied only to bonds with cash flows due in the second half of the publication month (thereby introducing a lag of at least one month[34]). GDP price deflators are usually published only quarterly, leading to a much longer lag for bonds that use such series to index cash flows. In addition to the expected time delay for an index to be published, issuers of indexed bonds often also allow an additional "safety margin" of a few weeks to cover the possibility of publication delays.

Second, a more significant lag can arise due to institutional arrangements for trading and settling bonds between coupon payment dates. Whenever a bond changes hands on a day other than a coupon payment date, its valuation will reflect the proximity of the next cash flow, and this is effected by the payment of accrued interest to compensate sellers for the period during which they have held the bond but for which they will receive no coupon payment. In most of the major index-linked bond markets, accrued interest is computed based on the convention first employed for Canadian RRBs. Accrued interest is based on cumulative movements in the CPI running from the last coupon date, and so it is not necessary to know the nominal value of the next coupon with certainty at all times. The daily rate of accrual varies from month to month in line with changes in the price index,[35] even between months within the same coupon period. The notable exception to this practice is the UK index-linked gilt market, in which the bonds are designed such that the nominal value of the next coupon payment is known at all times. Since coupons fall due semi-annually an eight-month lag must be employed, as this is the minimum period that allows the nominal accrued interest to be calculated with certainty for each and every potential settlement date within the current coupon period. Of the eight months, two allow for publication of the index (including a "safety margin") and the remaining six for the accrued interest calculation. In Italy the CTR issue of 1983 paid annual coupons with a one-year lag.

[34] Notwithstanding the fact that many price surveys used to construct indices are conducted throughout the month in question, so it is always debatable precisely how long a lag any particular publication date truly represents.

[35] For example, the difference between the CPI numbers for January and February determines the rate of nominal coupon accrual from 1 April to 1 May – this is usually referred to as a three-month indexation lag. This accrual convention is described in more detail in Appendix 6.2.

2.3.3 How to minimise the indexation lag

Of the two factors that can give rise to a lag in the indexation of bond cash flows, the publication delay, though unavoidable, can be minimised by a choice of price index that is published frequently (preferably at least monthly) and with a short lag – one of the main reasons why the CPI is usually used.

Some issuers have carefully considered the method for calculating accrued interest in order not to extend the lag much beyond that necessary to allow for the publication of the index. The method introduced by the Canadian authorities for their RRBs (first issued in 1991) and which is now used in the majority of major markets employs a lag of just three months. As detailed above, accrued interest using this convention is computed based on cumulative movements in the CPI running from the last coupon date, and so it is not necessary to know the nominal value of the next coupon with certainty at all times. This cumulative measure of CPI growth is referred to as the *index ratio* and is used to compute inflation adjustments for both principal and coupons.[36]

One drawback with employing the Canadian-style method for calculating accrued interest is that the rate of accrual will in general vary from month to month within the same coupon period. One way to eliminate the accrued interest part of the indexation lag *entirely* would of course be to issue IZCBs – an approach advocated by Hetzel (1992), who further suggests that IZCBs could be issued and redeemed just after the middle of the month to minimise the delay between publication of the CPI and the payment of the bonds' cash flows.[37]

There are, however, several ways in which the lag can be reduced while retaining not only coupon payments but also a constant rate of nominal accrual throughout each individual coupon period. As noted earlier, in order to compute the nominal value of a coupon before it starts to accrue, a lag longer than the period between consecutive coupon payments is required. One way to reduce the lag is to issue indexed bonds with more frequent coupon payments. For instance, while conventional bonds in Australia and New Zealand pay semi-annual coupons, indexed bonds in these markets pay coupons quarterly. Shen (1995) suggests that indexed bonds could be issued with monthly coupons, thereby reducing the necessary length of the indexation lag for a UK-style indexed bond from eight months to three. However, as Price (1997) points out, high-frequency coupon bonds are likely to be administratively burdensome and so are rarely issued. Also, in markets where indexed bonds can be stripped, increasing the frequency of coupon payments will reduce the size – and hence almost certainly the liquidity – of the resultant coupon strips.

While reducing the length of the indexation lag is perhaps the most obvious way to obtain an improvement in the quality of the inflation protection offered by indexed bonds, it is not the only way. A more complex solution is proposed by Barro (1994), who suggests an alternative method for index-linking gilts while effectively retaining the eight-month lag.[38] Barro suggests that inflation in the six months prior to a coupon or

[36] A detailed explanation of these calculations can be found in Appendix 6.2. This method of indexation has also been adopted by many other government debt agencies, including those of France, Sweden and the USA.

[37] Hetzel (1992) refers to the USA in particular although his observation applies more generally, since CPI publication schedules are similar in many industrialised countries.

[38] Although Barro's formulation is actually for an index-linked gilt with a six-month lag (for ease of exposition) the methodology can easily be extended to indexed bonds with any length lag. More details of Barro's proposal appear in Appendix 2.2.

principal payment should be proxied by giving double weight to the previous six months (the most recent for which data are available when the coupon must be fixed) rather than by including in the calculation the six months before the bond's issue date, since the former is likely to be more representative of current inflation rates. However, the seasonal patterns inherent in many CPI series means that this may not always be the case – indeed, employing such an indexation technique might serve to amplify seasonal effects, in which case it would prove undesirable. The Bank of England decided against introducing "Barro-style" index-linked gilts on the grounds that such a move would risk segmentation of the market between gilts with different indexing techniques[39] – to change the indexation methodology on existing issues was deemed infeasible.

Barro's method uses inflation from the previous coupon interval to proxy the rate in the current period. This idea can be taken one step further by the use of an explicit inflation forecast to determine index values for those months that have passed but for which official numbers have yet to be published. Such a procedure might be difficult to implement in practice, since common agreement would have to be reached as to how the forecast index numbers were to be calculated. Alternatively, a verifiably independent third party could be employed to produce the data, either by using its own forecasting techniques or by surveying forecasts from a number of other institutions. In 1972 Brazil introduced an index adjustment that was partly based on official government expectations of inflation. This gave the Brazilian authorities substantial latitude to influence interest rates and bond prices through its forecasts of future inflation. Jud (1978) reports that the government so underestimated the rate of inflation that in 1973 the *ex post* real rate of return on a 4% one-year index-linked government bond was only 1.6%. As a result, in 1974 the authorities reverted to the use of only lagged realised inflation to adjust indexed bond cash flows.[40]

2.3.4 Full or partial indexation?

Another issue that arises in the design process is the decision whether to fully or only partially index the cash flows. Investors may prefer partially indexed bonds if they provide a better hedge for their liabilities, and it can take several different forms. For instance, some governments have issued indexed securities that protect investors from a fall in the nominal value of their cash flows in the event of deflation. In France the *Rentes Giscard* bond paid a guaranteed annual coupon of "not less than 7%", while in New Zealand each inflation adjustment used to set the semi-annual coupons for Index-Linked Government Stock was defined to be the maximum of the six-month change in the CPI and zero, thus ensuring that investors were protected against the possibility of declining nominal cash flows in periods of deflation.[41]

When the US Treasury launched its inflation-indexed securities in 1997 it decided to provide a "deflation floor" in the form of a guarantee that each bond's redemption payment would never be less than the original par amount,[42] thus serving to protect the nominal value of the principal should deflation occur over the bond's lifetime. Follow-

[39] Following discussion at its conference on index-linked debt in 1995 – see Bank of England (1996).
[40] Indexation in Brazil is discussed in more detail in Chapter 7.
[41] More information on these bonds appears in Chapter 7.
[42] See Department of the (US) Treasury (1997a, p. 4).

ing the US lead, indexed bonds in France, Italy, South Africa and Sweden[43] also employ deflation floors.

In the UK, the DMO considered the merits of deflation floors as part of its consultation on index-linked gilt redesign in 2001.[44] While noting that the inclusion of a deflation floor would provide consistency with bonds in other large markets, the DMO cited several reasons why it would be reluctant to introduce such a feature. Most importantly, a deflation floor would reduce the value to the government of index-linked gilts in its debt portfolio since their "deficit-smoothing" properties would be reduced in certain economic scenarios.[45] Second, to include such a feature would require legislation and, furthermore, would rule out any possibility of index-linked coupon and principal strip fungibility in the future. The DMO also asserted that investors would place little value on any deflation floor, on the basis that over the preceding 50 years the longest period of deflation in the UK had been for a mere 21 months during the late 1950s.

Although perhaps the most common manifestation of partial indexation, the deflation floor is not the only variant to have been used in the design of index-linked bonds. In the UK the 1995 Pensions Act requires defined benefit pension schemes to index mature pensions entitlements to RPI inflation, with a 5% per annum cap and a 0% per annum floor on that uplift.[46] While the Act was still at the discussion stage, some commentators indicated that its introduction might give rise to potential demand from pension funds for a new type of indexed security. Referred to as *Limited Price Indexation* (LPI) bonds, this new product class was envisaged to have coupon and principal payments indexed to the increase in the RPI, albeit with a cap at 5% and a floor at 0%, and thereby provide an ideal hedge for the corresponding pension fund liabilities.[47]

Despite the potential demand that the Pensions Act created for this new product, it was not until 2001 that LPI issuance began, with sterling-denominated LPI bonds being issued that year by the European Investment Bank, as well as by water and electricity utilities.[48] The UK authorities have also debated on more than one occasion whether or not to issue LPI government bonds. However, on each occasion they have decided against going down such a path, on the grounds that the introduction of securities with a new structure might damage the liquidity of the existing index-linked gilt market. The introduction of inflation caps would also reduce the deficit-smoothing properties produced by the presence of index-linked bonds in a government's debt portfolio, in much the same manner as would the existence of deflation floors, another factor behind the DMO's reluctance.[49] Besides, the existence of a large and reasonably liquid index-linked government bond market, coupled with a growing

[43] Only the design of the more recently issued (coupon-paying) Swedish indexed bonds incorporates a deflation floor.
[44] See UK Debt Management Office (2001d).
[45] One major advantage to governments of indexed debt is the perceived correlation between the rate of inflation and economic growth, which serves to reduce nominal debt payments in periods of low growth (and vice versa). See Chapter 4 for more details.
[46] This Act took effect on 6 April 1997. In June 2003 Andrew Smith, the Secretary of State for Work and Pensions, announced draft legislation to replace the 1995 Pensions Act. In particular, the proposed legislation includes a reduction of the inflation cap from 5% to 2.5%.
[47] While the "pre-retirement" liabilities of most *defined benefit* pension funds in the UK are effectively linked to wages, "post-retirement" liabilities are linked to consumer prices.
[48] More information on these bonds appears in Chapter 6.
[49] See UK Debt Management Office (2002a).

indexed derivatives market, should enable investment banks to offer "tailor-made" products for pension funds and other clients. The structure of LPI bonds is discussed in more detail in Chapter 8.

The range of potential implementations of partial indexation is vast, but in general its use is driven either by specific investor demand or by particular concerns of an issuer that outweigh any increased costs arising from the divergence from pure inflation linking. In the past other forms of partial indexation have been employed by the authorities in both Brazil and Israel.[50] For instance, in the mid-1970s Israeli indexed bonds were partially adjusted at the rate of 80% or 90% of the change in the CPI. Also, in the 1970s the inflation adjustment for Brazilian indexed bonds was at one time defined to be a weighted average of past inflation and a fixed rate of 15%.

2.4 THE IMPACT OF TAX REGULATIONS

Since government issuers of indexed bonds often also have the power to choose (at least in part) the tax regime that will apply to their securities, the tax regime is considered here to be a design feature. Tax regulations can affect indexed bonds in two ways: first, if cash flows are taxed on a nominal rather than a real basis, then post-tax *real* yields are uncertain; second, the rules determining the timing of tax payments on the inflation uplift component of the principal will tend to make some designs of indexed bonds more attractive to investors than others.

2.4.1 Uncertainty of post-tax real yields

Real value certainty is the most important characteristic of indexed bonds. Taxable investors will, however, be concerned with *post-* rather than pre-tax real returns. While perfectly indexed bonds guarantee the certainty of pre-tax real returns, any tax system that fails to distinguish between the two components of an indexed bond's nominal income – the real return and the inflation uplift – will reintroduce inflation risk.[51] Under such a system, even if pre-tax real yields do not change, an increase in inflation will raise the nominal yield on indexed bonds, thereby increasing an investors' tax liability and so lowering their post-tax real return.

The following example from Shen (1995) helps to illustrate this concept. Consider an indexed bond guaranteed to yield a 3% (pre-tax) real return. As the first scenario in Table 2.9 shows, if inflation averages 1% over the bond's lifetime, the pre-tax nominal return is 4%. At a 30% flat tax rate the tax burden is 1.2% (30% of the 4% nominal yield), giving a post-tax nominal yield of 2.8%. Subtracting inflation results in a post-tax real return of 1.8%. Now consider the case where inflation in fact averages 7% (scenario 2) and the pre-tax nominal return rises to 10%. This gain in the nominal yield also increases the investor's tax burden to 3% and so reduces the post-tax nominal yield to 7%, the same as the inflation rate. Thus, the post-tax real yield declines to zero. So,

[50] See Chapter 7 for more details.

[51] Nevertheless, this is a feature of the tax system employed in most countries where indexed bonds are issued.

Table 2.9 The effect of taxes on indexed and conventional bonds

Scenario number	Type of bond	Inflation rate (%)	Pre-tax real yield (%)	Pre-tax nominal yield (%)	Tax burden at 30% marginal tax rate (%)	Post-tax nominal yield (%)	Post-tax real yield (%)	Change in post-tax real yield (%)
		(1)	(2)	(3) = (1) + (2)	(4) = (3) × 30%	(5) = (3) − (4)	(6) = (5) − (1)	(7) = change in (6)
1	Indexed	1.0	3.0	4.0	1.2	2.8	1.8	–
2	Indexed	7.0	3.0	10.0	3.0	7.0	0.0	−1.8
3	Nominal	1.0	3.0	4.0	1.2	2.8	1.8	–
4	Nominal	7.0	−3.0	4.0	1.2	2.8	−4.2	−6.0

Reproduced from Shen (1995, p. 51), by permission of Pu Shen.

even a bond with no indexation lag exposes taxpaying investors to inflation risk under the tax regime described here.

To ensure that the real value of the post-tax cash flows is fully guaranteed, the nominal adjustments due to inflation must be exempt from tax. However, since the tax rate will be applied to the full *nominal* income derived from conventional bonds, such rules give preferential treatment to an indexed bond that provides the same *ex post* nominal yield and as such may prove to be undesirable. Also, in certain inflation environments, employing such rules could substantially decrease the authorities' tax take relative to alternative regimes and thus markedly reduce the cost-saving arguments for the issuance of indexed bonds. An alternative solution that goes some way toward tackling the problem is proposed by Campbell and Shiller (1996), who suggest that a government could create indexed bonds with inflation adjustments that more than compensate for inflation, so that post-tax cash flows are stabilised for investors in targeted tax brackets.

However, although the tax system can reintroduce inflation risk for indexed bonds, it is still considerably less than that for conventional bonds. For a nominal security the decline in the post-tax real yield caused by an increase in inflation is one for one, while for an indexed bond the decline is scaled by the tax rate. This effect is illustrated by the example in Table 2.9. Suppose an investor is faced with the choice of an indexed bond with an *ex ante* pre-tax real yield of 3% and a nominal bond with a pre-tax nominal yield of 4% and that the investor has similar expectations regarding inflation as those implied by the prevailing market prices. In the scenario under which this expectation is borne out, both instruments provide the same pre- and post-tax returns (scenarios 1 and 3). If, however, inflation turns out to be 7% (i.e., 6 percentage points above expectations), the post-tax real yield on the indexed bond is reduced by 1.8 percentage points (scenario 2), while the post-tax real yield on the conventional bond is reduced by the full 6 percentage points (scenario 4). As both Hetzel (1992) and Shen (1995) point out, one advantage of applying the same tax treatment to indexed and conventional bonds is that information about inflation expectations embodied in their relative prices should not be distorted by tax effects. This issue is discussed further in Chapter 5.

2.4.2 The effect of income accrual rules

In addition to the issue of whether indexed bonds' nominal or real cash flows should be taxed, there is also the question of when tax should be levied on the inflation uplift on the principal. In several countries (including Australia, Canada and the USA) this uplift is treated as current income for tax purposes. This creates no particular problem for holders of interest indexed bonds, since all the inflation compensation is paid through ongoing coupon adjustments. However, applying this rule to capital (or zero-coupon) indexed bonds results in tax on the inflation uplift component of the principal being levied on an annual basis, even though the uplift itself is not paid out until maturity. As Campbell and Shiller (1996) note, under such a system the taxes owed on CIBs could potentially exceed the coupon income from the bond, leading to a series of negative annual net cash flows.

Taxing income that has not yet been received (so-called "phantom" income) risks restricting the set of investors who will find it efficient to hold CIBs to those who are exempt from taxes, such as pension funds. However, the alternative of deferring tax payments on the inflation adjustment until maturity would again favour indexed bonds over their conventional counterparts and could result in a significant loss in revenue for the government. Interestingly, this is the approach that the US Treasury applies to its indexed savings bonds that have been issued to the retail market since 1998. In the UK, the principal inflation uplift on index-linked gilts is tax-free, widening the appeal of the bonds to investors other than tax-exempt institutions.[52]

2.5 OPTIONS ON INDEXED BONDS

In principle, it is possible to buy or write options on indexed bonds in just the same way as for other classes of securities. Such options can either take the form of a contract traded separately from the underlying bond or be embedded in the structure of the security itself as an additional feature to the benefit of the issuer or in order to attract investors. The former are discussed in detail in Chapters 8 and 9, while this section provides an introduction to the latter – bonds with embedded options. Since the three most common forms of option-bearing *conventional* bonds are callable, puttable and convertible bonds, this section considers the corresponding indexed instruments. To date, however, issuance of indexed bonds with such characteristics has been relatively rare and has largely been confined to the corporate sector.

2.5.1 Callable bonds

A *callable bond* is a security that can be redeemed early (or "called") at the discretion of the issuer on a single date, or on one of a set of dates, specified at issue. Should its yield level fall below its coupon rate, the issuer can redeem the bond at par and refinance their debt by selling a new bond paying lower coupons.[53] Callable indexed bonds have been issued by corporations in both Spain and Peru. A call option on an indexed bond can also take the form of a restriction (or cap) on the size of the cash flow payouts, as in the case of the LPI bonds briefly mentioned above and described in detail in Chapters 8 and 9.

2.5.2 Puttable bonds

A *puttable bond* has the opposite feature to that embedded in a callable bond – it is the investor rather than the issuer that has the right to exercise the option, which in this case is to *sell* the bond back to the issuer at a predetermined price. In Australia both the South Australian Government Financing Authority (SAFA) and the Treasury Corporation of Victoria (TCV) have issued index-linked puttable bonds. While the two TCV issues are both IABs, the SAFA has issued a puttable CIB as well as a puttable IAB.[54] Such options allow an investor to "put", or sell, the bond back to the issuer on specific dates and at specific real yields. The option is of value to the investor because it

[52] Despite this, pension funds are still the dominant holders of index-linked gilts.
[53] This is a slight simplification since it ignores the time value of the option.
[54] For full details of these bonds see BZW (1992, p. 118).

Table 2.10 Put option details for the Treasury Corporation of Victoria (TCV) 2030 Indexed Annuity Bond (IAB)

Put date	Put yield (%)
15 Dec 2002	5.90
15 Dec 2007	5.80
15 Dec 2012	5.80
15 Dec 2017	5.80
15 Dec 2022	5.80
15 Dec 2027	5.80

offers protection against adverse movements in real yields, while at the same time guaranteeing liquidity at certain dates in the future. Table 2.10 illustrates the nature of the put option embedded in the TCV 2030 bond, which was issued on 15 June 1992. Moss and Preston (1997) discuss how to price puttable indexed bonds.

2.5.3 Convertible bonds

A *convertible bond* gives an investor the right to exchange the bond for another security at one or more dates either before or at maturity. Convertible and puttable bonds are therefore very similar – the primary difference being whether the holder receives cash or another security on exercising their option. For corporate issues of convertible bonds the option usually gives the right to convert the bond into equity, while government convertible issues typically confer the right to exchange one bond for another.

In May 1983 the UK government issued £1 billion of a convertible index-linked gilt issue ($2\frac{1}{2}$% Index-linked Treasury Convertible 1999). This bond gave investors the option to convert all or part of their holdings into a conventional gilt ($10\frac{1}{4}$% Conversion 1999) on any one of three dates.[55] In the event, 97% of the bond was converted at the first available opportunity and a further 2.8% on the subsequent conversion dates, leaving only a small amount of the bond unconverted (£1.7mn) which ran to maturity. The ratios of notional amounts for each of the conversion dates were fixed at issue: £100 nominal of the conventional bond would be receivable per £100 nominal of the index-linked bond converted.[56] In Austria, Immo-Bank issued a corporate indexed convertible bond in 1995 which matures in 2010 and offers holders the right to convert their holdings into shares.

2.6 METHOD OF ISSUE

Because of the relative quantities of bonds involved, the mechanics of selling debt is more of an issue for governments than for corporations. At present, government bonds

[55] 22 November 1983, 22 May 1984 or 22 November 1984.

[56] In other words, the value of the principal of the indexed bond was not indexed for the purposes of the conversion. Precise details of the terms of this bond can be found in Bank of England (1983).

are issued by a wide variety of techniques, including auctions, subscriptions, taps and private placements, and extensive research by both academics and debt managers continues in order to identify the optimal technique. Much of this work focuses exclusively on the choice between single and multiple price auctions.[57] While much of the analysis regarding the issuance of conventional bonds is directly applicable to their indexed counterparts, there are some additional factors that need to be considered.

2.6.1 Pricing

When an issuer offers a new type of financial product for the first time, the primary difficulty faced by investors and issuers alike is to price it with no comparable instrument trading in the secondary market for reference. This is likely to be a particular problem for indexed bonds, both because of their comparative rarity and because of their relative structural complexity. One way for an issuer to overcome the pricing problem is to sell indexed bonds (initially at least) by auction,[58] thereby transferring the responsibility for pricing the bond to investors. By retaining the right to not fully allot the bond should bids be deemed too low – or even by stating explicitly the minimum acceptable price before issue – the issuer can maintain some degree of control over the issue price.

Pricing considerations tend to favour the single or uniform price auction format to that of the multiple price auction. At a single price auction all successful bidders receive their allocations at the clearing price, whereas at multiple price auctions bidders pay the price they actually bid. Use of the multiple price format will tend to favour more sophisticated bidders, who are likely to have more information and be better equipped to price new instruments, and hence may discourage the participation of smaller investors. In contrast, small investors are more likely to participate at a single price auction since they know that any bonds they attain should be at a competitive rate (i.e., the clearing price).

The importance of the pricing problem can be graphically illustrated by a couple of examples. In the UK, in order to avoid pricing difficulties, the Treasury initially issued index-linked gilts by single price auction. However, as Price (1997) reports, the market actually found pricing the first index-linked gilt difficult, with bids at the first auction ranging from £80 to £130. Since the entire issue was allocated at one price (par), some investors were saved from an exceptionally large "winners' curse".[59] Similar problems were encountered by those participating at the early auctions of CIBs by the Australian government. However, because the Australian auctions were conducted on a multiple yield basis[60] there were significant variations in the allocation prices at each auction. For instance, at the February 1986 auction, the range of accepted yields for the 20-year

[57] Two particularly good papers on auction theory are Klemperer (1999) and Chari and Weber (1992).

[58] An alternative way of transferring the responsibility of price setting to the market is to sell the bonds through a syndicate.

[59] At a multiple price auction, bids are filled from the highest down until all securities to be issued are allocated. This means that to have received an allocation a bidder must necessarily have paid at or above the lowest accepted price. An investor who bids excessively above the market will suffer what is known as the *winners' curse* – "winning" at the auction, but paying a significant premium above the clearing price.

[60] In most countries, auctions of index-linked bonds are conducted on a real yield rather than a price basis. For simplicity, rather than referring to such auctions as "single (or multiple) price auctions on a yield basis", the simpler terminology "single (or multiple) yield auctions" is used here and elsewhere in this book.

CIB was 200 basis points.[61] In South Africa the first one or two auctions of a new indexed bond are held on a single yield basis to aid price discovery, before a switch to the multiple yield format for subsequent reopenings.

2.6.2 Cost-effectiveness and market development

Another important consideration is which method is likely to produce the most revenue for the issuer. Although much academic literature exists on the relative merits of single or multiple price auctions there is no clear consensus as to which format will tend to minimise issuance costs.

Despite the prevalence of government bond auctions, other issuance techniques also have their advantages. For instance, selling bonds by tap allows an issuer to time debt sales to coincide with any increase in demand and corresponding rise in market prices and, as such, potentially reduce its interest costs. However, on the downside, such a policy tends to mean that individual bonds and the overall size of a market can be built up only gradually. Perhaps more importantly, this increase in flexibility may come at the expense of transparency, which in turn may lead the market to demand a premium and thereby inflate issuance costs in the long run.

In contrast, there are a number of reasons why auctions may create the potential to sell more debt at a similar or lower cost than that achievable through the use of taps. The preannouncement of an auction gives end investors more time to plan for new supply; "When-Issued" (WI) trading helps price discovery and reduces risks to those bidding in the auction, and the "event" of the auction itself might attract additional traders and hence improve liquidity. Of course, the downside to a fixed auction schedule is the lack of flexibility to react to any large, unpredictable changes in demand. Although some government debt issuers still employ taps (the Danish government being one notable example), nowadays the consensus among most debt management agencies is that a preannounced auction programme is the most cost-effective mechanism over the long run. Indeed, all the major government issuers of indexed bonds employ auctions at least some of the time – see below.

2.6.3 Consistency with other instruments

A priori, it would seem desirable to use the same technique for issuing indexed bonds as that already in place for their conventional counterparts. This simplifies operating procedures for the issuer and has the advantage that the technique used for index-linked issuance is one with which investors are already familiar. However, the less liquid nature of indexed bonds and their relative novelty as a product may mean that such an approach is inappropriate. Indeed, such consistency has been eschewed by government debt managers in several countries. For instance, in the UK, index-linked gilts are sold by single price auction while conventional gilts are sold using the multiple price format.

[61] The results of early CIB auctions by the Australian government are discussed in more detail in Chapter 6.

Table 2.11 Techniques used for issuing indexed government debt

Country	Current issuance technique*	Basis of issue
Australia	Multiple price auction	Real yield
Canada	Single price auction	Real yield
France	Syndication/Multiple price auction	Real price
Iceland	Multiple price auction	Real yield
Israel	Multiple price auction	Price
New Zealand	Single price auction	Real yield
South Africa	Single/Multiple price auction	Real yield
Sweden	Multiple price auction	Real yield
UK	Single price auction	Price
USA	Single price auction	Real Yield

* Note: At the time of writing, index-linked issuance had been suspended in both Australia and New Zealand.

2.6.4 What happens in practice?

Auctions are the predominant method of issue among the major issuers of indexed debt, as Table 2.11 shows, with only the French government deviating slightly from this pattern by using a syndicate system for the initial issue of most of its indexed bonds.[62] However, while there is clear consensus on the merits of auctions, the same cannot be said regarding the use of a multiple or single price format. It should also be noted that several of the largest issuers of indexed bonds have changed their method of issuance on at least one occasion, illustrating that the best choice for a fledgling index-linked market may not necessarily be optimal once the asset class becomes more established.

2.7 SUMMARY

Although all inflation-indexed securities are designed with the same aim, to provide investors with certain real returns, this chapter has shown that there are several ways in which this goal can be achieved. There are a number of important constraints on issuers that can materially affect the structure of such securities. The choice of index is important; both the integrity and acceptability of the index itself as well as its publication frequency have a real impact on the properties of instruments with payments linked to it. This choice, and the resulting cash flow structure, is often determined by demand from end investors and driven by the nature of their liabilities. Tax regulations can also play an important role, even more so perhaps than is the case in markets for other securities; even if an instrument provides certain pre-tax real returns, aspects of the taxation regime often result in post-tax real returns being uncertain. These factors have led to a wide variety of sometimes quite complex instruments being developed to meet what is, in principle, a straightforward requirement – real income certainty.

[62] While the first four French indexed bonds were all launched by syndication, the fifth bond (the latest at the time of writing), 2.5% OAT*i* 2013, was in fact launched by auction. See Section 6.3 for more details.

Appendices

A2.1 CALCULATING THE BASE ANNUITY PAYMENT FOR INDEXED ANNUITY BONDS (IABs)[63]

The equation for deriving the base annuity payment for an annual paying n-year IAB under an assumption of a real interest rate of r is:

$$B = \frac{F}{a_n}$$

where: B = base annuity payment

F = face value of the bond

r = annual real interest rate (decimal) (e.g. $r = 0.03$ for interest rate of 3%)

$$w = \left(\frac{1}{1+r}\right)$$

$$a_n = w + w^2 + w^3 + \cdots + w^n = \left(\frac{1-w^n}{r}\right)$$

Example

Consider the example of an annual paying IAB of 10-year maturity under a 4% real interest rate assumption. The base payment for this is calculated as follows:

$$F = 100$$

$$r = 0.04$$

$$w = \left(\frac{1}{1+0.04}\right) = 0.961\,538$$

$$a_n = \left(\frac{1-0.961\,538^{10}}{0.04}\right) = 8.110\,896$$

Therefore:

$$B = \frac{100}{8.110\,896} = 12.33$$

[63] Based on BZW (1992, p. 125).

A2.2 BARRO'S PROPOSAL FOR REVISING THE INFLATION ADJUSTMENT OF PAYMENTS ON INDEX-LINKED GILTS[64]

Barro (1994) suggests a modification that could be made to the indexation procedure used in the UK in order to provide better protection against inflation. Of necessity this method uses an indexation lag of eight months, but for ease of explanation a six-month lag is used (as in Barro, 1994).

Consider an n-period index-linked gilt that is issued at date 0, with semi-annual coupon payments at 1, 2, ..., n. Let c be the annual coupon rate and π_i be the inflation rate for the RPI between dates $i-1$ and i, as shown in Figure A2.1. Ignoring the two-month lag that arises from the compilation and publication of the RPI ensures that π_i will be known at the start of period i.

The schedule of cash flows under the method of indexation employed by the UK DMO is given in the second column of Table A2.1. The third column of the table illustrates what the cash flows would be under perfect indexation (i.e., the hypothetical ideal with no inflation indexation lag). A comparison between these two sets of cash flows shows that the errors under the current system derive from the lag by one period in each of the terms $1+\pi_i$ – for example, the second coupon is defined as $\frac{c}{2}(1+\pi_0)(1+\pi_1)$ compared with the ideal of $\frac{c}{2}(1+\pi_1)(1+\pi_2)$. The mistake in the last $1+\pi_i$ term in each expression (i.e., the one furthest to the right) is inevitable since the nominal payments have to be expressed one period in advance. More generally, in the formula for coupon t in the third column, the term $1+\pi_t$ is unknown at the time that the nominal value of this coupon is announced, and so $1+\pi_{t-1}$ is used instead. Thus the formula for coupon t in the second column commits a string of unnecessary errors in that the earlier $1+\pi_i$ terms are also lagged by one period relative to those shown in the third column. Barro's proposal is to use the indexation method illustrated in the fourth column of the table.

The first coupon payments shown in the second and fourth columns – $\frac{c}{2}(1+\pi_0)$ – are the same; each deviates from the ideal value shown in the third column because $1+\pi_0$ appears instead of $1+\pi_1$. However, since π_1 is known when the nominal value of the second coupon payment is set, Barro reasons that it is unnecessary to allow this mistake to persist for the second (and subsequent) payments. Thus, the fourth column uses $\frac{c}{2}(1+\pi_1)(1+\pi_1)$, instead of $\frac{c}{2}(1+\pi_0)(1+\pi_1)$ from the second column, to determine the second payment. The substitution of $(1+\pi_1)$ for $(1+\pi_0)$ means that the initial error – created by the gap between π_1 and π_0 – does not persist beyond the first

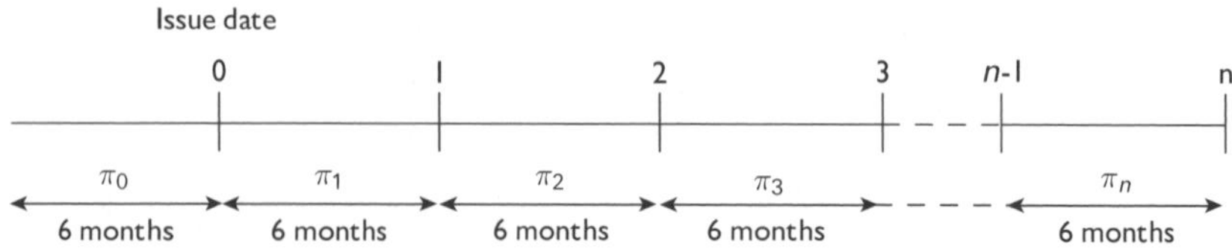

Figure A2.1 Illustration of the indexation lag

[64] Reproduced from Chapter 7 of *Estimating and Interpreting the Yield Curve* (Anderson *et al.*, 1996) by permission of the authors and John Wiley & Sons Ltd.

Table A2.1 Index-linked gilt payments under different indexation schemes

Payment	Current system	Perfect indexation	Barro proposal
Coupon 1	$\frac{c}{2}(1+\pi_0)$	$\frac{c}{2}(1+\pi_1)$	$\frac{c}{2}(1+\pi_0)$
Coupon 2	$\frac{c}{2}(1+\pi_0)(1+\pi_1)$	$\frac{c}{2}(1+\pi_1)(1+\pi_2)$	$\frac{c}{2}(1+\pi_1)(1+\pi_1)$
Coupon 3	$\frac{c}{2}(1+\pi_0)(1+\pi_1)(1+\pi_2)$	$\frac{c}{2}(1+\pi_1)(1+\pi_2)(1+\pi_3)$	$\frac{c}{2}(1+\pi_1)(1+\pi_2)(1+\pi_2)$
$\vdots$	$\vdots$	$\vdots$	$\vdots$
Coupon t	$\frac{c}{2}(1+\pi_0)(1+\pi_1)\ldots(1+\pi_{t-1})$	$\frac{c}{2}(1+\pi_1)(1+\pi_2)\ldots(1+\pi_t)$	$\frac{c}{2}(1+\pi_1)\ldots(1+\pi_{t-2})(1+\pi_{t-1})(1+\pi_{t-1})$
$\vdots$	$\vdots$	$\vdots$	$\vdots$
Coupon n	$\frac{c}{2}(1+\pi_0)(1+\pi_1)\ldots(1+\pi_{n-1})$	$\frac{c}{2}(1+\pi_1)(1+\pi_2)\ldots(1+\pi_n)$	$\frac{c}{2}(1+\pi_1)\ldots(1+\pi_{n-2})(1+\pi_{n-1})(1+\pi_{n-1})$
Redemption	$100(1+\pi_0)(1+\pi_1)\ldots(1+\pi_{n-1})$	$100(1+\pi_1)(1+\pi_2)\ldots(1+\pi_n)$	$100(1+\pi_1)\ldots(1+\pi_{n-2})(1+\pi_{n-1})(1+\pi_{n-1})$

Reproduced from *Estimating and Interpreting the Yield Curve* (Anderson *et al.*, 1996) by permission of the authors and John Wiley & Sons Ltd.

payment. The second $1 + \pi_1$ term for the second coupon in the fourth column necessarily still differs from the ideal value in the third column, which contains $1 + \pi_2$.

Barro's proposal is equivalent to saying that, for a given point in time, inflation over the preceding six months should on average provide a better predictor of inflation over the subsequent six months than inflation from an earlier period. In other words, for any t, π_{t-1} should be a better predictor of π_t than π_0. Seasonal patterns in the RPI may mean that this is not unambiguously the case.

3
Why Invest in Indexed Debt?

There are a number of reasons why investors might wish to include inflation-indexed bonds in their portfolios. This chapter considers the main attractions to investors and financial intermediaries of buying indexed bonds and highlights some of the reasons why, in practice, they are not always the cure-all that theory might suggest. It concludes by examining some of the financial assets that investors might hold as alternatives to indexed bonds.

3.1 REDUCING INFLATION RISK

People save for just one reason, to defer consumption. Central to investment decisions is therefore a measure of the *real* value of such deferred spending. In this light, when comparing the properties of inflation-indexed bonds with those of conventional bonds and indeed with those of all other asset classes, their major benefit is clear: a much reduced exposure to unexpected changes in the level of prices. To illustrate the importance of this property, both Hetzel (1992) and Shen (1995) provide graphic examples of the substantial inflation risk that investors have faced in the conventional US Treasury market. Shen (1995) reports the case of an issue bought in 1955 by the US Treasury: a 40-year conventional bond with a 3% coupon. Because the actual average inflation rate over the life of the bond turned out to be 4.4%, investors who bought the bond when it was issued and held it to maturity would have "earned" a negative real return (−1.4%) on this investment. Indexed bonds do not just offer real value certainty, they also (under normal circumstances) guarantee a *positive* real return.

Since the purchase of inflation-indexed bonds reduces the real risk of a portfolio so it must increase the nominal risk,[1] and for this reason indexed bonds appeal most to those investors for whom real value certainty is the more important. Since financial assets are often acquired as a means to hedge future financial commitments, preferences here are likely to be determined by the nature of such liabilities. For instance, since banks generally have nominal liabilities they might be expected to have a preference for assets providing nominal value certainty, whereas pension funds may attach greater value to real assets to offset any inflation-indexed annuity commitments. Indeed, in many countries, the single largest group of indexed bondholders consists of pension funds and insurance companies. Data on the UK index-linked gilt market, for example, suggest that pension funds and insurance companies hold as much as 75% of the market.[2] This is due in part to the 1995 Pensions Act which stipulates, *inter alia*, that many funds must guarantee that any future benefits to which their members are entitled

[1] Since inflation-indexed bonds offer real value certainty while conventional bonds provide nominal value certainty.
[2] Source: OECD (2002).

increase by Retail Prices Index (RPI) inflation, with a 5% per annum cap and a 0% per annum floor on that uplift – so-called *Limited Price Indexation* (LPI).[3] Price (1997) and the OECD (2002) report a similar situation in the Canadian Real Return Bond (RRB) market, where the majority of the outstanding debt is held by large pension funds and non-taxable insurance portfolios with a significantly smaller proportion in individual tax-sheltered retirement savings plans. Market participation in Australia's Treasury indexed bond market is also concentrated in superannuation and insurance portfolios. As Section 3.7 discusses, large holdings of indexed bonds by such "buy-and-hold" investors is likely to reduce the liquidity of the secondary market and so reduce the attractiveness of the asset class to investors who value liquidity.

Indexed bonds can also appeal to individual investors. In addition to providing an alternative to a standard pension plan, indexed bonds can be used by those preparing for large future capital expenditures (e.g., purchasing a house or sending children to college) for which it is desirable that such savings are not eroded by unexpected inflation. In its marketing programme prior to the launch of its Treasury Inflation-Protection Securities (TIPS) series in 1997, the US Treasury cited this as one of the primary attractions of inflation-indexed securities for individuals.[4] Personal investors certainly form an important part of the UK index-linked gilt market: as of October 2002 there were over 55,000 registered holders of index-linked gilts of which almost 68% could be identified as personal investors,[5] although unsurprisingly this proportion falls below 2% when measured in terms of the nominal value of bondholdings.

Bootle (1991) argues that, although indexed bonds are specifically designed to protect investors from increases in the price level, they are at their most useful in situations of moderate to high inflation, since in a hyperinflationary environment the continued integrity of the price indices themselves would probably be in some doubt. Also, in such a climate even a short lag in indexation can leave investors seriously under-compensated.

3.2 RELATIVE STABILITY OF RETURNS

In principle, inflation-indexed bonds represent a less risky class of asset than conventional bonds or equities, since their real returns are much less affected by unexpected changes in inflation.[6] In the UK, where inflation-indexed securities have been in existence long enough to lend some validity to historical studies of this nature, there is indeed some evidence that real returns on index-linked gilts have proved less variable than those on their conventional counterparts. This is illustrated by Figures 3.1–3.3, which compare quarterly real holding period returns on index-linked and conventional gilts of different maturities between 1982 and 2001.[7]

[3] In June 2003 the UK government announced plans to reduce the LPI cap to 2.5%. See Chapter 6 for more details.
[4] See Department of the (US) Treasury (1996b).
[5] According to data provided by the Registrar's Department at the Bank of England.
[6] Since in practice inflation-indexed bonds are not perfectly indexed their returns become more dependent on inflation as they approach maturity – see Chapter 5.
[7] For information on the construction of this data set see UK Debt Management Office (2002d). In the UK market, *short* is used to denote bonds with residual maturities of up to 7 years; *medium*, bonds with maturities of between 7 and 15 years; and *long*, bonds with maturities of over 15 years.

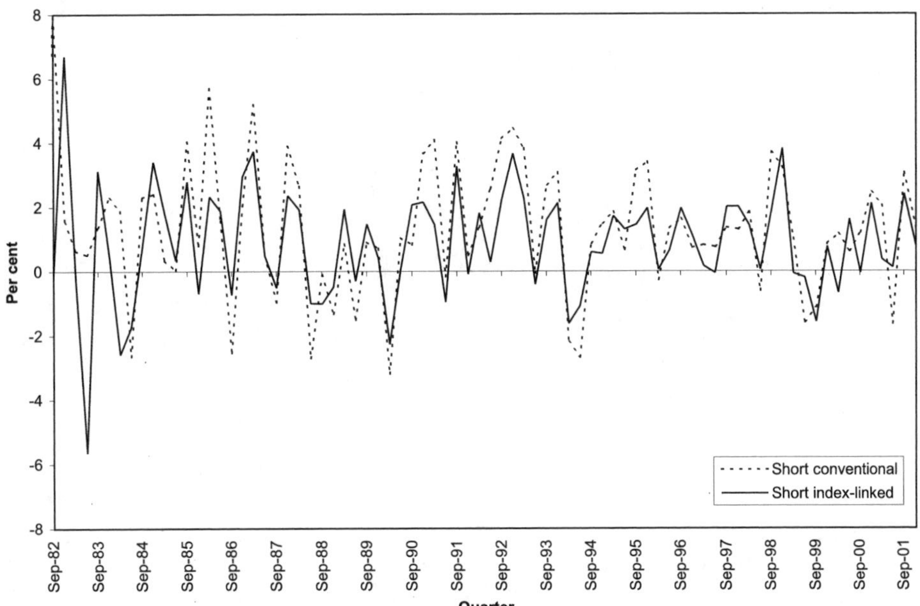

Figure 3.1 Quarterly real holding period returns for short maturity gilts
Data sources: Bank of England and UK Debt Management Office

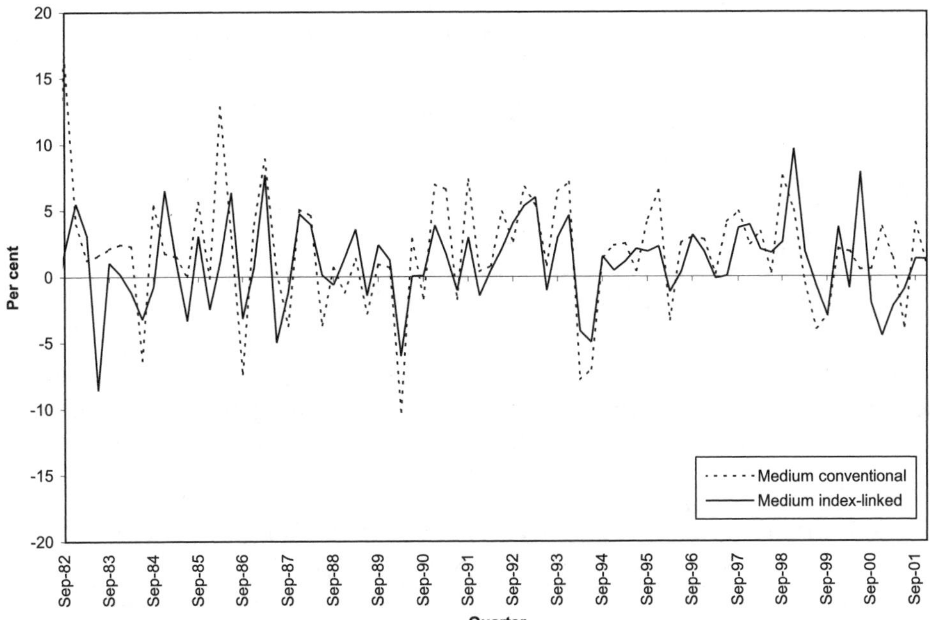

Figure 3.2 Quarterly real holding period returns for medium maturity gilts
Data sources: Bank of England and UK Debt Management Office

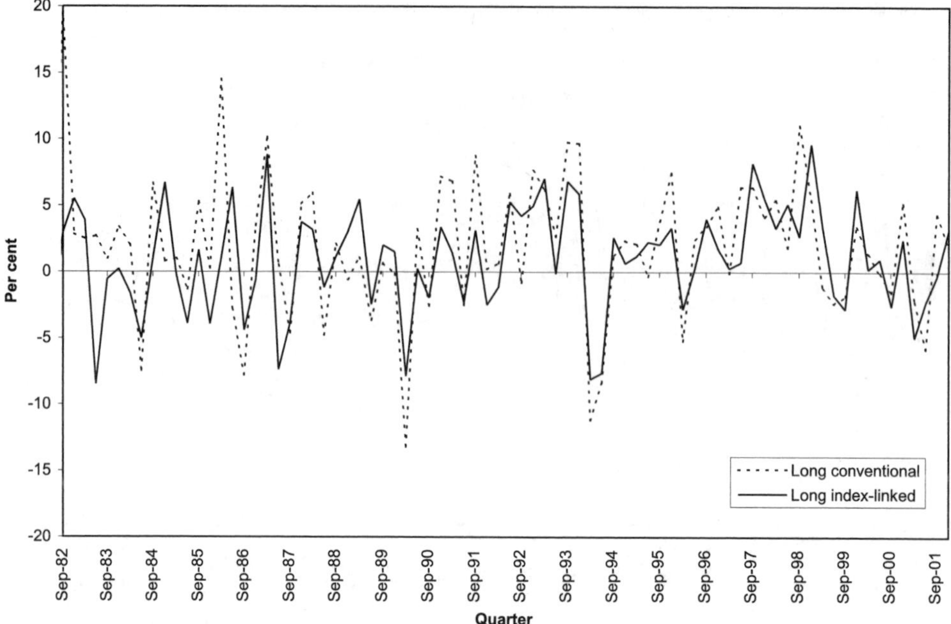

Figure 3.3 Quarterly real holding period returns for long maturity gilts
Data sources: Bank of England and UK Debt Management Office

Table 3.1 Volatility of real holding period returns (HPRs) in the UK

	Annualised standard deviation of real HPR (%) (Q3 1982–Q4 2001)	
Maturity	Conventional gilts	Index-linked gilts
Short	4.15	3.52
Medium	8.71	6.59
Long	10.75	8.14
Average	7.87	6.09

Data sources: Bank of England and UK Debt Management Office.

Table 3.1 shows annualised standard deviations for each of the above, as one measure of volatility. Clearly, over the period in question, the returns on index-linked gilts were noticeably less volatile than those on conventional gilts.

3.3 PERFORMANCE RELATIVE TO CONVENTIONAL BONDS AND EQUITIES

In principle, indexed bonds should provide lower returns than alternative assets, such as conventional bonds or equities, quite simply because they are less risky. In the UK a comparison of returns on index-linked gilts to those on other assets between 1983 and

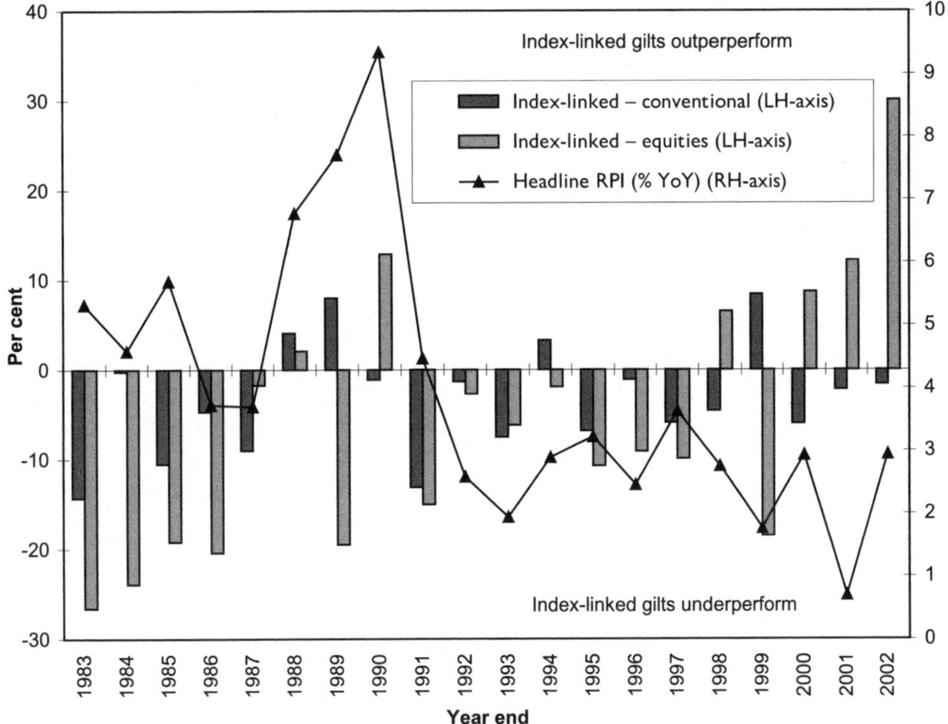

Figure 3.4 Total annual real return of index-linked gilts versus conventional gilts and equities (1983–2002)

Data source: Barclays Capital (2003b)

2002 shows that – on average – this has indeed been the case. Over this period index-linked gilts produced an average annualised real return of just 3.6% per annum, while the real returns on conventional gilts and UK equities were 6.7% and 8.3%, respectively.[8] However, the poor performance of index-linked gilts over this period may reflect additional factors: first, over the period under study inflation expectations[9] declined significantly while inflation was persistently overpredicted by the market, thus increasing the *ex post* real returns on conventional gilts relative to index-linked gilts. Second, *ex ante* real yields on indexed gilts had risen – possibly reflecting either a reduction in an initial scarcity premium or simply investor demand for a higher return – reducing mark-to-market realised real returns.

While one might expect indexed bonds to underperform conventional bonds when inflation is falling, in inflationary environments they are often considered likely candidates to outperform conventional bonds and possibly even equities. This can be corroborated, in the UK at least, by an examination of the annual returns of index-linked gilts relative to those of both conventional gilts and equities over the period from 1983 to 2002 (illustrated in Figure 3.4). Although index-linked gilts clearly underperformed for most of this period, there are some years during which they

[8] Source: Barclays Capital (2003b).

[9] As measured by break-even inflation rates – see Chapter 5 for more details.

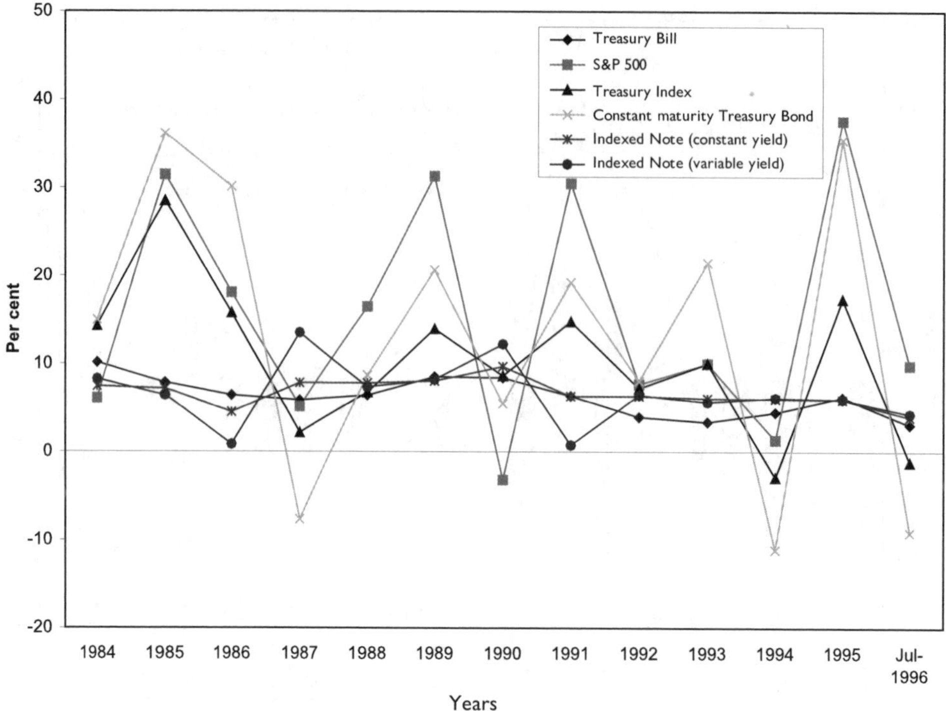

Figure 3.5 Hypothetical nominal return of inflation-indexed notes versus actual returns of alternative assets (% per annum)
Data source: Abuhoff and Malik (1996)

produced noticeably superior returns compared with the other asset classes. For instance, index-linked gilts outperformed conventional gilts from the beginning of 1988 to mid-1990, presumably as a result of the sharp increase in inflation following the "Lawson boom" of 1987/88. More recently, central banks around the world cut rates during 2001 and 2002 – in some cases rapidly – in reaction to global economic weakness. Initially, these moves benefited nominal bonds, with inflation-indexed bonds failing to keep pace as investors began to price in the risk of a prolonged period of disinflation in industrialised countries. As these fears began to recede and commodity prices began to rise in early 2003, so the situation reversed and index-linked bonds began to outperform – a situation that may prove to persist should the global economy recover and in turn cause inflationary pressures to reignite. These episodes evidently support the assertion that investors are attracted to indexed bonds in periods of emerging inflation risk.

Abuhoff and Malik (1996) carry out an interesting assessment of how indexed bonds in the USA might have performed prior to 1996, had they been available, relative to other asset classes. The authors assume that real yields and inflation are negatively correlated and that the relationship between the two is based on the simple rule that real yields rise (or fall) by 10% of the decrease (or increase) in the annual inflation rate over a two-month period. The data displayed in Figure 3.5 and summarised in Table 3.2 compare the historical returns from Treasury bills, Treasury bonds (both the Treasury

Table 3.2 Statistics comparing the hypothetical nominal return of inflation-indexed notes with actual returns of alternative assets over the period January 1984 to July 1996 (% per annum)

	Treasury bills	S&P 500	Treasury index	Constant maturity Treasury bond	Indexed note (constant yield)	Indexed note (variable yield)
Average	6.25	15.57	10.42	13.25	6.71	6.63
Standard deviation	2.14	13.20	8.45	16.08	1.54	3.65
Sharpe ratio	2.93	1.18	1.23	0.82	4.37	1.82

Data source: Abuhoff and Malik (1996)

long bond index and a constant maturity long bond) and equities (the Standard & Poor's 500 Index) with those of a hypothetical 10-year inflation-indexed note over the period from January 1984 to July 1996. Returns for the inflation-indexed note are computed under two assumptions: a yield that varies using the inflation–real yield relationship described above and a constant real yield (of 325 basis points) over the Consumer Price Index (CPI).

Over this period the average hypothetical total return on the indexed note under both scenarios was lower than that on all other assets except three-month Treasury bills. Under the constant yield assumption, the volatility (standard deviation) of its return was the lowest of all the assets, although as would be expected this increased when price risk was introduced (the variable yield scenario). This contrasts with the high volatility of returns on equities – a standard deviation of 13.2%, indicating that in any one year the real rate of return has a significant chance of being much lower (or indeed much higher) than the average return of 15.6%. So to the extent that expected real yield volatility is low then the Sharpe ratio[10] of indexed bonds can be higher than that of other asset classes, and even under more conservative assumptions the Sharpe ratio is at least comparable.

Barclays Capital (2002b) takes the Sharpe ratio analysis one step further and uses *efficient frontier analysis* to investigate what role index-linked bonds play in a diversified portfolio. The aim of such studies is to identify an optimal portfolio allocation across a target group of asset classes for different levels of risk, and the Barclays Capital analysis concludes that inflation-indexed bonds strongly dominate gold as a "low risk" asset in a portfolio with conventional bonds and equities. Moreover, they go on to contend that, since investors should only be concerned with the *real* return on their portfolios, such studies overstate the riskiness of index-linked bonds and hence understate their relative attractiveness.

3.4 TOTAL RETURN OPPORTUNITIES

Inflation-indexed bonds may attract total return investors or arbitrageurs seeking to exploit either the yield spread between indexed and conventional bonds, or the spread

[10] The *Sharpe ratio* of an asset is its return over a given period divided by the volatility of the return over the same period. This is the most commonly used statistic to compare returns across different asset classes.

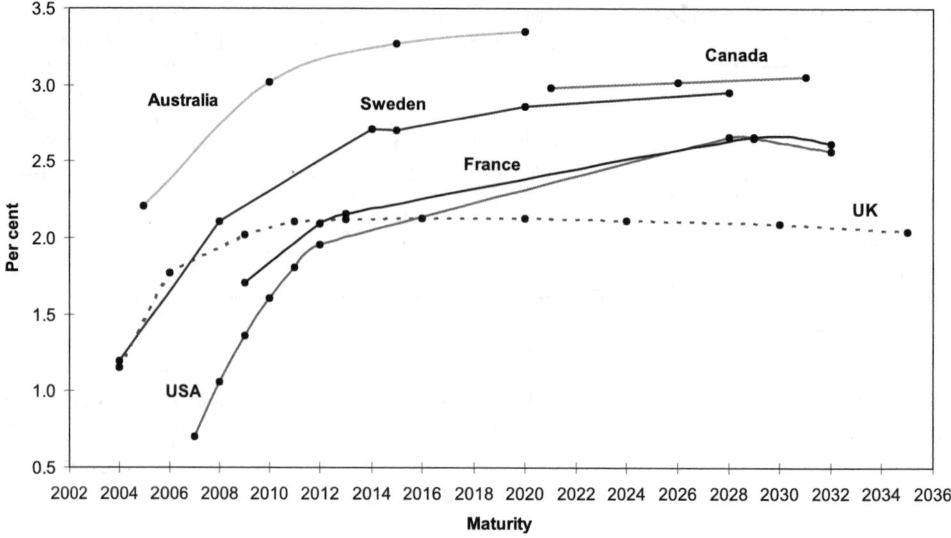

Figure 3.6 Global real yields (as at 31 March 2003)
Data sources: UK Debt Management Office and Bloomberg

between bonds from different indexed bond markets. In theory, with floating exchange rates and a high degree of capital mobility, real yields in different countries should only diverge to the extent that a real appreciation/depreciation is expected and reflected in the exchange rate.[11] However, despite this theoretical case for similar real yields across the globe, Figure 3.6 illustrates that the reality is somewhat different.

Basta *et al.* (1996) suggest that prior to the launch of the US market there was little enthusiasm in the investment community for entering into real yield spread trades, reflecting the fact that the relative illiquidity of the markets made it difficult to assess how much of any real yield differential was due to an illiquidity premium and how much was driven by economic fundamentals.[12] More fundamentally, measurement of inflation can vary greatly from country to country. Even if there were a "true" global inflation rate that was the same across countries, if it was measured differently then quoted real yields (such as those presented in Figure 3.6) would also be different.[13]

Notwithstanding the above, as the markets for real bonds have matured both in the USA and in Europe, such cross-market analysis is becoming more important to global investors. Indeed, the increased liquidity in these two markets in particular has led to an ever greater number of "global" mandates that allow investment fund managers to

[11] Assuming Purchasing Power Parity (PPP) (i.e., that the baskets of goods used in the consumer price indices in different countries are perfectly substitutable). In reality PPP is unlikely to hold at all times. Also, economies can sometimes be distinguished by perceptions that they have different *expected* real returns on capital employed, which in turn would tend to cause real interest rates to diverge, at least in the short term. Again, in the medium term and assuming efficient markets for capital and labour, such differences might be expected to disappear.

[12] Chapter 5 examines other reasons why real rates might vary between different indexed bond markets. Statistics on the liquidity of major indexed bond markets appear in Chapter 6.

[13] Real yields will also differ between countries if different market conventions are employed in their computation – see Bank of England (1998).

invest in inflation-indexed bonds from outside their domestic market in order to improve expected returns. Moreover, the rapid development of the markets for inflation derivatives is also drawing the various markets closer together and adding to the overall transparency. The extent to which different real yields are applicable to different economies looks likely to be a fruitful area of study as these markets continue to grow.

3.5 DURATION AND OTHER CASH FLOW CONSIDERATIONS[14]

One of the attributes of an indexed bond is that the nominal size of its coupon cash flows increases over its life.[15] Relative to a conventional bond issued at the same time and with the same maturity date, the early cash flows on an indexed bond will be smaller and the final (principal) cash flow will be greater. As such, indexed bonds are unlikely to attract investors seeking high income, but should appeal more to those looking for full capital realisation at maturity.[16] Based on the traditional definition of *duration* as the present value weighted average maturity of the cash flows, the duration of indexed bonds will generally be longer than that of conventional bonds with the same maturity. Thus switching from the latter to the former on a cash-neutral basis can be viewed as a way to effectively increase the duration of the investment.

When considering the conventional market in isolation, switching a bond for another with greater duration necessarily increases the investor's risk profile, since duration provides a basic measure of the relative sensitivity of the bonds' prices with respect to changes in yields. Thus it is common practice to compare two bonds (or indeed to compare a bond to a particular liability profile) on the "risk-neutral" basis of duration. More care is required when extending this approach to include indexed bonds, because their nominal valuations are determined by (at least) two separate factors: changes in the real interest rate and changes in inflation expectations.[17] The (real) duration of an indexed bond is usually taken to be the first of these – the price sensitivity with respect to changes in the *real* interest rate. In contrast, the price sensitivity of conventional bonds is measured with respect to a change in the *nominal* interest rate.[18] Indeed, the use of these conventions implies that the quoted "duration" of indexed bonds will always be greater than that of similar maturity conventional bonds, assuming inflation is non-zero and positive on average over their lifetimes. This feature of the most commonly used measure of "duration" for indexed bonds means that great care must be used when applying standard bond analytical techniques directly to the index-linked market. Chapter 5 describes this and other aspects of risk measurement in more detail.

[14] Discussion in this section is based on the Capital Indexed Bond (CIB) structure – the most common form of indexed bond. Chapter 2 described how the duration of a CIB differs from that of other types of indexed bonds.

[15] Assuming that the inflation rate is (on average) positive.

[16] Chapter 2 briefly outlined the reinvestment risk and duration characteristics of inflation-indexed bonds.

[17] For conventional bonds it is impossible (without additional information or assumptions) to distinguish whether changes in nominal yields are caused by changes in the real rate or inflation expectations.

[18] For a more detailed discussion of this issue readers are referred to Dudley *et al.* (1996).

3.6 TAXATION

The treatment of indexed bonds within tax legislation is likely to play an important role in determining the investor base. Chapter 2 has already examined in detail the two key areas in which taxation rules can affect indexed bonds: first, if cash flows are taxed on a nominal rather than a real basis then the *post-tax* real yields on indexed bonds are uncertain. While this will not affect tax-exempt investors (namely, pension funds in many countries) this feature obviously penalises indexed bonds relative to conventional securities for those investors subject to tax on their bondholdings. Second, the rules that determine the tax treatment of the inflation uplift may either encourage or deter investors from holding indexed rather than conventional bonds. For instance, in the UK the principal inflation uplift on index-linked gilts is tax-free, so a taxpaying investor facing the choice between index-linked and conventional gilts with the same expected gross real return will receive a better *ex ante* net return by purchasing the former. Although long-term tax-exempt savings institutions tend to dominate the index-linked gilt market, at shorter maturities (up to about 10 years) there is strong interest from the personal sector. It is not clear why private investors should focus primarily on the short end of the curve: this may be because individuals are averse to the greater price risk inherent in higher duration instruments, or simply that they typically have shorter investment horizons than institutions with long-term liabilities. Another contributory factor could be the transactions costs involved with trading the securities – though this is less likely to be a major consideration for "buy-and-hold" investors. Whatever the reasons, this preference coupled with the tax rules has led to a situation where the marginal holder of shorter dated index-linked gilts is likely to value them on a post-tax basis, in marked contrast to the situation at longer maturities, where it is tax-exempt investors who dominate.

In many countries (including Australia, Canada and the USA), the increase in the principal of an indexed bond due to inflation is treated as current income for tax purposes. Taxing "phantom" income in this way can in principle lead to negative net cash flows (when the tax due on the principal inflation uplift exceeds the net coupon payments), a rule that would seem likely to limit the demand for indexed bonds to tax-exempt investors or those taxpayers with access to tax-deferred accounts.[19] Basta *et al.* (1996) develop a simple example to highlight this effect: domestic US investors in the top income tax bracket (and thus liable to a 39.6% marginal rate of tax) who own a hypothetical $3\frac{1}{4}$% 10-year indexed note[20] would be liable to pay more each year in tax than the income they would receive should US inflation rise above 5%. This is illustrated by Figure 3.7, which shows the post-tax real returns on this hypothetical bond for investors facing different marginal tax rates. The ability to utilise a tax-deferred account materially impacts the outcome: for example, were an investor in the 39.6% tax bracket to place this indexed note in such an account, the post-tax real return based on a 5% inflation outturn would rise from 0.03% to 0.73%. In 1998, in order to foster retail interest in its indexed securities, the US Treasury introduced inflation-indexed

[19] With a tax-deferred account, payment of income tax is deferred until the income is withdrawn from the account.

[20] These calculations were done prior to the coupon on the first 10-year US Treasury Inflation-Indexed Note being known. The coupon on this note was actually set at $3\frac{3}{8}$% – very close to the rate used in this study.

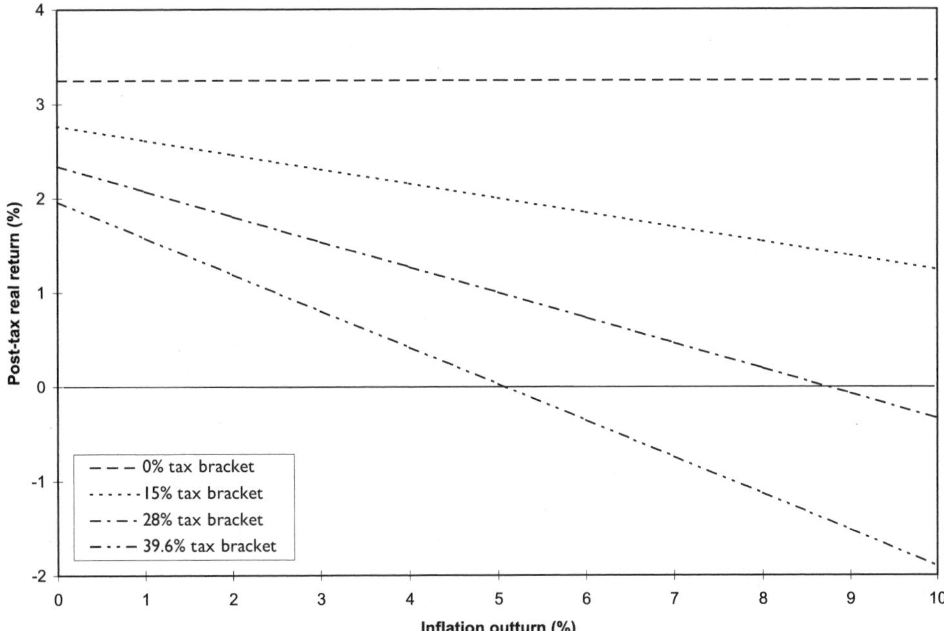

Figure 3.7 Post-tax real returns on a 10-year $3\frac{1}{4}\%$ inflation-indexed note (purchased at par)
Data source: Basta *et al.* (1996)

savings bonds (so called *I-Bonds*) on which tax is deferred until the securities are cashed in.[21]

3.7 LIQUIDITY

Two of the main factors that can deter investors from purchasing inflation-indexed bonds are their tax treatment and their lack of liquidity compared with other investments. In fact, these issues can sometimes be connected because the tax regime applied to indexed bonds will influence the investor base, which in turn may restrict the development and hence liquidity of the market. For instance, since many tax regimes effectively treat the inflation uplift on inflation-linked bonds' principal payments as income, this may reduce demand to a narrow sector of investors – namely, those who are exempt from taxes, such as pension funds, and those with access to tax-preferred investment vehicles.[22] As well as potentially limiting the expansion of an indexed bond market, such rules can also cause bonds to become concentrated in the hands of buy-and-hold investors, thus further reducing liquidity. However, even in the UK, where the tax regime is among the more favourable for taxpayers, the market has still been dominated by tax-exempt institutions.

One of the problems caused by an illiquid market is that investors may require a

[21] I-Bonds are discussed briefly in Section 6.6. For more details see Department of the (US) Treasury (1998b).
[22] Such as tax-deferred accounts in the USA, for example.

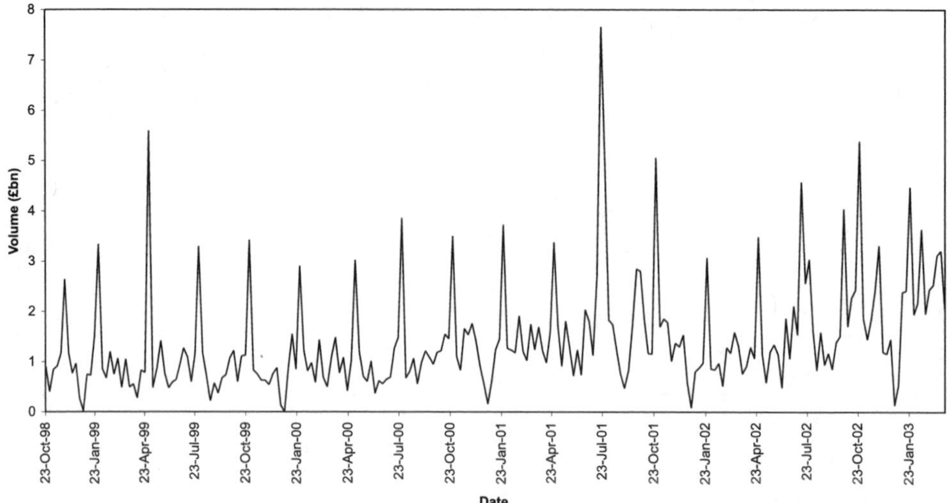

Figure 3.8 Index-linked gilt weekly turnover (all Gilt-edged Market Makers [GEMMs]) (October 1998–March 2003)
Data source: UK Debt Management Office

liquidity premium for holding bonds, thus increasing the cost to issuers.[23] Low liquidity is likely to reduce demand from those investors with relatively short horizons as well as those looking to arbitrage the market; buy-and-hold investors will be less concerned about liquidity since typically they will trade less frequently. The UK market – despite currently being one of the world's more liquid – illustrates the relative illiquidity of indexed bonds when compared with their nominal counterparts. Two of the most commonly used indicators of liquidity are turnover and the size of bid–ask spreads. Analysing UK data for 2002/03 shows that turnover (measured by market value) in the conventional gilt market was approximately 20 times greater than that of index-linked gilts,[24] even though on aggregate the conventional gilt market was only around three times greater in size. It is interesting to note that the volume of primary issuance in 2002/03 represented about 4.4% of the total index-linked gilt market turnover, while in the conventional gilt market it represented just 1.0%. The significant increase in turnover around the (quarterly[25]) index-linked gilt auctions is graphically illustrated by Figure 3.8.

The relative illiquidity of index-linked gilts is also revealed by the bid–ask spreads charged by dealers – widely accepted to be significantly wider than those for conventional gilts, as dealers are less likely to be able to close out any assumed positions as rapidly.

[23] Having to pay such a liquidity premium would to some degree offset the inflation risk premium that issuers might be looking to save by issuing indexed rather than conventional debt – see Chapter 4.

[24] Source: UK Debt Management Office (DMO). Ways in which issuers of indexed bonds can improve the liquidity of the secondary markets for their bonds are discussed in Chapter 4.

[25] Since April 2003 index-linked gilt auctions have been held more frequently – see Section 6.5.

3.8 OTHER POTENTIAL DETERRENTS TO INVESTING IN INDEXED BONDS

In addition to those detailed above, there are several other reasons why investors may be discouraged from purchasing indexed bonds. For example, Fisher (1928) suggests that people are accustomed to thinking of money as a standard of value and consequently do not understand or trust indexation. Campbell and Shiller (1996) advance another interpretation of such "money illusion"; that in a low-inflationary environment people do not see the need to protect themselves against the possibility of future increases in the general level of prices. It is only in countries with a history of high and volatile inflation that the merits of indexed bonds are truly recognised – witness the presence of indexation in countries that have experienced hyperinflation (e.g., Brazil, Chile and Israel).

Index mismatching may also deter investors from purchasing indexed bonds. For instance, while indexed bonds almost invariably have cash flows tied to consumer prices, would-be investors might have liabilities linked to an alternative measure of inflation. The larger this discrepancy between the two measures the larger the inflation basis risk an investor takes on when purchasing the bonds. Uncertainty over possible revisions to the price index may also discourage investors. Both of these issues were discussed in Chapter 2. They are also areas for which derivative markets have developed and now play a significant role – see Chapter 8.

3.9 ALTERNATIVES TO INDEXED BONDS

Real value certainty is the most important characteristic of inflation-indexed bonds. However, it is sometimes argued that indexed bonds are unnecessary, since there are other assets that allow investors to eliminate inflation risk. For instance, some suggest that a strategy of purchasing and rolling over Treasury bills[26] is a close substitute for investing in long-term indexed bonds, while others have likened indexed bonds to equities or property based on the protection each investment offers against inflation.[27] Despite such claims, empirical evidence paints a different picture. This section examines these potential alternatives[28] to indexed bonds and explains why none is capable of offering investors fixed long-term real yields that are as free from inflation risk.

3.9.1 Treasury bills

One alternative to purchasing long-term indexed bonds is to buy short-term fixed rate instruments, such as one or three-month bills or short-term nominal bonds, and continually roll over the investment into new short-term debt instruments as the origi-

[26] A similar strategy would be to purchase Floating Rate Notes (FRNs) (i.e., longer maturity bonds with floating coupons that are set with reference to Treasury bill yields or to rates on other money market instruments). The main difference between a strategy based on FRNs and that based on rolling over bills is that with the former there is much less reinvestment risk. Spiro (1989) provides a more detailed comparison of the properties of inflation-indexed securities and FRNs.

[27] This may help to explain why fund managers have generally been slow to recognise indexed bonds as a separate asset class.

[28] Since the inadequacy of the inflation protection offered by long-term conventional bonds was discussed earlier in this chapter it will not be revisited here.

nals mature. Such a portfolio should be less exposed to inflation risk than one consisting of their long-term counterparts simply because the nominal yield of a Treasury bill portfolio will reset to the market rate whenever the portfolio rolls over. At each nominal reset the interest rate achieved for the upcoming investment period should reflect the real yield demanded by the market at the time, which with such short dated instruments will be heavily influenced by the central bank's monetary policy rate settings and the *ex ante* expected inflation rate.

However, instead of locking into a known, fixed long-term real yield (as with the purchase of a long-term indexed bond), investors following such a strategy will face uncertainty over future short-term returns, both nominal and real. Indeed, investors will instead receive something close to the cumulative short-term real interest rate effectively targeted by the central bank over the investment period – a rate that is actively varied by the monetary authority in response to conditions in the wider economy. Moreover, since the yield curve in most markets has tended to be upward-sloping, such an approach has suffered historically as real yields on Treasury bills have on average proven to be very low. For example, figures for the US market[29] indicate that over the period from 1926 to 1995 the average *realised* annual real yield on 20-year Treasury bonds was 2%, while the comparable figure for one-month Treasury bills was just 0.6%. Such a strategy might also be expensive to execute due to the potential transactions costs involved.[30] Finally, statistics suggest that Treasury bills have in fact proved to be a poor inflation hedge: for example, the correlation between real returns on Treasury bills and inflation in the USA over the period from 1926 to 1995 is −0.75.[31] This poor level of inflation protection is illustrated by Figure 3.9, which shows the realised real rate of return on one-year US Treasury bills over the period from 1953 to 1982.[32]

Looking forward, as more and more central banks focus on explicitly targeting inflation, it may well turn out to be the case that simply rolling bills over will prove to be a better inflation hedge than in the past, not least as these instruments may be the very tool the central bank is using to attain its goal. However, this strategy will still be susceptible to the requirements of the central bank, and so the real returns generated will always be volatile.

3.9.2 Equities

Equities are often thought to be fairly close substitutes for indexed bonds as the two asset classes have similar cash flow structures: in both cases dividend payments and capital value will tend to rise over time as the price level generally increases. However, as Bootle (1991) notes, there are four fundamental differences between the two. First, the factors that cause a stock's dividends and capital value to rise over time are not purely inflation-related, as is the case for indexed bonds. Other real economic factors will also affect equities, the most significant being economic growth. Assuming a constant share of profits in GDP (and a constant ratio of dividends to profits), dividends

[29] See Ibbotson Associates (1996).
[30] There is also a risk that it might not always be possible to roll over Treasury bill holdings.
[31] Source: Ibbotson Associates (1996).
[32] Figure 3.9 also demonstrates the volatility of real returns on Treasury bills. Over the period examined, the average annual return was 1.03% while the standard deviation was 2.46%. Focusing just on the period 1973–1982 illustrates this volatility to even greater effect – the mean and standard deviation being 0.12% and 4.05%, respectively.

Figure 3.9 Inflation and realised real returns on US 1-year Treasury bills
Data source: Weiner (1983)

and capital values will grow in real terms at the rate of economic growth and so provide a nominal return that is over and above that due to inflation. Of course, in practice, changes in the share of profits in GDP do occur and so complicate the causal links – an issue that Bootle discusses at some length.

Second, the liquidity of indexed bonds is likely to be very different from that of equities. Also, an indexed bond offers a real return that is known with certainty (if held to maturity)[33] while that on an equity is not, and so indexed bonds are likely to provide a lower relative return, reflecting a certainty premium. The fourth difference noted by Bootle is that a well-balanced portfolio of equities may perform in a radically different fashion to investments in individual equities.[34] Finally, the tax regime may be such that the relationship between pre- and post-tax returns is also different for the two asset classes.

It is perhaps not surprising that equities have proved to be a poor hedge against inflation, since it is only one of several factors that might determine their performance. Indeed, empirical evidence suggests that real returns on equities might actually correlate negatively with inflation. For example, using US data, Ibbotson Associates (1996) estimate the correlation between inflation and the real yield on the S&P 500 over the

[33] Subject to the caveats discussed in Chapter 2.
[34] Since an individual company's equity is exposed both to risks associated with the company itself as well as those associated with the market as a whole.

period from 1926 to 1995 to have been −0.22. Similarly, Shen (1995) reports that over the post-war period the correlation with inflation for the S&P 500 was −0.30. These statistics are more consistent with the hypothesis that real equity valuations are actually more likely to fall as inflation becomes more prevalent, reflecting investors' fears that the authorities are likely to hold nominal interest rates higher. In such circumstances firms tend to reduce investment as their expected returns for potential projects need to be greater to offset the increased cost of capital, and similarly consumers have an increased incentive to save as opposed to purchase goods – two factors that will probably reduce expected dividend payments and therefore lower equity values. A more detailed comparison between equities and indexed bonds appears in Barclays Capital (2003b).

3.9.3 Property

Although property prices may not be influenced by many of the economic factors that tend to affect the equity market, they are subject to their own forces of supply and demand. Commercial property prices are influenced by the overall level of economic activity, for instance, as well as the financial circumstances of companies that own or rent property. History suggests that property prices will almost certainly suffer if there is an economic downturn. Demographic trends and immigration patterns can also play a role, not to mention government planning policies that may not always be based solely on economic considerations. As Bootle (1991) notes, indexed bonds are also much more marketable than property – in difficult times in the property market there may be no meaningful market price since dealings may have all but ceased. In addition, the transactions costs involved in trading property are likely to be significantly higher than those in the bond market.

3.10 SUMMARY

Inflation-indexed bonds provide investors with an asset that is largely free from inflation risk and whose real returns have, over time, demonstrated significantly lower variability relative to those available from other asset classes. They clearly have a number of features that in practice may discourage investors: they are typically less liquid than nominal bonds, are often taxed disadvantageously and have historically tended to underperform other assets. However, no other asset class is able to provide such a level of protection against the erosion of purchasing power – a feature that can make inflation-indexed bonds a valuable addition to an investment portfolio.

4 Why Issue Indexed Bonds?

The arguments for and against issuing indexed bonds have received comprehensive coverage in the academic literature over the years. In a survey of US economists carried out in 1992,[1] when asked whether the government should issue inflation-indexed bonds, 36.4% of respondents said no, 32.1% said yes and 26.3% said yes subject to certain provisos. This clearly illustrates the contentious nature of the subject. The significant increase in the asset class globally since the survey was conducted would seem to suggest that the bias has now shifted firmly in their favour. This chapter assesses the main attractions that indexed debt holds for both governments and private sector issuers and concludes by examining possible explanations why, despite their increasing popularity, indexed bonds are still much less prevalent than their conventional counterparts on the global stage.

4.1 WHY GOVERNMENTS ISSUE INDEXED BONDS

During the 1960s and 1970s indexed bonds were predominantly issued by governments of countries experiencing inflationary problems, as a means both to preserve their access to long-term capital markets and to extend the maturity of their debt. More often than not in such cases it would seem that the governments in question had little choice but to issue indexed debt. In contrast, most of the countries that have begun issuing indexed bonds in the last two decades did so having already established a commitment to low inflation and have looked to indexed debt to produce cost savings and to enhance the credibility of their monetary policy. This section examines all these motivations in more detail.

4.1.1 Reducing borrowing costs: the role of inflation expectations

It has long been argued that governments can reduce their borrowing costs by issuing inflation-indexed bonds. Although lowering the cost of state sector funding simply transfers interest costs between different elements of society and so may not in itself be desirable,[2] it is certainly in the interests of the fiscal authorities themselves – not least because in many countries they are charged with an explicit mandate to minimise the cost of financing the government's debt. Of the countries that have begun to issue indexed bonds in the last 20 years, Australia, Canada, France, New Zealand, South

[1] Alston *et al.* (1992) carried out an extensive survey of US economists. Of the 1350 economists approached, 464 (34.4%) responded. The survey consisted of 40 questions about a range of economic issues.
[2] See Campbell and Shiller (1996).

Table 4.1 Average real holding period returns (HPRs) of UK government bonds

Maturity	Annualised mean real HPR (%) (Q3 1982–Q4 2001)	
	Conventional gilts	Index-linked gilts
Short	5.38	3.56
Medium	7.72	4.14
Long	8.06	4.06
Average	7.06	3.92

Data sources: Bank of England and UK Debt Management Office.

Africa, Sweden, the UK and the USA have all cited potential cost savings as one of their primary motivations.

Cost savings could arise in several ways. Indexed debt provides *ex post* cheaper funding than conventional debt if inflation turns out to be lower than the market had expected at the time of issuance. For instance, suppose that the market expects inflation to be 5% per year and that a government has the choice of issuing either indexed bonds with a real interest rate of 3% or conventional bonds with a nominal interest rate of 8%. By issuing conventional bonds the government locks itself into paying a nominal interest rate of 8% on its debt. If instead it issues indexed bonds and inflation turns out to be only 4%, for example, then the realised nominal interest rate will be only 7%, representing a 1% *ex post* cost saving per annum.

The perception that inflation expectations were too high was one of the reasons that the authorities in both Sweden and the UK began to issue indexed bonds. An indication of the cost savings that the UK government has made by taking this route can be obtained by comparing the real holding period returns of indexed and conventional government bonds from 1982 to 2001. As Table 4.1 shows, the returns on index-linked gilts in that period have been on average around 300 basis points lower than those on conventional gilts,[3] suggesting that indexed debt in the UK has on average provided cheaper funding than conventional debt. Similarly, in a report published in 2002, the Swedish National Debt Office estimated that the decision to issue index-linked bonds had saved the government SEK 8 billion since they were first issued in 1994.[4]

So if a government believes that future inflation will be lower than that implied by market prices of nominal and indexed bonds, then it will expect to be able to reduce its debt-servicing costs through indexed issuance. However, why might the market overestimate future inflation? One explanation might be that, although a government may not be any better at economic forecasting than the market, inflation is ultimately a variable that the authorities can set policy to control, and so they may have better information than the market regarding their ability and commitment to reduce it. However, one would not expect the market to systematically overpredict inflation in the long run and, in the event that inflation turns out higher than had been

[3] UK Debt Management Office (2002d, pp. 43–52) provides an explanation of how these returns were calculated.
[4] Source: Swedish National Debt Office (2002a).

expected, conventional bond issuance would of course have been the cheaper alternative.[5]

4.1.2 Reducing borrowing costs: saving the inflation risk premium

By issuing index-linked as opposed to conventional bonds, governments can also make an *ex ante* saving on the inflation risk premium component of nominal bond yields – the premium in bond yields demanded by investors to reflect uncertainty about future inflation. In offering almost complete real value certainty, the inflation premium attached to indexed bonds should be negligible compared with that on their conventional counterparts.

Early academic studies using bond prices to draw inferences about market expectations of future interest and inflation rates often assumed the inflation risk premium on nominal bonds to be insignificant, or at the very least constant (see Chapter 5). More recent research has shown that it is important to distinguish the inflation risk premium from the real term premium and that both may vary over time.[6] Campbell and Shiller (1996) use two alternative techniques for estimating the inflation risk premium in the US market and conclude that for a five-year nominal zero-coupon bond a best guess would be between 50 and 100 basis points. Gong and Remolona (1996) also use US data to measure the inflation risk premium, obtaining a figure of 100–300 basis points for a 5-year bond and 50–150 basis points for a 10-year bond. Their estimates vary substantially for different time periods – in some the risk premium was three times that in others. Converting these figures into cost savings, Gong and Remolona compute that had all of the 10-year Treasury notes issued between the period from February 1984 to November 1995 been indexed rather than nominal, the US Treasury would have saved approximately 20% of its expected borrowing costs simply by not paying an inflation risk premium.[7]

A problem with such studies as the two cited above is that they were necessarily carried out in the absence of inflation-linked bond price data, since US Treasury Inflation-Protection Securities (TIPS) were first issued in 1997. For this reason many authors have turned their attentions to the UK index-linked gilt market with its history stretching back to 1981. Foresi *et al.* (1997), for example, obtain separate estimates of the inflation risk premia for nominal and index-linked gilts. The difference between these estimates suggests a potential yield saving of about 250 basis points at the 10-year horizon and about 300 basis points at the 20-year horizon. In an extensive study Brown (1998) suggests an estimate for the inflation risk premium in the UK of between 100 and 200 basis points, depending on maturity. However, at that time other market practitioners were quoting lower figures: for instance, Roberts (1997) estimates the premium at 25 basis points for short-dated gilts rising to 50 basis points for longer maturities, while Adams (1996) suggests a premium of about 100 basis points under normal market conditions. Arora *et al.* (1997) estimate that over

[5] Once a government has committed itself to issuing indexed bonds it would be difficult for it to cease at a future date simply because its inflation expectations had overtaken those of the market. Such a course of action could among other things lead to a rise in the yields on nominal bonds and hence an increase in the overall cost of financing in the long run.

[6] Cost savings from issuing indexed bonds will only come from the elimination of the inflation risk premium.

[7] Sack and Elsasser (2002) and Craig (2003) conclude that in practice the government has actually faced increased borrowing costs since introducing its TIPS programme in 1997 – see below.

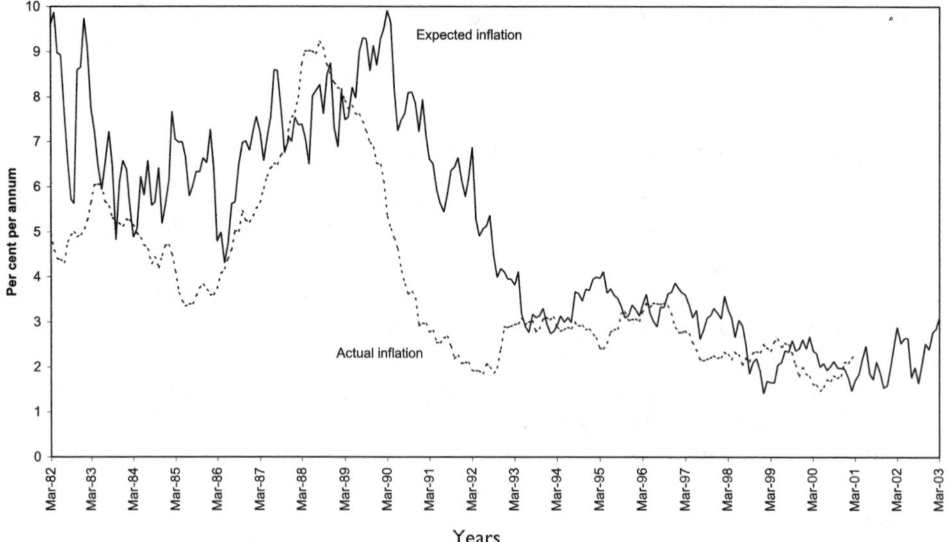

Figure 4.1 Inflation over a two-year horizon: market expectations versus inflation outturn
Note: for example, annualised inflation between end March 2001 and end March 2003 is plotted against the correspondig 2-year inflation expectation at end March 2001.
Data sources: Bank of England and the Office of National Statistics

the period from October 1990 to November 1996 the "effective" risk premium (i.e., the combination of the inflation risk premium and the convexity effect[8]) at the 10-year horizon ranged between 166 and 243 basis points. Based on this analysis of the UK, the authors compute an effective risk premium for the USA in 1997 of between 21 and 35 basis points.

Breedon and Chadha (1997) compare estimates of expected inflation (derived using the Bank of England's inflation term structure model[9]) with realised inflation over different time horizons.[10] Although the Bank's implied inflation curve shows that the market seems to have predicted future *changes* in inflation reasonably well, it has fairly consistently overestimated the *level* of inflation – as illustrated in Figure 4.1. The authors attribute the average forecast error of about 180 basis points[11] to either the inflation risk premium or expectational errors,[12] or to a combination of the two. Although it is difficult to categorically distinguish between these two explanations, Breedon and Chadha point to evidence that suggests that the inflation risk premium rationale is the more likely.

Kandel *et al.* (1996) estimate the inflation risk premium for the Israeli bond market for two different sample periods. The first period ran from September 1984 to March 1992 and included the period of high and volatile inflation of 1984/85

[8] See Chapter 5 for an explanation of the convexity effect.
[9] Discussed in Chapter 5.
[10] Further research on the predictive power of the spread between the returns on nominal and indexed bonds – this time focused primarily on the Canadian market – appears in Spiro (2003). The author concludes that this measure of inflation expectations is a poor predictor of inflation – expectations in the Canadian market appear to be backward-looking and best approximated by average inflation over the preceding seven to ten years.
[11] Based on data up to 1996.
[12] That is, over the sample period investors consistently overpredicted inflation.

(the monthly inflation rate peaked at over 1500% per annum in 1984), while the second period began in August 1985 (immediately after the Israeli government introduced its economic stabilisation programme[13]) after which inflation was much lower and more stable. The estimates obtained for the two periods are 34 basis points per month and 5 basis points per month, respectively, providing some evidence that the inflation risk premium does indeed vary both with time and with the rate of inflation itself.

In addition to computing estimates for the inflation risk premium in the UK, Foresi *et al.* (1997) also obtain estimates for the Swedish bond market, though their analysis was hampered by the fact that at the time there were only two indexed bonds. In a low-inflation scenario they estimate the premium to be 400 basis points at the 10-year horizon and 500 basis points at the 20-year horizon, while in a high-inflation scenario the figures fall to 130 and 160 basis points, respectively, perhaps a little counter-intuitively. The authors also estimate the cost savings arising from the issue of the CTR (Certificato del Tesoro Reali) bond in Italy in 1983, a subject discussed in some detail in Chapter 7.

Although the figures from the studies quoted above suggest that the inflation risk premium is significant and that indexed bonds may have produced cost savings for governments, there are reasons why these figures should be interpreted carefully. First, existing indexed bond markets are generally less liquid than their conventional counterparts.[14] This relative illiquidity is likely to manifest itself in the form of a liquidity premium that, if it exists, will at least partially offset the inflation risk premium. A common assumption is that the liquidity premium is much smaller than that due to inflation, since the former will also be reflected in wider bid–ask spreads. However, should the opposite be the case, indexed issuance would actually increase the cost to governments of servicing their debt, all else being equal. This would seem to have been the case in the USA since the Treasury introduced its TIPS programme in 1997. Craig (2003) estimates that break-even inflation rates derived from comparing 10-year nominal Treasury bonds and TIPS have averaged approximately 1.90% over the period from 1997 to 2002. When this is compared with survey data, which suggests inflation expectations were relatively constant at around 2.50% over the same period, and with the actual outturn for the Consumer Price Index (CPI) of approximately 2.60% per year, it would be very hard to conclude that the inflation risk premium was even positive. The inference from this is that there have been other factors, whose impact has been to more than offset any inflation risk premium inherent in nominal bond yields over the period of this study. The author suggests that, although there is evidence that liquidity in the TIPS market has improved markedly since 1997, the existence of a liquidity premium for TIPS yields is the most likely explanation for this phenomenon. Second, other factors can give rise to differences in the returns between conventional and indexed bonds, such as differential tax treatment and the market's valuation of *convexity*. The issue of disentangling the convexity effect from the inflation risk premium is discussed further in Chapter 5.

The introduction of the euro in 1999 has given rise to a further source for potential cost savings. Government debt issuers within the Euro-zone are now competing much

[13] A discussion of which appears in Chapter 7.

[14] Reasons why this might be the case were discussed in Chapter 3.

more actively with each other than was previously the case, and this has led to some issuers attempting to carve out niche markets for themselves or innovating in order to attract investors. The French Trésor took the bold move of launching its inflation-indexed securities programme just months ahead of the launch of the euro, and thus became the first government issuer of indexed bonds in the Euro-zone.[15] Although domestic demand for such securities did not appear to be especially strong at the time, by taking this step the Trésor was able to obtain the advantages associated with being "first mover" in the market. With its original issue now redenominated in euros and with additional bonds indexed to Euro-zone inflation, the Trésor has strengthened its primacy over an ever growing market, a position that over time might be expected to help lower its overall borrowing costs.

4.1.3 Risk management

There are two broad approaches that a government can take toward managing the risk of its debt portfolio. The first is based on the argument that a government should structure its debt to facilitate the provision of insurance between different groups in society, or between one generation and the next. Through the issuance of indexed bonds, governments are in a position to provide securities that are both free from credit risk and from purchasing power risk. Indexed debt can enable relatively unsophisticated small investors, with limited access to financial markets, to protect themselves against both inflation and credit risk. It also provides a useful hedge for such institutions as pension funds with inflation-indexed liabilities. As Chapter 3 has shown, the risk–return characteristics of indexed bonds cannot yet be replicated by combinations of other assets, so by offering such securities the government can help complete the market and possibly reduce its funding costs at the same time. Government issuance of indexed debt should also encourage the private sector to follow suit, by providing a pricing benchmark as well as a hedging tool.

The second approach often utilised by governments is to structure its debt profile with the aim of hedging its finances against the effects of potential future shocks.[16] Optimal taxation theory suggests that it is desirable to minimise fluctuations in tax rates over time. When a government has primarily nominal debt, changes in the price level will obviously change its real value – which in turn must be matched by changes in taxation levels and/or changes in the rate of debt issuance. On the other hand, to the extent that inflationary pressures are more likely to be evident during economic upswings – periods in which government finances might be expected to be relatively strong – the existence of indexed debt will help a government to stabilise its real financing cost and thereby reduce the need for tax changes. Barro (1996) argues that, for an economy with no random fluctuations in government financing, the ideal form of government debt would be indexed perpetual bonds, which would provide a uniform stream of real coupons *ad infinitum*. However, Bohn (1996) maintains that the optimal structure of government debt should be a mixture of nominal and indexed bonds, arguing that nominal debt can serve as an insurance cushion since its real value can

[15] France remained the sole government issuer of euro-denominated inflation-indexed bonds until the Spring of 2003 when the Greek government came to the market – see Chapter 7.

[16] See, for example, HM Treasury (2002, p. 9).

decline when the government faces fiscal pressures, assuming of course these problems are accompanied by a sustained period of inflation. The provision of a diverse range of financial instruments also has the potential to create a broad investor base, thereby helping to ensure that the government can maintain debt sales in a variety of economic climates.

4.1.4 Inflation-indexed bonds and monetary policy

The existence of indexed debt removes one of the main incentives for a government to adopt inflationary policies (namely, the possibility of reducing the real value of its outstanding liabilities) and so may lead to a reduction in the inflation risk premium paid on subsequent issues of conventional debt. Indeed, Hanke and Walters (1994) claim that one of the reasons why the US Treasury was slow to issue indexed bonds was to keep open the possibility of reducing the real value of the Federal debt via inflation. However, while the existence of indexed debt removes this incentive to inflate, it does not in itself provide any encouragement for a government to take active steps to reduce inflation. Insofar as the real value of its debt is concerned, a government with a fully inflation-indexed debt portfolio will be entirely indifferent to the rate of inflation in the wider economy. A decision to issue indexed bonds is only likely to enhance policy credibility if there is already an established monetary policy framework and long-term inflation track record.

The ability to compare returns on indexed bonds offered by the market with those on nominal bonds can provide policy makers with important information on real interest rates and inflation expectations, which in turn can provide insights into the market's assessment of the credibility of monetary policy. From this perspective policy makers have long been advocates of indexed bonds. The following is an extract from Federal Reserve Board Chairman Alan Greenspan's testimony to the US House of Representatives in June 1992:[17]

> *Without doubt, the substantial uncertainty facing monetary policy would be reduced somewhat if the market were able to provide a reliable measure of current inflation expectations. Indeed, the paired issuance of indexed and unindexed debt at various maturities might make it possible to offer some information on the market's expectations for the path of inflation well into the future.*

In the UK, the Bank of England has been publishing estimates of inflation expectations derived in this manner since May 1993. Similar analysis is produced by policy makers in other countries with indexed bonds including Australia, Canada and Israel. Chapter 5 provides more detail regarding the techniques used to derive such measures. Several papers by policy makers and academics have outlined ways in which issuers of indexed bonds could make the task of extracting information on inflation expectations easier. For instance, Hetzel (1992) echoes Chairman Greenspan's comments by suggesting that the US Treasury issue zero-coupon bonds – an equal proportion being conventional and index-linked to enable perfect maturity pairing – with maturity dates a year apart and ranging from one year to twenty years.

[17] Source: Greenspan (1992).

4.1.5 Maintaining long-term capital markets in difficult economic conditions

Although more recent issuers of indexed bonds have generally rationalised their decision on the grounds discussed above, it is important not to overlook the fact that earlier issuers were often forced to index their debt by the threat to their ability to access long-term capital markets in the face of high and variable inflation. In such an environment it is rational for potential long-term investors to demand instruments that offer near-guaranteed positive real rates of return. Hence the reason that many governments in this position have chosen to issue index-linked debt, with varying degrees of success – see Chapter 7 for more details.

4.2 WHY PRIVATE CORPORATIONS ISSUE INDEXED BONDS

Many of the reasons why private sector entities might choose to issue indexed rather than conventional debt are clearly the same as those for governments. For example, corporate treasurers who hold the view that expectations of future inflation (as priced by the market) are too high will consider the issuance of inflation-indexed bonds to be an attractive option, in just the same way as would public sector fiscal authorities with a similar inflation outlook. Even without such an explicit view on the path of future inflation, the diversification of a company's debt portfolio can improve its risk–return characteristics – just as it can for a government. The utility sector in the UK has provided a number of examples of companies that have followed such an approach and structured their funding to tap a number of different sources, including of course through the use of index-linked bonds.[18]

However, there are other factors that potential private sector issuers face that are not always explicitly factored into a government's issuance analysis. For example, when structuring the liability portfolio, debt agencies typically consider the government finances on aggregate – they rarely employ a bottom–up approach to match individual bonds to specific liabilities. Corporations, on the other hand, may have incentives to match liabilities explicitly with expected future assets, primarily to reduce uncertainty but also to aid transparency – both factors that increase investor confidence. For this reason, organisations with assets whose nominal cash flows are expected to increase broadly in line with the general level of prices over time are prime candidates to issue indexed bonds to hedge the inflation risk.[19] Even without specifically indexed liabilities, a company's management may find the notion of knowing with certainty their *real* cost of finance to be an attractive one. Even for those treasurers who prefer to think in nominal terms, an index-linked bond has the distinguishing feature that its first nominal coupon payments will be small relative to an equivalent fixed rate conventional bond, but that they will grow over time. This feature could be attractive to issuers who have

[18] Examples of UK companies that have taken this approach include BG Transco, Glas Cymru (Welsh Water) and Anglian Water – see Barclays Capital (2002b). The use of indexed bonds by utilities in the UK is discussed in Chapters 6 and 8.
[19] Some of the practicalities associated with structuring liabilities to match more exactly a specific stream of indexed cash flows are discussed in Chapters 8 and 9.

limited income to pay dividends in the short term, but whose income is expected to increase over time.

Non-government issuers may also feel that they can benefit by issuing to meet a source of unsatisfied demand, since they often have more flexibility than governments over the timing and structure of their liability management activities. For example, within a month of the first issue of inflation-indexed notes by the US Treasury in January 1997 a handful of private sector issues were brought to the market. The majority of these bonds did not appear to have been brought by "natural" issuers (i.e., those with easily identifiable inflation-indexed assets). This implies either that they themselves felt that the market pricing of the inflation-indexed securities was too expensive, with real yields being too low, or that they were able to find other entities of that opinion to bear this risk. Since then, the development and increasing maturity of the market for inflation derivatives has broadened the range of these kinds of opportunities.

Moreover, private sector issuers are of course not obliged to design their instruments in precisely the same manner as the prevailing government bonds. In the same way that it seems likely that a developed government bond market is required as a precursor to the establishment of a corporate bond market,[20] it also seems logical to assume that private sector bonds will predominantly have the same features as the underlying government bonds. Although this is often indeed the case, there are many instances in which issuers have deviated from the standard bond design – to better match either their own assets or the liabilities of potential purchasers. A good example of the latter situation is the concept of *Limited Price Indexation* (LPI) in the UK pension industry. To meet their LPI pension liabilities (pension commitments that must be increased in line with the RPI [Retail Prices Index] but with a cap and a floor) UK index-linked gilts are not the perfect match for pension funds, since the bonds' cash flows reflect the uncapped RPI. A number of institutions have taken advantage of this mismatch by issuing LPI bonds to meet this natural demand. Again, this is an area in which the derivatives markets have grown to play an important role and thus enabled much greater participation by private sector issuers, since they can now employ swap contracts to ensure that they have no exposure to risks beyond those with which they feel comfortable. Chapters 8 and 9 discuss a number of such issues in more detail.

4.3 THE RELATIVE SCARCITY OF INDEX-LINKED BONDS

A number of explanations have been offered for why indexed bonds are not more prevalent. The main argument used by governments against issuing them has been that such a course of action might be viewed as a signal of reduced commitment to price stability since, if inflation is easier to live with, then there will be less resolve to maintain stable prices. Bootle (1991) notes that the authorities in the UK were certainly once of this view – the Radcliffe Report of 1959 pronounced that indexation would amount to a "confession of failure". Certainly, by providing such protection for

[20] This issue is discussed in more detail in Section 4.3.

bondholders a government is reducing the political lobby against inflation. It is interesting to note that for some years now the Israeli authorities have preferred to issue nominal bonds for precisely this reason: the belief that by expanding the group of agents with a vested interest in the maintenance of low and stable inflation, pressure will be brought to bear on the authorities to this end – see Yariv (1997).

Another criticism sometimes levelled at the concept of indexation is that its very existence could itself fuel inflation – an argument that has often been used in the past by the German Bundesbank.[21] Wojnilower (1997) puts forward a similar objection, arguing that "for a small budgetary gain at best, indexed bonds court an ugly risk that is intrinsically unlimited and, given long enough, almost certain to materialise." He reasons as follows: by issuing indexed bonds, the government is offering the public the opportunity to bet on inflation in return for a presumed interest saving (in the form of the inflation risk premium). If inflation does not accelerate, the government (and hence the general public) realises its savings, while indexed bondholders lose. On the other hand, should inflation accelerate,[22] indexed bondholders gain at the expense of those taxpayers that did not take part in the "bet".[23] Although this is unlikely to be a major issue while there are few indexed bonds in existence or the inflation increase is small, Wojnilower argues that as quantities of indexed bonds grow (as they are likely to in an inflationary environment) objections to indexed bonds from non-bondholders are more likely to surface. Under the extreme scenario in which the whole national debt had been converted to indexed bonds, raising funds to compensate the multitude of investors in the event of inflation would be a "wrenching process, bound to culminate in recession, hyperinflation, or both". There have indeed been several countries in which a policy of indexation could be deemed to have "failed". However, in such cases indexation was typically widespread, affecting all aspects of the economy (its use was not confined to the financial markets), and so such policies could alternatively be viewed as having exacerbated existing inflationary problems rather than creating them.

Hanke and Walters (1994) note that the US Treasury consistently cited a lack of demand as one reason for not issuing indexed bonds. However, this view is at odds with others, such as Weiner (1983), who have argued that their absence reflected supply-side problems more than a lack of demand. Another of the US Treasury's concerns with indexed government debt, and one that it happened to share with the Swedish authorities at one point,[24] had been that its issuance might *balkanise* the bond market – causing a situation in which an issuer creates too many categories of debt and thereby reduces overall liquidity. However, as noted earlier, Hanke and Walters (1994) claim that the main reason the Treasury was loath to issue indexed bonds was a desire to retain the option of reducing the real value of the Federal debt by allowing inflation to rise.

Another reason frequently offered in the past for the dearth of indexed bond issues in the USA is the question of legality. In 1933 the "Gold Clause" Joint Congressional Resolution was passed, banning indexation to gold prices. Although the first sentence of this law specifically prohibits gold clauses and so does not pertain to indexation *per se*, McCulloch (1980) claims that "most legal scholars have agreed that the wording

[21] See, for example, Deutsche Bundesbank (1998, p. 27).
[22] Wojnilower elaborates on why he thinks that this is the more likely outcome.
[23] This argument is not symmetrical since taxpayers do not have a choice as to whether or not they pay taxes.
[24] See Persson (1997).

of the second sentence of the Resolution [reproduced below] is sufficient to invalidate a price index clause if literally construed." He reports a case in 1939 during which the US Supreme Court made it clear that the second sentence of the law should indeed be "literally construed", "read by itself" and "torn out of context" thereby casting a doubt over whether inflation-indexed clauses would be enforceable:

> *Every obligation, heretofore or hereafter incurred, whether or not any such provision is contained therein or made with respect thereto, shall be discharged upon payment, dollar for dollar, in any coin or currency which at the time of the payment is legal tender for public and private debts.*

Although the 1933 Resolution may have discouraged the issuance of indexed bonds, it certainly did not stop it entirely – Weiner (1983) provides details of two such bonds that were issued after the 1939 Supreme Court case. In October 1977 Congress passed the Helms Amendment which revoked the 1933 Resolution and so removed any shadow of doubt over the legality of indexed bonds in the USA. However, the passing of this Amendment did not result in a rush of indexed bond issues, suggesting that there were other reasons behind the lack of supply. Interestingly, the USA is not alone in having had legal obstacles to the existence of an index-linked bond market. In the past other countries have taken an even firmer stance against indexation – in particular, the issuance of indexed bonds used to be explicitly banned in both Finland and Germany.[25]

The tax system in some countries can provide a further set of obstacles to the issuance of corporate indexed bonds. Of particular significance is whether a tax system allows inflation adjustments to be tax-deductible for the issuer. Bootle (1991) attributes the limited development of a private sector indexed bond market in the UK during the 1980s to the tax regime that applied prior to 1989. This system, which he describes as "vague or penal or both", treated private sector indexed bonds as conventional securities issued at a discount rather than as a separate asset class. However, although the tax rules in the UK were substantially revised in both 1989 and 1996 – steps that should have encouraged firms to consider more seriously the possibility of indexed debt – private sector issuance remained limited throughout the 1990s. This issue is discussed further in Chapter 6.

Wojnilower (1997) argues that the general lack of private sector issuance is because no company can make its indexing promise credible; only governments can guarantee to be able to honour such promises. To quote one of his examples, "how can a cereal maker promise to pay higher interest if grain prices explode?" Some other possible explanations for the lack of private indexed issues are put forward by Fischer (1983): that issuers suffer from money illusion, or that borrowers' inflation expectations have been systematically higher than those of lenders. He postulated that corporate profits tend to be lower in periods of high inflation, and so the issuance of indexed debt would force companies to have to make interest payments at points in the economic cycle when they can least afford them. Spiro (1989) suggests further that corporations are fundamentally risk-averse and, as such, are unlikely to take decisions that might cause them to incur higher real funding costs than their direct competitors in spite of the advantages of knowing with certainty their real cost of funding. Index

[25] See Chapter 7 for more details of the situations in these countries.

mismatching – discussed at length in Chapter 2 – may also have been a contributory factor.

Campbell and Shiller (1996) suggest that, were a government to issue indexed bonds, the private sector would be more likely to follow suit. There are several reasons why this might be the case: first, the government would need to engage in a public relations campaign beforehand. By issuing indexed bonds after the government, private corporations would benefit from the government's publicity campaign, reducing the extent (and therefore the cost) of marketing the generic instrument that they themselves would otherwise need to undertake. The government bonds would also give private issuers and their underwriters an instrument with which to hedge their own bonds, as well as providing them with a pricing benchmark. Evidence from the French market seems to confirm that governments have an important role to play in fostering a market for privately issued indexed debt.

The reputation of indexed bonds as an illiquid asset class has deterred some governments from launching an indexed bond programme, due primarily to concerns over the volume of issuance that might be necessary to establish a suitably liquid secondary market. Yet it can be difficult for a corporate bond market to gain sufficient depth without such government sponsorship, since without it only those investors with indexed liabilities have access to a suitable hedge to enable them to take on a position. Indeed, this is precisely the situation in many markets, where positions in indexed bonds can only be partially hedged through the use of nominal bonds – far from ideal given the different risk–return characteristics of the two classes of bonds, as Chapter 3 has illustrated. Without the ability to hedge effectively some of the fundamental risk it is far harder for the market to "underwrite" any proposed indexed bond issue, thus increasing the cost to any potential issuer.

A number of other possible solutions have been put forward in an attempt to address this problem of poor liquidity. In particular, an indexed bond futures contract should provide a good hedging vehicle for indexed bonds – just as existing bond futures contracts do for nominal bonds – and hence the establishment of such exchange-traded derivatives would almost certainly improve the liquidity of the market. However, when the possibility of an index-linked gilt futures contract for the UK market was considered during the 1990s the idea was not implemented, on the grounds that a reasonably liquid cash market was a precondition for the establishment of a successful futures contract – a classic "chicken and egg" situation.[26] In the USA, although the Chicago Board of Trade (CBOT) introduced futures contracts based on Treasury indexed notes in 1997, they were withdrawn shortly thereafter due to a lack of investor interest[27] – possibly because the TIPS market had yet to reach a sufficient level of liquidity to support such contracts.

As Abuhoff and Malik (1997) observe, another way to improve liquidity is to create bonds at different maturities and thereby enable traders to hedge a position in one indexed bond with one in another, although this gives rise to curve risk. Again, to some degree this comes down to the question of sponsorship – a government that makes a concerted effort to establish a bond market will typically issue a number of instruments

[26] See Bank of England (1996).

[27] The CBOT launched two contract specifications in July 1997: a 10-year contract that was withdrawn in March 1998 and a 5-year contract that was withdrawn in June 2000. In addition it launched a 30-year contract in April 1998 that was also withdrawn in June 2000.

with a variety of maturities for this very reason. Liquidity will also tend to improve as more countries introduce indexed bonds, since this is likely to lead to more cross-country trading and a general increase in awareness of the asset class internationally.

4.4 SUMMARY

There are several reasons why issuers of bonds might find indexed securities attractive. First, they provide an issuer with the potential to reduce its cost of funding versus issuance of fixed-rate nominal debt. This could arise either through saving the inflation risk premium embedded in nominal bond yields or by the issuer correctly anticipating that inflation will be lower than the market is expecting. For governments, indexed bonds provide a vehicle that enables them to manage risk more effectively through revenue and expenditure smoothing. Indexed government bonds also serve a social welfare function in providing the public with an asset that is free from both credit risk (in the case of highly rated sovereign issuers) and purchasing power risk, and their existence enables monetary authorities and other observers to derive measures of inflation expectations that can be used in the formulation of monetary policy.

Despite such seemingly compelling reasons for issuing indexed bonds, in practice the markets have been slow to develop. In some countries it has been legal issues that have restricted their growth, in others the concern that such issuance might balkanise the existing debt market. Experience also shows that indexed bond markets are generally less liquid than their nominal counterparts, so reducing the potential cost savings from issuance if the market charges an "illiquidity premium". Nevertheless, experience in both France and the USA has shown just how rapidly the markets can become established given sufficient investor demand and suitable government sponsorship.

Indeed, in many countries a corporate index-linked market has only developed following the introduction of indexed securities by the government. Other reasons for the slow growth in corporate index-linked markets in the past may have been unfavourable tax regimes or the fact that there was only a small group of natural issuers of inflation-linked products. However, with the rapid expansion of the indexed derivatives markets, particularly in the Euro-zone and the UK, government and corporate issuers alike can now much more easily exploit index-linked markets in periods when they provide a cheap source of funding.

5 Inflation and Real Interest Rate Analysis

The existence of a complete and efficient nominal debt market reveals the nominal interest rates at all future dates faced by borrowers and investors alike. Moreover, the rates available at any particular point in time represent those demanded by the marginal investor,[1] and as such reveal to some extent this investor's expectations of future nominal interest rates. In exactly the same way, the existence of a complete and efficient real debt market provides the *ex ante* real interest rates faced by borrowers and investors who want to avoid exposure to the effects of inflation, at the same time providing at least some information about their expectations of future real interest rates.

If two such markets exist, on any particular date the *ex ante* nominal and real interest rates available on loans at any future date are directly observable. If at least some investors participate in both markets, then the difference between nominal and real rates must to some extent reflect those participants' expectations of future inflation. In fact, in a world where future interest rates (both nominal and real) are known with certainty the difference between nominal and real interest rates is exactly equal to the (certain) inflation rate over the same period.

So the existence of complete and efficient nominal and real debt markets provides information not only on the *ex ante* nominal and real interest rates available at any particular time but also on participants' expectations of future nominal and real interest rates and of future inflation rates. In practice, however, future interest rates are not known with certainty and many debt markets are not complete and efficient; so, it is not always a straightforward exercise to observe nominal and real interest rates – let alone to use them to derive estimates of market participants' inflation expectations.

The prices of real and nominal bonds not only depend on expectations of real and nominal interest rates but also on tax regimes, market liquidity, the choice of index, the indexation method for real bonds and so on. There is much in the academic literature developing methods to identify the term structure of nominal interest rates and from it to derive estimates of the market's expectations of future interest rates – Anderson *et al.* (1996) provide a detailed survey. More recently, with the increased issuance of sovereign index-linked debt and the increased emphasis placed by monetary authorities on the control of inflation, this literature has broadened to look at the use of indexed bond prices to identify the term structure of *real* interest rates and estimates of inflation expectations.

This chapter surveys a number of estimation methods, highlighting the advantages and pitfalls of each. Section 5.1 describes how index-linked bond prices are used to measure real yields. Section 5.2 shows how these measures can be improved by using the prices of nominal bonds to pin down real rates of interest more accurately and at the

[1] Also, those willing to be paid by the marginal borrower.

same time provide estimates of inflation expectations in the market. Section 5.3 surveys how some of these techniques have been put to use by researchers in the literature.

5.1 MEASURES OF REAL INTEREST RATES

As with measures of nominal interest rates there are two issues here: the first is to identify the term structure of real interest rates accurately in the absence of a perfect real bond market and the second is the use of such term structures to derive estimates of expected future real interest rates.

The full market price P_N of a nominal bond paying a regular nominal coupon C_N and nominal redemption payment R_N at maturity is given by the bond price equation:[2]

$$P_N = \sum_{j=1}^{n} \frac{C_N}{(1+y_j)^j} + \frac{R_N}{(1+y_n)^n} \tag{5.1}$$

where y_j represents the spot interest rate on a loan repayable at date j. Similarly, the full market price P_R of a real bond[3] paying a regular real coupon C_R and real redemption payment R_R at maturity is given by the equation:

$$P_R = \sum_{j=1}^{n} \frac{C_R \prod_{i=1}^{j}(1+\pi_i)}{(1+r_j)^j \prod_{i=1}^{j}(1+\pi_i)} + \frac{R_R \prod_{i=1}^{n}(1+\pi_i)}{(1+r_n)^n \prod_{i=1}^{n}(1+\pi_i)} \tag{5.2}$$

where π_i is the rate of inflation between date i-1 and i. Because this real bond is perfectly indexed, the indexation factors scaling up the cash flows (in the numerator) exactly match those discounting the cash flows to obtain a price (in the denominator). These cancel to give:

$$P_R = \sum_{j=1}^{n} \frac{C_R}{(1+r_j)^j} + \frac{R_R}{(1+r_n)^n} \tag{5.3}$$

reducing the relationship between the price of a real bond, its real cash flows and real interest rates to exactly the same form as that between the price of a nominal bond, its nominal cash flows and nominal interest rates (Equation 5.1).

In reality, index-linked bonds are not perfectly indexed to inflation. Most fundamentally, the index used to inflate the cash flows may not be an accurate measure of "true" inflation. Most index-linked bonds currently in existence are linked to a consumer price index. As discussed in Chapter 3, for many classes of investors consumer price inflation is unlikely to be the most relevant measure – pension funds, for example, often have liabilities linked to wage growth (in addition to those linked to consumer prices), and so only a bond indexed to a measure of wage inflation will provide them with a real bond that truly allows them to hedge such liabilities. In this case the inflation

[2] For ease of exposition the first coupon payment is assumed to be paid in exactly one period's time, with all cash flows separated by identical time intervals.

[3] All the analysis in this chapter is with reference to the Capital Indexed Bond (CIB) structure – see Chapter 2.

terms in Equation (5.2) cannot cancel one another because the measure used in the numerator to scale up cash flows will not be the same as the one used by investors in the denominator to discount them. Even for those investors for whom the Consumer Price Index (CPI) is the relevant one, there is often debate over how this index is best constructed. For example, monetary authorities in the UK monitor at least four measures: the standard Retail Prices Index (RPI), the Retail Prices Index excluding mortgage interest (RPIX), the same index excluding mortgage interest and indirect taxes (RPIY) and the Harmonised Index of Consumer Prices (HICP).[4] Whereas the nominal cash flows of index-linked gilts are defined using the RPI measure, the government's inflation target is currently defined with reference to RPIX.[5] If RPIX is viewed to be the "true" measure of consumer price inflation in the UK, then index-linked gilts will be imperfect real bonds to the extent that RPI differs from RPIX.

A more practical issue is that inflation is not observed either continuously or contemporaneously. In most countries, price indices are published monthly and even the most rapid publication is 10 to 15 days after the end of the month in question. Moreover, the necessity in some countries for the nominal value of each coupon to be known before it begins accruing can increase the lag significantly – the most notable example being the UK where index-linked gilt cash flows are indexed to the RPI with an eight-month lag.[6] As discussed in Chapter 2, interpolation techniques are used in a number of markets – such as in the USA, Canada, France and Sweden – to minimise the indexation lag, but the fact that indices are published only monthly and with a delay means that the indexation on these bonds is still far from perfect. Estimates of real interest rates from index-linked bond prices that do not correct for any such imperfect indexation will therefore also be imprecise.

A number of techniques of varying sophistication exist to compute measures of *ex ante* real interest rates, the more common of which are detailed below.

5.1.1 Real gross redemption yields

Just as a gross redemption yield on a nominal bond can be computed as its internal rate of return, the real gross redemption yield for a perfectly index-linked bond is its (real) internal rate of return. Given an index-linked bond's price (as well as its real coupon and redemption payments) its real redemption yield is calculated from Equation (5.3) by setting $r_1 = r_2 = \cdots = r_n = \bar{r}$ and then solving iteratively for $\bar{r}$:

$$P_R = \sum_{j=1}^{n} \frac{C_R}{(1+\bar{r})^j} + \frac{R_R}{(1+\bar{r})^n} \tag{5.4}$$

In practice, Equation (5.4) should never be applied directly because bonds are not perfectly indexed.[7] Since most index-linked bonds are affected by an indexation lag,

[4] See Beaton and Fisher (1995) for a detailed comparison of the first three of these indices: RPI, RPIX and RPIY. A similar situation exists in many other countries.
[5] In a speech to the House of Commons on 9 June 2003, Chancellor of the Exchequer Gordon Brown announced his intention to redefine the Bank of England's inflation target in terms of Eurostat's HICP, as part of a broader package of measures intended to better prepare the UK's economy for possible adoption of the euro. At the time of writing this change is expected to come into force in late 2003.
[6] This design was implemented to best suit the tax rules in place during the early 1980s, when the bonds were first issued.
[7] The appendices to Chapter 6 list the actual bond price–yield equations used in the larger index-linked markets.

their computed real yields are dependent on an assumption about future inflation rates. To see why this is the case, consider an (imaginary) index-linked bond with an indexation lag equal to its coupon period. Its bond-pricing equation would be similar to Equation (5.2), but the indexation of payments would start one period earlier:

$$P_R = \sum_{j=1}^{n} \frac{C_R \prod_{i=0}^{j-1} (1+\pi_i)}{(1+r_j)^j \prod_{i=1}^{j} (1+\pi_i)} + \frac{R_R \prod_{i=0}^{n-1} (1+\pi_i)}{(1+r_n)^n \prod_{i=1}^{n} (1+\pi_i)} \tag{5.5}$$

In this case, the indexation terms in the numerator and the denominator do not completely cancel one another:

$$P_R = \sum_{j=1}^{n} \frac{C_R(1+\pi_0)}{(1+r_j)^j(1+\pi_j)} + \frac{R_R(1+\pi_0)}{(1+r_n)^n(1+\pi_n)} \tag{5.6}$$

Given the bond's price P_R, the inflation rate π_0 and the real coupons and redemption payment (C_R and R_R), the real gross redemption yield is then computed by setting $r_1 = r_2 = \cdots = r_n = \bar{r}$ and $\pi_1 = \pi_2 = \cdots = \pi_n = \bar{\pi} = 3\%$ (for example) and then solving for $\bar{r}$ as before:

$$P_R = \sum_{j=1}^{n} \frac{C_R(1+\pi_0)}{(1+\bar{r})^j(1+\bar{\pi})} + \frac{R_R(1+\pi_0)}{(1+\bar{r})^n(1+\bar{\pi})} \tag{5.7}$$

Although it can be confusing when looking at index-linked bonds for the first time to see that their yields are dependent on an assumed inflation rate, the reason is clear from Equation (5.7). The longer the lag and the shorter the residual maturity, the more impact this inflation assumption will have on the bond's computed yield. In the UK, index-linked gilt yields are usually quoted assuming a constant future inflation rate of 3%. Table 5.1 shows the yields for two index-linked gilts with very different residual maturities under different inflation assumptions. A 2 percentage point increase in the

Table 5.1 Quoted real yields on selected index-linked gilts based on different inflation assumptions*

Assumed annual inflation rate (%)	Real yield on 2% Index-linked Treasury 2006 (based on a price of £261.56) (%)	Real yield on 2% Index-linked Treasury 2035 (based on a price of £102.40) (%)
0.0	1.575	2.036
1.0	1.403	2.012
2.0	1.233	1.988
3.0	1.065	1.965
4.0	0.898	1.941
5.0	0.734	1.918

* The quoted bond prices are the Gilt-edged Market Makers Association (GEMMA) reference prices as at close of business 31 March 2003. The yields were calculated by the UK Debt Management Office assuming a settlement date of 1 April.

inflation assumption from 3% to 5% reduces the computed real yield by around 33 basis points for the 3-year bond, but by only 5 basis points for the 32-year bond.

As discussed in detail in Chapter 2, many countries avoid distortions of this magnitude by interpolating between observed inflation numbers to reduce the indexation lag – the USA, Canada, France and Sweden being notable examples. However, in order to compute real yields in these markets it is still necessary to make some assumption about inflation, and so the observed real yields are still approximations to "true" real rates. In practice, because indexed bonds in most major markets are issued on a real yield basis the authorities have to publish an official price–yield equation for settlement purposes. For simplicity these official formulae assume that the expected inflation terms in the price–yield relationship cancel entirely, leaving:

$$P_R = \sum_{j=1}^{n} \frac{C_R(1+\pi_0)}{(1+\bar{r})^j} + \frac{R_R(1+\pi_0)}{(1+\bar{r})^n}$$

$$\Rightarrow \quad P_R = (1+\pi_0)\left[\sum_{j=1}^{n} \frac{C_R}{(1+\bar{r})^j} + \frac{R_R}{(1+\bar{r})^n}\right] \tag{5.8}$$

Although an approximation, this simplification makes the formula easier to use and ensures that it bears a strong resemblance to the corresponding conventional bond formula (with which market participants are probably already familiar). The longer the indexation lag, the greater an approximation this represents. One practical problem with using a formula for settlement that requires an inflation assumption is that everyone involved would have to agree on the inflation assumption to use. In any case, although the official formula in most markets may be a simplification, it is likely that more sophisticated market players will derive their own analytical techniques based on Equation (5.6) to circumvent these issues.

5.1.2 Hedge ratios: the duration and "beta" of inflation-indexed bonds

In standard nominal bond mathematics, a bond's *duration* is defined to be the average maturity of its cash flows, weighted by present value. Duration is a key concept in risk management because it is a measure of price sensitivity – two par bonds with the same duration will experience the same price move for a given parallel shift in nominal yields. It is therefore natural to try to extend this analysis to index-linked bonds, but unfortunately this is not as straightforward as might be hoped.

Typically, the modified duration[8] of a real bond is taken to be its (normalised) price sensitivity with respect to its *real* yield:

$$\textit{Modified duration} = -\frac{1}{P}\frac{dP}{dr} \tag{5.9}$$

While this concept has some use when analysis is limited to index-linked bonds, more care has to be taken in any comparison with their nominal counterparts. The reason for this statement is clear from the Fisher equation:[9] a nominal bond has sensitivity both to

[8] More precisely, duration is defined to be the average maturity of the cash flows weighted by present value. Equation (5.9) defines a very closely related quantity referred to as *modified duration*.

[9] See Equation (5.12), for example. The effects of risk premia are disregarded for ease of exposition.

Table 5.2 Examples of estimates of beta for selected index-linked bonds*

Index-linked bond	Central estimate of beta	95% confidence interval	
		Lower	Upper
US $3\frac{3}{8}$% TIIN January 2007	0.37	0.26	0.48
FR 3% OAT*i* July 2009	0.39	0.26	0.52
UK $2\frac{1}{2}$% Index-linked Gilt May 2009	0.32	0.18	0.46

* Estimated using (non-annualised) monthly yield change data.
Data source: Barclays Capital (2002b, pp. 67–72).

the real interest rate and to the expected inflation rate, and so its duration measures the bond's sensitivity to some combination of both these factors.[10] Since the duration of a real bond as set out above is defined with respect to only the real interest rate, any comparison of the two asset classes based solely on these standard definitions is clearly inconsistent. An analysis of this nature implicitly assumes that expected inflation rates are either zero or constant, in which case inflation-indexed bonds would be redundant.

Without recourse to such standard measures of risk it has become common practice to describe the *beta* of index-linked bonds with respect to their conventional counterparts, in the same way and for much the same purpose as equity analysts compute the beta of individual stocks with respect to an index – to construct hedge ratios. A stock's beta reflects the correlation between its price and that of the broader market.[11] So the higher a stock's beta, the more volatile its price (and vice versa); a stock with a beta of zero is generally characterised as uncorrelated with other equities and a stock with a negative beta tends to move in the opposite direction to the general level of share prices. Estimates of stock betas therefore provide useful measures with which to quantify the risk of a given portfolio, which fund managers can use to quantify their exposure relative to benchmark indices. They are also used to construct *beta-neutral* trading strategies that enable investors to trade one set of equities versus another (or against index futures) while keeping the overall risk of their portfolio constant.

There is no single correct method for calculating the beta of an index-linked bond, as indeed is the case for stocks, but in general a mixture of historical and theoretical analysis is used. Historical data can be processed in many different ways: by varying the time period, the bonds selected (both nominal and real) and so on, each of which will impact beta estimates. Even the horizon of the analyst can play a part: if a "hold-to-maturity" strategy is under consideration, then a beta computed using interest rate *level* data is the more appropriate, but for those more concerned with the day-to-day riskiness of a portfolio then betas computed using interest rate *changes* might be useful. By way of illustration, for the three largest markets, Barclays Capital (2002b) presents estimates based on monthly changes that are reproduced in Table 5.2. Although the central estimates for the beta of each of the three bonds are reasonably similar, it is

---

[10] Siegel (2002) describes this feature as *double-duration*, to distinguish between the distinct hedging properties of nominal and inflation-indexed bonds.

[11] More precisely, the beta represents the sensitivity of the stock price to a unit move in the broader market (usually taken to be represented by an index) and is often computed as the coefficient from a standard linear regression.

interesting to note their apparent instability as represented by the statistical confidence intervals around the estimates.

Estimates such as those presented in Table 5.2 are typically based on straightforward regression analysis, and so there is clearly room for more rigorous theoretical underpinnings. There is no *a priori* reason why a bond's beta should not vary through time, or with the level of interest rates, or with the level of inflation. A fundamental difference between the beta of an index-linked bond compared with that of an equity is that the former has an interpretation over and above simply being the relative volatility of the asset. Unless a beta of precisely one is chosen, any beta-hedged combination of nominal and real bonds can be decomposed into a break-even inflation position plus an outright position in the nominal market. This insight is often used to help establish a suitable value for beta. For example, as central banks turn more and more to inflation targeting and accumulate experience in doing so, it may be reasonable to presume that inflation will not be permitted to run persistently at rates significantly different from the authorities' central target. In such an environment it may therefore be sensible to estimate a bond's beta to be at least partially dependent on the level of break-even inflation rates (fully adjusted of course for all the technicalities of the market, the different indices, etc.), so that it approaches unity as break-even inflation rates move above levels that are perceived to be "sustainable". Such an approach clearly involves more than a little subjectivity, but ignoring fundamentals and basing beta estimates purely on historical data runs the risk that future conditions turn out to be different from those observed in the past.

5.1.3 The term structure of real interest rates

The difficulties in interpreting a series of gross redemption yields on nominal bonds with different maturities as the term structure of interest rates are well known: cash flow timing, tax effects and differing liquidity between issues can distort the picture. For example, an investor purchasing a benchmark issue rather than an off-the-run issue with the same duration may be prepared to pay more for the former because of the additional liquidity it provides. An investor who pays tax on coupon income but not on capital gains will prefer low-coupon bonds that provide more of their return in the form of the latter, causing low-coupon bonds to trade at a premium should such a taxpayer be the marginal investor. Even if all such distortions can be accounted for, bonds do not define the full maturity spectrum; so some form of interpolation is required to uncover the market interest rate at a term for which there is no existing bond. Academics and practitioners have developed a whole range of both parametric and non-parametric modelling techniques to fit a term structure curve to a set of nominal bond prices – Anderson *et al.* (1996, Chapter 2) again provide a comprehensive survey.

The same problems exist when attempting to estimate a term structure of real interest rates from a set of index-linked bond prices and are compounded by the indexation lag and the fact that there are in general far fewer index-linked than nominal issues. Nevertheless, a number of the techniques used to fit a term structure of nominal interest rates can be amended to fit a term structure of real interest rates to index-linked bond prices. For example, McCulloch (1971, 1975) developed an essentially non-parametric approach to estimating the nominal term structure using prices of conventional bonds by defining the discount function $\delta(t)$ as a linear combination of suitably chosen basis functions $f_1(t), \ldots, f_k(t)$:

$$\delta(t) = 1 + \sum_{j=1}^{k} \alpha_j f_j(t) \tag{5.10}$$

where the coefficients $\alpha_1, \ldots, \alpha_k$ are determined by linear regression on bond price data.

Deacon and Derry (1994b) show how this same procedure can be used to fit a term structure of real interest rates using UK index-linked gilt price data, and this methodology can easily be amended to cater for the different indexation techniques employed in other markets. Such techniques still require assumptions about future inflation to determine a term structure, again because of the inflation lag, although there are a number of ways to handle the problem. These are discussed in the remainder of this chapter.

5.2 MEASURES OF INFLATION EXPECTATIONS

Imperfect indexation of cash flows means that an index-linked bond can be viewed as a combination of two instruments: a perfectly indexed real bond and a non-indexed nominal bond. This can be illustrated using the hypothetical case of the index-linked bond with cash flows lagged by one coupon period described in Equation (5.5). Suppose the penultimate coupon has just been paid on such a bond, leaving only the final coupon and redemption cash flow. Equation (5.5) becomes:

$$P_R = \frac{C_N}{(1+r)(1+\pi)} + \frac{R_N}{(1+r)(1+\pi)} \tag{5.11}$$

The remaining cash flows are now not indexed at all (they are fixed in nominal terms[12]) and so such a bond is priced in exactly the same way as a standard nominal bond. This observation leads to a solution to the indexation problem – by using data from the nominal bond market to price the non-indexed portion of an index-linked bond, its "true" real yield can be better observed. Underlying this approach is the well-known *Fisher identity* linking *ex ante* nominal (y) and real (r) interest rates with the expected inflation rate π^e:

$$(1+y) = (1+r)(1+\pi^e)(1+\rho) \tag{5.12}$$

where ρ is a risk premium that reflects the uncertainty of future inflation.[13] This approach is richer than it first appears: given a value for the inflation risk premium ρ, Equation (5.12) provides a link between the nominal and index-linked bond price equations that allows the real interest rate r and the expected inflation rate π^e to be solved simultaneously. This is the general approach taken in much recent research, with varying degrees of sophistication. This section outlines the various techniques that use nominal and index-linked bond prices to uncover r and π^e. The final section describes how these have been used to draw inferences about real rates of interest and expectations of inflation.

[12] Hence the subscript N in Equation (5.11).

[13] The Fisher identity can take a number of forms, but Equation (5.12) is the most relevant for the discussion here.

5.2.1 Break-even inflation rates

The simplest way to measure expected inflation is to pick a pair of nominal and index-linked bonds with the same maturity, to ignore any problems caused by imperfect indexation and to define expected inflation as the yield on the nominal bond less the yield on the index-linked bond:

$$\bar{\pi}^e = \bar{y} - \bar{r} \tag{5.13}$$

where $\bar{y}$ and $\bar{r}$ are the gross redemption yields on the nominal and index-linked bond, respectively. This technique produces an estimate of the *average* expected rate of inflation $\bar{\pi}^e$ from today until the maturity of the bonds. This is certainly a quick way to obtain a rough approximation to the inflation expectations of market participants, but there is an obvious inconsistency here: to compute the real redemption yield $\bar{r}$ on an imperfectly index-linked bond an initial assumption about $\bar{\pi}^e$ needs to be made. Whatever value of $\bar{\pi}^e$ results from Equation (5.13) depends on the assumed level of $\bar{\pi}^e$ used in the initial computation of $\bar{r}$. This problem is more serious the shorter the maturity of the chosen bonds, because the nominal component of an imperfectly index-linked bond becomes more significant as it ages.

To avoid this inconsistency in $\bar{\pi}^e$, break-even inflation rates can be computed as follows:[14] first, compute the nominal yield on the nominal bond in the usual way, and then compute the real yield on the index-linked bond using an initial guess at the expected inflation rate $\bar{\pi}_0^e$. Assuming $\rho = 0$, the Fisher identity (Equation 5.12) is applied to obtain a new estimate of the expected inflation rate π_1^e.[15] In turn, this new estimate π_1^e is now used to recompute the real yield on the index-linked bond and thus obtain a new estimate of the expected inflation rate π_2^e. This iterative technique is applied until it converges on a single value π^e, thus ensuring consistency.

There are clearly some shortcomings with the break-even rate methodology. It can be difficult to find a conventional and an index-linked issue with exactly the same maturity dates, so that it is often only possible to match bonds with *approximately* the same maturity. There are situations in which such a mismatch could distort any estimates of inflation expectations that arise: for example, in the case of a steeply sloped nominal yield curve, two nearby nominal bonds could have significantly different yields. More importantly, when selecting only two bonds from the market not only is a large amount of information (from the prices of other bonds) being ignored but also any estimate of inflation expectations is at risk of being distorted by any idiosyncrasies of the chosen bonds. For instance, using a benchmark nominal bond rather than an equally nearby "off-the-run" issue with a higher yield will affect the resulting estimate of the break-even inflation rate.

Despite these problems, this methodology (or some variation on it) is often the only option available – particularly in markets where very few sovereign index-linked bonds

[14]Note that although the market convention for computing real yields of Canadian Real Return Bonds (RRBs) – as well as those of the US Treasury Inflation-Protection Securities (TIPS), French OAT*i*s and many other inflation-linked bonds – assumes that all terms in π cancel, a more consistent break-even inflation rate is obtained if the formula is expanded based on Equation (5.7) and the iterative algorithm is applied as described below.

[15]The Fisher identity should be amended to take account of the coupon frequency of the bond. For example, in markets where bonds pay coupons semi-annually the following variation is commonly used to compute break-even inflation rates:

$$(1 + y/2) = (1 + \pi^e)^{1/2}(1 + r/2)$$

Note also that there is no reason why ρ must be set equal to zero.

exist. In Canada, for example, where there are currently only four RRBs (maturing in 2021, 2026, 2031 and 2036, respectively) there is little more analysis that can be done in this respect. The Bank of Canada monitors the levels of break-even inflation rates in its quarterly *Review* (e.g., Côté *et al.*, 1996[16]). Similarly, Heenan (1991) applies this technique to study inflation expectations in Australia and Yariv (1994) uses the same method with data from Israel's capital markets.

5.2.2 The "Inflation Term Structure"

In countries with a more developed index-linked debt market, more detailed and efficient estimates of the market's inflation expectations can be obtained by, first, constructing term structures of nominal and real interest rates and, then, using these as the basis for estimates of inflation expectations. This has a number of advantages over simply picking pairs of bonds and estimating break-even inflation rates as described above: there is no longer the problem that pairs of bonds may have only approximately the same time to maturity – in fact, a pair of nominal and real rates from any maturity along the length of the curve can be selected and analysed. Also, using estimated term structures helps to remove the possibility of distortions arising from the choice of individual bonds (due to tax rules, "on-the-run" [benchmark] status and so on) – assuming of course that the modelling techniques used are rich enough to extract successfully the true underlying term structures of interest rates from noisy bond price data. Finally, estimating a term structure of inflation means that instantaneous implied rates at any future date can be computed in precisely the same way that implied forward interest rates are derived from an estimated par (or zero-coupon) yield curve.

The Bank of England has been publishing the results of such analysis in its quarterly *Inflation Report* since May 1993 (see Figure 5.1). The initial implementation[17] involved the use of an iterative routine: having estimated the nominal term structure in the usual way, an initial inflation term structure is specified (e.g., 3% across all maturities) and then from these two curves a term structure of real interest rates is obtained.[18] Applying the Fisher identity (Equation 5.12)[19] to each pair of points along the nominal and real forward rate curves gives a new estimate of the inflation term structure, from which a new implied real rate curve can be obtained. This iterative procedure is continued until the inflation term structure converges to a single curve. In general this iterative process is well behaved, but it should be noted that there is nothing explicit in this methodology to ensure convergence.[20]

Evans (1998) introduces the innovation of an *index-linked yield curve*, as distinct from the "true" real yield curve, to reflect the fact that index-linked bond yields are imperfect measures of real yields. His formulation allows for the relationship between the three forward rate curves – nominal, real and inflation – to be defined explicitly and thus

[16] For further information see Ragan (1995).

[17] See Deacon and Derry (1994a).

[18] The choice of algorithm to fit both the nominal and real term structures can have a material impact on the resulting forward inflation curve. The Bank of England has over time used a number of curve-fitting methodologies, most recently one developed from Waggoner's "Variable Roughness Penalty" model (1997).

[19] Setting ρ equal to zero for simplicity, although this need not be the case (see below).

[20] A feature that can lead to unstable estimates of the inflation term structure if the process is not well specified – see Gilbert (1995).

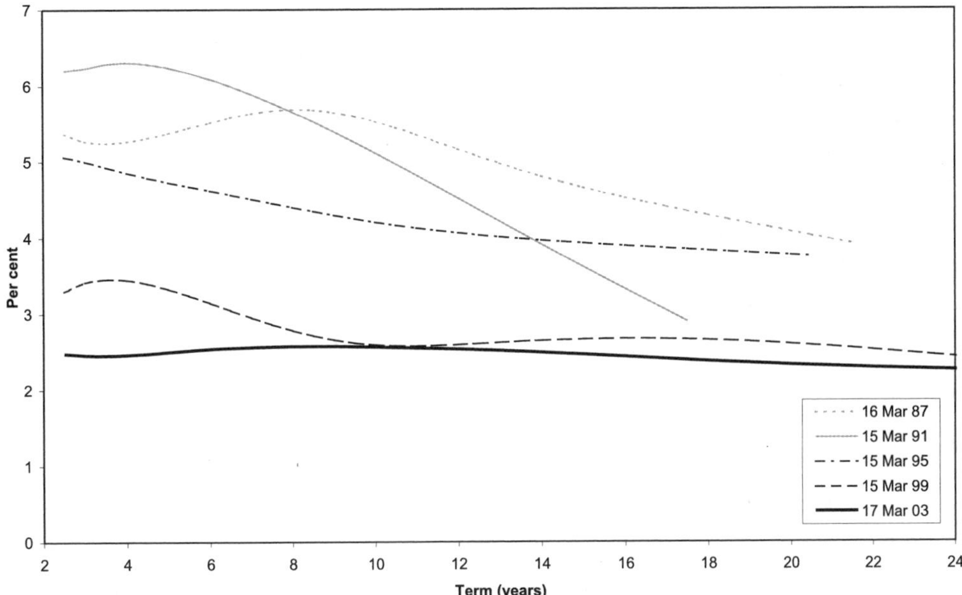

Figure 5.1 Examples of the UK implied forward inflation rate term structure
Data source: Bank of England

avoids the iteration process inherent in the Bank's original specification.[21] Anderson and Sleath (2003) describe a number of technical adjustments that are required to apply Evans' approach directly to the UK gilt market and show that over time its implementation achieves more stable results than the iterative approach.[22] The forward inflation rate curves published by the Bank of England since late 1999 have been constructed in this manner.

5.2.3 The inflation risk premium and bond convexity[23]

Having estimated a term structure of implied forward inflation rates, it is tempting to interpret this directly as describing the market's expectations of inflation at any point in the future. The desire to do this is clear from the point of view of investors (who may decide how to invest on the basis of how the market's view of future inflation differs from their own), monetary authorities (as market expectations about future inflation can play an important part in monetary policy decisions) and academics – all of whom otherwise lack measures of inflation expectations from any source other than survey data. However, there are two problems with making such a leap: bonds are convex instruments and nominal bonds are usually thought to carry an inflation risk premium

[21] Cairns (1998) details a different approach to achieve a similar result.
[22] Although some of this improvement seems likely to be due to the choice of more flexible models for the nominal and real term structures.
[23] See Anderson *et al.* (1996, chap. 8) for a more rigorous analysis of the problems caused by the inflation risk premium and the convexity of the bond price equation.

to compensate investors for the risk that higher than expected inflation will decrease the real valuation of the bonds.

The first of these problems is a purely mathematical phenomenon. The bond price equation (Equation 5.1) implies that the price of a bond P is a *convex* function of interest rates $y_1, \ldots, y_n$. *Jensen's inequality*, a well-known result from statistical theory, states that for a random variable X and a strictly convex function $g(.)$ then:

$$E[g(X)] > g[E(X)] \tag{5.14}$$

To see the impact of Jensen's inequality on the interpretation of bond yields, consider a simplified version of the nominal bond price (Equation 5.1) with only one future payment (worth £1) remaining:

$$P = \frac{1}{(1+y)} \tag{5.15}$$

An investor could price this bond using either one of the following equations:

$$P = E\left[\frac{1}{(1+y)}\right] \tag{5.16a}$$

$$P = \frac{1}{(1+E[y])} \tag{5.16b}$$

Now, because Equation (5.15) is convex, Jensen's inequality (Equation 5.14) shows that for the same expected interest rate y over the lifetime of the bond, Equation (5.16a) would produce a larger price than Equation (5.16b). In other words, an investor using Equation (5.16a) to price a bond would demand a lower yield than the investor using Equation (5.16b), simply because the bond price equation (Equation 5.15) is convex.[24] If investors used Equation (5.16b), then the expected interest rate $E(y)$ would equal the forward rate by construction. However, Cox *et al.* (1981) demonstrate that Equation (5.16a) is the only one consistent with the *rational expectations hypothesis* – the basis of all modern finance theory – and so Jensen's inequality necessarily drives a wedge between implied forward rates and expected future interest rates, causing the former to underestimate the latter.

The second problem is more straightforward to understand (namely, that risk-averse investors faced with uncertain future interest rates will demand an interest rate risk premium to compensate them for taking that risk). In other words, the yield demanded by a risk-averse investor to hold a fixed income bond will be higher than that implied by the same investor's expectations of the path of interest rates over the security's lifetime. So, to the extent that holders of bonds are risk-averse, implied forward interest rates will overestimate the market's expectations of interest rates.

Jensen's inequality and the likely existence of interest rate risk premia mean that implied real and nominal forward rates cannot be directly interpreted as expected real and nominal interest rates, so the difference between them cannot be directly interpreted as expected inflation rates. However, there are two points worth emphasising.

First, because it is the difference between nominal and real forward rates that is being computed, estimates of inflation expectations will be distorted only in so far as the risk

[24] Equation (5.16a) is usually referred to as the *local expectations hypothesis* whereas Equation (5.16b) represents the *unbiased expectations hypothesis*.

premium and convexity effects are different between nominal and index-linked bonds. Since inflation is the major factor that affects nominal but not real bond prices, it seems reasonable to assume that the difference between nominal and real interest rate risk premia is primarily an inflation rate risk premium. Also, because both nominal and real bonds have convex price functions, the difference between the inflation term structure and the true path of inflation expectations due to Jensen's inequality will be smaller than that between the implied nominal forward rate curve and the true path of expected nominal interest rates.

Second, the inflation rate risk premium and bond convexity will bias the inflation term structure in opposite directions – in other words, to the extent that these effects are of the same order of magnitude they will offset each other. It is a heroic assumption to propose that they offset exactly, as many researchers (including two of the authors of this book) have done in the past. Nevertheless, it may well be the case that such effects are often of second-order importance because they at least partially offset one another.

5.3 ANALYSIS OF REAL INTEREST RATES AND INFLATION EXPECTATIONS

There are a number of uses to which the tools outlined so far in this chapter can be put. The existence of index-linked bonds to identify *ex ante* real yields and the ability to combine this information with prices of nominal bonds – both to improve these real interest rate estimates and to provide estimates of the market's inflation expectations – have formed the basis of a number of research articles. This section surveys some of them, highlighting the benefits and deficiencies of the techniques described earlier in this chapter and some of the uses to which they have been put.

5.3.1 Real interest rates

Some of the earliest research sought to use information from the index-linked gilt market in the UK (the first significant index-linked bond market) to extract information about real rates of interest. Before the existence of such instruments, the only way economists could measure real interest rates was to combine nominal interest rates with estimates of inflation expectations taken either from survey data or from econometric models. The study by Arak and Kreicher (1985) was one of the first that used information from nominal bond prices to correct index-linked gilt yields for the indexation lag in order to obtain robust estimates of *ex ante* real interest rates. They used a technique that is essentially a linearisation of the break-even inflation rate methodology and concluded that real yields uncorrected for the lag can overestimate true real interest rates by up to 50 basis points. They recognised that their technique also provides estimates of inflation expectations under an assumption of no inflation risk premium but concentrated on obtaining accurate measures of the real interest rate.

Woodward (1988) points out that an error with Arak and Kreicher's analysis led them to underestimate real yields by 15% to 25% and, in his own analysis (Woodward, 1990), uses the break-even inflation rate methodology (without Arak and Kreicher's linearisation) to compute real yields corrected for the indexation lag. Woodward

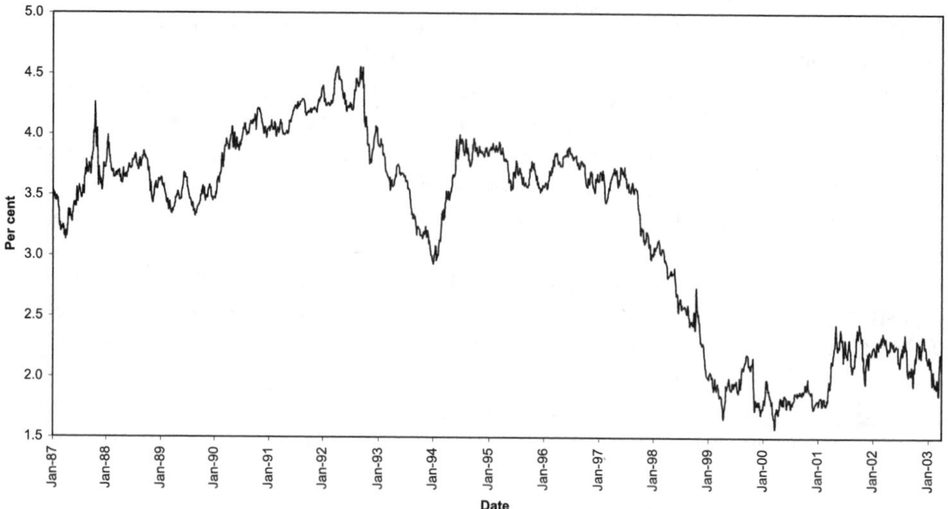

Figure 5.2 Real yield on UK $2\frac{1}{2}$% Index-linked Treasury 2024 (January 1987–March 2003)
Note: A 3% inflation assumption was used from January 1998 and a 5% assumption prior to that
Data source: UK Debt Management Office

enhances the work of Arak and Kreicher in two further ways: by matching index-linked bonds to "par-equivalent" conventional bonds with precisely the same maturity (estimated from a simple yield curve model) and by considering post-tax rather than pre-tax returns to adjust for any distortions caused by tax regimes.[25] Of course, by using a model to correct for these two factors any improvement may be offset by deficiencies in the modelling procedure itself. Both Arak and Kreicher (1985) and Woodward (1990) highlight the importance of index-linked bonds to policy makers to signal whether a change in nominal rates represents a change in real rates and/or a change in inflation expectations (or the risk premium). They also highlight how, contrary to most economic theory, real interest rates appear to vary (with a 300 basis point range in long-dated UK gilt yields between 1987 and 2003 – see Figure 5.2) and, in the UK at least, can remain at levels somewhat higher than the real growth rate of the economy for significant periods of time. Both studies also assume that the inflation rate risk premium is zero – in the case of Arak and Kreicher this is because their main purpose was to estimate real interest rates, and they recognised that any misspecification of the inflation rate risk premium was more likely to corrupt estimates of inflation expectations rather than estimates of real interest rates. Woodward confirms this using a simple simulation study but also argues that the inflation risk premium is small because his estimates of inflation expectations over the period 1982–1990 are already lower than survey measures over the same period, and the introduction of a significant risk premium would lower these estimates still further.

[25] For each period the technique computes the tax rate that minimises the sum of squared residuals in a post-tax yield curve model. Therefore the marginal tax rate can (and does) vary from period to period, with Woodward (1988, table 1, p. 381) reporting a range of tax rates from 14% to 40%.

Levin and Copeland (1993) explicitly measure the inflation rate risk premium by making assumptions about the expected paths of future inflation and real interest rates. They assume that the real interest rate is expected to be constant in the future, that the rate of inflation is expected to decay from its current level to some future long-run equilibrium level and that the marginal rate of tax on all securities is the same (but can vary from period to period). This enables them to estimate the constant *ex ante* real rate of interest, the expected path of the inflation rate, the marginal tax rate and the inflation rate risk premium simultaneously for each period in their estimation sample, using prices of conventional and index-linked bonds in a cross-sectional regression. The estimates of the inflation risk premium that Levin and Copeland derive are mostly negative, recognising that this residual term is a combination of the risk premium and the effect of convexity on bond prices (see Section 5.2) whose effects work in opposite directions. Although Levin and Copeland are reluctant to draw this conclusion, their study appears to suggest that the effects of convexity outweigh the inflation rate risk premium.[26] However, their estimates of the real interest rate, like those of Woodward (1990) using an earlier sample, broadly increase over time.

Robertson and Symons (1993) build on these approaches to come up with a term structure of real interest rates, as opposed to a constant real rate (Levin and Copeland, 1993) or a set of "adjusted" real interest rates (Arak and Kreicher, 1985; Woodward, 1988, 1990). By linearly expanding the index-linked bond price–yield equation (e.g., Equation 5.7) around each bond's gross redemption yield, a piecewise linear term structure is obtained which is then smoothed to obtain a reasonable term structure of real interest rates. They assume that the marginal tax rate is zero for both nominal and index-linked markets[27] and that the inflation risk premium is small (citing Levin and Copeland, 1993; Woodward, 1990). They adjust for the indexation lag by decomposing an index-linked security into a pure real bond and a nominal bond (the latter representing the imperfect indexation of UK index-linked gilts) and price the nominal bond component using a nominal term structure model. Consistent with the earlier studies they also note that real yields in the UK increased from the early 1980s to the early 1990s (and suggest that events in Eastern Europe over this period may have significantly increased the real cost of capital in Europe as a whole). They also conclude that longer term real interest rates have been more stable than short-term rates, observing that this finding is consistent with the hypothesis that monetary policy cannot affect real interest rates in the long term, only in the short term.

Brown and Schaefer (1994) provide a theoretically rigorous methodology for fitting the term structure of real interest rates. They develop an earlier model for fitting the term structure of nominal interest rates (Schaefer, 1981), explicitly accounting for both the impact of tax regulations and seasonality in the UK's RPI.[28] They note the stability of long-term real interest rates (as do Robertson and Symons, 1993) and the rise in real rates through the 1980s mentioned earlier. They also note that the term structure of real interest rates is usually "humped", a point noted previously by Woodward (1990). They

[26] Although in theory this will depend on the maturity of the bonds in question and the volatility of inflation (and hence nominal interest rates) – an area not explored here.

[27] They justify this assumption by claiming that pension funds (which are exempt from tax in the UK) dominate the index-linked gilt market. Also they use only high-coupon nominal bonds in their estimation, considered to be held primarily by tax-exempt institutions due to the tax regime in force in the UK at the time (e.g., Schaefer, 1981).

[28] The latter is achieved by fitting a seasonal ARIMA time-series model to historic RPI data, a statistical technique that identifies trends and cycles in data series – see, for example, Chatfield (2003).

go on to fit the well-known theoretical one-factor model due to Cox, Ingersoll and Ross (1985) to real interest rate data and conclude that it does much better at fitting real interest rates than it does nominal rates – in particular, the model's prediction that long-term interest rates are constant is borne out by real interest rate data from the UK over this time period. However, although the model fits data well in any given period, its parameters prove to be unstable over time. Two aspects of the study are questioned by Aziz and Prisman (2000) who claim that the methodology used to fit the term structure (due to Schaefer, 1981) is prone to systematic bias and that concentrating on pre-tax returns in a segmented market, such as the UK, also induces distortions. By focusing instead on *post*-tax returns and implementing a least-squares algorithm to construct real yield curves[29] the authors confirm Brown and Schaefer's (1994) main result that the Cox, Ingersoll and Ross (CIR) model fits the data well and report more stable model parameters over time.

Jarrow and Yildirim (2003) use a different theoretical term structure framework, due to Heath, Jarrow and Morton (HJM) (1992), applied to a different market – that for TIPS in the USA. The paper formulates a three-factor arbitrage-free term structure model to fit inflation, real and nominal yield curves to market prices of TIPS and conventional Treasury securities. The authors demonstrate that the framework is as robust as the original HJM model when applied to nominal bonds and illustrate its potential usefulness – particularly to the derivatives markets – by using it to price an option on CPI-U (Consumer Price Index for All Urban Consumers). This is one of the first studies of its kind to be applied to a market outside the UK and would be immediately extendable to other markets with bonds of a similar design, such as those of France, Canada and Sweden.

All but the last of the above studies have been carried out using data from the UK index-linked gilt market, since it is still the richest source of historical real interest rate data. However, the development of other markets has begun to shed some light on another important economic question: theory suggests that, in the long run at least, there should be a single global real cost of capital and thus a single *ex ante* real interest rate across the world. By looking at real interest rates from index-linked securities across different markets, it should be possible to identify the extent to which this is true.

So far, this appears to be the domain more of practitioners rather than academics (e.g., Basta *et al.*, 1994, pp. 12–13; Deacon and Andrews, 1996, p. 24), but superficial observation suggests that there might indeed be some convergence in real yields in different markets – see Figure 5.3.[30] Even if there were a single global real interest rate, structural features of individual markets and instruments could lead to differences in real rates. For example, differences in taxation regimes, market liquidity, credit considerations and indexation methods (and, of course, the indices themselves and how they are constructed) could lead to different observed real interest rates across countries. More fundamentally, for there to exist a single global real rate it would require investors to be truly global and willing to "arbitrage" any observed real yield differences.

---

[29] Based on a technique to fit the nominal term structure developed by Litzenberger and Rolfo (1984).

[30] Since Figure 5.3 shows historic unadjusted real yields (i.e., quoted in the usual convention for each market), interpreting them as real *interest rates* is subject to all the earlier caveats.

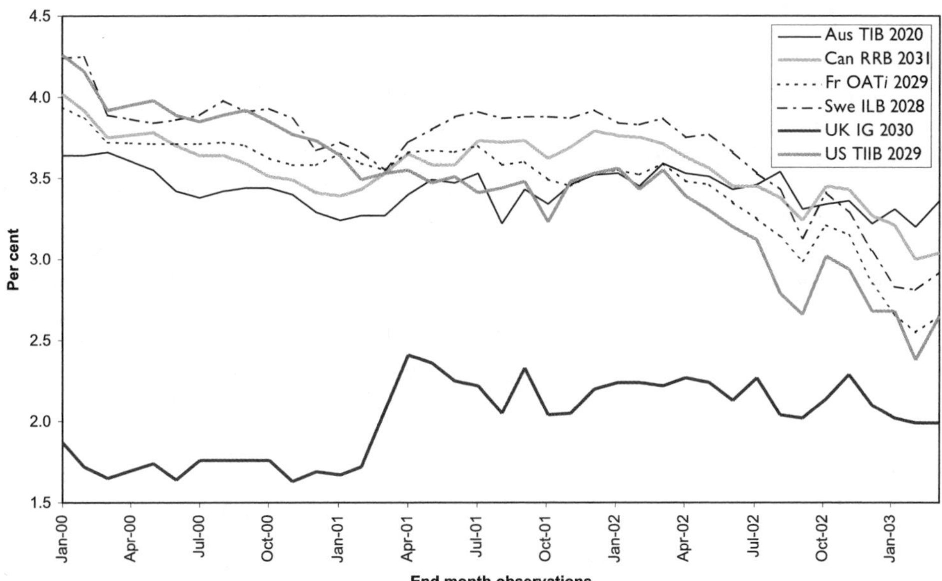

Figure 5.3 International real yields on inflation-indexed government bonds (January 2000–March 2003). *Note*: The UK yield is based on a 3% inflation assumption

Data source: Barclays Capital.

TIB = Treasury Indexed Bond; RRB = Real Return Bond: OAT*i* = Indexed Obligations assimilables du Trésor; ILB = Index-linked Treasury Bond; IG = Index-linked Gilt; TIIB = Treasury Inflation-Indexed Bond.

5.3.2 Measures of inflation expectations

More recently, the emphasis of research has shifted away from the estimation of real interest rates to measuring expectations of future inflation. Of course, some of the earlier studies also provided estimates of inflation expectations: Arak and Kreicher (1985) note that "for those who are willing to assume (boldly) that the uncertainty premium is zero" their methodology provides estimates of inflation expectations. Woodward (1990) is prepared to assume that the uncertainty premium is not significantly different from zero and interprets his (slightly modified) break-even inflation rates as the average expected inflation rates to different horizons. Although the estimation of expected inflation rates was not the primary aim of either of these studies, they have subsequently been used as the basis of practitioner studies to evaluate their usefulness in this area. As part of an exercise to investigate the relevance of index-linked securities to the US authorities, de Kock (1991) questions whether the existence of an index-linked gilt market in the UK has provided policy makers with any additional information about the private sector's inflation expectations and concludes that very little benefit is gained as the inflation expectations measure has consistently poorly predicted actual inflation. Hetzel (1992, p. 19) reinterprets de Kock's results: "Would evidence that investors predict inflation poorly affect the value to the central bank of a yield-gap measure of expected inflation? The answer would appear to be no. What matters in determining the real rate of interest is what inflation rate financial markets expect, not whether *ex post* they predicted inflation accurately." Indeed, the Bank of Canada (e.g., Côté *et al.*, 1996) use precisely this information from their domestic bond market to help measure the inflation expectations of Canada's private sector.

Levin and Copeland (1993) was one of the first studies that expressly set out to measure market participants' expectations about the future path of inflation rates. As discussed above, they impose the constraint that the inflation rate decays from its short-run level to some long-run equilibrium level, and their results show that long-run inflation expectations declined over their sample period (1982–1991). More recent studies have attempted to develop a less constrained term structure of inflation expectations by using curve-fitting techniques. Such an approach allows for the construction of inflation forecasts for any future date, rather than simply the average expected inflation rate from today to a set of horizons matching the maturity dates of existing index-linked securities. Robertson and Symons (1992) develop their methodology for estimating the term structure of real interest rates (described above) to estimate a term structure of inflation expectations and, again assuming that the inflation rate risk premium is approximately zero, use it to study the market's reaction to sterling's forced exit from the European Exchange Rate Mechanism (ERM) during September 1992. They conclude that *ex ante* short real rates were held artificially high by sterling's membership of the ERM and that, while long-term real rates remained constant, the expected long-term inflation rate rose significantly on sterling's exit.

Deacon and Derry (1994a) develop a more general approach that enables a term structure of inflation expectations to be constructed from underlying term structures of real and nominal interest rates, again assuming that the inflation rate risk premium is zero. This methodology can be characterised as a "break-even inflation rate term structure" – an inflation rate term structure that is consistent with the term structures of nominal and real interest rates and accounts for the indexation lag inherent in index-linked securities. This technique, with the enhancements described in Anderson and Sleath (2003), forms the basis of the "inflation term structure" that the Bank of England publishes in its quarterly *Inflation Report* and uses to help measure the private sector's expectations of future inflation. Wilcox and Zervos (1994) develop a similar approach, again based on the observation that an imperfectly indexed security is a hybrid between a nominal bond and a perfectly indexed "real" bond and so estimate a term structure of inflation expectations that accounts correctly for the indexation lag. They apply their technique to dates surrounding sterling's exit from the ERM – reaching broadly the same conclusions as Robertson and Symons (1992) – as well as to dates either side of the UK general election in April 1992, when the Conservative government was unexpectedly re-elected and inflation expectations across the maturity spectrum decreased significantly.

The major problem with interpreting the output from any of the above approaches as representing inflation expectations is the (often implicit) assumption that the combined effect of the inflation rate risk premium and the convexity of the bond price equation (deriving from Jensen's inequality – see above) cancel each other out, at least approximately. If the inflation rate risk premium is significantly larger across the yield curve than the effect due to Jensen's inequality, then all the above techniques[31] will overstate inflation expectations – since ρ in Equation (5.12) is assumed to be zero when it is in fact positive – and *vice versa*.

[31] Except that due to Levin and Copeland (1993) who explicitly measure this effect.

Estimating the size of this effect is plainly an empirical issue, as the inflation risk premium and the convexity effect (whose magnitude will depend on the volatility of expected future interest rates) are likely to vary through time and across markets. A number of studies point to different conclusions: for example, Levin and Copeland (1993) suggest that the combined effect leads to a negative value for ρ in Equation (5.12), implying that the convexity effect outweighs the risk premium significantly. Schaefer (1996), although not discussing the potential size of the inflation risk premium, indicates that the convexity effect is likely to dominate, particularly at longer maturities. Conversely, comparing a number of single-factor yield curve models, Anderson *et al.* (1996, chap. 8) suggest that the effect of Jensen's inequality is much less significant, whereas a number of other studies suggest that the inflation risk premium can be sizeable. For example, Chu *et al.* (1995) suggest that the inflation risk premium in the UK has been as high as 2.5% and cite other studies with similarly large estimates. Foresi *et al.* (1997) also estimate the inflation rate risk premium on UK 10-year government bonds to be around 2.5%.[32] The work of Gong and Remolona (1996) hypothesised that the US government had been paying a significant risk premium by issuing nominal rather than index-linked debt, although Craig (2003) suggests this has not been borne out in practice since the Treasury began issuing TIPS in 1997. These studies, and others addressing the issue of estimating risk premia, were discussed in more detail in Chapter 4.

A variation on the term structure methodology that internalises the estimation of inflation risk premia and convexity effects is proposed by Evans (1998).[33] As discussed above, by explicitly modelling index-linked bonds as a combination of perfectly indexed "real" bonds and nominal bonds, Evans identifies an additional covariance term in the Fisher Equation (5.12) to explicitly differentiate "real" and imperfectly indexed bonds. Aside from his observations regarding the Bank of England's "Inflation Term Structure", he concludes that the risk premium is time-varying (as have a number of studies before him, most notably Campbell and Shiller, 1991), implying that the assumption of $\rho = 0$ in Equation (5.12) can produce misleading estimates of the market's inflation expectations.

A different avenue of research addresses the question of whether the market actually predicts future changes in inflation and interest rates correctly. Traditionally, in markets without index-linked securities, these studies have concentrated on whether changes in the slope of the nominal yield curve are accurate predictors of future changes in interest rate policy (e.g., Mishkin, 1990; Frankel, 1982). Breedon and Chadha (1997) compare these with data generated by the Bank of England's inflation term structure model to see whether the latter forecasts future inflation better than more traditional methods. Their results are positive, though not overwhelmingly conclusive, suggesting that these term structures "seem at least as good (and probably better over longer horizons) at forecasting future changes in inflation." From the results of this study it would appear that *changes* are forecast better than *levels*, perhaps another signal that the risk premium and convexity do not cancel each other out all of the time.

[32] In fact, this study computes the nominal and real bond inflation risk premia separately and reports estimates of 300–350 basis points and 100 basis points, respectively.
[33] A similar approach is proposed by Gilbert (1995).

The relatively recent introduction of TIPS has limited the scope for similar analysis to be applied to data from the USA. Sack (2000) represents an early study in this regard, combining data from the nominal strips market[34] with both prices of TIPS and a simple mean-reverting model of the inflation rate to generate a time series of constant maturity 10-year inflation expectations. He observes that almost all market reaction to macroeconomic events is reflected through changes in nominal interest rates, resulting in estimates of inflation expectations that are far more volatile than either survey forecasts or the level of the CPI itself. For this reason the author cautions against attempts to interpret high-frequency changes in such measures as being representative of changes in inflation expectations.[35]

5.4 SUMMARY

This chapter has described a number of approaches in the academic and practitioner literature that use the prices of index-linked and nominal bonds to make inferences about real interest rates, expectations of future inflation rates and the sizes of the inflation risk premium and the convexity effect. Although such techniques can provide useful insights, there are a number of serious caveats that need to be borne in mind when interpreting the data, not least the uncertainty surrounding the size (and even the sign) of the combined effect of the inflation risk premium and the convexity effect. Nevertheless, institutions around the world – not least central banks – are increasingly applying these techniques to obtain data from which to draw inferences about real interest rates and the market's expectations of inflation, which in turn are used to aid policy decisions.

[34] On the grounds that the strips had similar liquidity characteristics to TIPS over the sample period in question.
[35] A similar conclusion is drawn by Shen and Corning (2002).

6
Major International Indexed Bond Markets

An extensive literature has developed that describes the properties of inflation-indexed bonds as well as techniques for extracting estimates of market expectations from the prices of such instruments, but there are few reviews of the markets themselves.[1] This chapter and the one that follows draw on such reviews in combination with information sourced directly from many of the issuers of indexed government bonds to provide a comprehensive description of the world's indexed bond markets. The information that appears here dates from around March 2003 and, to the best of the authors' knowledge, represents a full account of the markets at that time. Although the main focus of attention is indexed *government* bonds, some reference is also made to securities issued by public corporations, quasi-government authorities and the private sector.

This chapter focuses on the six countries with the most developed international markets for indexed government debt: Australia, Canada, France, Sweden, the UK and the USA – the same set of markets used to construct global bond indices, such as those published by Barclays Capital[2] and other investment banks. Table 6.1 presents summary statistics for the six markets, while Figure 6.1 illustrates how their combined size has grown since the first edition of this book was published in January 1998.

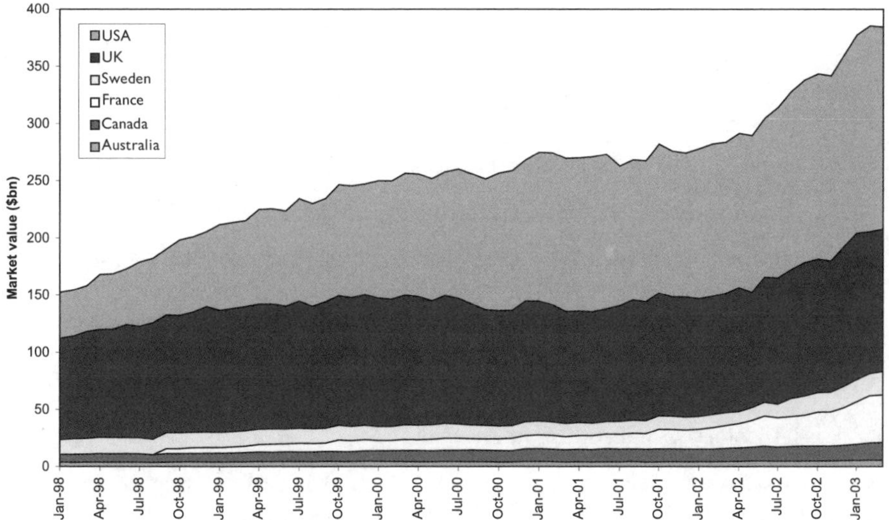

Figure 6.1 Growth of the major inflation-indexed government bond markets (January 1998–March 2003)

Data source: Barclays Capital

[1] Two notable exceptions are Page and Trollope (1974) and Price (1997), which both provide detailed coverage of this subject.

[2] See BZW (1997) for a description of the criteria on which the Barclays Capital indices are based.

Table 6.1 Summary of major international indexed government bond markets (as at 31 March 2003)

	Australia	Canada[a]	France	Sweden	UK	USA
Market value (US$bn)	5.5	15.5	41.8	20.5	124.4	176.7
Number of bonds in issue[b]	4	4	5	6	10	10
Longest maturity	2020	2036	2032	2028	2035	2032
Average (semi-annual) real yield (%)	3.27	3.01	2.27	2.71	1.91	2.18
Coupon frequency	Quarterly	Semi-annual	Annual	Annual	Semi-annual	Semi-annual
Frequency of price index publication	Quarterly	Monthly	Monthly	Monthly	Monthly	Monthly
Indexation lag	See[c]	3 months	3 months	3 months	8 months	3 months
Current method of issue	Multiple yield auction	Single yield auction	Multiple real price auction[d]	Multiple yield auction	Single price auction	Single yield auction
Quotation convention for trading	Real yield	Real price	Real price	Real yield	Nominal price	Real price
Strippable?	No	Yes, coupons are not fungible	No	No	No	Yes, coupons are fungible

Data sources: the authors and Barclays Capital.
[a] The market value and yield figures for Canada are based on the three bonds that existed at the end of March 2003, but the other rows in the table reflect the fact that a fourth bond maturing in 2036 was launched in June 2003.
[b] Bonds with less than US$100mn nominal outstanding and those with less than one year to maturity are excluded from these statistics.
[c] The formula is based on the average percentage change in the CPI over the two quarters ending two quarters prior to that in which the next interest payment falls.
[d] Although multiple price auctions are the French government's main means of issuing indexed bonds it sometimes issues new bonds through a syndication process.

6.1 AUSTRALIA

6.1.1 A brief history of indexation in Australia

Australia's first index-linked security was a CPI-linked Capital Indexed Bond (CIB) launched by the State Electricity Commission of Victoria in August 1983. In July 1985 the Commonwealth Government entered the market with an issue of four Treasury Indexed Bonds (TIBs) – two CIBs, issued by auction and two Interest Indexed Bonds (IIBs), issued by tap immediately after the CIB auction.[3] The government's rationale

[3] The IIBs had the same maturities as the CIBs, but were sold in much smaller quantities.

for issuing inflation-indexed bonds was threefold: to provide cost-effective financing (including a reduction in the overall risk of the government's debt portfolio), to lengthen the average maturity of government debt[4] and to complement its retirement incomes policy by offering an "inflation-proof" asset to pension and insurance funds.

After the first issue, further TIB auctions were held at approximately three-month intervals, each issue consisting of two CIBs and two IIBs.[5] These were multiple yield auctions, with accepted bids being converted into a settlement price using a standard formula published by the Australian Treasury.[6] The market initially found it hard to value the new securities, and there were wide ranges of bids at the early bond sales, with the most extreme result occurring in the February 1986 auction for which the range of accepted yields for the 20-year bond was 200 basis points.[7] The variability in the range of accepted yields at the early TIB auctions is illustrated in Figure 6.2.

From 1987 several quasi-government authorities began issuing indexed bonds. Initial offerings were in the CIB format, but in 1988 annuity-style indexed securities were introduced. These could take one of two forms; either Indexed Annuity Bonds (IABs) or Credit Foncier Bonds (CFBs). The nominal cash flows on a CFB are identical to those on an equivalent IAB. However, while the latter is viewed for tax purposes as a stream of revenues with no principal attached (each payment thereby treated as income resulting from the purchase of an annuity), the corresponding CFB's cash flows are considered to represent the repayment of debt, and hence each payment is deemed to consist of both principal and interest components. The instruments are therefore subject to different tax treatment.[8]

When the Australian government's finances moved into surplus in 1988, it ceased issuing new indexed bonds and actually repurchased some of the existing bonds as part of its debt reduction policy. Due to a lack of investor demand it was not until 1993 that the Treasury resumed its index-linked issuance programme. Under the new programme only CIBs have been issued, reflecting the earlier limited interest in IIBs. Because of the poor results from the early multiple yield auctions of the 1980s, the Treasury decided as a short-term measure to issue TIBs by fixed yield subscription through a dealer panel. After five issues using this system the panel was disbanded in July 1994,[9] since when the authorities have reverted to multiple yield auctions (though only one bond is now sold at each auction[10]).

Although the timing of these auctions was initially determined by perceived demand, in the 1997/98 financial year the Treasury introduced a more regular issuance schedule with auctions being held every six to eight weeks.[11] The intention was to provide greater certainty regarding the timing of indexed bond auctions and so allow investors to plan better their acquisitions of TIBs. It was hoped that in turn this would ultimately increase demand for the asset class and thereby improve the cost-effectiveness of indexed debt issuance for the government.[12] The authorities always retained the right

[4] The maturities of the bonds issued at the first auction were 10 and 20-years.
[5] Most of these were reopenings of existing bonds rather than new issues.
[6] The price–yield formula for CIBs appears in Appendix 6.1.
[7] Real yield bids in the February 1986 auction ranged from 5.4% to 7.4%. A complete record of CIB issuance appears on the Australian Office of Financial Management's website: www.aofm.gov.au
[8] For a more detailed comparison of IABs and CFBs see BZW (1992).
[9] See The Treasury (Australia) (1994a).
[10] The only exception being the auction of 23 September 1999, at which both the 2015 and the 2020 TIBs were sold.
[11] *Note*: in Australia the financial year ends on 30 June.
[12] See The Treasury (Australia) (1998, p. 10).

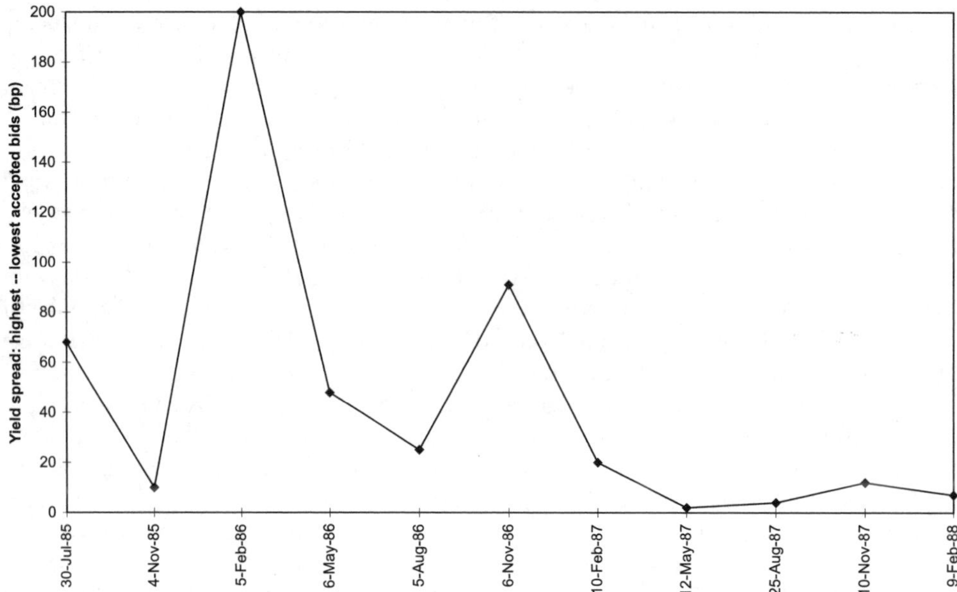

Figure 6.2 Range of accepted bids at auction for Australian Commonwealth 4% Capital Indexed Bond (CIB) 2005

Data source: Reserve Bank of Australia

to cancel an auction if they perceived there to be insufficient demand from the market, a right they have exercised on occasion.[13] A further change was introduced in 2000/01, from which point the index-linked auction calendar was announced at the start of each financial year and auction dates were chosen to follow the (quarterly) TIB coupon payment dates to aid coupon reinvestment.[14] Figure 6.3 shows the bid-to-cover ratios for all auctions since August 1994, as well as margins between yields achieved at auction and those prevailing in the secondary market. The largest such spread – 12 basis points – occurred in November 1999, reflecting the 28 basis point range of accepted bids at the auction.

As Figure 6.4 illustrates, growth in the market has slowed significantly in recent years due to the sharp fall in the Commonwealth government's financing requirement. At the end of March 2003 the total nominal amount of TIBs outstanding was approximately Aus$6.6bn[15] which, as Table 6.2 shows, represented around 10.7% of the Commonwealth Government Securities (CGS) denominated in Australian dollars,[16] or 9.8% of the gross outstanding government debt. Although at the start of the 2002/03 financial year the Treasury had indicated that it expected to issue Aus$200mn nominal of TIBs during the year,[17] in practice just Aus$150mn nominal was issued due to the cancellation of the May 2003 auction.

[13] Several auctions were cancelled on these grounds in both 1998/99 and 1999/2000 – see The Treasury (Australia) (1999, p. 11) and Australian Office of Financial Management (2000b, p. 22).

[14] See Australian Office of Financial Management (2000a).

[15] Or Aus$8.5bn including the inflation uplift.

[16] Excluding Commonwealth government holdings.

[17] See Australian Office of Financial Management (2002).

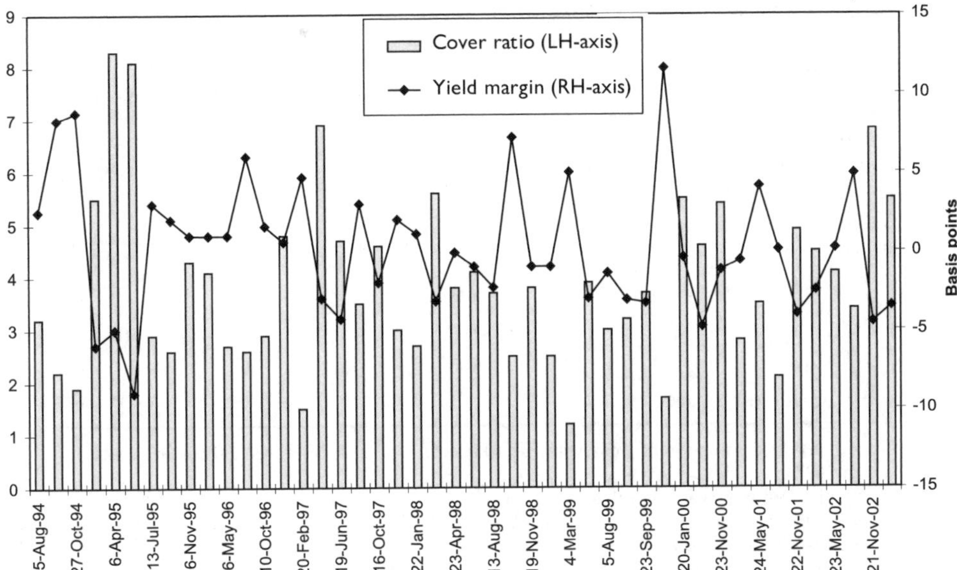

Figure 6.3 Australian Treasury Indexed Bond (TIB) auctions (August 1994–March 2003), bid-to-cover ratio and clearing yield spread. *Note*: yield spread is the auction clearing yield minus the prevailing secondary market yield

Data source: Australian Office of Financial Management

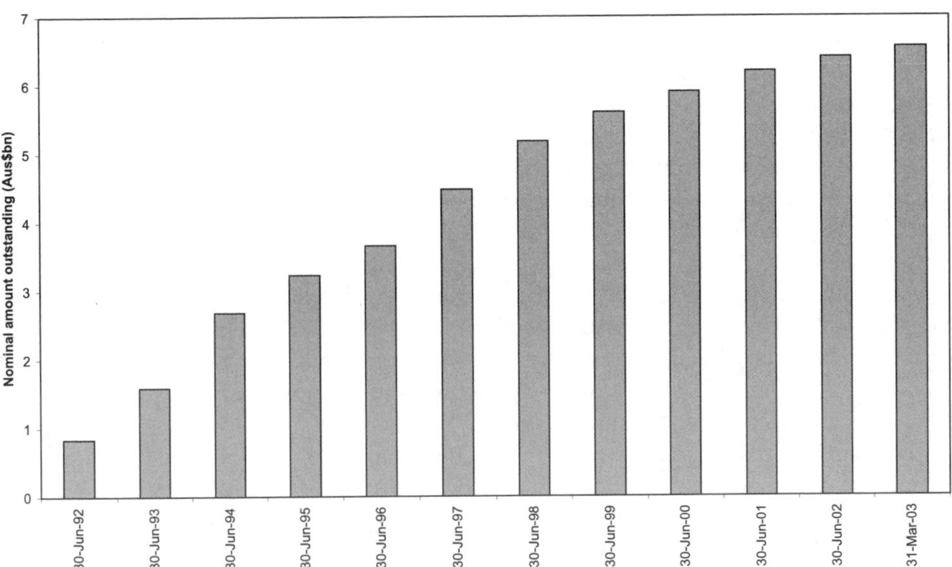

Figure 6.4 Growth in the Australian Treasury Indexed Bond (TIB) market

Data source: Australian Office of Financial Management

Table 6.2 Australian Commonwealth Government Securities (CGS) outstanding

Instrument	Nominal amount (Aus$ thousand)
Treasury Bonds[a]	49,334,231
Treasury Notes	1,997,000
Treasury Indexed Bonds (TIBs)	6,551,845
Assumed debt[b]	401,467
Other[c]	223,269
Total Aus$ denominated CGS	58,507,812
Total foreign currency-denominated CGS[d]	304,023
Total[a]	58,811,835
Gross outstanding debt	63,948,915

Reproduced by permission of the Australian Office of Financial Management (figures as at 31 March 2003).
[a] Excludes Commonwealth holdings.
[b] Debt assumed by the Commonwealth from the Federal Airports Corporation and Snowy Mountains Hydro-Electric Authority.
[c] Overdue CGS, State Domestic Raisings and State Tax-Free Stock.
[d] Valued at end-month exchange rates.

By 2002 the reduction in the size of the CGS market resulting from the combined effect of the Australian government's medium-term fiscal strategy (introduced in its 1996/97 budget) and its sale of state assets had led market participants to question its future viability. The ratio of Commonwealth general government net debt to GDP had fallen from a peak of 19.1% in 1995/96 to just 5% in 2001/02, representing a debt repayment of Aus$60bn over this period. In recognition of these concerns the Australian Treasury published a discussion paper in October 2002 that reviewed the CGS market and outlined its preference to eliminate government debt.[18] While recognising that the CGS market plays a number of important roles in the economy, the Review argued that the private sector could undertake at least some of these. It went on to propose that the continued maintenance of a debt market would require the accumulation of a substantial portfolio of assets and thereby expose the government to large financial risks, potentially distort Australian markets and raise significant governance concerns. With this exercise the Treasury had in effect placed the onus on others to demonstrate the benefits of the status quo and to provide evidence that the private sector would be unable to adapt to an environment without a government bond market. As might be expected, sentiment on this issue ran high: for example, Macquarie Research (2002) provides a detailed critique of the proposals and argues that "the place of the CGS in financial markets (is) as significant as are highways and freeways to the national road transport system. In the final analysis, the economy and the community could still function without highways and freeways, but why try to?"

The Treasury received around 40 written submissions to its proposals and held over 120 consultation meetings involving more than 90 domestic and international market

[18] See (Australian) Department of the Treasury (2002).

participants and organisations. The outcome of the Review was published on 13 May 2003 as part of the 2003/04 budget.[19] It concluded that to close the CGS market would lead to slightly higher interest rates due to the higher costs associated with managing interest rate risk without a Treasury bond futures market, and so the government decided to maintain a sufficiently liquid bond market to support the Treasury futures contracts. In order to minimise the resultant accumulation of financial assets, the government decided to limit future issuance to nominal Treasury bonds, and as a result the TIB programme was suspended on 1 July 2003.

6.1.2 The structure of the Commonwealth Treasury Indexed Bond (TIB) market

Table 6.3 provides a listing of the current Commonwealth government index-linked issues. As in other countries, TIBs are significantly less liquid than their nominal counterparts, a fact highlighted by turnover data for the 2001/02 financial year. In this period the total turnover of Commonwealth government fixed coupon bonds was Aus$543,666mn, compared with just Aus$8,543mn for TIBs.[20] The principal reason for such poor liquidity seems to be that investors tend to buy TIBs with the intention of holding them until redemption. Indeed, a survey by the OECD (2002) found that the top 15 investors in the market together hold around 90% of the total. These investors are predominantly domestic superannuation funds and insurance companies, with only limited overseas interest in the market due to disadvantageous withholding tax rules.

Although the Commonwealth government is the dominant issuer of Australian indexed bonds, its securities represent only about half of the market. In addition, the Australian market has a large number of smaller inflation-indexed issuers including state governments, quasi-government authorities, electricity companies and financiers of private projects. For instance, both the Melbourne Cricket Club and the Sydney Harbour Tunnel Company have issued indexed bonds. In addition to the four formats of indexed bond already discussed, Australian CIBs and IABs have also been issued with embedded put options, though not by the Commonwealth government.[21]

All Australian IIBs bar one are tied to the CPI,[22] the exception being an Australian Overseas Telecommunications Corporation issue which is linked to average weekly earnings. Both CIBs and IIBs pay coupons on a quarterly basis, with cash flows indexed to the average percentage change in the CPI over the two quarters ending in the quarter that is two quarters prior to that in which the next interest payment falls. For example, for interest payments due in February 1997 the adjustment was based on the average quarterly movement in the CPI over the two-quarter period ending in September 1996. This indexation methodology implies that changes in the general level of consumer prices from up to 11 months prior to any payment date are reflected

[19] See (Australian) Department of the Treasury (2003) Statement 7: Budget funding.

[20] Source: Australian Financial Markets Association (2002).

[21] The put option gives the investor the chance to put, or sell, the bond back to the issuer on specific dates and at specific real yields, thus providing protection against adverse movements in real yields while guaranteeing liquidity at discrete points of time in the future. Chapter 2 gives more details on the structure of such bonds.

[22] The CPI used is the "Weighted Average of Eight Capital Cities: All Groups Index". The last review of its construction was completed by the Australian Bureau of Statistics in September 1998.

Table 6.3 Australian Commonwealth Government Treasury Indexed Bonds (TIBs)

Type of bond	Coupon (%)	Maturity date	Date of first issue	Nominal amount outstanding (Aus$ million)
CIB	4.00	20 Aug 2005	30 Jul 1985	531.79
IIB	4.25–5.80	20 Aug 2005	30 Jul 1985	0.05
CIB	4.00	20 Aug 2010	9 Feb 1993	1,452.00
CIB	4.00	20 Aug 2015	17 May 1994	2,095.80
CIB	4.00	20 Aug 2020	14 Oct 1996	2,472.20

Data source: Australian Office of Financial Management (figures as at 31 March 2003). CIB = Capital Indexed Bond; IIB = Interest Indexed Bond.

in the calculation of the cash flow. The formulae for CIB cash flows are detailed in Appendix 6.1. The full nominal interest payments (i.e., both the real coupon and corresponding inflation uplift) are subject to income tax under Australian tax rules. Tax on the capital uplift on the principal is calculated and paid annually on the year on year increase in the uplifted redemption value.

6.2 CANADA

The Canadian authorities contemplated issuing indexed bonds during the early 1980s when, on the eve of the 1984 election, Prime Minister John Turner announced his intention to issue them. In the event he failed to get re-elected, and as a consequence the Canadian government did not begin issuing Real Return Bonds (RRBs) until December 1991.[23] RRBs were introduced as a means of minimising the risk associated with inflation – both for the government, by stabilising the real cost of borrowing, and for investors, by fixing the real rate of return. Indexed bonds were also seen as both an additional source of funding as well as one that could produce cost savings for the government.[24] Mitchell (1996) reports a further motive: to introduce a means to measure market expectations of the future path of inflation.

While RRBs were initially distributed by fixed price subscription through a syndicate of lead managers, more recent issues have been by single yield auction to primary dealers.[25] The authorities opted for this format to help reduce the risk to investors of submitting a mispriced bid and thereby encourage wider participation in the market-making process.[26] The Canadian authorities have to date issued four RRBs, all of which were originally 30-year bonds at issue. As Table 6.4 and Figure 6.5 illustrate, each bond has been reopened over a period of approximately four years before the

[23] See Spiro (1989).

[24] Branion (1995) reports that RRBs have indeed produced cost savings, since realised inflation has on average been lower than that priced into comparable conventional bonds.

[25] For the terms and conditions of RRB auctions see Department of Finance, Canada (1998).

[26] Branion (1995) reports that limited secondary market trading makes it harder for potential investors to price RRBs than conventional bonds.

Table 6.4 Issuance of Canadian Real Return Bonds (RRBs)

Issue date	Bond issued	Nominal amount issued (Can$mn)	Method of issue	Real yield (%)
10 Dec 1991	4.25% 2021	700	Syndicate	4.250
14 Oct 1992		500	Syndicate	4.750
3 May 1993		325	Syndicate	4.550
1 Dec 1993		600	Syndicate	4.099
22 Feb 1994		600	Syndicate	3.423
21 Jun 1994		400	Syndicate	4.499
15 Sep 1994		500	Syndicate	4.691
15 Dec 1994		500	Syndicate	4.770
2 Feb 1995		350	Syndicate	5.054
8 May 1995		300	Auction	4.578
4 Aug 1995		400	Syndicate	4.848
7 Dec 1995	4.25% 2026	300	Auction	4.595
6 Mar 1996		350	Auction	4.880
6 Jun 1996		400	Auction	4.760
9 Sep 1996		400	Auction	4.785
6 Dec 1996		400	Auction	3.980
12 Mar 1997		500	Auction	4.110
9 Jun 1997		500	Auction	4.500
8 Sep 1997		400	Auction	4.230
8 Dec 1997		400	Auction	4.032
9 Mar 1998		400	Auction	4.200
8 Jun 1998		400	Auction	3.910
8 Sep 1998		400	Auction	4.180
7 Dec 1998		400	Auction	4.190
8 Mar 1999	4.00% 2031	400	Auction	4.310
8 Jun 1999		300	Auction	4.080
7 Sep 1999		300	Auction	4.030
6 Dec 1999		300	Auction	4.020
6 Mar 2000		350	Auction	3.980
5 Jun 2000		350	Auction	3.790
5 Sep 2000		350	Auction	3.660
11 Dec 2000		350	Auction	3.450
5 Mar 2001		350	Auction	3.405
11 Jun 2001		350	Auction	3.590
24 Sep 2001		300	Auction	3.730
10 Dec 2001		350	Auction	3.748
18 Mar 2002		350	Auction	3.750
10 Jun 2002		400	Auction	3.510
16 Sep 2002		300	Auction	3.317
9 Dec 2002		400	Auction	3.410
17 Mar 2003		300	Auction	2.769
9 Jun 2003	3.00% 2036	400	Auction	2.915

Data source: Bank of Canada (figures as at 9 June 2003).

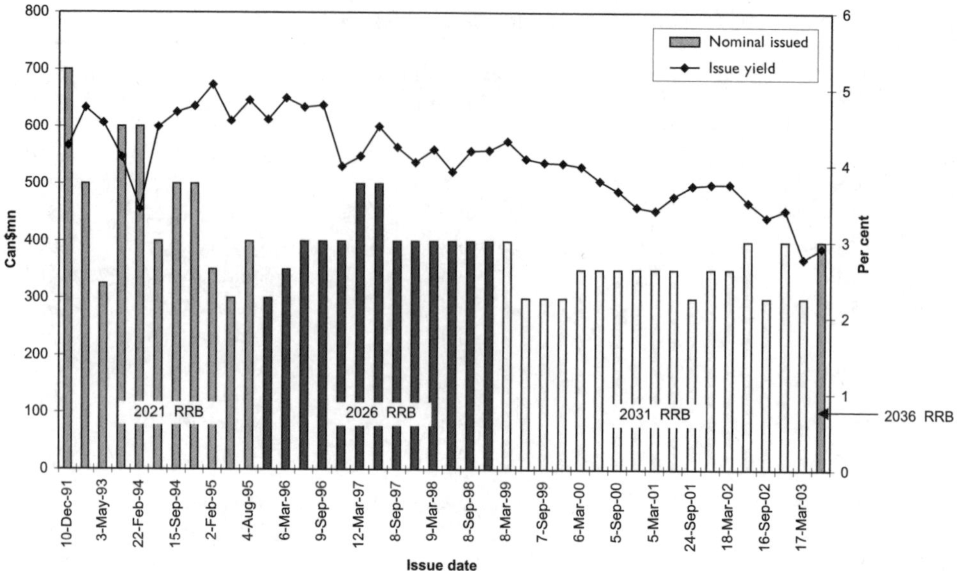

Figure 6.5 Canadian Real Return Bond (RRB) issuance (December 1991–June 2003), nominal amount and real yield at issue
Data source: Bank of Canada

launch of a new issue. Figure 6.6 shows how the 30-year benchmark real yield has varied since the introduction of the RRB programme in 1991.

RRBs are CIBs that pay semi-annual coupons. The innovative manner in which accrued interest is defined for RRBs enabled the Canadians to employ a shorter (three-month) lag than that used in comparable markets at the time, such as those in Australia and the UK. This indexation methodology has since been adopted by several other debt managers, most notably those of France, Italy, Sweden and the USA. In contrast to the situation in the Australian and UK markets, where accrued interest for each business day is computed pro rata based on the nominal size of the next coupon payment (which must therefore always be known), interest accrual on Canadian RRBs is based on cumulative movements in the CPI since the last coupon date. This cumulative measure is referred to as the *index ratio* and is also used to compute the inflation adjustments to both the RRB coupons and the principal.

The index ratio for a given settlement date is defined to be the ratio of the appropriate *reference CPI* divided by the bond's reference CPI at issue. The reference CPI for the first day of any calendar month is defined to be the published index level for the month three months prior, so the reference CPI for 1 June corresponds to the published index level for March, the reference CPI for 1 July corresponds to that published for April, etc. The reference CPI for any other date is calculated by linear interpolation between the index levels for the first days of the months each side of the date in question.[27]

[27] A more detailed description can be found in Appendix 6.2.

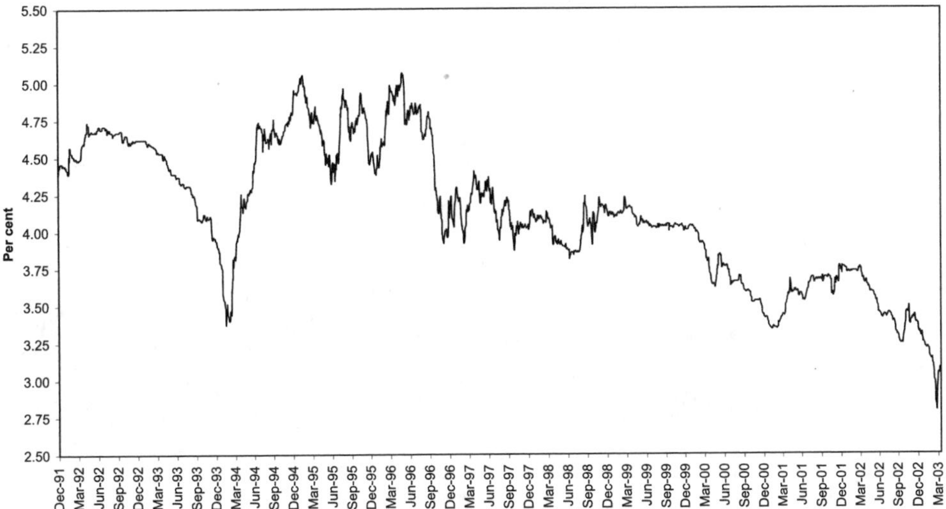

Figure 6.6 Real yield of the benchmark 30-year Canadian Real Return Bond (RRB)
Data source: Bank of Canada

Table 6.5 Canadian Real Return Bonds (RRBs)

Coupon (%)	Maturity date	Date of first issue	Nominal amount outstanding (Can$mn)
4.25	1 Dec 2021	10 Dec 1991	5,175
4.25	1 Dec 2026	7 Dec 1995	5,250
4.00	1 Dec 2031	8 Mar 1999	5,800
3.00	1 Dec 2036	9 Jun 2003	400

Data source: Bank of Canada (figures as at 9 June 2003).

Details of the four current RRBs are summarised in Table 6.5. Although each is eligible to be stripped into separate indexed cash flows, as at 30 April 2003 just 2.9% of the 2021 RRB was held in stripped form. The Canadian Depository for Securities (CDS) has intimated that, given sufficient demand, it would put in place the administrative procedures to funge coupon strips from different RRBs based on the method employed by the US Treasury – more details of which appear in Grieves and Sunner (1999).

For RRBs the full nominal interest payments (including the inflation uplift) are taxable. Also, for each given tax year, a bondholder must declare as income the amount by which the compensation for inflation on the principal has increased, even though this accrual is not paid out until the bond matures.[28] Possibly as a result of this feature of the Canadian tax system, RRBs are predominantly held by tax-exempt institutions such as pension funds and life insurance companies. During the

[28] For more details on the tax treatment of RRBs visit the Canadian Department of Finance website: www.fin.gc.ca/invest/taxtreat-e.html

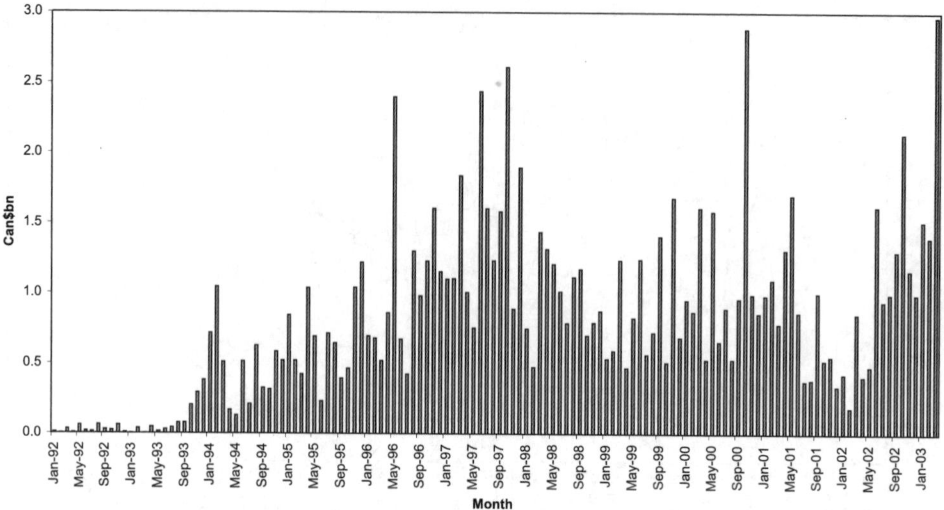

Figure 6.7 Monthly turnover of Canadian Real Return Bonds (RRBs) (January 1992–March 2003)

Data source: Bank of Canada

mid-1990s, for instance, 60% of the outstanding amount of RRBs was held by just 10 pension funds.[29] Individual RRB investors typically hold them in the form of Registered Retirement Savings Plans (RRSPs) in order to defer the tax.

Not surprisingly, the buy-and-hold nature of RRB investors has meant that secondary market trading of the bonds has been limited. Figure 6.7 shows the monthly turnover of RRBs since the inception of the market. Even at its peak in March 2003 turnover represented only 18% of the amount of outstanding RRB debt – a fraction of the comparable figure for conventional bonds. The lower trading volume is also evident in the bid–offer price spread in the secondary market – typically 25 cents per Can$100 for an RRB, compared with about 10 cents for a conventional 30-year bond. The OECD (2002) notes that market makers have in the past tended to avoid RRBs due to the lack of an effective hedge, although the situation has improved since the formation of the US indexed bond market in 1997.

Since 1991 the size of the RRB market has steadily risen, and by the end of March 2003 it stood at Can$18.8bn including the inflation uplift (or Can$16.2bn excluding it), constituting about 4.5% of the Canadian marketable government debt portfolio – see Figure 6.8. However, despite auctioning RRBs on a regular quarterly basis for some years now, the authorities have found it difficult to increase the size of auctions beyond Can$400mn nominal. Mitchell (1996) attributes this to the poor performance of RRBs relative to conventional Canadian government bonds, coupled with the fact that investors have failed to appreciate the different nature of the two asset classes. In an attempt to address the second of these points the Canadian authorities launched an education programme targeted at pension plan sponsors in 1996.

[29] Source: OECD (2002, p. 64).

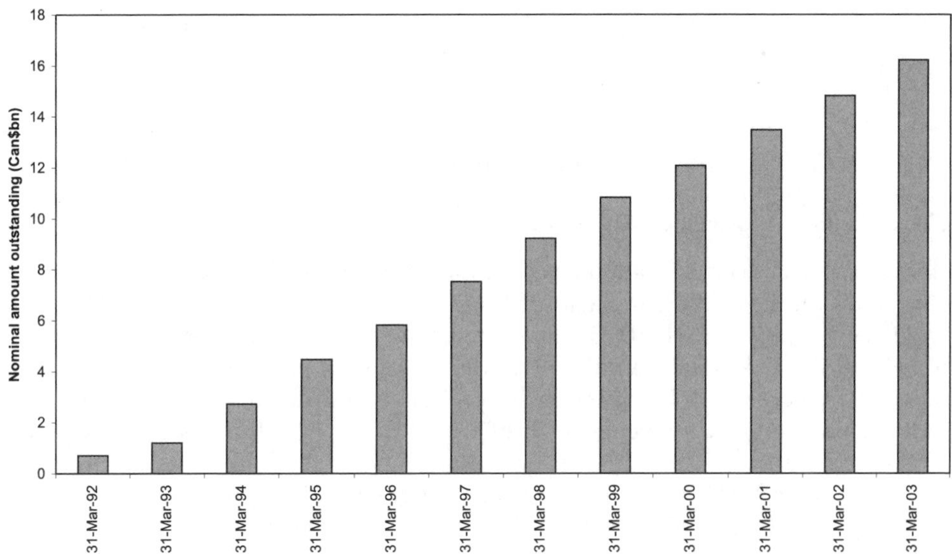

Figure 6.8 Market capitalisation of the Canadian Real Return Bond (RRB) market
Data source: Bank of Canada

Following the launch of the first inflation-indexed note by the US Treasury in 1997, the Canadian government considered the introduction of shorter maturity securities (a 10-year issue being perhaps the most likely) in order to capitalise on the additional interest in the RRB market generated as a result of the US programme.[30] However, no doubt influenced by the preference of the existing investor base for long-maturity assets, the decision was made to continue with the issuance of 30-year bonds.

The Department of Finance's published debt strategy for 2003/04[31] outlines plans to reduce the share of its debt in the form of fixed rate bonds from 66% to 60% over the next five years, in order to achieve debt cost savings. To maintain a well-functioning government debt market these changes will be implemented gradually through increases in the Treasury bill programme coupled with reductions in the bond programme (including the use of buy-backs). For the 2003/04 fiscal year as a whole, the Canadian government plans gross bond issuance totalling approximately Can$40bn, of which about Can$1.5bn will be in RRBs. However, consistent with its desire to reduce the proportion of fixed rate debt, the Department of Finance has announced its intention to review the entire RRB programme following consultations with market participants. It is interesting to note that for the first RRB auction of 2003/04 (held in June 2003) the authorities decided to launch a 3% coupon 2036 RRB, the first new RRB for over four years.

Despite the fact that the central government has now been issuing indexed bonds for over 10 years, few other Canadian issuers have followed its lead. The notable exception

[30] This interest stemmed in part from the fact that the design of US Treasury inflation-indexed securities is based on that of Canada's RRBs.

[31] See Department of Finance, Canada (2003).

is Quebec Province, which has issued three CPI indexed bonds with maturities of between 20 and 30 years.

6.3 FRANCE

6.3.1 The history of indexation in France

Historically, the use of indexation has been widespread in France with various different types of linkage having been implemented. The first indexed bond arrived in 1925 with a state issue tied to the exchange rate, and a second with the same design followed in 1937. However, it was not until the 1950s that indexation in France became commonplace. After the Second World War the French capital market was moribund, due predominantly to a fundamental lack of confidence in the franc coupled with the unhealthy condition of the public finances. Only issues that offered especially advantageous terms were likely to succeed in such an environment, and so the authorities were led to experiment with indexed bonds in order to raise revenue.

In 1952 the government issued the *Rentes Pinay* bond, which had a redemption value linked to the Paris market price of the 20-franc Napoleon gold coin. The bond paid a tax-free 4.5% coupon and was originally scheduled to mature in 2012, though it was also redeemable at annual drawings through a sinking fund. In 1956 the government issued a new style of bond which offered a fixed redemption value but with interest calculated at 5% per annum plus 0.05% for every point by which industrial production exceeded the 1955 level. Another government issue that year paid a fixed interest rate but had a redemption value linked to the annual change in the average value of the price indices of fixed and variable interest French securities. A state issue in 1957 had yet another form of indexation, with both interest payments and the redemption value linked to changes in the equity price index. Throughout the 1950s a number of public corporations and nationalised industries followed the government's lead and issued index-linked bonds, which tended to be linked to their product prices and so generated a diverse range of index-linked securities. Table 6.6 provides a few examples.

Following the devaluation of the franc in 1958 the government initiated an economic stabilisation programme, which explicitly banned most forms of indexation for fear that the combination of rising import prices resulting from the devaluation coupled with the widespread use of indexation would lead to spiralling inflation. Although it was still lawful to issue bonds indexed to the product price, output or profits of the borrower, in practice the authorities effectively prevented all new indexed issues bar one and even froze the premium payable under indexation clauses on existing private issues at the level payable on 31 December 1958.

During the 1960s, as a result of the political stability created by de Gaulle, the government's finances improved significantly, and in 1968 the general ban on indexation in France was lifted.[32] Issuance of public sector indexed bonds did not resume until 1973, however, when the government brought a 4.5% conversion option from the 1952 and 1958 *Rentes Pinay* bonds[33] as a means of reducing their servicing costs, which had

[32] Although the ban stayed in force for bonds linked to inflation.
[33] Like the 1952 loan, the 1958 state loan was also known as *Rentes Pinay* since it too was linked to the price of the 20-franc Napoleon gold coin.

Table 6.6 Some examples of early French indexed bond issues

Issue Date	Issuer	Indexation
1952	Electricité de France	Interest and redemption value linked to the average price to the consumer of 100 kilowatt hours of electricity
1953	Société Nationale de Chemins de Fer	Interest and redemption value linked to the cost of second class rail travel ("free" tickets could be taken in lieu of interest)
1953	Gaz de France	Interest and redemption value linked to the average price of 25 cubic metres of gas
1955	Regié Renault	Interest and redemption value linked to the increase in company sales
1957	Electricité de France	Redemption value included a premium related to the growth in electricity production
1958	Charbonnages de France	Interest and redemption value linked to the price of coal

Data source: Bank of England.

become considerable. Also in 1973 the government introduced a new form of indexed bond: referred to as the *Rentes Giscard*; this 15-year Fr 6.5 billion bond paid an annual coupon of "not less than 7%". Capital and interest were guaranteed to maintain a minimum fixed relationship between the gold content of the franc at the time of issue and that of the EEC Unit of Account used for the Common Agricultural Policy. On 31 December each year the relative values were reviewed and, if there had been any change to the detriment of the franc, the interest and capital of the bond were adjusted accordingly.[34]

Unfortunately, from the point of view of the French government, the demise of the Unit of Account in March 1979 triggered a clause in the *Giscard* bond's prospectus which stipulated that forthwith the bond's cash flows would be linked to the market price of gold. As a result its price rose rapidly, and by January 1980 the bond was trading at seven times face value.[35]

6.3.2 The introduction of inflation-indexed OATs (Obligations assimilables du Trésor)

In the period between 1977 and the mid-1990s there were no further public issues of index-linked bonds in France. However, as part of its financing programme for 1997 the Trésor indicated that it was considering a resumption of index-linked issuance in order to reduce borrowing costs.[36] On 3 December 1997, Dominique Strauss-Kahn, the Minister of the Economy, Finance and Industry, confirmed the government's intention

[34] A similar bond – the *Rentes Barre* – was issued in 1977.
[35] For more information on gold indexed bonds see Kettell (1982, p. 201).
[36] See Ministère de l'Économie et des Finances (1996).

to become the first major sovereign issuer in continental Europe to issue inflation-indexed bonds. The following extract from Strauss-Kahn's speech elaborates on the authorities reasoning:[37]

> *I am convinced that linking a small proportion of government debt to inflation will be in the interest of both the government and the investors. As an issuer, the government's interest lies in direct benefits that will accrue to it from the sale of a risk premium and indirect benefits that this product will produce by making the whole of its debt more attractive and thereby reducing its debt burden. The investors' interest lies in the added diversification and protection against economic risks provided by the new product.*

As well as the stated objective of cutting borrowing costs, an additional motivation for this innovative step was undoubtedly to enhance France's claim to have the dominant bond market in Europe following the introduction of the single currency in 1999. However, before any indexed bonds could be launched it was necessary to pass legislation to establish a legal framework for their issuance. Strauss-Kahn also had to contend with criticism from Jean-Claude Trichet, the Governor of the Banque de France, who was vocal in his opposition to the proposal,[38] and in the event legislation was not enacted until July 1998.

While the necessary legal steps were being taken the Trésor consulted the market on issues regarding instrument design, and one of the toughest choices was which index to use. Although there were a number of other possible contenders, the real decision came down to a choice between a French CPI index and one to reflect inflation across the Euro-zone. While indexation to a domestic measure of inflation would certainly provide a better liability match for the government, it could potentially have limited the bonds' appeal outside France. Governor Trichet advocated indexation to Euro-zone inflation to reflect the fact that changes in consumer prices in France would be closely related to those in other countries preparing to adopt the single currency. However, as noted by Barclays Capital (2002b), the final decision almost certainly came down to practicalities, since at the time there were several material disadvantages to Eurostat's European Harmonised Index of Consumer Prices (Euro-HICP) for the EMU area: in particular it was a relatively new and untested index with no track record, its coverage was incomplete and there was a fear of revision risk. Faced with such difficulties, a consensus formed in favour of using a measure of domestic inflation, although some commentators suggested that the Trésor might keep its options open by inserting a prospectus clause to permit a switch to Euro-HICP at a later date.[39] Similar problems are likely to have discouraged the use of French HICP, the CPI calculated under European harmonised standards by Eurostat.

In the event, the authorities opted to link the bonds to INSEE's measure of French national CPI, excluding tobacco.[40] It was hoped that French inflation might be regarded as a good proxy for European inflation over the full term of the bonds and thereby encourage demand from other Euro-zone countries. The index excluding tobacco, rather than INSEE's standard CPI index, was chosen because under French law[41] all government contractual arrangements with a link to inflation (including the

[37] See Strauss-Kahn (1997).
[38] See Graham and Luce (1997).
[39] See Majoul and Nehls (1998).
[40] INSEE is the French National Institute of Statistics and Economic Studies.
[41] Act No. 92-60, dated 18 January 1992.

statutory minimum wage) must not be indexed to a measure that includes the price of tobacco – further legislation would have been required for the standard CPI to have been used. Another important feature of the chosen index was that future changes to its composition and calculation methodology were expected to be modest. Concerns over such changes to the calculation and composition of indices had become an important issue around the globe following the publication of the Boskin report in 1997, which had suggested that US CPI might overstate true inflation by as much as 1.1%. However, in the case of the French CPI, official estimates suggested that the "Boskin effect" was much smaller, at between 0.10% and 0.25%.[42]

The Trésor decided to base the design of its inflation-indexed bonds on that of Canada's RRBs, though with annual rather than semi-annual interest payments. Like their Canadian counterparts, the French securities are CIBs bonds with a three month indexation lag. Following the US Treasury's lead, the Trésor opted to include a guarantee that the redemption payment on its bonds would not be less than the original par value (i.e., a guarantee that protects the nominal value of the principal should deflation occur over the bond's lifetime).[43] However, as there are slight differences between the definition of the index ratio for French indexed bonds and that used in the US market, investors would not necessarily assign exactly the same financial value to the deflation floors on securities in the two markets, all other things being equal.[44] Additionally, the Trésor announced that its indexed bonds would be eligible to be stripped, once issuance had reached a critical mass.

The first French government indexed bond – 3% OAT*i* 2009 – was launched on 15 September 1998 and was sold through a syndication process led by Banque Nationale de Paris, Barclays Capital and Société Générale.[45] Ahead of the launch the Trésor announced that it would sell a minimum of Fr 20 billion nominal of the bond, although in the event demand was so strong that Fr 24bn was issued.[46] The issue came to market at a slight premium (a price of 100.18) and shortly afterwards rose to 100.75 in the secondary market. By the end of the month its price had fallen back to 100.22.[47]

As Figure 6.9 shows, 79% of this issue was sold within France, primarily to insurance companies and retirement funds. The remaining 21% was purchased by non-domestic investors, of which more than half came from continental Europe and the rest from the UK or the USA. Domestic demand for the bonds is likely to have been boosted by the government's announcement two months earlier that the benchmark savings rate, the *Livret A*, would henceforth be linked to consumer prices. This change in regulation meant that inflation-indexed bonds would provide a natural liability match for those institutions offering such savings plans. De Beaupuy (1998) reports that domestic investors had approximately $116bn invested in *Livret A* savings schemes at that time.

The tax treatment of inflation-indexed OATs is similar to that of their conventional counterparts. Domestic retail investors are taxed on the uplifted annual interest payments as well as on any capital gain realised either at redemption or when the bond is

---

[42] Source: Trésor (1998, p. 10).

[43] Note that the same protection does not apply to the coupon payments. For full details of the terms and conditions of the French securities readers should refer to Trésor (1998).

[44] Appendix 6.3 details how the index ratio is constructed for French bonds and highlights this difference.

[45] In addition to these three lead managers, the syndicate also comprised the 17 other French primary dealers.

[46] Equivalent to approximately €3.7bn on redenomination on 1 January 1999.

[47] See Barclays Capital (1998d).

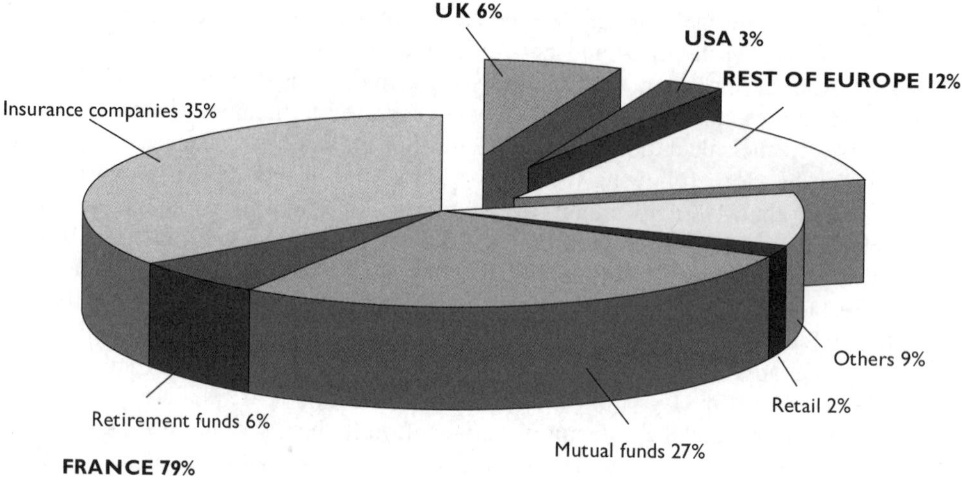

Figure 6.9 Placement of the first tranche of 3% OAT*i* 2009 at issue on 15 September 1998
Data source: Trésor

sold. Like retail investors, French-resident institutional investors are taxed on interest received. However, unlike retail investors, they may be required to pay some tax on their capital gains before the bond redeems or is sold.[48]

The second OAT*i* sale occurred on 5 November 1998, when a further Fr 4.47bn nominal of 3% OAT*i* 2009 was sold.[49] This and all subsequent reopenings of the bond have been by multiple price auction. The bid-to-cover ratio at the auction was 2.80 and the average yield was 3.126%,[50] a rate that reflected the cheapening of the bond during October – see Figure 6.10. Two weeks after the auction Benoit Jolivet, the President of the French social security debt repayment fund CADES,[51] announced its intention to issue indexed bonds, though most likely not until after the introduction of the euro. Further commitment to the sector came on 23 November when Anne Le Lorier, Head of Monetary and Financial Affairs at the Trésor, announced plans to create an index-linked yield curve through the issuance of OAT*i*s at several maturities, and that securities both shorter and longer than the 2009 bond would be considered.[52]

On 1 January 1999, 3% OAT*i* 2009 was redenominated in euros along with all fixed-rate OAT securities and thereby was established as the first euro-denominated inflation-linked government bond. For 1999 – the first full year of OAT*i* issuance – the Trésor announced that it expected to sell approximately €6 billion in OAT*i* bonds as part of an issuance programme totalling €80bn. The first inflation-indexed auction of the year occurred on 4 February when a further €675mn nominal of the 2009 issue was

[48] More details on the tax treatment of inflation-indexed OATs are available on Agence France Trésor's (AFT) website: www.aft.gouv.fr
[49] Equivalent to approximately €681 million on redenomination on 1 January 1999. Ahead of the auction the Trésor had announced its intention to sell between Fr 3bn and Fr 5bn of the bond.
[50] The formula used by the French authorities to derive yield from price appears in Appendix 6.3.
[51] *Caisse d'Amortissement de la Dette Sociale (CADES)* was established in January 1996 to refinance deficits accumulated by the French social security system between 1994 and 1998.
[52] See *Reuters News* (1998).

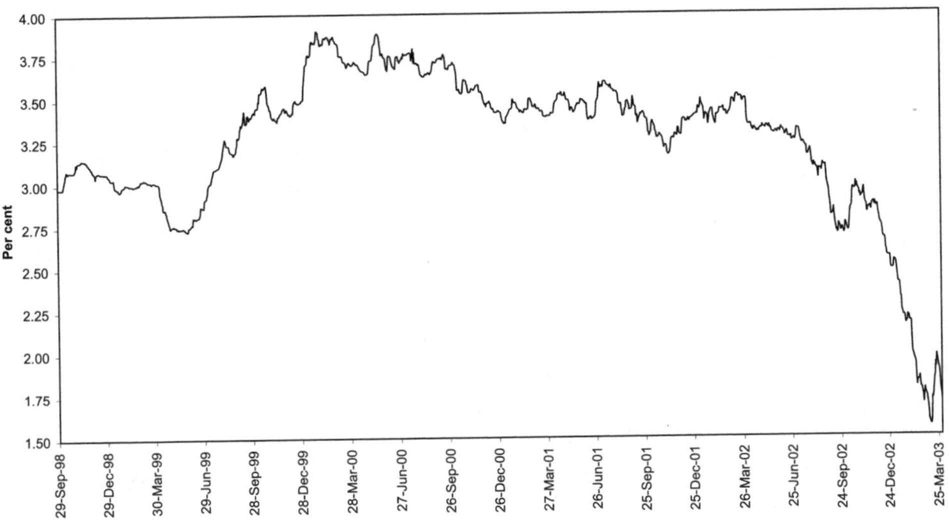

Figure 6.10 Real yield of 3% OAT*i* 2009
Data source: Bloomberg

sold. Strong demand for the bond was reflected in a bid-to-cover ratio of 2.85 and an average yield of 3.01%.

Another important change that took place in early 1999 was the introduction by INSEE of a new methodology for computing the CPI. In addition to rebasing the index, INSEE also undertook a major reshaping of the CPI basket.[53] Improvements aimed at reducing the "Boskin bias" included a better coverage of sales and rebates, the extensive use of geometric means and better monitoring of price/quality effects for new products. INSEE estimated that these changes would shave 0.1% off CPI inflation per year and improve the index's correlation with Eurostat's harmonised French CPI.[54]

Since January 1999 it has been possible for retail investors to purchase holdings of 3% OAT*i* 2009 through the Trésor's OAT private individual placement programme. This programme was launched in September 1994 as a means of boosting long-term savings. Under the scheme the Trésor reserves a part of its OAT issuance each year for sale to retail investors. This amount is underwritten by selected primary dealers (SVTs) and leading commercial banks, each of which signs rolling one-year distribution agreements with the government. The annual amount underwritten by each institution is offered for sale throughout the year. Although about €195mn nominal of 3% OAT*i* 2009 was issued through the programme in 1999, in each successive year there has been a decline in the volume sold and just €1.9mn nominal was sold during 2002.[55]

Interest in the sector was further boosted in March 1999 when CADES launched its first inflation-indexed bond – 3.15% CADES*i* 2013.[56] CDC Marchés, Crédit Agricole Indosuez and Société Générale were lead managers, BNP and Barclays Capital were

[53] INSEE changes the base year of its CPI every 5 to 10-years in order to keep the index relatively uniform over time.
[54] Further details of the changes in the index and its impact on the indexation calculations for the 2009 OAT*i* bond can be found in France Trésor (1999), as well as in Appendix 6.3.
[55] 3% OAT*i* 2009 remains the only inflation-indexed OAT eligible to be sold through this programme.
[56] For more details see CADES (1999).

co-lead managers and the bond was priced at a yield of 14 basis points over the 2009 OAT*i*. As strong demand for this AAA-rated bond became evident through the syndication process the issue size was raised from the €1bn initially planned to €1.5bn. The index and bond structure adopted were identical to that of the OAT*i* and, similarly, the CADES bond also pays its redemption payment and annual dividends on 25 July. The maturity of this (and indeed subsequent) issues has demonstrated CADES's policy to complement the issuance strategy of the Trésor, and the secondary markets for bonds of both issuers are supported by the same group of primary dealers.

Following further successful auctions of 3% OAT*i* 2009 in April and May 1999, Jean Lemierre, head of the Trésor, told reporters that the government planned to increase the size of its inflation-linked bond programme due to the strength of investor demand.[57] Monsieur Lemierre also indicated that the launch of a second OAT*i* was under consideration, although no details were given at the time. In July a new unit – *France Trésor* – was established within the Trésor to handle both debt and cash management. Finance Minister Strauss-Kahn announced that the two immediate priorities for this new group would be to launch the new OAT*i* that autumn and to consider a scheme under which retail investors could purchase OATs over the Internet.

The new bond – 3.40% OAT*i* 2029 – was launched on 21 September 1999 and was sold by syndication following a two-week pre-marketing period. It shared the same instrument design and coupon date as the 2009 OAT*i* and was also indexed to French CPI excluding tobacco. Although the minimum size for the launch was fixed at €2.5bn, in the event demand was such that France Trésor was able to sell €2.8bn of the bond. It is interesting to compare the investor breakdown between this syndication and that of the earlier issue. While foreign investors had accounted for 21% of purchases at the launch of 3% OAT*i* 2009, in the case of the new 2029 bond this proportion almost doubled to 41%. Unlike the first bond this new security was issued into a bear market, and following the launch its yield rose steadily from 3.41% to a peak of 3.60% on 25 October before falling off slightly. However, the fall in price could not be attributed solely to the general market environment since it also represented an underperformance relative to the OAT*i* 2009.[58]

In January 2000 France Trésor announced that OAT*i* issuance would constitute approximately 5% of its planned issuance programme for the forthcoming year,[59] which represented approximately €4.5bn. January also saw CADES reaffirm its commitment to the asset class with the €500mn launch of a new 3.80% CADES*i* 2006 bond, issued at level yield to the 2009 OAT*i*. The issue was well timed, since a sharp pick-up in economic growth had generated a degree of unease over the potential for rising inflationary pressures. The carry and the break-even inflation rate on the issue looked attractive, which partially explains why more than half of it was bought by international investors. A large proportion of the issue was sold to European investors outside France, suggesting perhaps that they had begun to regard the French CPI as an adequate proxy for pan-European inflation. Given the strong demand for the bond, CADES quickly followed it up with a further €150 million tranche.

[57] See *Reuters News* (1999).
[58] See Barclays Capital (1999).
[59] See France Trésor (2000a).

During the course of 2000, France Trésor auctioned further tranches of both OAT*i*s, on several occasions selling both bonds on the same day. At a symposium in July, Laurent Fabius, Minister of the Economy, Finance and Industry, announced his intention to transform France Trésor into a Debt Agency accountable directly to the Treasury Director, with the additional resources necessary to engage in more active debt management.[60] In addition, he announced that France Trésor had been tasked with rapid implementation of an interest rate swaps portfolio and a reduction of the debt outstanding before the end of the year, the latter being made possible by the good fiscal outturns in 1999 and 2000. However, index-linked government bonds, such as the OAT*i* and TEC[61] securities, were excluded from the buy-back programme.[62]

6.3.3 Indexation to pan-European inflation – OAT€*i* bonds

The indicative financing programme for 2001 confirmed that France Trésor would continue to issue OAT*i*s on a regular basis,[63] and that it would examine the feasibility of different bond designs.[64] Notably absent from the published plans was any indication as to the volume of OAT*i* issuance envisaged for 2001. Speculation over the details of a new OAT*i* persisted until July, when Finance Minister Fabius announced the government's desire to launch a new set of securities indexed to pan-European inflation, partly as a means of widening its investor base. A week later, the AFT issued a working mandate to Barclays Capital, Deutsche Bank and SG Investment Banking to devise a strategy for developing the inflation-indexed bond market. In particular, the banks were asked to determine whether an opportunity existed to launch a new OAT with cash flows linked to the Euro-zone MUICP price index[65] and, if so, "how to harmoniously co-ordinate these new bonds with the existing OAT*i* linked to the French inflation index."

Indexation to Euro-zone inflation had been ruled out when the first OAT*i* was sold in September 1998 (see above), but the AFT now argued that, two years on, a lot of the original objections were no longer valid.[66] One of the main arguments against using the Euro-HICP index had been that it is subject to revision. However, the US Treasury faces a similar problem with the index used to determine cash flows on Treasury Inflation-Protection Securities (TIPS) and had introduced a solution during the course of 2000. Under the US system – which the AFT decided to adopt in its entirety for its Euro-HICP indexed bonds – cash flows are indexed with reference to the *first* published value of the index for a given month, regardless of whether or not it is subsequently revised. A second objection, that the coverage of the Euro-zone index had been incomplete, was also felt to no longer be relevant. Indeed, the European Central Bank had been using just such a measure as the basis of its inflation target since the formation of the single European currency in 1999.

[60] This agency – the Agence France Trésor (AFT) – was established on 8 February 2001.
[61] The Taux de l'Échéance Constante à 10 ans or TEC 10 is a floating OAT indexed to long benchmark nominal rates.
[62] See France Trésor (2000b).
[63] Also, in an attempt to more closely match supply with demand, France Trésor announced that it would modify its OAT*i* auction policy to enable it to sell OAT*i* bonds on the afternoon of an OAT or BTAN auction. Until this point OAT*i* auctions had only been held on the afternoon of OAT auctions.
[64] See France Trésor (2000c).
[65] The Monetary Union Index of Consumer Prices (MUICP) is the official title of Eurostat's Euro-zone HICP index.
[66] See Agence France Trésor (2002a), available on the AFT website: www.aft.gouv.fr

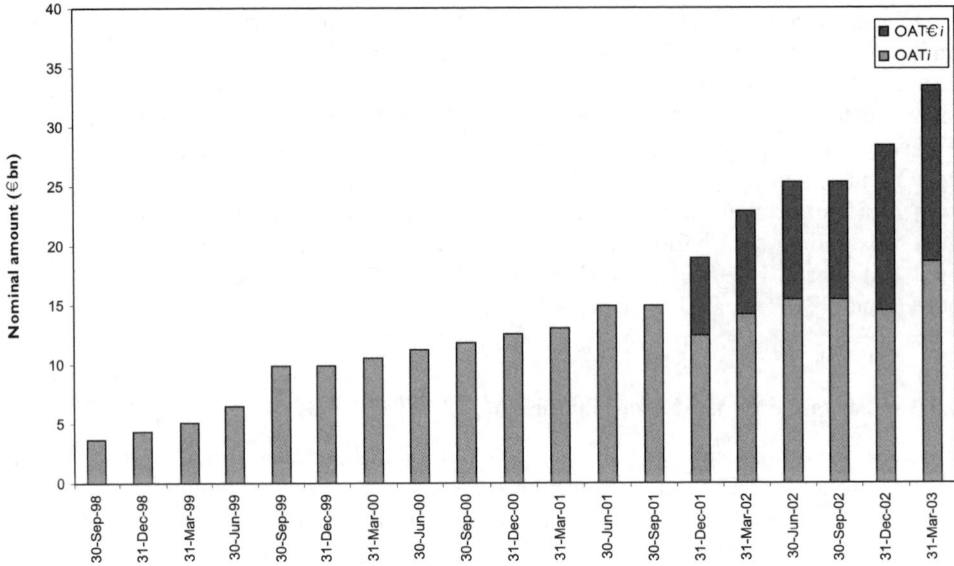

Figure 6.11 Growth of the market for French inflation-indexed OATs
Data source: Agence France Trésor.

Once the investment banks had reported their recommendations, Finance Minister Fabius announced his intention to proceed with the launch of a new OAT indexed to Euro-zone HICP excluding tobacco. The exact details of the new bond were given to investors at the start of a promotional phase ahead of the 25 October launch and, aside from the choice of index used to construct cash flows, the bond's design is identical to that of the earlier OAT*i* securities: with a three-month indexation lag, a deflation floor and annual coupons payable on 25 July. The AFT issued €6.5bn nominal of the new 3% OAT€*i* 2012 bond, which comprised €4bn in direct subscriptions sold at a real yield of 2.98% as well as €2.5bn created as a result of investors exchanging holdings of the 3% OAT*i* 2009 bond at a spread of 30 basis points. Of the direct subscriptions, French investors purchased €1.1bn (27%) of the issue, those from other Euro-zone countries a further €1.5bn (38%) and the residual €1.4bn (35%) was sold to purchasers from outside the Euro-zone. This launch was an important development for the Euro-zone bond market and was well publicised with an advertising campaign in the specialist press as well as through a series of roadshows.

The importance of indexed securities in the French government's debt portfolio continued to grow, and in its financing programme for 2002 the AFT announced that inflation-indexed bonds would constitute about 10% of gross issuance (approximately €8.5bn) for the upcoming financial year.[67] Although such a high volume of issuance seemed ambitious, representing as it did an increase of 49% over 2001 funding, in practice the French government was in fact able to sell €10.4bn nominal of inflation-indexed OATs during 2002[68] (see Figure 6.11). The AFT also announced plans to

[67] With the potential for more, should buy-backs or switches be held over the course of the year. See Agence France Trésor (2001).
[68] Or €9.5bn when measured in terms of net issuance.

reopen the OAT€i 2012 by auction at least once a quarter in order to strengthen the bond's position as a European benchmark and that, in consultation with the primary dealers, it would study whether to issue new Euro-HICP indexed bonds. The authorities also made clear that the option to reopen existing OAT*is* was a further possibility.

The first inflation-indexed sale of the year came on 10 January 2002 when the AFT tapped all three of its indexed bonds. Ahead of the auction it had announced its intention to issue a total of between €0.7bn and €1.2bn nominal. Overall demand at the auction was strong, but there was significantly more interest in the OAT€*i* than for the other two bonds with bids for it accounting for €2.4bn nominal of the total €3.8bn. In particular, market analysts attributed the lack of demand for the OAT*i* 2029 to expectations that a new 30-year OAT€*i* would be launched during the course of the year. These expectations were confirmed by the AFT in July, when it announced the issue of a mandate to four investment banks to determine the best time to launch a new long-dated OAT€*i* and how best to minimise its impact on the existing bonds.

The launch of the new 3.15% OAT€*i* 2032 bond took place in October 2002. This followed the same format as that employed for the introduction of the 2012 OAT€*i* the previous October: a syndicated deal with investors able to bid either outright or in exchange for holdings of the 2029 OAT*i*. The AFT issued €4bn nominal of the new OAT at a yield of 3.20% (€3.08bn in direct subscriptions and €0.92bn from exchanges at a spread of 11 basis points below the OAT*i* 2029), with bids totalling €5.97bn. There was a slightly higher proportion of direct subscriptions from French investors than at the launch of the 2012 OAT€*i*, with these accounting for €1.06bn (34%) of the €3.08bn sold directly. Investors from other Euro-zone countries accounted for €0.99bn (32%) with the remaining €1.03bn (34%) sold to purchasers from outside the Euro-zone.

Despite record sales of inflation-indexed OATs during 2002, the AFT was not the only notable issuer in the market. In June 2002, CADES issued its first new indexed bond for two and a half years. In line with its earlier issues, this bond was indexed to French CPI excluding tobacco and paid annual interest on 25 July. The initial issue size of this 3.40% 2011 bond was €600mn, but due to strong demand another €400mn was tapped in July and a further €500mn in November. As a result, by the end of 2002, the total amount of CADES' inflation-indexed debt had reached €6.6bn, equivalent to approximately 23% of its total outstanding debt. The proportion of indexed bond issuance was even more significant for the year 2002, representing €1.5bn of a €4bn issuance programme. CADES reports strong international interest in its indexed bonds – a tap of the 2006 bond in early 2003 saw more than 70% go to international investors, primarily from the UK and Switzerland.

The AFT's successful launch of its 2032 OAT€*i* bond in October 2002 was one of the reasons behind its decision to increase index-linked issuance further in 2003.[69] The AFT indicated its intention to issue both French CPI and Euro-zone HICP-linked bonds during 2003 and that combined these would account for at least 10% of *net* issuance over the year, equivalent to €11bn nominal (potentially more, should buy-backs or switches occur). As part of this programme the AFT made it clear that it would "regularly tap the 2032 OAT€*i* in order to strengthen the European benchmark status of the line." The first issuance of the year came on 9 January when the AFT

[69] For full details see Agence France Trésor (2002b).

re-opened three of the four bonds, including the 2032 OAT€*i*, issuing a total of over €2.2bn nominal. As Table 6.7 shows, despite being by far the largest auction that the AFT had held to date, demand remained strong – particularly for the shorter maturity bonds.

Shortly after this auction the AFT surprised the market with the announcement of a new 2013 OAT indexed to French CPI ex-tobacco to be launched in February. This was the first new OAT*i* to be issued for three and a half years and was also to be the first indexed OAT to be launched by auction rather than syndication. The authorities' commitment to maintain and develop the market for bonds indexed to domestic inflation alongside that for Euro-HICP bonds is graphically illustrated in Figure 6.11.

The new issue was well timed, as it came during a surge in demand for French CPI indexed bonds following a relaxation of accounting regulations for French insurance companies. Under the old rules insurance companies were allowed to report only realised gains in their annual accounts. For holders of inflation-indexed bonds this meant that only the nominal coupons (which are typically lower than for equivalent conventional bonds) could be reported, but not any principal inflation uplift that had accrued during the year. As a result, despite the fact that insurance companies might be considered to be natural investors in indexed bonds, the old regulations had proved to be a significant deterrent.[70]

In launching a new OAT*i* the AFT had provided an important signal to the market of its intention to continue supporting and developing in parallel the markets for both types of bond, OAT€*i* and OAT*i*. While some issuers have resisted pressure to issue more than one type of indexed security for fear that it might fragment liquidity, the AFT has taken a diametrically opposed view. By offering two products the AFT has been able to appeal to a wider investor base as well as providing an opportunity for investors to hedge and arbitrage between the two real yield curves. Although the market is less liquid than its conventional counterpart, as indeed is the case for index-linked bond markets globally, the AFT has indicated that it believes liquidity to be adequate. As Figure 6.12 shows, secondary market turnover has grown considerably over the last four years. The ratio of daily turnover to the size of the market is about 1% and bid–offer spreads are around two basis points across the curve.[71]

By the end of March 2003 the uplifted nominal size of the indexed OAT market had grown to €34.6bn (€33.4bn in nominal terms), of which around €19.6bn was in the form of OAT*i* bonds and €15.1bn in OAT€*i* bonds. Taken together this represented 4.6% of the total outstanding marketable government debt – see Figure 6.13. Table 6.8 provides full details of the five indexed OATs that were in issue at the end of March 2003. Although the AFT has indicated that inflation-indexed OATs of both types will be eligible for stripping should there be sufficient demand, to date this has yet to occur. As the indexed OAT market has grown, so other French institutions have also begun to issue inflation-linked bonds. The most significant of these is CADES, but other notable issuers include Caisse Nationale des Autoroutes (CNA) – a government-owned agency responsible for financing the French road network – and Réseau Ferré de France (RFF) – a public entity responsible for the rail infrastructure. The majority of

[70] For a more detailed discussion of this issue see Barclays Capital (2002a).

[71] Source: OECD (2002). In this survey the AFT reported a bid–offer spread of 2 basis points for both a €5 million trade in the 10-year OAT*i* and a €2.5mn trade in the 30-year OAT*i*.

Table 6.7 Issuance details of French OAT*i* and OAT€*i* bonds

Date of sale	Method of issuance	Bond(s) issued	Nominal amount issued (€ million)[a]	Average real yield (%)	Bid-to-cover ratio
15 Sep 1998	Syndication	3.00% OAT*i* 2009	~3,659	2.98	N/A
5 Nov 1998	Auction	3.00% OAT*i* 2009	~681	3.13	2.80
4 Feb 1999	Auction	3.00% OAT*i* 2009	675	3.01	2.85
1 Apr 1999	Auction	3.00% OAT*i* 2009	740	3.01	3.03
6 May 1999	Auction	3.00% OAT*i* 2009	571	2.75	2.89
1 Jul 1999	Auction	3.00% OAT*i* 2009	576	2.90	2.15
21 Sep 1999	Syndication	3.40% OAT*i* 2029	2,800	3.41	N/A
3 Feb 2000	Auction	3.00% OAT*i* 2009	629	3.85	3.25
6 Apr 2000	Auction	3.40% OAT*i* 2029	266	3.72	2.84
4 May 2000	Auction	3.00% OAT*i* 2009	259	3.72	3.26
		3.40% OAT*i* 2029	162	3.71	3.43
6 Jul 2000	Auction	3.00% OAT*i* 2009	367	3.74	2.63
		3.40% OAT*i* 2029	194	3.74	2.73
5 Oct 2000	Auction	3.00% OAT*i* 2009	546	3.71	3.57
		3.40% OAT*i* 2029	167	3.71	4.42
18 Jan 2001	Auction	3.00% OAT*i* 2009	499	3.42	2.53
5 Apr 2001	Auction	3.00% OAT*i* 2009	479	3.41	3.49
17 May 2001	Auction	3.00% OAT*i* 2009	690	3.40	3.37
21 Jun 2001	Auction	3.00% OAT*i* 2009	414	3.36	4.37
		3.40% OAT*i* 2029	282	3.54	2.97
25 Oct 2001	Syndication	3.00% OAT€*i* 2012	4,000	2.98	N/A
			2,500	2.98	N/A
		3.00% OAT*i* 2009	−2,500	3.28	N/A
10 Jan 2002	Auction	3.00% OAT*i* 2009	318	3.49	2.46
		3.40% OAT*i* 2029	270	3.60	2.95
		3.00% OAT€*i* 2012	787	3.25	3.59
21 Feb 2002	Auction	3.00% OAT*i* 2009	594	3.42	3.36
		3.00% OAT€*i* 2012	735	3.19	2.75
21 Mar 2002	Auction	3.00% OAT*i* 2009	589	3.50	3.40
		3.00% OAT€*i* 2012	662	3.28	2.53
2 May 2002	Auction	3.00% OAT*i* 2009	615	3.31	2.02
		3.00% OAT€*i* 2012	582	3.12	2.12
20 Jun 2002	Auction	3.00% OAT*i* 2009	181	3.23	4.90
		3.40% OAT*i* 2029	433	3.37	2.67
		3.00% OAT€*i* 2012	629	3.06	2.83
24 Oct 2002	Syndication	3.15% OAT€*i* 2032	3,080	3.20	N/A
			920	3.20	N/A
		3.40% OAT*i* 2029	−920	3.31	N/A
9 Jan 2003	Auction	3.00% OAT*i* 2009	1,310	2.43	3.71
		3.00% OAT€*i* 2012	324	2.41	5.46
		3.15% OAT€*i* 2032	587	2.70	2.04
6 Feb 2003	Auction	2.50% OAT*i* 2013	2,794	2.18	1.54

Data source: Agence France Trésor (figures as at 31 March 2003).

[a] Notes: (1) the total amount issued includes non-competitive allocations made both before and after the auction; (2) stock sold through the OAT private individual placement programme does not appear in this table and (3) nominal amounts for the September and November 1998 auctions are approximate as the stock sold at these auctions was originally denominated in French francs rather than euros.

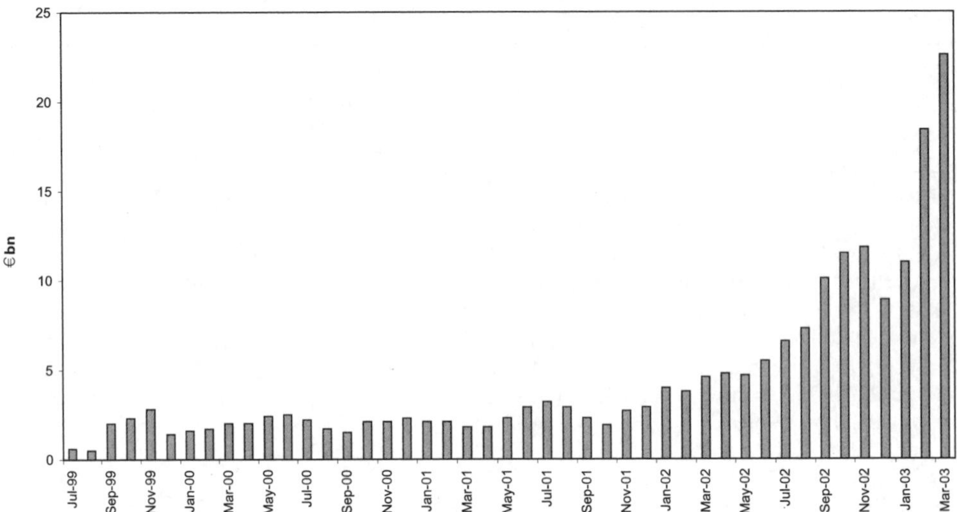

Figure 6.12 Secondary market turnover for OAT*i* and OAT€*i* bonds (three-month moving average)

Data source: Agence France Trésor

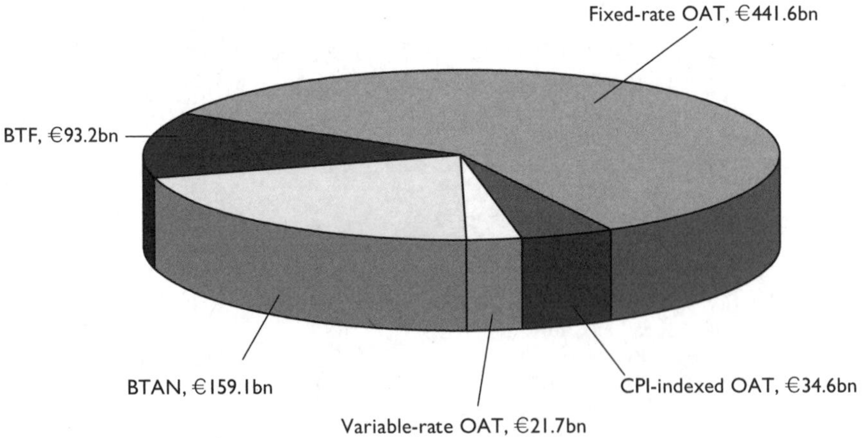

Figure 6.13 Composition of French government debt (as at 31 March 2003). *Note*: amounts for inflation-indexed OATs are quoted in terms of uplifted nominal

Data source: Agence France Trésor (2003)

OATs = Obligations assimilables du Trésor; BTFs = Bons du Trésor à taux fixe et à intérêts précomptés; BTANs = Bons du Trésor à taux fixe et à intérêts annuels; CPI = Consumer Price Index

"non-government" indexed bonds (including the CNA issue) are linked to French CPI ex-tobacco and share the indexed OAT's interest payment date of 25 July. A notable exception is the 2023 RFF bond which was issued in February 2003 and, at €1 billion nominal, was the first major non-AFT issue to be linked to Euro-HICP ex-tobacco.

Table 6.8 French OAT*i* and OAT€*i* Bonds

Bond	Maturity date	Date of first sale	Method of first sale	Nominal amount outstanding (€ mn)	Uplifted nominal amount (€ mn)
3.00% OAT*i* 2009	25 Jul 2009	15 Sep 1998	Syndication	12,157[a]	12,900
3.00% OAT€*i* 2012	25 Jul 2012	25 Oct 2001	Syndication	10,219	10,455
2.50% OAT*i* 2013	25 Jul 2013	6 Feb 2003	Auction	2,794	2,814
3.40% OAT*i* 2029	25 Jul 2029	21 Sep 1999	Syndication	3,654	3,861
3.15% OAT€*i* 2032	25 Jul 2032	24 Oct 2002	Syndication	4,587	4,601

Data source: Agence France Trésor (2003) (figures as at 31 March 2003).
[a] This includes stock sold through the OAT private individual placement programme.

6.4 SWEDEN

6.4.1 The formation of the Swedish government index-linked bond market

Sweden had briefly experienced indexation as early as 1952, with the issuance of a bond partially indexed to consumer prices launched by a public corporation. Lindh and Ohlsson (1992) report that indexation was employed again in the late 1970s, when a number of insurance companies offered loans linked to the CPI. In August 1977 Svenska Handelsbank issued a new type of security, the "indexed share" with a dividend linked to consumer prices. However, in the early 1980s the Swedish authorities imposed a ban on indexation which was not lifted until November 1991.[72] In April 1994, following consultations with both the government and the Riksbank,[73] the Swedish National Debt Office (SNDO) decided to embark on a programme of indexed bond issuance in order to reduce funding costs, to enhance the credibility of monetary policy, to broaden the range of available investment options and to provide a means of estimating market expectations of inflation. The SNDO reports that in practice, by 2002, inflation-indexed issuance had indeed "saved some SEK 8bn in accumulated funding costs since 1994."[74]

Although the SNDO issues conventional bonds by multiple price auctions, it opted to issue its first indexed bond by single price auction (on a yield basis) in order to reduce the risk faced by primary dealers by removing the "winner's curse".[75] The first issue was a 20-year zero-coupon bond indexed to the CPI (0% 2014, loan number 3001). Although the auction was covered, the SNDO judged that a large proportion of the bids were at unacceptably high yields and consequently issued only SEK 1.2bn of the SEK 3.5bn originally on offer. During the remainder of 1994 the SNDO held a further four auctions of the bond, though these proved equally disappointing and a sixth

[72] The government's concern was that widespread indexation might be interpreted as a signal that inflation had become acceptable and that the constituency opposed to inflation might be reduced.
[73] The Riksbank is the Swedish central bank. In order to ensure that debt management does not conflict with monetary policy, the SNDO is required to clear its debt management programme with the Riksbank on an annual basis; see Swedish National Debt Office (2002e).
[74] See Swedish National Debt Office (2002a).
[75] See Chapter 2.

auction was cancelled. Possible explanations for these poor results include the very long duration of the bond (20-years as opposed to 8 for the longest maturity conventional bond at the time), the unfamiliar auction format and a perception that the SNDO might not be fully committed to the development of a deep and liquid inflation-indexed bond market.

Toward the end of 1994 the SNDO announced its intention to issue shorter maturity indexed bonds, and in January 1995 SEK 500mn of a nine-year indexed zero-coupon bond (0% 2004, loan number 3002) was auctioned together with a further SEK 500mn of the existing 2014 bond. The SNDO also changed the method of issue to multiple price auction (again on a yield basis), thereby bringing the issuance technique for indexed bonds into line with that used to sell conventional bonds. Although the long bond reopening was well received by the market and fully allocated, almost half of the shorter bond remained unsold.

Following the auctions in January, the SNDO decided to sell small quantities of the bonds at weekly auctions for the remainder of 1995 (typically SEK 100–300mn of the shorter bond and SEK 400–800mn of the longer bond) in an attempt to encourage the development of the market. The nine-year bond continued to be less popular than the longer bond and was in fact withdrawn from auction on more than one occasion due to lack of demand. While up to this point bonds had been sold only to the institutional market, in June 1995 the SNDO began to sell indexed securities to private investors. Rather than introduce a separate retail product at this early stage in the market's development, the SNDO opted to broaden the appeal of the existing market by allowing private investors to purchase its marketable bonds through primary dealers after each auction.[76] Distinct inflation-indexed retail products did not become available until 1997 (see below).

On 5 January 1996 the SNDO announced that its two indexed zero-coupon bonds would, for an unspecified period, be issued by tap rather than by regular auction. This change in issuance procedure was combined with the introduction of more formal market-making obligations for the primary dealers. SEK 17.9bn of the two bonds were sold in the five weeks following the first tap, compared with just under SEK 29bn by auction for the whole of 1995. In the light of this success, the SNDO introduced three new indexed bonds (two of which were coupon-paying bonds, see below) during 1996 and announced a reduction in conventional debt issuance. Figure 6.14 illustrates the significant increase in index-linked sales that arose as a result of this switch to tap issuance, which occurred in conjunction with a significant reduction in real yields demanded by investors to hold index-linked bonds.

6.4.2 The development of the market toward international standards

In October 1996, the SNDO Director General, Thomas Franzén, announced a scaling back of indexed bond issuance, claiming "...we can say we have established the instrument." As Figure 6.14 shows, this led directly to a slowdown in the growth of the market. Two innovations that might have been expected to aid liquidity were introduced in October 1997 by Skandinaviska Enskilda Banken (SEB), one of the

[76] For more information see Swedish National Debt Office (1995).

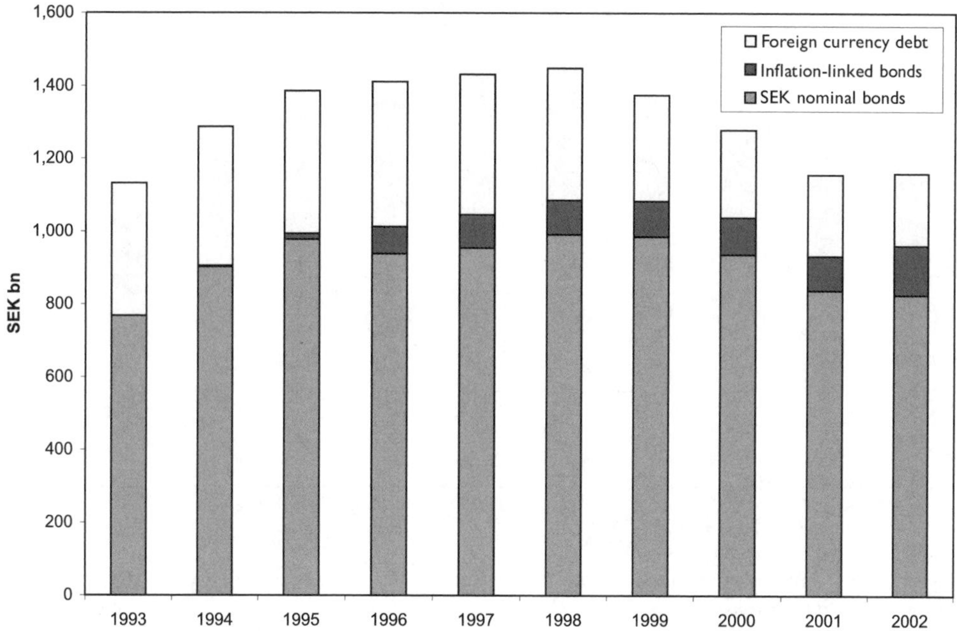

Figure 6.14 Changes in the composition of Swedish central government debt
Data source: Swedish National Debt Office

authorised dealers in Swedish index-linked bonds: CPI futures contracts and real rate swaps.[77] However, like the indexed bond futures introduced in the USA by the Chicago Board of Trade (CBOT), the Swedish equivalent proved to be short-lived and was withdrawn in 1999. That said, SEB (and others) continue to execute real rate swaps on an Over The Counter (OTC) basis – something that has helped facilitate the growth in the Swedish corporate indexed bond market (see below).

Since its coupon-bearing indexed bonds had proven to be much more popular than their zero-coupon counterparts, the SNDO decided to change the composition of its debt portfolio in their favour. On 23 June 1998 it held the first index-linked switch auction, the source bond being loan number 3001 (0% 2014) and the destination security a new 3.5% index-linked bond maturing in 2028 (loan 3103). The decision to issue a long-maturity bond was influenced by the SNDO's desire to widen the appeal of its index-linked bonds to international investors. Although only 50% of the SEK 5bn of the new bond on offer was sold, the sale established the switch auction as an important mechanism by which the SNDO could restructure its index-linked debt portfolio.

In April 1999 the SNDO announced several reforms to the inflation-indexed bond market.[78] In particular, issuance by tap ceased and was replaced by multiple yield auctions on the grounds that the market was now mature enough to accommodate

[77] See Alaton (1997a, b).
[78] See Swedish National Debt Office (1999a).

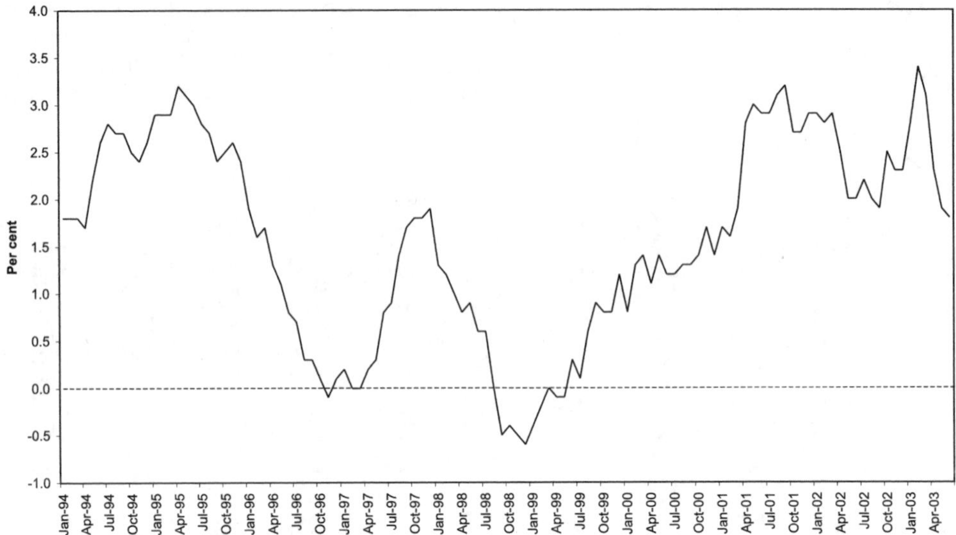

Figure 6.15 Annual percentage change in the Swedish Consumer Price Index (CPI)
Data source: Statistics Sweden

the change. The SNDO felt that this change would improve the predictability of supply and hence improve the operation of the secondary market. Auctions were initially held on a quarterly basis, and in any given quarter inflation-linked bonds were auctioned on three consecutive days – outright auctions on the first and third days, with a switch auction in between.

Along with the decision to reintroduce auctions, the SNDO also announced its intention to introduce a deflation floor on the principal payment of any new inflation-indexed bonds that it issued. Again, the main rationale behind the change was to harmonise the Swedish market with the practice already established in the USA and France, although another factor is likely to have been that demand for inflation-indexed bonds had again begun to decline following several months of negative inflation rates – see Figure 6.15. The first bond with a deflation floor, loan number 3104, was introduced in the period 19–23 April when it formed the destination bond for a conversion from loan 3103. Both securities have the same coupon (3.5%) and maturity date (1 December 2028) and terms were set at even yields for the two bonds. On 28 April, a new 2015 bond with a deflation floor (loan number 3105) was introduced via switch auction from loan number 3001 (0% 2014).

Accompanying the introduction of the deflation floor was a further technical change to the design of Swedish inflation-linked bonds. The SNDO announced that the 3104 and 3105 bonds (as well as all future inflation-linked new issues) would have an individual base index for pricing, established at the time of issue. This contrasts with the earlier inflation-linked bonds that all share a common base index dated from 1994. As a result, new issues from April 1999 onward do not have historic accrued inflation since 1994 built into their cash flows. While the introduction of the 3104 and 3105 bonds established medium- and long-maturity inflation-linked bonds with deflation floors, the SNDO opted in addition to continue to reopen the "old style" short-maturity 3101 bond.[79]

Demand for inflation-linked bonds in Sweden continued to be variable despite these substantial changes, and in August 1999 two outright auctions were cancelled due to lack of investor interest. As a result, further innovations were announced by the SNDO in December 1999.[80] Central to these changes was the desire to improve investor awareness, and thereby trading volume, of inflation-linked bonds. In practical terms this involved taking active steps to broaden the investor base, partly through the SNDO's own publicity campaigns and partly in the form of co-ordinated programmes with the primary dealers. To help achieve this aim a new dealer and commission system was introduced that increased the demands on the dealers, while at the same time providing them with higher levels of compensation. The new demands included a requirement that all dealers submit a detailed business plan to outline how they planned to broaden the investor base. Four firms were appointed as authorised inflation-linked bond dealers for 2000, and the SNDO annually reviews their status.[81]

To complement these structural changes, the SNDO further amended its auction schedule. Since February 2000 its monthly auctions have taken the form of outright, switch or reverse auctions (or any combination of the three), with auction events sometimes split over more than one day per month. Extensive and regular use of these various formats over a period of several years has enabled the SNDO to restructure its inflation-linked bond portfolio by concentrating its debt into a handful of bonds, thereby building up their volume and liquidity. In June 2002 the SNDO reported that it saw no need to carry out further portfolio restructuring and that it would revert to a debt management strategy based purely on outright issuance.[82] Figure 6.16 illustrates the maturity profile of the Swedish government's inflation-linked bond portfolio at end March 2003 and highlights how the bonds typically have much longer maturities than their nominal counterparts.

In June 2002 the SNDO also announced that, following discussions with market participants, it had decided to allow a degree of flexibility over the amount of an index-linked bond sold at any given auction. Under this new system a fixed size need not be announced ahead of each auction, but instead a target interval may be specified, such as SEK 500 – 1000mn. The SNDO also consulted on a proposal to revert to selling inflation-linked bonds by single price auction, although in the event it was decided to retain the multiple price format since market reaction to this suggestion was mixed. As a further illustration of its desire to develop and improve its indexed bond market an independent financial consultant was commissioned to survey investors, asset managers and financial advisors on their attitudes toward the asset class – the findings from which are summarised in Swedish National Debt Office (2002b).

In order to help maintain secondary market liquidity the SNDO offers three facilities to its authorised dealers. Perhaps the most important is the index-linked bond switch facility that enables dealers to switch bonds on a duration-neutral basis, although due

[79] In addition to the measures already discussed, the SNDO's April 1999 announcement also noted its intention to reduce the size of the 3003 bond (0% 2001) through direct repurchases and/or switch trades into other indexed bonds.
[80] See Swedish National Debt Office (1999b).
[81] Until January 2003 a post-auction non-comp facility was offered to the authorised dealers. Under this system each could buy an additional 20% of the allotted volume of the bond bought at the auction.
[82] See Swedish National Debt Office (2002b).

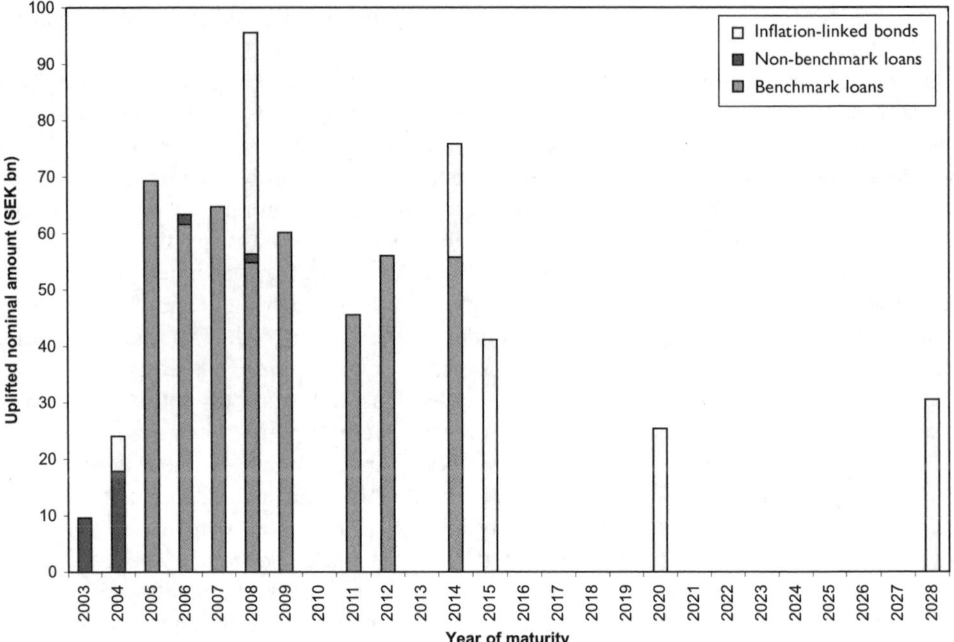

Figure 6.16 Maturity profile of SEK-denominated Swedish government bonds (as at 31 March 2003)
Data source: Swedish National Debt Office

to the deliberately penal terms set by the SNDO this facility only tends to be used as a last resort. Each authorised dealer is also permitted to borrow up to SEK 200mn of inflation-indexed bonds via repurchase agreement ("repo") at 25 basis points below the Riksbank's overnight rate. Third, poor liquidity in loan 3002 (0% 2004) led the SNDO to introduce a new repurchase procedure for the bond in October 2002. Although SEK 9.24bn of the bond had already been bought back through reverse auctions during 2001, the third such auction was not covered and as a direct result the decision was taken in March 2002 to suspend the reverse auction programme. The terms of the new, continuous buy-back offer made clear that, while the SNDO was prepared to support the market by providing liquidity, it was not prepared to do so at any price. It announced that "terms will not be based on indicative market prices for inflation-linked bonds, but mainly on nominal bond prices. They are set to be attractive to the SNDO in terms of cost. The price will be adjusted in order to limit the usage of the facility."[83]

6.4.3 Recent developments

The size of the index-linked bond market received a significant boost during 2002, when the Riksdag (Swedish parliament) decided to convert assets of three state entities: the Swedish Nuclear Waste Fund (KAF), the Premium Pension Authority (PPM) and the

[83] See Swedish National Debt Office (2002d).

Deposit Guarantee Board (IGN). Assets held in the form of cash balances at the SNDO were converted to Treasury bonds, which resulted in the creation of SEK 41.5bn of bonds on 1 July 2002, SEK 34.1bn of which were inflation-linked, with allocations spread (unevenly) across all the existing securities.[84] This represented a 33% increase in the nominal size of the inflation-linked government debt outstanding at the time and a corresponding rise of 0.6 years in its duration.

In its funding programme for 2003, the SNDO announced a very sharp rise in inflation-linked issuance – up from SEK 9bn in 2002 to SEK 15bn in 2003.[85] The decision to increase the supply of indexed bonds, not just for 2003 but over the longer term, was a reflection of the rising demand for the product. However, the SNDO sounded a note of caution and indicated that the future rate of growth would be based on both perceived demand for the product as well as an ongoing analysis of the relative borrowing cost compared with other types of debt, with due consideration for risk. Such cost analysis in Sweden is hampered by the lack of long-term nominal bonds, as Figure 6.16 illustrated. The development of the inflation-indexed sector could also be affected should Sweden decide to join EMU. On several occasions the SNDO has indicated that it would almost certainly continue to link its bonds to domestic consumer prices in the event of Sweden's entry into EMU,[86] arguing that domestic inflation would be likely to become more volatile, should Sweden adopt the euro and so increase the value of inflation-linked bonds to domestic investors. Also, bonds linked to Swedish CPI would provide a better hedge for the government since their finances are linked more closely to that index than to any pan-European measure.

Barclays Capital (2002d) examines the reasons behind the rising demand for inflation-linked bonds in Sweden. Institutional demand has increased with the part-privatisation of the National Pension system, coupled with a growing realisation that older, defined benefit schemes are underweight inflation-linked debt. Demand is also likely to have increased as a result of the conversion of the KAF's cash balance into government bonds, since KAF is expected to continue to make provision for decommissioning costs in the future and thereby will be required to undertake further purchases of indexed bonds. In addition to demand from domestic pension funds and insurance companies, the SNDO reports a growing interest from foreign investors. Against this backdrop early 2003 saw real yields in Sweden fall to historically low levels – see Figure 6.17.

By the end of March 2003 the size of the inflation-indexed government bond market was SEK 163bn in terms of uplifted nominal value (or SEK 148bn in nominal terms) and, as Figure 6.18 shows, indexed bonds constituted around 13.3% of total central government debt.[87] As such, of the six countries examined in this chapter, Sweden has the second highest proportion of its debt in the form of inflation-linked bonds, after the

[84] Except loan 3002 (0% 2004), which had been the subject of a buy-back programme earlier in the year, and loan 3103. For more details see Swedish National Debt Office (2002c).

[85] See Swedish National Debt Office (2003a). During 2003 the SNDO confirmed its intention to maintain issuance at SEK 15bn for 2004 also. In addition, it also invited views on the introduction of stripping facilities for its inflation-linked bonds (Swedish National Debt Office, 2003c, pp. 10–11).

[86] See, for example, Thedéen (2003).

[87] Note: from the beginning of 2003 the Swedish government introduced a new method of measuring central government debt. The new measure is based on an estimate that includes derivative instruments valued at their nominal final value in accordance with the same principles in effect for countries already in the Euro-zone. For inflation-linked bonds the implication is that accrued inflation is now included in figures recording outstanding debt. For each bond the uplifted figure is calculated as the product of the nominal amount outstanding and the index ratio.

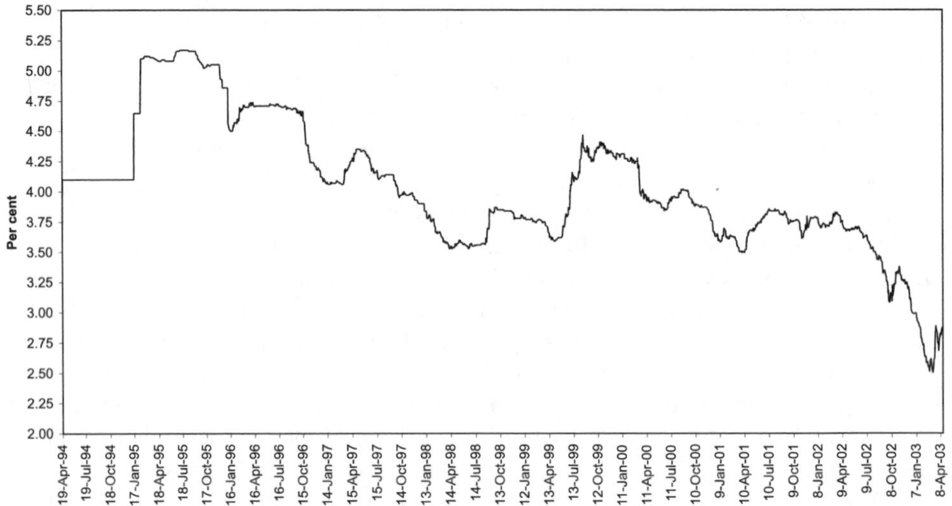

Figure 6.17 Real yield on Swedish government 0% Index-linked Treasury Bond 2014 (loan number 3001)
Data source: Swedish National Debt Office

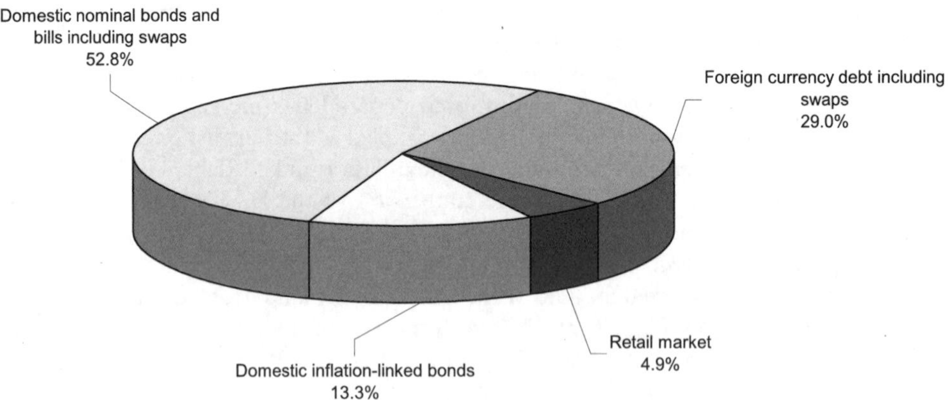

Figure 6.18 Composition of Swedish central government debt (as at 31 March 2003)
Data source: Swedish National Debt Office

UK. As in other indexed bond markets, trading in the secondary market (which takes place on a real yield basis) is much less frequent than in the nominal bond market. For example, daily turnover during 2002/03 averaged around SEK 750mn and an average trading lot for customer trades was around SEK 200mn for short-dated indexed bonds and around SEK 100mn for longer-dated bonds.[88]

As of March 2003 the Swedish indexed government bond market consisted of seven bonds: the two original indexed zero-coupon bonds and five capital indexed bonds, two of which feature a deflation floor. Details of these bonds are provided in Table 6.9,

[88] Source: Swedish National Debt Office.

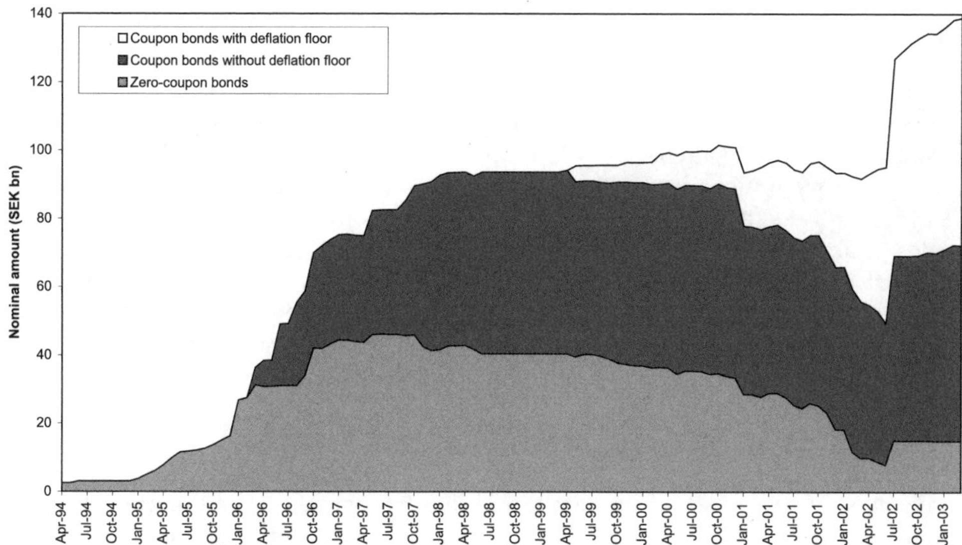

Figure 6.19 Composition of Swedish government inflation-linked marketable debt by instrument type (April 1994–March 2003)

Data source: Swedish National Debt Office.

Table 6.9 Swedish Index-linked Treasury Bonds

Loan number	Coupon (%)	Maturity date	Deflation floor?	Date of first sale[a]	Nominal amount outstanding (SEK mn)	Uplifted nominal amount (SEK mn)
3002	0.00	1 Apr 2004	No	16 Jan 1995	5,535.610	6,206.175
3101	4.00	1 Dec 2008	No	3 Mar 1996	34,868.870	39,273.631
3001	0.00	1 Apr 2014	No	19 Apr 1994	18,570.235	20,093.845
3105	3.50	1 Dec 2015	Yes	28 Apr 1999	38,214.000	41,141.491
3102	4.00	1 Dec 2020	No	3 Jun 1996	22,484.115	25,383.152
3103	3.50	1 Dec 2028	No	23 Jun 1998	3.000	3.373
3104	3.50	1 Dec 2028	Yes	19 Apr 1999	28,372.500	30,492.665

Data source: Swedish National Debt Office (2003b) (figures as at 31 March 2003).
[a] These are the dates on which the bonds were sold rather than the settlement dates.

while Figure 6.19 shows how the composition of the inflation-linked sector by instrument type has changed since the beginning of the issuance programme in 1994. The coupon-bearing bonds all pay coupons annually on 1 December, the indexation lag for all bonds is three months[89] and the index is applied in the same way as for Canadian RRBs and US TIPS. Details of the indexation calculation and the price–yield equations appear in Appendix 6.4. For all indexed bonds the inflation uplift on the principal is taxable only on sale or on redemption – not annually as is the case in the USA, for example.

[89] The SNDO sometimes refers to the lag as being $2\frac{1}{2}$ months rather than 3 months, since cash flows on all Swedish indexed bonds are paid on the first day of the month and the price index is published in the middle of the month.

As Figure 6.18 shows, at end March 2003 the retail market represented 4.9% of total Swedish central government debt.[90] The SNDO offers retail investors (individuals, small companies and small organizations) three main savings alternatives: Treasury instruments (Treasury bills, nominal government bonds and inflation-linked government bonds), National Debt Savings Accounts and Lottery bonds. The facilities available to retail investors for the purchase of nominal bonds were improved during 2002 through the launch of online sales, to enable non-institutional investors to buy bonds at auction (at the average allotted yield) via the Internet. This facility will be extended to Treasury bills and inflation-linked bonds during 2003.[91] In addition the SNDO offers inflation-indexed National Debt Savings Accounts.[92] These were introduced in 1997 and take the form of inflation-linked zero-coupon bonds with maturities of five or eight years. In line with marketable bonds, a deflation floor was introduced for new accounts in April 1999.

To date, only a limited corporate inflation-linked bond market has developed in Sweden. At the end of March 2003, issuance stood at approximately SEK 6bn[93] and represented less than 4% of the total Swedish inflation-linked bond market. The few bonds issued so far have all been linked to domestic consumer prices and the majority have been launched with an initial maturity of between 8 and 20 years. The issuers represent a diverse range of business activities and include: Electrolux (the manufacturer of electrical appliances), Fysikhuset Stockholm KB (a construction company), Investor AB (an investment fund), Statens Bostadsfinansieringsinstitut (a government agency) and Volvo (the vehicle manufacturer).

6.5 UNITED KINGDOM

6.5.1 A brief history of the index-linked gilt market

Indexation in the UK was advocated by several prominent economists as far back as the 19th and early 20th century, although their efforts were to no avail. Even John Maynard Keynes was unable to persuade the British government to issue indexed bonds, when he presented his case to the Royal Commission on National Debt and Taxation in 1924. A similar lack of enthusiasm was apparent in the *Report of the Committee on the Working of the Monetary System* (Radcliffe Committee, 1959), which declared that indexation would constitute "a confession of failure" in the face of inflation.[94]

By the early 1970s rising inflation (see Figure 6.20) meant that holders of nominal debt were experiencing a significant erosion of the real value of their assets. For instance, Rutterford (1983) calculates that the market value of one particular undated gilt (a perpetual government bond) halved in real terms between 1965 and 1971. As a result, the *Report of the Committee to Review National Savings* (Page Committee, 1973) recommended the launch of indexed national savings certificates

[90] Note that in Figure 6.18 retail holdings of Treasury instruments are not reported in the retail market category.
[91] In 2002 retail investors purchased SEK 20mn of inflation-linked bonds.
[92] Fixed and floating rate accounts are also available.
[93] Source: Bloomberg.
[94] See the Radcliffe Committee (1959).

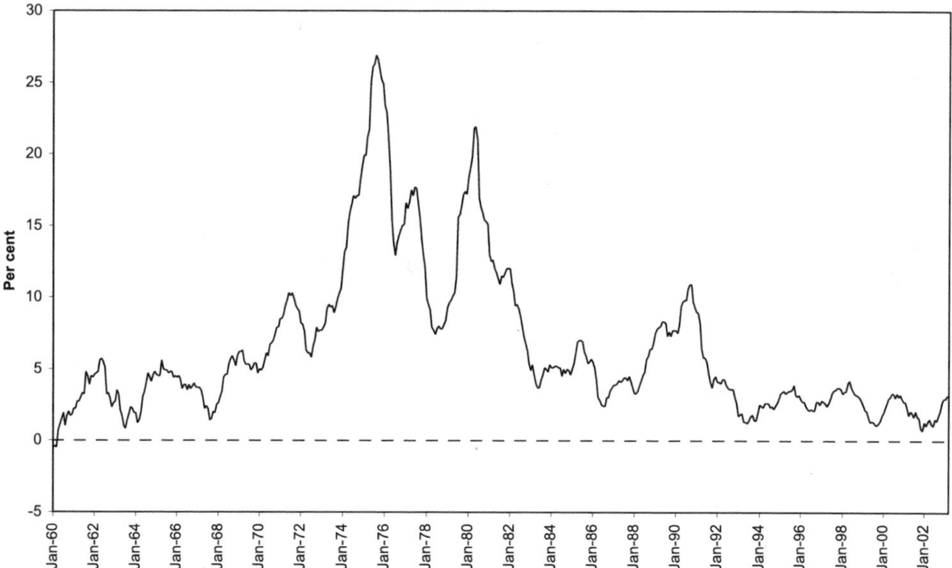

Figure 6.20 Annual percentage change in the UK Retail Prices Index (RPI)
Data source: Office of National Statistics

aimed at small investors.[95] In 1975 the government acted on this advice and began issuing non-marketable national savings contracts with returns linked to the Retail Prices Index (RPI). Investment in these certificates was initially limited to pensioners (thus earning them the nickname "granny bonds"), although this restriction was later removed.[96]

The Wilson Report of 1980 highlighted further sources of anxiety with regard to the potential effects of inflation on the UK financial system.[97] A chief concern was the existence of a substantial number of high coupon bonds issued during the 1970s that left the government vulnerable to the risk that the real burden of its debt interest would rise, should interest rates fall. The authors also emphasised the adverse effects of inflation on the real value of investors' savings. Given the important role played by pension funds in the gilt market and their need to provide pensions based on earnings, the Wilson Report recommended that the government should issue earnings-indexed gilts eligible for purchase only by pension funds.[98]

In March 1981, doubtless influenced by the Wilson Report, the government issued its first index-linked gilt. For the reasons outlined in Chapter 2, rather than index to average earnings, the Treasury opted instead to use the more widely accepted RPI.[99]

---

[95] See Page Committee (1973).

[96] At the end of March 2003 a total of £8.0bn index-linked national savings certificates were outstanding. For more information on this product see National Savings and Investments (2002).

[97] See Wilson Committee (1980).

[98] For a more detailed account of the background to the first issue of index-linked gilts, readers should refer to Rutterford (1983).

[99] For details on the construction of the RPI see Baxter (1998), available on the website of the Office of National Statistics: www.statistics.gov.uk.

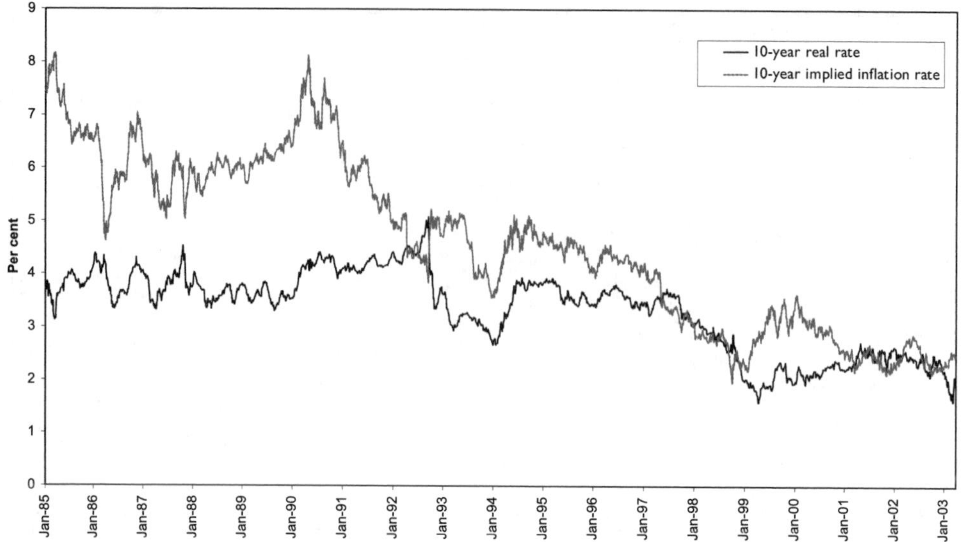

Figure 6.21 UK 10-year real zero-coupon rates and implied average inflation rates (January 1985–March 2003). *Note*: these rates were produced by the Bank of England's yield curve model, details of which can be found in Anderson and Sleath (2003)
Data source: Bank of England

Ownership of the bonds was initially limited to pension funds (as suggested by Wilson[100]), but these restrictions were lifted in March 1982. The official reasons given for introducing indexed bonds were threefold: to reinforce belief in the government's anti-inflation policy, to reduce the cost of funding by saving the inflation risk premium and to improve monetary control by increasing the flexibility of funding.[101] De Kock (1991) reports that these advantages were partially offset by a number of disadvantages, including the possibility that the introduction of index-linked gilts might depress equity prices as well as reduce corporate financing opportunities.

In practice, the issuance of index-linked gilts has indeed increased the diversity of the government's debt portfolio and can be demonstrated to have generated a significant reduction in the cost of funding. This is likely to be due in part to a reduction of inflation risk, but more importantly because market expectations of inflation have exceeded the inflation outturn for much of the period since the bonds were launched. As Figure 6.21 shows, by 2001 long-term expectations of inflation (as measured by the RPI) had settled at around $2\frac{1}{2}$% per annum, consistent with the Bank of England's long-run target level,[102] suggesting that there was no longer a significant inflation risk premium built into the prices of conventional gilts. Although this movement in relative

[100] Wilson's recommendation was not the only factor influencing this decision. Bootle (1991) reports that the authorities were unsure how existing tax rules would be applied to index-linked gilts. By initially limiting the ownership of index-linked gilts to pension funds (who pay no tax on bondholdings in the UK) the authorities gained time to introduce the necessary reforms to the tax system.

[101] See HM Treasury (1981). Rutterford (1983) examines each of these reasons in detail.

[102] The inflation target is currently based on the growth rate of RPIX (RPI excluding mortgage interest) rather than RPI, but in practice these two measures tend to be very similar on average over an economic cycle. In June 2003 Chancellor Gordon Brown announced his intention to switch the Bank's target to one specified in terms of the HICP measure.

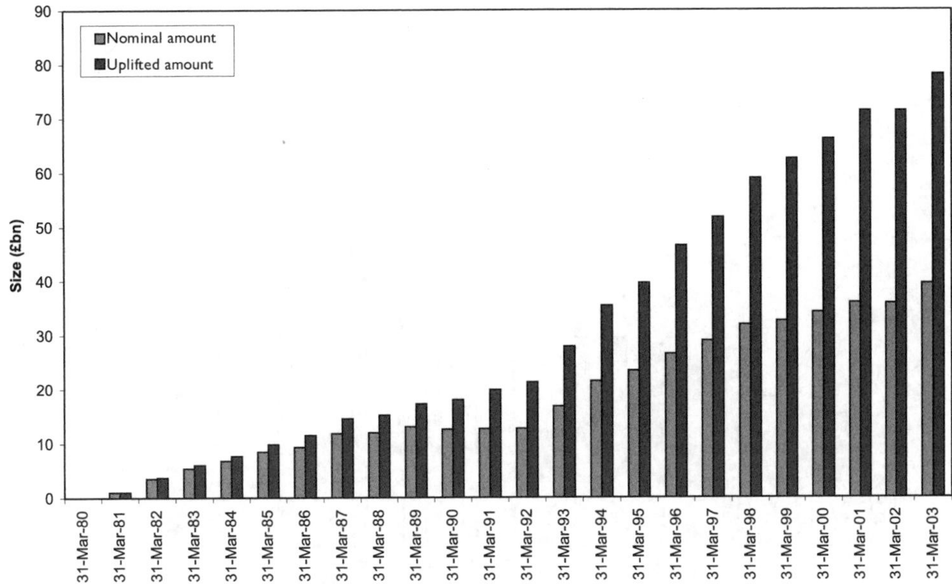

Figure 6.22 Growth of the UK index-linked gilt market. *Note*: the inflation uplift for an index-linked gilt is the inflation that has accrued on the principal since it was first issued. For example, the inflation uplift on a particular index-linked gilt at 31 March 2003 would be the RPI level in July 2002 (eight months before March 2003) divided by the index level eight months before the bond's original issue date. The eight-month delay is because of the lag in indexation
Data source: UK Debt Management Office

valuations of nominal and index-linked gilts reduces the cost advantages to the government of issuing the latter, HM Treasury has indicated its intention to maintain supply for several reasons – not least due to the "fiscal insurance" properties of indexed bonds as well as the diversification benefits that they offer.[103]

The first index-linked gilt, a 15-year bond, was issued on 27 March 1981 by single price auction. The coupon for new gilt issues (both conventional and index-linked) is not fixed at auction but is decided beforehand, and for the first index-linked gilt the real coupon of 2% was chosen as it fell within a range of actuarial assumptions about future real returns on gilts.[104] Within 18 months of this launch a further 6 index-linked gilts had been issued, with original maturities ranging from 6 to 29 years. As Figure 6.22 shows, the market grew significantly during the early 1980s, although later the same decade the government's finances had moved into surplus and as a result a programme was initiated to repurchase some nominal bonds. Although index-linked gilts did not form part of the buy-back programme, along with conventional gilts they were subject to a freeze in issuance between October 1988 and January 1991. Figure 6.23 highlights how the proportion of index-linked gilts in the government debt portfolio rose during this period. Issuance resumed as the government's budget moved back into deficit during the early 1990s. The proportion of index-linked gilts increased noticeably

[103] See HM Treasury (2001, pp 5–6).
[104] Source: HM Treasury (1981).

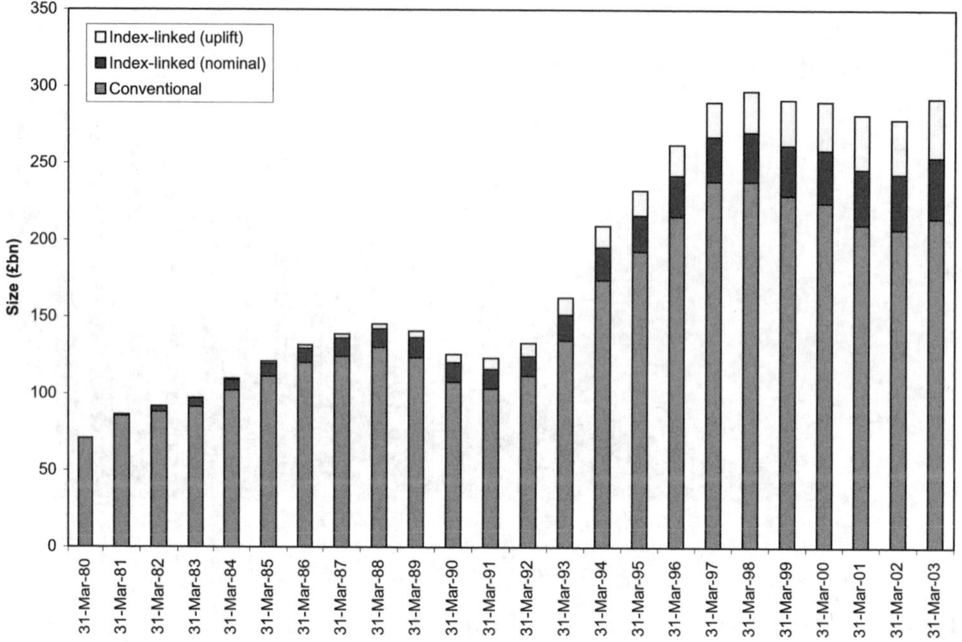

Figure 6.23 Growth of the aggregate UK gilt market
Data source: UK Debt Management Office

again in 2000/01 when a surplus in government finances led the authorities again to buy back conventional gilts, this time repurchasing a total of £4.1bn (cash) through a programme of reverse auctions, while maintaining index-linked issuance.[105]

In 1988, following several auctions at which significant amounts of index-linked gilts remained unsold, it was decided to abandon auctions as the chosen sales process in favour of taps, with the aim of timing issuance to coincide better with market demand. Another significant step to improve liquidity was taken in March 1998, with the announcement of the Treasury's commitment to a minimum gross supply of £2.5bn cash of index-linked gilts each financial year for the foreseeable future.[106] This commitment has indeed been renewed each subsequent year and has served to provide the market with a degree of certainty with regard to the supply of index-linked gilts. Liquidity has also been aided by a policy of building up large issue sizes through the reopening of existing bonds, rather than the launch of new ones. The impact of this strategy is illustrated by the fact that between September 1992 and July 2002 the nominal size of the market increased from £15bn to £38bn, with the average bond size rising from £1.1bn to £3.8bn nominal, even though no new bonds were launched during the period. This policy was pursued initially by the Bank of England and more recently by the UK Debt Management Office (DMO), which took over responsibility for management of the government's debt portfolio in April 1998, and since March 1999 issuance has been further limited to index-linked gilts with maturities of 2009 and

[105] For details of this programme see UK Debt Management Office (2001e, pp. 18–19).
[106] See HM Treasury (1998).

longer. As an additional means of providing liquidity, the DMO has established repo facilities for both for conventional and index-linked gilts.[107]

By 1998 the authorities believed that the market was sufficiently mature to support auctions and so in June, following a consultation process with the market by the Bank and HM Treasury, the DMO published proposals for their reintroduction.[108] It was felt that a pre-announced auction programme would improve the predictability and transparency of issuance and thereby lead to a focusing of demand and increased liquidity. The decision was also influenced by the US Treasury's successful introduction of inflation-indexed security auctions in January 1997.

At the same time the DMO decided to specify a group of specialist index-linked market makers, in order to minimise the likelihood of so-called "fair-weather" market-making behaviour, and thereby reduce the risk that any individual Gilt-edged Market Maker (GEMM) simply opts to participate in the index-linked gilt market only when it appears profitable to do so. A particular concern was that a GEMM might seek to purchase a high proportion of the bonds available at index-linked auctions without making a commitment to provide liquidity in the secondary market and thereby make it harder for others to perform the latter function. The specialist index-linked market maker list was therefore introduced in September 1998 and initially consisted of eight firms, although by March 2003 this had increased to eleven.[109] The DMO did however continue *for a time* with its established policy of acting as "market maker of last resort".[110]

The DMO announced that auctions would be on a single price basis, initially at least, in order to encourage the IG GEMMs to build up short positions with some comfort that they could be covered at an auction price common to the rest of the market. It was thought that this format would also help to ease risks associated with the lack of a suitably liquid hedging instrument, as well as broadening participation. As with conventional gilt auctions, the DMO offered a non-competitive bidding facility for market makers of up to 10% of the nominal amount being auctioned. For index-linked auctions (only), the non-competitive allotment is allocated to market makers on the basis of the share of bonds allotted to their competitive bids at the previous three auctions. This measure was intended to be an incentive for market makers to participate competitively, in order to earn the right to place non-competitive bids at future auctions.

The first auction in this new programme was held on 25 November 1998 when £450mn nominal (approximately £825mn in cash terms) of $2\frac{1}{2}$% index-linked Treasury stock 2013 was sold. It proved to be a reasonable success with a bid-to-cover ratio of 2.29 and an allotment price of £183.20 (equivalent to a real yield of 2.42%), 72 pence down on the previous evening's GEMMA[111] closing price.[112] Since then the DMO has

[107] For more details on these facilities see UK Debt Management Office (2000).

[108] See UK Debt Management Office (1998).

[109] The firms on this list are referred to as IG GEMMs. An up-to-date list of IG GEMMs appears on the DMO website: www.dmo.gov.uk

[110] This facility was intended to assist market makers who were unable to sell their index-linked holdings to others in the secondary market. Under this policy the DMO was prepared to bid individual market makers for their bonds. In November 2001 the DMO withdrew this facility in order to bring its relationship with index-linked market participants more into line with that for conventional gilts. It was replaced by a reverse tap facility to mirror that already in place to sell bonds, thus enabling the DMO to buy back and cancel bonds (for "market management purposes" only) in conditions of extreme market dislocation. For more details see UK Debt Management Office (2001f).

[111] Gilt-edged Market Maker Association.

[112] The DMO's formula for calculating yields from prices for index-linked gilts appears in Appendix 6.5.

Table 6.10 Results of index-linked gilt auctions (November 1998–March 2003)

Auction Date	Index-linked Gilt	Nominal amount Issued (£ mn)[a]	Cash raised (£ mn)	Bid-to-cover ratio	Real yield (%)[b]
25 Nov 1998	$2\frac{1}{2}$% IL 2013	450	824	2.29	2.42
27 Jan 1999	$2\frac{1}{2}$% IL 2024	450	817	1.83	2.01
28 Apr 1999	$4\frac{1}{8}$% IL 2030	500	897	0.94	1.97
28 Jul 1999	$2\frac{1}{2}$% IL 2011	375	846	1.93	2.19
27 Oct 1999	$2\frac{1}{2}$% IL 2016	370	757	2.65	2.34
26 Jan 2000	$2\frac{1}{2}$% IL 2024	370	692	2.54	1.93
3 May 2000	$2\frac{1}{2}$% IL 2020	375	821	2.30	1.92
26 Jul 2000	$2\frac{1}{2}$% IL 2013	435	850	1.94	2.18
25 Oct 2000	$4\frac{1}{8}$% IL 2030	450	851	2.07	1.87
24 Jan 2001	$2\frac{1}{2}$% IL 2016	470	1,028	3.16	2.08
25 Apr 2001	$2\frac{1}{2}$% IL 2011	400	901	1.92	2.59
25 Jul 2001	$2\frac{1}{2}$% IL 2024	500	910	1.48	2.29
24 Oct 2001	$2\frac{1}{2}$% IL 2016	445	948	2.63	2.39
24 Jan 2002	$4\frac{1}{8}$% IL 2030	500	882	1.98	2.23
24 Apr 2002	$2\frac{1}{2}$% IL 2020	425	893	2.19	2.39
10 Jul 2002	2% IL 2035	950	929	1.38	2.09
25 Sep 2002	2% IL 2035	900	891	0.95	2.04
24 Oct 2002	$2\frac{1}{2}$% IL 2013	450	890	3.01	2.40
22 Jan 2003	$2\frac{1}{2}$% IL 2020	425	961	2.59	2.03

Data source: UK Debt Management Office.
[a] These figures include any non-competitive allocation to the IG GEMMs (Index-linked Gilt Gilt-Edged Market Makers) and retail investors, as well as any stock sold to the Commissioners for the Reduction of the National Debt (CRND). For information about the CRND visit www.crnd.gov.uk
[b] Calculated using a standard 3% inflation assumption.

held index-linked auctions on a quarterly basis, although for the 2003/04 financial year it has announced its intention to increase the frequency in line with the increased borrowing requirement.[113] With the reintroduction of auctions it was decided that index-linked taps should be used only to help mitigate the effects of temporary excess demand in a particular bond or sector. As such, the DMO indicated that it would only tap index-linked gilts in exceptional circumstances and since auctions were reintroduced has never done so. Table 6.10 gives the results for all outright index-linked gilt auctions since November 1998 and Figure 6.24 compares the real yield with the bid-to-cover ratio at each auction.[114]

In addition to outright auctions the DMO can also hold index-linked switch auctions, proposals for which were published in a DMO market consultation paper in March 2001.[115] The catalyst for this initiative was the event of 2% IL 2006 dropping out of the FTSE "Over Five Year" index-linked gilt index in July 2001,[116] and the anticipation

[113] Eight index-linked auctions are scheduled at irregular intervals over the 2003/04 financial year.
[114] Real yields are calculated using a 3% inflation assumption.
[115] See UK Debt Management Office (2001a).
[116] When its residual maturity fell below 5 years.

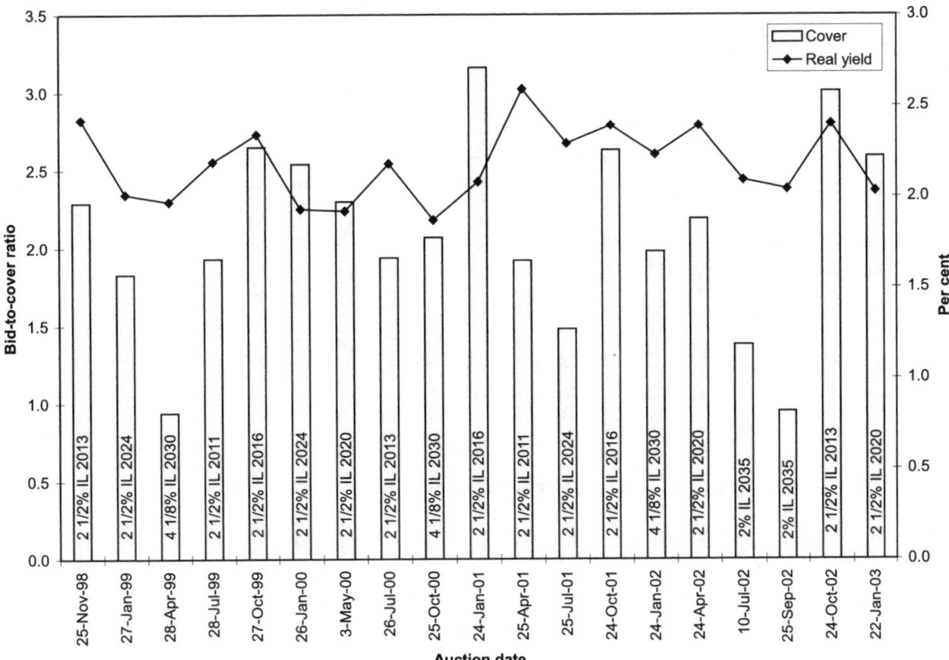

Figure 6.24 Real yield and bid-to-cover ratio at index-linked gilt auctions (November 1998–March 2003)
Data source: UK Debt Management Office.

that significant distortions might be caused by a number of passive index-tracking funds attempting to switch their holdings into longer-dated index-linked gilts through the secondary market at the same time. Having published its response to the consultation paper in May, the DMO held its first index-linked switch auction on 19 July 2001[117] – timed to ease the impact of the change in composition of the FTSE index. Indeed, the destination bond,[118] $2\frac{1}{2}$% IL 2016, was chosen to match the duration of the index as closely as possible in a further effort to reduce market impact. Six days later the DMO held an outright auction of the $2\frac{1}{2}$% IL 2024 bond to provide a further opportunity for index trackers to lengthen the duration of their portfolios. Table 6.11 shows the effect that these events had on the modified duration of the FTSE index.

This episode serves to illustrate how the DMO can "manage the market" and attempt to reduce the potential for serious dislocations. To date, the DMO has held no further index-linked switch auctions, since the rationale for their use and that for conventional gilt switch auctions have deliberately been kept quite distinct – the latter (introduced in October 1999) are intended primarily to assist in building up the size of individual conventional bonds at a pace faster than that achievable through outright

[117] At the switch auction £500mn nominal of 2% IL 2006 was switched into around £561mn nominal of $2\frac{1}{2}$% IL 2016. For the full details see UK Debt Management Office (2001c).
[118] Although some market participants had indicated a preference for switch auctions with multiple destination bonds during the consultation process, the DMO decided that this would add too much complexity and uncertainty to the process and thus opted to provide a single destination bond.

Table 6.11 The evolution of the modified duration of the FTSE index-linked gilt indices in July 2001

Index	Before index change	After index change and switch auction	After outright auction
All index-linked gilts	10.73	10.85	10.95
Over five-year index-linked gilts	11.78	12.51	12.59

Data source: Merrill Lynch (2001).

auctions alone, while the former are employed solely for market management purposes and as such are likely to occur relatively infrequently.[119]

6.5.2 The structure of the index-linked gilt market

Chapter 2 made brief reference to the design of index-linked gilts – and in particular to their unique indexation lag. All index-linked gilts are capital indexed bonds that pay semi-annual coupon payments and none have deflation floors.[120] Unlike indexed bonds in most markets, in the UK the inflation uplift on the principal is tax-free, potentially widening the appeal of index-linked gilts beyond just tax-exempt institutions, though it does mean that a distinction has been drawn in the tax regime between the treatment of indexed and nominal bonds.

An eight-month indexation lag is employed – two months to allow for the compilation and publication of the RPI and a further six months to ensure that the nominal size of the next coupon payment is known at the start of each coupon period – in order to compute accrued interest. Since this represents a longer lag than that employed in other major markets, changes to the instrument structure have been proposed on a number of occasions.[121] For instance, Chapter 2 described a proposal put forward by Professor Robert Barro in 1995 to modify the indexation lag on new index-linked gilts to provide better inflation protection. More recently, the DMO carried out a detailed consultation exercise in 2001[122] with regard to the potential introduction of a new design for index-linked gilts ahead of the first issuance of a new bond for 10 years. The growth in international markets for index-linked securities had led to increasing convergence to a "standard" design, based on that pioneered by the Canadian authorities in 1991 and subsequently adopted in France, Italy, Sweden, the USA and other markets. With a three-month indexation lag this structure provides investors with better inflation protection than that available from index-linked gilts and their eight-month lag. Although the majority of respondents agreed that the Canadian design was an improvement over

[119] Another difference between index-linked switch auctions and their conventional counterparts is that the former are held on a single price basis (in line with outright index-linked gilt auctions), while the latter are on a multiple price basis. Other differences are highlighted in the DMO's consultation response – see UK Debt Management Office (2001b).

[120] The only index-linked gilt to differ from the standard format was a convertible index-linked gilt that was issued in 1983 and which redeemed in 1999. The conversion feature gave investors the option to convert their holdings into a conventional gilt – an offer which almost all holders of the bond exercised. Full details on the conversion terms appear in Chapter 2.

[121] The UK suffers in some sense from being the "pioneer" index-linked bond market, with later issuers able to improve on the instrument design used in the UK.

[122] See UK Debt Management Office (2001d). The authorities had previously raised the issue of instrument design as part of the consultation on the reintroduction of index-linked gilt auctions in 1998.

that of existing index-linked gilts,[123] many expressed the concern that the launch of a new style of security could create a two-tier market, with liquidity being concentrated in the new-style bonds at the expense of the existing issues.

In light of the mixed reactions that its proposals received the DMO decided to retain the existing design, although it did take the opportunity to introduce some changes to the prospectus terms for future new issues. The most significant was to the "indexation clause": instead of an explicit provision for the early redemption of index-linked gilts affected by an index change, for new bonds the prospectus places the onus on an independent institution to propose a satisfactory replacement index, should the original cease to exist. This, it was argued, would bring the UK more into line with other major markets and reduce the potential for disruption in the event that the early redemption clause is ever triggered.[124]

As part of the same consultation exercise, the DMO also sought to gauge potential demand for a facility for stripping index-linked gilts. However, reflecting the limited utilisation of the equivalent facility for conventional gilts since its introduction in December 1997, few respondents indicated any interest in the formation of a market for index-linked strips. The DMO therefore concluded that such a development would be premature, but signalled that it would consider aligning the coupon dates of new issues in order to help facilitate the introduction of a strips market in the future, should demand materialise.

At the end of March 2003 the nominal size of the index-linked gilt market stood at £39.5bn, or £78.1bn when the inflation uplift was added. As Figure 6.25 shows, index-linked gilts (in uplifted terms) constituted 25.4% of total government marketable debt, which means that the UK has the highest proportion of indexed debt of the major government bond markets. Table 6.12 provides information on the 11 index-linked gilts in existence at end March 2003,[125] while Figure 6.26 illustrates their maturity distribution along with the secondary market real yields on 31 March 2003.[126] For the 2003/04 financial year the DMO is planning to raise around £6.5bn in cash through index-linked gilt sales, representing 14% of gross gilt issuance for the year.[127] Although this constitutes a much lower proportion of gilt issuance than in recent years, in cash terms it represents the most ambitious year's funding since 1993/94.

Although large in size, the index-linked gilt market has always been much less liquid than that for conventional gilts – a topic that was discussed at length in Section 3.7. A graphic illustration of this fact is provided by data from the DMO that rank gilts by turnover (see UK Debt Management Office, 2003b) – in the 13 weeks to 31 March 2003 no index-linked gilt featured in the top 20. The introduction of an index-linked gilt futures contract is a suggestion that has been put forward on a number of occasions in this context (e.g., at a conference hosted by the Bank of England in 1995[128]). However, the London International Financial Futures and Options Exchange (LIFFE) indicated

[123] The DMO reports that, while the overwhelming majority of respondents favoured the Canadian design, several respondents also suggested the issuance of *Limited Price Indexation* (LPI) bonds alongside standard RPI-linked bonds.

[124] For more details on this and the other changes made by the DMO refer to UK Debt Management Office (2002a).

[125] The full issuance history of each index-linked gilt appears on the DMO website, www.dmo.gov.uk

[126] By 31 March 2003 the final coupon and the redemption payment on $2\frac{1}{2}$% IL 2003 had been fixed, and so it was effectively trading as a conventional bond (with a nominal yield), hence its exclusion from Figure 6.26. Real yields on the other index-linked gilts are calculated using the market standard 3% inflation assumption.

[127] For details of the DMO's planned issuance programme for 2003/04 see HM Treasury (2003). The issuance target for index-linked gilts represents the DMO's estimate of annual end-user demand – see UK Debt Management Office (2003a).

[128] "The UK index-linked gilt market: Future development", see Bank of England (1996).

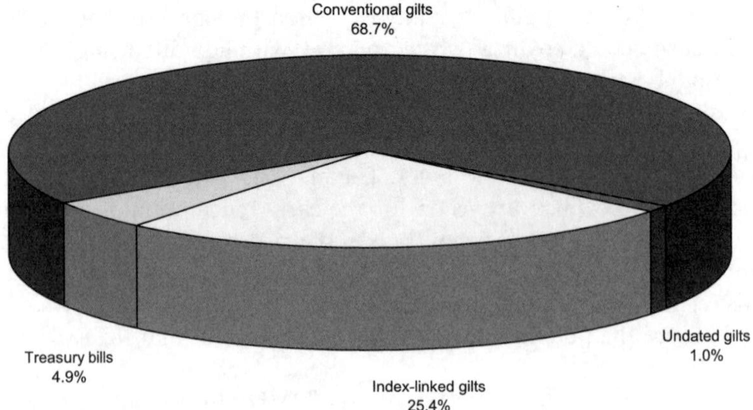

Figure 6.25 Composition of UK government debt (as at 31 March 2003). *Note*: amounts for index-linked gilts are quoted in terms of uplifted nominal
Data source: UK Debt Management Office (2003b)

Table 6.12 UK Index-linked Gilts

Index-linked gilt	Maturity date	Date of first issue	Nominal amount outstanding (£ mn)	Uplifted nominal amount (£ mn)
$2\frac{1}{2}$% IL 2003	20 May 2003	27 Oct 1982	2,734	6,165
$4\frac{3}{8}$% IL 2004	21 Oct 2004	22 Sep 1992	1,338	1,736
2% IL 2006	19 Jul 2006	8 Jul 1981	2,037	5,157
$2\frac{1}{2}$% IL 2009	20 May 2009	19 Oct 1982	2,673	5,970
$2\frac{1}{2}$% IL 2011	23 Aug 2011	28 Jan 1982	3,942	9,301
$2\frac{1}{2}$% IL 2013	16 Aug 2013	21 Feb 1985	5,172	10,199
$2\frac{1}{2}$% IL 2016	26 Jul 2016	19 Jan 1983	6,055	13,050
$2\frac{1}{2}$% IL 2020	16 Apr 2020	12 Oct 1983	5,093	10,798
$2\frac{1}{2}$% IL 2024	17 Jul 2024	30 Dec 1986	5,401	9,727
$4\frac{1}{8}$% IL 2030	22 Jul 2030	12 Jun 1992	3,171	4,129
2% IL 2035	26 Jan 2035	11 Jul 2003	1,850	1,875

Data source: UK Debt Management Office (figures as at 31 March 2003)

that it would not consider such a move until the underlying cash market was more liquid – a "chicken-and-egg" situation. In the meantime the OTC derivatives market in indexed bonds and forward inflation has been growing rapidly in the UK, a topic which is discussed in detail in Chapter 8.

6.5.3 The market for non-government index-linked bonds in the UK

Despite the fact that the index-linked gilt market has grown relatively quickly since its inception in 1981, there has only been significant corporate and supranational sterling

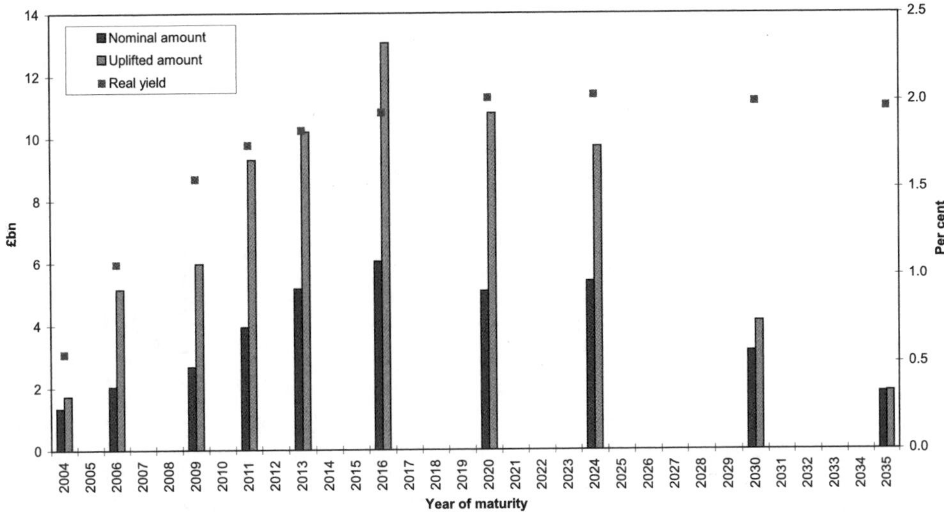

Figure 6.26 Maturity profile and real yields of index-linked gilts (as at 31 March 2003)
Data source: UK Debt Management Office

index-linked issuance since the late 1990s[129] – see Figure 6.27. Several reasons have been offered for the recent increase in activity in the sector. The first is the change in tax regime that was implemented in 1996, which allowed the uplift in the principal value of an index-linked bond to be set against corporate tax liabilities and thereby made corporate issuance of index-linked debt more tax-efficient than had previously been the case.[130]

Another likely factor behind the increase in corporate issuance is the privatisation of many public sector corporations during the 1980s and 1990s. In order to maintain a balance between the interests of consumers and those of shareholders the government created regulatory regimes based on price controls, often defined with links to the rate of inflation. As the revenue streams for these companies are thus inflation-linked it is logical for them to consider issuance of index-linked debt, and a number of gas, electricity and water companies have taken this option. Furthermore, the 1990s also saw the development of the Private Finance Initiative (PFI) as a means for the government to finance the construction of public sector facilities, such as hospitals and roads. The structure of PFI deals is described in more detail in Chapter 8, but the presence of inflation-linked cash flows in such finance deals has led to a wave of private sector issuance of indexed debt.

Historically, defined benefit pension plans in the UK have tended to invest a relatively high proportion of their assets in equities, despite the fact that their liabilities are often viewed to resemble bonds more closely. The introduction of the Minimum

[129] Page and Trollope (1974) note one example of an indexed bond that was issued by a private corporation in the early 1970s, but this appears to have been a rare if not unique event.

[130] For bond *holders*, however, there is still a discrepancy between the tax treatment of index-linked gilts and index-linked corporate bonds. In the case of the latter, the inflation uplift is taxable (i.e., no inflation credit is applied).

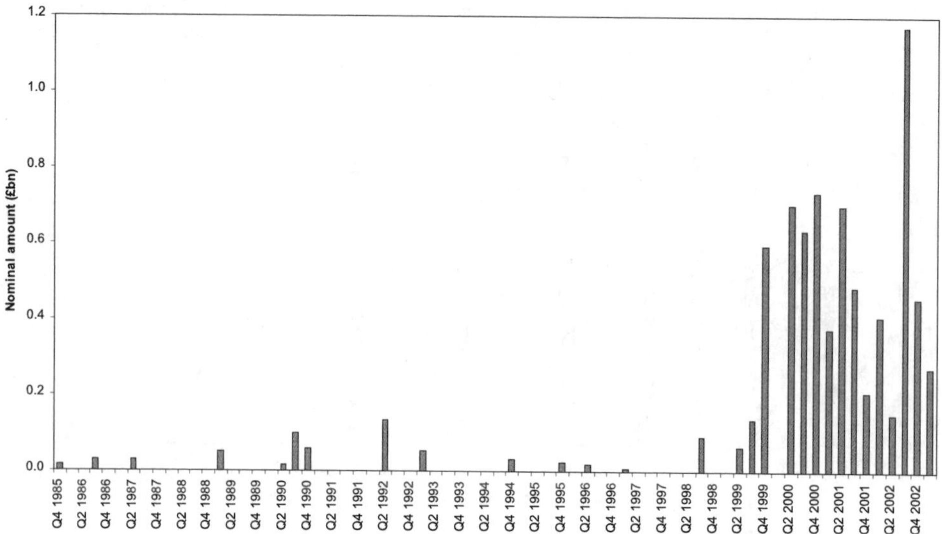

Figure 6.27 Issuance of sterling corporate and supranational index-linked bonds
Data sources: Bloomberg and UK Debt Management Office

Funding Requirement (MFR)[131] as part of the 1995 Pensions Act and, more recently, the proposed implementation of the FRS-17[132] Accounting Standard for corporations that sponsor such funds have both served to highlight this apparent asset–liability mismatch – particularly since the fall in global equity markets from their peaks in early 2000. This combination of factors has led to a collective shift in asset allocation away from equities to fixed income securities. Additionally, while these regulations mean that pension funds are encouraged but not compelled to hold inflation-linked bonds against their forecast inflation-linked pension payments, the same cannot be said of life assurance funds. Article 23 of the Third EU Life Directive stipulates that any inflation-indexed liabilities must be backed by closely matching assets,[133] thereby generating a further source of demand for both government and non-sovereign index-linked bonds.

This demand from pension funds and life insurance companies, coupled with low issuance of government debt in the years of budget surplus in the late 1990s, led to a significant reduction in real yields (as illustrated in Figure 6.21) and thereby increased the attractiveness to non-government entities of index-linked debt issuance. In 2001 the European Investment Bank (EIB) launched the first sterling LPI bond, quickly followed by several UK utility companies – an important development as LPI bonds offer a better match for many pension fund liabilities than standard RPI-linked bonds. Indeed, the issuance of government LPI bonds has been proposed on a number of occasions,

[131] The MFR was designed to ensure the solvency of pension funds by reference to the valuation of their assets and liabilities. It is due to be replaced, but however its replacement works it will not alter the essential nature of those liabilities that are index-linked.
[132] FRS denotes Financial Reporting Standard.
[133] See, for example, Hall (2001).

but each time the authorities have signalled their reluctance based on the concern that such a development might fragment liquidity across the two security types.[134]

By 2001, as a reflection of how well established corporate index-linked bonds had become in the UK, Barclays Capital decided that the asset class merited its own index. Their "Non-Gilt Linker Index" has sub-indices based on both credit rating and sector. There are currently four sector categories – agency/supranational, corporate, utility and wrapped, the latter covering bonds with an insurance guarantee as a credit enhancement.[135] By the end of March 2003 the nominal size of the market was over £7bn, equivalent to roughly 15% of the total UK index-linked market in nominal terms[136] and up from 2% just four years earlier. Developments in the sector are frequently highlighted in research publications from a number of investment banks.[137]

6.6 UNITED STATES OF AMERICA

6.6.1 A brief history of indexation in the USA

Although indexed bonds were first issued in the USA in 1742[138] it was not until 1997 that the US Treasury began issuing such securities. In the interim years there were just a handful of indexed bonds issued in the USA.[139] For instance, according to Baffi (1979), in 1782 the State of Virginia issued bonds linked to the prices of land and slaves. Both Smithson *et al.* (1995) and Barone and Masera (1997) highlight an intriguing example of an indexed bond issue by the Confederate States of America in 1863. These "cotton bonds" paid coupons semi-annually and the principal was repayable by way of drawings. Barone and Masera report that "the bonds were denominated not in dollars but in French francs and pounds sterling (at the exchange rate of 25 francs to the pound). Subscribers could convert the bonds into cotton at a rate of exchange fixed at 6 pence per pound of cotton." This issue represents perhaps the only example of a dual currency cotton index bond that has been successfully brought to market.

Irving Fisher (a strong advocate of indexation) persuaded the Rand Kardex Company, which he had co-founded, to issue an indexed bond in 1925. The security was described as a "seven percent thirty year stabilised debenture bond, registered and safeguarded as to purchasing power of both principal and interest." Indexation was to the wholesale price index and coupon payments were made quarterly. However, the indexation procedure for the bond was unusual since a cumulative 10% change in the price level was required before the indexing provision became effective. Perhaps unsurprisingly the bond was not a success, though Fisher apparently attributed this to the market's lack of familiarity with the concept of indexed debt rather than a design fault on his part.[140]

---

134 This issue was discussed in Section 2.3. See also UK Debt Management Office (2002a) for more details.

135 Barclays Capital (2002c) provides more detail on the composition and construction of these indices.

136 The corporate sector would appear to be much less significant if measured in uplifted nominal terms, since most bonds have been issued only relatively recently and so will not have such a large element of accrued inflation as the majority of index-linked gilts.

137 See, for instance, Merrill Lynch (2002), one example of a regular series of publications analysing this market.

138 See Chapter 1 for a discussion of these bonds.

139 Some possible explanations for this lack of issuance were discussed in Chapter 4.

140 See Fischer (1975). Full details of the Rand Kardex issue appear in Pigou (1929, pp. 262–263).

Weiner (1983) describes two more indexed bonds that have been issued in the USA, one by the Christiansen Corporation in 1952 and a similar issue by the Utility Manufacturing Company some years later. In fact, Lindh and Ohlsson (1992) claim that in the USA there were only four indexed bonds issued in total between the early 1920s and the mid-1980s, but that several more were issued in 1988. The most significant issuer appears to have been the Franklin Savings Association,[141] which offered two types of CPI indexed securities from January that year. *Inflation-Plus CDs* were certificates of deposit that paid monthly interest payments that were calculated as the sum of a real rate of interest plus the change in the CPI during the previous month. These CDs were available with maturities of between 1 and 10 years: the longer the maturity the higher the real interest rate.[142] *Real Yield Securities (REALs)* were 20-year interest-indexed bonds that paid coupons of 3% per annum plus the change in the CPI, on a quarterly basis. According to Bodie (1990) two other financial institutions issued indexed bonds in 1988: in August the Anchor Savings Bank issued REALs and in September the JHM Acceptance Corporation issued indexed bonds with a nominal interest rate "cap" of 14% per annum.

6.6.2 The launch of the Treasury Inflation-Indexed Securities (TIIS) market

Spiro (1989) reports that indexed bonds were given serious consideration by the Treasury in 1981 and that the issue was raised again in 1984 when the administrator of the US Labor Department's Office of Pension and Welfare Benefit Programs urged the Treasury to issue inflation-indexed bonds for purchase by pension funds. Campbell and Shiller (1996) report that, although the US Congress had long argued in favour of the introduction of indexed debt, the Treasury had traditionally always opposed the idea. However, in May 1996 the Treasury ended much speculation by announcing its intention "to issue securities that provide protection against inflation as a multi-year experiment" in order to reduce the cost of government borrowing (by saving the inflation risk premium and completing the market) and to provide a means to observe market expectations of inflation.[143]

Over a four-month period following their May 1996 announcement the Treasury consulted more than 800 market participants on some of the more technical issues regarding the instruments' design, and the process culminated in a speech by President Clinton on 25 September setting out the full details of the Treasury's indexed securities programme.[144] In his speech, the President announced that the securities would be linked to CPI-U[145] and that the first issue, with a maturity of 10 years, would be issued in January 1997 by single yield auction.[146]

[141] Bodie (1997) reports that the Franklin Savings Association has since been shut down by the financial regulators and all the depositors have been paid off.

[142] Munnell and Grolnic (1986) report that the First City National Bank of Houston also issued CPI indexed CDs. These certificates – which were referred to as *Trans Texas Inflation Protectors* (TTIPs) – were first issued in 1984 and were targeted solely at pension funds.

[143] See Department of the (US) Treasury (1996a).

[144] See Department of the (US) Treasury (1996b).

[145] Or, to give it its full title, the "non-seasonally adjusted US City Average All Items Consumer Price Index for All Urban Consumers."

[146] This was the format in use for two and five-year conventional Treasury note auctions at the time, although conventional ten-year bonds were auctioned on a multiple yield basis. The US Treasury has since moved to the single yield auction format for issuing all its securities.

On 4 December 1996 Professor Boskin reported to the US Senate on his study into the accuracy of the CPI as a measure of consumer price inflation. His main conclusion was that the US CPI typically overstated the true rate of increase in consumers' cost of living by about 1.1 percentage points annually. Publication of the report created much uncertainty among potential indexed bond purchasers, concerned that CPI-U might either undergo downward adjustment at some stage or be replaced entirely by a more representative measure of consumer price inflation. The Treasury responded in late December with an announcement that the January auction would be postponed, in order to finalise the terms and conditions for the sale of the new securities (and in particular to clarify the position of bondholders should the index be revised) as well as to allow investment firms time to review them. In the event the auction was rescheduled for 29 January 1997, representing a postponement of three weeks.

The official documentation produced by the Treasury states that, in the event that the applicable CPI is discontinued, fundamentally altered in a manner materially adverse to the interests of investors or altered by law in a similarly detrimental manner, the Bureau of Labor Statistics (BLS) will substitute an appropriate index.[147] However, from the outset the Treasury made it clear that changes to the CPI calculation methodology or coverage, arising either from the Boskin recommendations or from the recently completed BLS work on CPI measurement, would constitute "technical" rather than "fundamental" changes.

On 21 January 1997 the size of the forthcoming *Treasury Inflation-Indexed Note* (TIIN)[148] auction was announced and "When-Issued" (WI) trading began. Since the market had in general expected an issue size of \$5bn for the new security, the Treasury's announcement that it would in fact be \$7bn came as a surprise to many.[149] The WI period for the indexed note was set at eight days, one day longer than for conventional US Treasuries, in order to allow a little extra time for price discovery.

Ahead of the WI period analysts had forecast that the indexed note would trade at a real yield[150] of between $3\frac{3}{8}$% and $3\frac{5}{8}$%, though in the event WI trading opened at 3.55% before dropping to a low of 3.27% within just a few hours. However, as Figure 6.28 shows, the yield subsequently rose steadily until by the auction it was quoted at 3.485%. WI activity was fairly light, which apparently reflected the dealers' reluctance to sell the bond short – due primarily to concerns regarding liquidity of the issue.

The note was sold with a clearing yield of 3.449% at the auction on 29 January, with low and median yields of 3.20% and 3.40%, respectively. The coupon rate of $3\frac{3}{8}$% was set at the auction by rounding the clearing yield down to the nearest eighth. Bids for the indexed note totalled more than \$37bn, representing a cover ratio for the auction of

---

[147] See Department of the (US) Treasury (1997a).

[148] In January the Treasury announced that it had decided to call the new instruments Treasury Inflation-Indexed Securities, rather than Treasury Inflation-Protection Securities or TIPS (the original name that it had given the securities), but "TIPS" has become the market's preferred nomenclature for these bonds. As for conventional Treasury securities, TIIS with an original maturity of up to 10-years are referred to as *notes*, while those with an original maturity of over 10 years are referred to as *bonds*.

[149] In addition, the Treasury sold \$350mn to the Federal Reserve Banks at the clearing yield for their own account, in exchange for maturing securities.

[150] While WI trading of the indexed notes is on a real yield basis, secondary market (post-auction) trading is on a real price basis (the clean price excluding the inflation uplift).

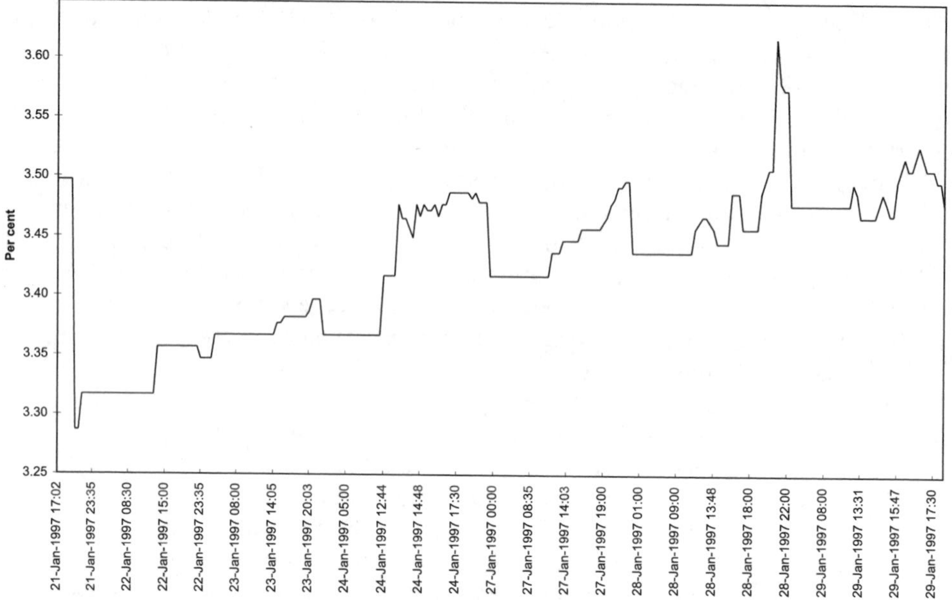

Figure 6.28 Intra-day real yield data for the "When-Issued" (WI) period ahead of the first 10-year Treasury Inflation-Indexed Note (TIIN) auction (21–29 January 1997)
Data source: Bloomberg

5.31, which was more than double the typical cover at auctions of conventional 10-year Treasury notes.

The Treasury auctioned a further \$8bn of the 10-year note on 8 April, with a clearing yield of 3.65% (some 20 basis points higher than at the January auction) combined with a significantly lower cover ratio of 2.26. Various explanations have been offered for this relatively weak result compared with the inaugural auction: the general weakness of the US bond market at the time was one contributory factor, since nominal bond yields had risen by about 25 basis points since January in anticipation of increases in the official "Fed Funds" interest rate, as was the fact that the indexed note now looked poor value when compared with similar securities in other markets (principally Canada). Bernstein and Gardner (1997) suggest that several large hedge funds and speculators were present at the first auction but not at the second and so concluded that subsequent auctions were more likely to follow the pattern of the April auction. Figure 6.29 shows the real yield history for the 2007 indexed note since its introduction.

The Treasury's third indexed note auction took place on 9 July 1997. Following the advice of its bond market advisory panel the Treasury opted to issue a new 5-year indexed note ($3\frac{5}{8}$% TIIN 2002), based on an expectation that the shorter maturity might prove to be more popular with individual investors and those investment banks that specialised in derivative products based on indexed notes. Indeed, it would appear that some players moved out of the ten-year indexed note into the new five-year note during the WI period, with the expectation that it would be easier to swap the latter's cash flows into Libor. The five-year note was also expected by many to prove less vulnerable to uncertainty over revisions to the CPI – so-called "Boskin Commission Risk". In the

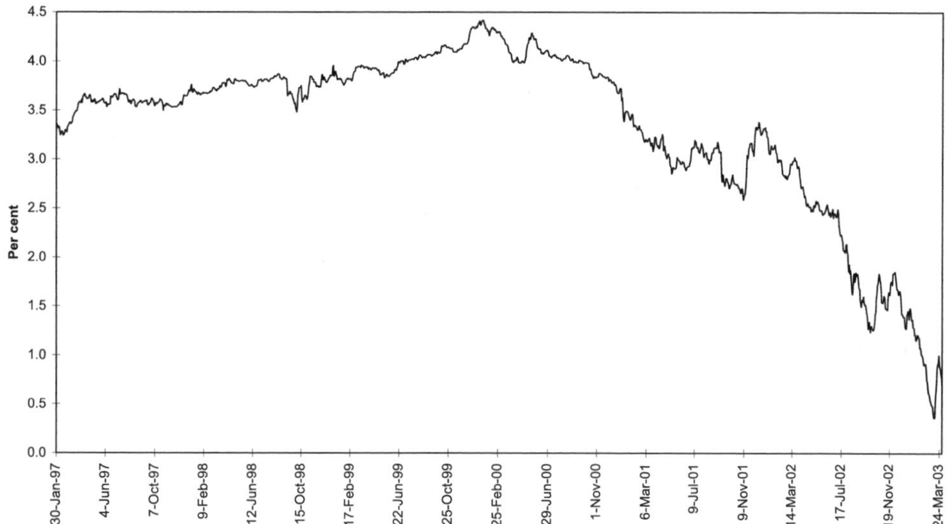

Figure 6.29 Secondary market real yield on US $3\frac{3}{8}$% Treasury Inflation-Indexed Note (TIIN) 2007

Data sources: Bloomberg and Barclays Capital

event, although the cover ratio at the $8bn auction was a healthy 3.31, the clearing yield of 3.744% was higher than the market had anticipated[151] and the spread between the median and clearing yield was larger than at the previous two ten-year auctions. This mixed reaction to the issue was largely attributed to investors' perceptions that US inflation would remain low for some time to come, though it is also likely to have reflected reaction to the Treasury's announcement in June describing plans to expand further the indexed securities market.[152] The combined effect of the falling US deficit and this planned increase in index-linked bond issuance resulted in the Treasury scaling back its planned ten-year conventional note programme in 1997, a policy shift reiterated by Deputy Secretary Lawrence Summers in a speech that September.[153]

The five-year indexed note was reopened in October 1997 when a further $8 bn nominal was auctioned. Interest in the security was greater than at the previous auction, no doubt partly in response to Alan Greenspan's warning given during congressional testimony that inflation still posed a threat to the economy. The cover ratio at this auction was up from 3.31 to 3.56 and the clearing yield of 3.60% was this time lower than many in the market had anticipated. In spite of this improved result the Treasury has not issued a five-year indexed note since, announcing in September 1998 its intention to concentrate indexed issuance at longer maturities.[154] Summary statistics from all the inflation-indexed security auctions appear in Table 6.13, while Figure 6.30 compares the real yield with the bid-to-cover ratio at each auction.

[151] See Bloomberg (1997b).
[152] See Department of the (US) Treasury (1997b).
[153] See Bloomberg (1997c).
[154] See Bloomberg (1998b).

Table 6.13 Results of US Treasury inflation-indexed security auctions (January 1997–March 2003)

Auction date	Security issued	Nominal amount issued ($mn)[a]	Real yield (%)	Bid-to-cover ratio
29 Jan 1997	$3\frac{3}{8}$% TIIN 2007	7,353.017	3.449	5.31
8 Apr 1997	$3\frac{3}{8}$% TIIN 2007	8,402.618	3.650	2.26
9 Jul 1997	$3\frac{5}{8}$% TIIN 2002	8,401.066	3.744	3.31
8 Oct 1997	$3\frac{5}{8}$% TIIN 2002	8,411.717	3.600	3.56
8 Jan 1998	$3\frac{5}{8}$% TIIN 2008	8,408.613	3.730	2.94
8 Apr 1998	$3\frac{5}{8}$% TIIB 2028	8,402.158	3.740	2.58
8 Jul 1998	$3\frac{5}{8}$% TIIB 2028	8,404.017	3.680	2.38
7 Oct 1998	$3\frac{5}{8}$% TIIN 2008	8,400.538	3.650	1.92
6 Jan 1999	$3\frac{7}{8}$% TIIN 2009	8,530.979	3.898	3.12
7 Apr 1999	$3\frac{7}{8}$% TIIB 2029	7,350.408	3.899	2.10
7 Jul 1999	$3\frac{7}{8}$% TIIN 2009	7,368.472	4.040	2.10
6 Oct 1999	$3\frac{7}{8}$% TIIB 2029	7,368.469	4.138	1.92
12 Jan 2000	$4\frac{1}{4}$% TIIN 2010	6,316.921	4.338	3.07
12 Jul 2000	$4\frac{1}{4}$% TIIN 2010	5,001.620	4.030	2.35
11 Oct 2000	$3\frac{7}{8}$% TIIB 2029	5,000.084	3.953	1.98
10 Jan 2001	$3\frac{1}{2}$% TIIN 2011	6,000.430	3.522	1.68
11 Jul 2001	$3\frac{1}{2}$% TIIN 2011	5,000.004	3.500	1.90
10 Oct 2001	$3\frac{3}{8}$% TIIB 2032	5,000.011	3.465	2.23
9 Jan 2002	$3\frac{3}{8}$% TIIN 2012	6,000.004	3.480	2.39
10 Jul 2002	3% TIIN 2012	10,010.395	3.099	2.43
9 Oct 2002	3% TIIN 2012	7,000.047	2.260	1.36
8 Jan 2003	3% TIIN 2012	6,000.109	2.340	2.22

Data sources: Department of the (US) Treasury and Bloomberg. TIIN = Treasury Inflation-Indexed Note; TIIB = Treasury Inflation-Indexed Bond.
[a] Includes stock awarded to the Federal Reserve Banks for their own account in exchange for maturing securities, as well as stock sold to foreign official institutions.

Following its established pattern of quarterly indexed note issuance,[155] the first auction of 1998 took place in January and was for $8bn nominal of a new 2008 indexed note. However, at the next auction in April the Treasury opted to launch its much anticipated first 30-year indexed bond. As at the previous four auctions, the nominal size to be issued was again set at $8bn. With inflation running at close to its lowest level for several decades (see Figure 6.31) early 1998 did not, on the surface of things, appear to be an ideal time to issue indexed securities, although this concern was mitigated somewhat by the choice of a bond of long maturity and hence one that would be less affected by short-term inflation expectations.

[155] Although indexed securities were initially auctioned on a quarterly basis the frequency was reduced during the years of a fiscal budget surplus (discussed later). The Treasury returned to a quarterly schedule in May 2003.

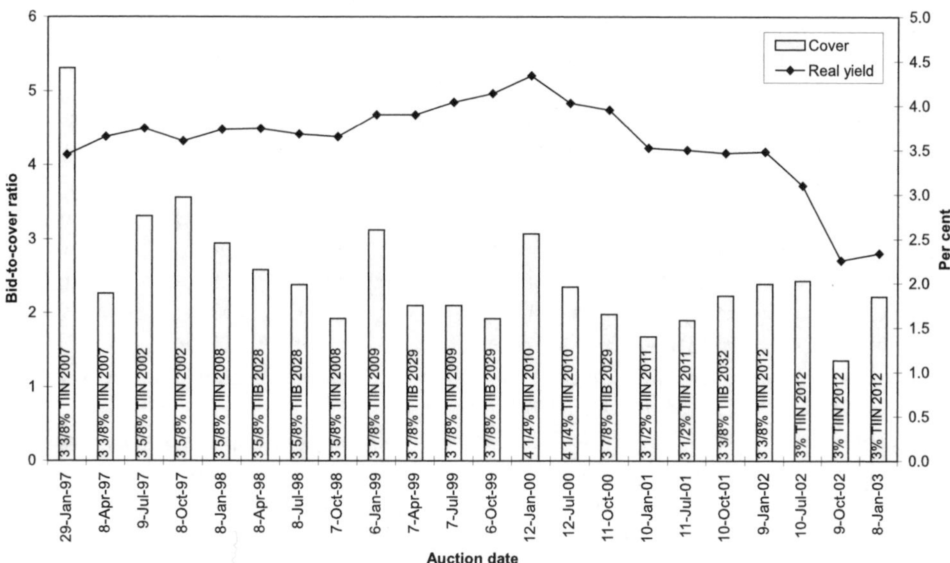

Figure 6.30 Real yield and bid-to-cover ratio at Treasury Inflation-Indexed Security (TIIS) auctions (January 1997–March 2003)
Data source: Department of the (US) Treasury

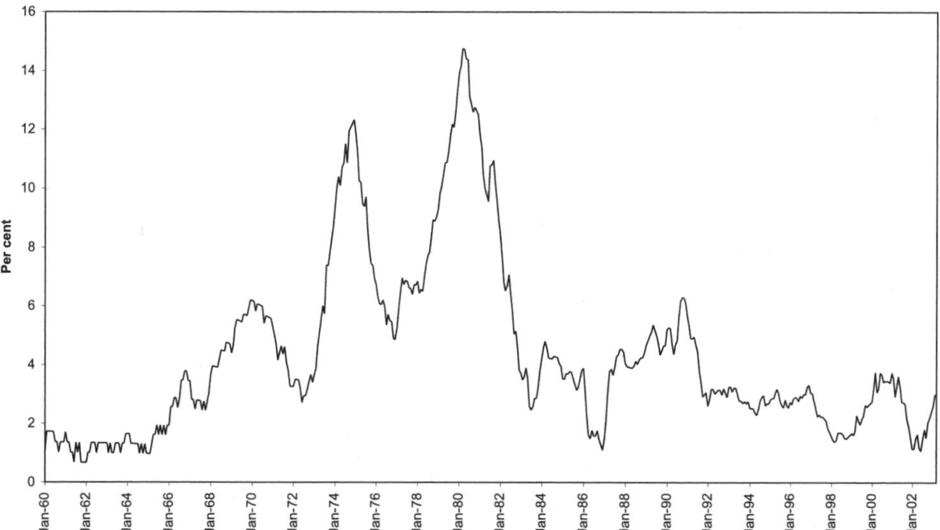

Figure 6.31 Annual percentage change in the US Consumer Price Index for All Urban Consumers (CPI-U)
Data source: Bureau of Labor Statistics

Consequently, market sentiment going into the auction was mixed; some analysts speculated that it could be the most successful TIPS auction to date, while others reported virtually no institutional interest. Valuation of the bond proved to be similarly contentious, with at least one market maker of the view that the new bond would trade cheap to the 2008 indexed note while others expected the opposite.[156] Although the cover ratio for the auction of 2.58 was relatively low, the clearing yield of 3.740% was in line with expectations, coming just below the median 3.753% yield anticipated by analysts surveyed by *Bloomberg News*[157] and 4.8 basis points below the 2008 note. Indeed, by the end of April the new 30-year security had richened to trade at a yield spread 9 basis points dear to the 10-year TIIN.[158]

Shortly after the auction the BLS published its proposed changes to the calculation of the CPI, to take effect from January 1999. These amendments were part of a series of ongoing technical changes that have subsequently reduced the CPI's annual growth rate significantly, perhaps by as much as 0.65%.[159] In February 2000 the US General Accounting Office published a report entitled *Consumer Price Index: Update of Boskin Commission's Estimate of Bias*, in which four of the original members voiced their opinions on the effect of the BLS improvements.[160]

July 1998 saw a reopening of the 2028 indexed bond, and in September the Treasury unveiled its planned inflation-indexed issuance programme for 1999. Along with the announcement of its intention to discontinue 5-year indexed notes (see above), the Treasury indicated its intention to issue 10-year indexed notes in January and July and 30-year indexed bonds in April and October. Further interest in the sector was generated by an announcement on 23 November 1998 that the Federal Reserve Bank of New York had bought $437mn of inflation-indexed securities through one of its regular coupon pass operations.[161] Although the Fed regularly purchased indexed securities at auction and may have already purchased further holdings through coupon passes, this was the first coupon pass at which *only* indexed securities were eligible. Bonds purchased by the Fed in this manner are added to its permanent reserves, implying that these operations effectively reduce the supply of TIPS available to the market. Although most analysts saw the Fed's purchase as a natural progression in the development of the product, there was some speculation that the Fed's motivation was to stimulate interest in indexed securities on behalf of the Treasury. According to Wade (1998) such intervention puts at risk one of the original aims of the TIPS programme – the existence of an asset class that provides market signals of inflation expectations. Fed statistics show that it held $12.8bn nominal of indexed securities as at 7 May 2003, with the largest holding, $2.49bn of the 2028 bond, representing 13.1% of that issue.[162]

6.6.3 The expansion of the TIIS programme in the fiscal surplus years

Gary Gensler, Assistant Treasury Secretary responsible for financial markets, indicated in February 1999 that the Treasury might need to sell fewer government securities at less frequent auctions in forthcoming years due to the continued improvement in the US government's fiscal budget and that the authorities would also consider the intro-

[156] See Barclays Capital (1998a).
[157] Source: Bloomberg (1998a).
[158] Source: Barclays Capital (1998b, p. 10).
[159] Source: Barclays Capital (2002b).
[160] See US General Accounting Office (2000), which is available on the GAO's website: www.gao.gov. A useful critique of this report appears in Merrill Lynch (2000).
[161] See Bloomberg (1998c).
[162] Source: www.ny.frb.org/pihome/statistics/soma.shtml. The holdings figures represent a combination of bonds purchased at auction and those purchased through coupon passes.

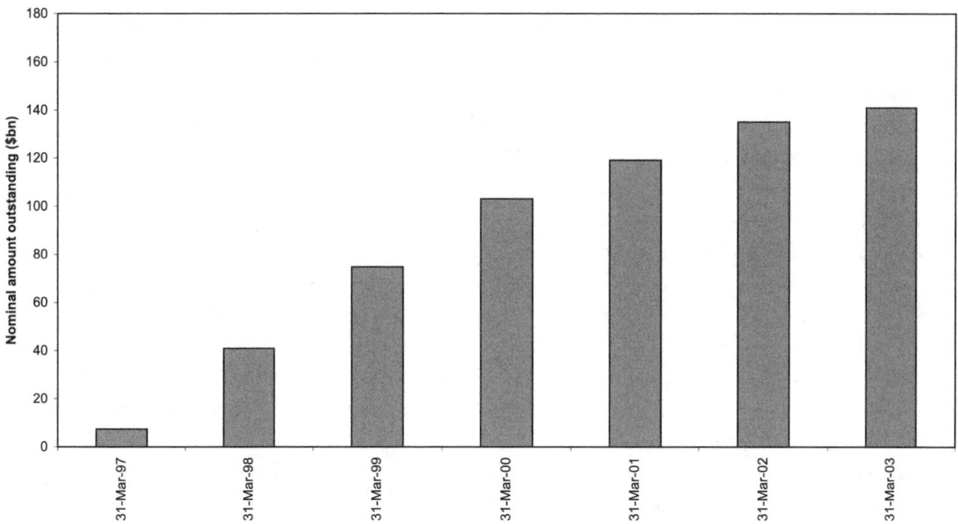

Figure 6.32 Growth in the US Treasury Inflation-Indexed Securities (TIIS) market
Data source: Department of the (US) Treasury

duction of buy-backs as a tool to help manage the debt portfolio. Despite already having significantly reduced annual issuance of bills, notes and bonds, as well as having eliminated some issues and retired debt, the Federal budget moved into surplus during the 1998 fiscal year to the tune of approximately $70bn. This was the first occasion in three decades that the US government had run a budget surplus and its forecast surplus for 1999 was even higher at over $79bn. In response, the Treasury announced plans to reduce the frequency of its nominal 2-year note and 30-year bond auctions, but confirmed its intention to proceed with the three remaining indexed security auctions planned for 1999 – albeit each reduced in size to $7bn from the usual $8bn. The April and October auctions saw the establishment of a new 2029 indexed bond, while the July auction was a reopening of the 2009 indexed note that had initially been launched the previous January.

The amount of securities on offer was cut further at the January 2000 auction, which was for $6bn of a new 2010 indexed note. The security was issued with a $4\frac{1}{4}$% coupon, reflecting the rise in US real yields that had occurred during the course of 1999 – see Figure 6.29. In its February 2000 financing announcement the Treasury outlined how it intended to continue reducing the size of the public debt in the light of the continued Federal surplus:[163] in addition to yet another reduction in issuance of nominal securities, plans to introduce cash buy-backs of bonds with maturities of 10 years or more were unveiled. The 30-year indexed bond auction in April was also cancelled and the planned size of 10-year indexed note auctions was again reduced from $6bn to $5bn. The slowdown in the growth of the TIIS market in recent years is illustrated in Figure 6.32.

[163] See Bloomberg (2000).

The vulnerability of indexed bond markets to errors in the calculation of the underlying price index was highlighted in September 2000, when the BLS announced that a miscalculation of the CPI had occurred and as a result the index values for the period from January to August would have to be revised and republished. The error related to the calculation of quality adjustments for reported changes of air-conditioning equipment in rental properties. Initially, there was speculation that a significant revision, perhaps up to +0.3%, would have to be made to the headline series, though in the event the change turned out to be less than 0.1%.[164] The revisions disadvantaged investors who had sold indexed securities prior to the BLS announcement as well as those who had received interest payments during the year since, under the official terms and conditions for all TIPS, neither group will have been entitled to additional compensation.[165] As a direct consequence of this episode the Treasury opted to reopen the 2029 indexed bond for a second time at the October auction "to preclude any computational issues regarding the Reference CPI that would be associated with the issuance of a new security".[166] This came as a surprise to many who had expected a new 2030 indexed bond to be launched in line with the established precedent that each indexed security was reopened just once.

Throughout 2001 there was much speculation and uncertainty surrounding the future of the TIIS programme. In February the Treasury Borrowing Advisory Committee of the Bond Market Association (BMA) repeated an earlier recommendation that the Treasury cease issuing 30-year indexed bonds, and then in May it went further and suggested that the whole TIIS programme should be suspended.[167] The Committee justified its recommendation as follows:

> *To date, calculations suggest that the Treasury has made $1.5billion extra in coupon payments under the program compared to what would have been paid if nominal securities had been issued. Other estimates of the incremental cost of the program are even higher. Continued issuance of indexed securities in an era of large budget surpluses only exacerbates the liquidity problem in the benchmark nominal debt programs.*

In the event the Treasury decided to continue with the TIPS programme, although three weeks after its October auction of a new 2030 indexed bond it announced that both 30-year nominal and indexed bond issuance would be discontinued. This development was largely unexpected, not least as it came as expectations began to form that government finances were set to sharply deteriorate in the years ahead. Indeed, many analysts were now beginning to forecast a small deficit for 2002, in contrast to the large surplus envisaged for the same year just months earlier.[168] The market reacted strongly to the news, with bonds staging their biggest one-day rally since the stock market crash of October 1987.[169]

In his Quarterly Refunding Statement for February 2002, Assistant Secretary Brian

[164] The All-Items index for August 2000 was revised up from 172.7 to 172.8.
[165] See Barclays Capital (2000).
[166] See Department of the (US) Treasury (2000b).
[167] See Treasury Advisory Committee of the Bond Market Association (2001), a critique of which appears in Barclays Capital (2001a).
[168] For example, analysts at one investment bank reported that they had revised their estimate for the 2002 budget balance from an initial $176bn surplus to a deficit of approximately $25–50bn – see Barclays Capital (2001b).
[169] Bloomberg (2001) reports that the nominal 30-year Treasury bond gained $5\frac{7}{32}$ points, pushing its yield down by 33 basis points. The price action may have been exacerbated by the accidental release of the information 20 minutes early on the Treasury website.

Roseboro confirmed that the Treasury itself also envisaged small budgetary deficits for both 2002 and 2003 and went on to note that both the size and frequency of auctions were under review, along with the policy governing the reopening of 10-year indexed notes.[170] The statement also confirmed that the Treasury intended to continue with the buy-back programme initiated in March 2000.[171] Three buy-back operations were scheduled for the quarter ahead and, in an interesting move, the Treasury announced that at the second of these it would repurchase up to $250mn nominal of inflation-indexed bonds in addition to $750mn nominal of conventional securities.[172] This buy-back took place on 18 April and $225mn nominal and $25mn nominal of the 2029 and 2028 bonds, respectively, were repurchased. This was the first and only time that TIIS were included in a buy-back operation; the programme itself was suspended after the third operation of the quarter on 25 April.

6.6.4 Recent developments in the market for inflation-indexed securities in the USA

The Treasury used the May 2002 quarterly refunding announcement as an opportunity to publicise further changes to the TIIS programme.[173] In response to a suggestion by the BMA it indicated its intention to shorten the WI period for TIPS auctions to two days with effect from July. It also announced that the new 10-year indexed note scheduled for launch at that auction would subsequently be reopened twice, in both October and January. This would make it the first TIIS to be auctioned three times, aside from the 2029 bond that had been reopened a second time purely in response to the confusion surrounding the calculation of the CPI in late 2000 (see above). Although the BMA had advised equal-sized auctions the Treasury instead opted to "front-load" supply, with $9bn nominal of 3% TIIN 2012 auctioned at the July auction[174] followed by $7bn and $6bn at the subsequent reopenings in October 2002 and January 2003, respectively.[175] This increase in supply reflected the further deterioration of the fiscal situation: in February 2001 the government had forecast a surplus of $238bn for the 2002 fiscal year, but by July 2002 its projection had been revised to a deficit of $165bn – a change in forecast equivalent to approximately 4% of GDP.

The second half of 2002 also saw the Treasury launch a key initiative to promote inflation-indexed securities. During the remainder of 2002 and in 2003, Assistant Secretary Brian Roseboro and his deputy, Timothy Bitsberger, both spoke at a variety of conferences and seminars to describe the development of the TIIS programme over the preceding five years as well as to encourage greater awareness of the asset class. In his address to the BMA's Inflation-Linked Securities Conference in New York in June 2003,[176] Bitsberger highlighted that a much higher percentage of 10-year indexed notes has been allocated to "longer term" investors, such as pension funds, than is the case for 10-year nominal Treasury notes – see Figures 6.33 and 6.34.

---

[170] See Department of the (US) Treasury (2002a).

[171] For the terms and conditions of buy-back operations see Department of the (US) Treasury (2000a).

[172] See Department of the (US) Treasury (2002b).

[173] See Department of the (US) Treasury (2002c).

[174] In addition, more than $1bn nominal of the indexed note was sold to the Federal Reserve – see Department of the (US) Treasury (2002d).

[175] The redemption in July 2002 of the five-year TIIN was a further reason for front-loading supply in this manner, to give investors in the 2002 note the opportunity to reinvest in the TIIS market.

[176] See Bitsberger (2003).

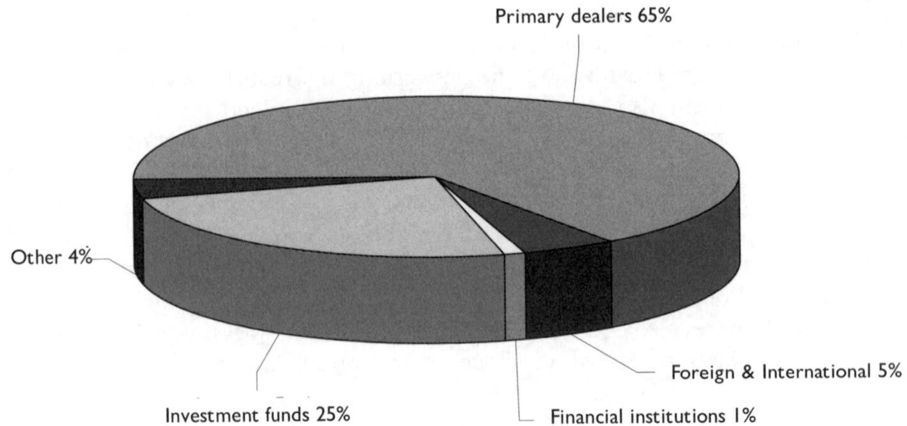

Figure 6.33 Distribution of competitive auction awards of 10-year inflation-indexed notes (based on July 2002, October 2002 and January 2003 auctions). *Notes*: investment funds includes investment managers, mutual funds and hedge funds; financial institutions includes non-primary dealers, depository institutions and insurance companies; other includes individuals, non-financial companies and other financial companies
Data source: Department of the (US) Treasury

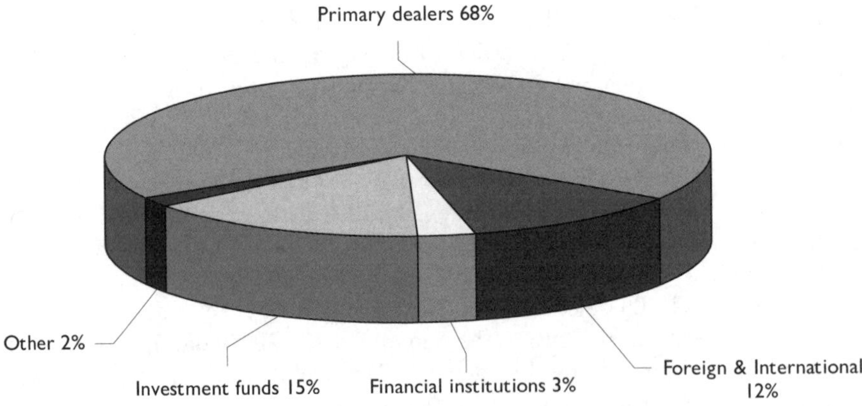

Figure 6.34 Distribution of competitive auction awards of 10-year fixed rate nominal notes (based on August 2002, November 2002 and February 2003 auctions). *Notes*: investment funds includes investment managers, mutual funds and hedge funds; financial institutions includes non-primary dealers, depository institutions and insurance companies; other includes individuals, non-financial companies and other financial companies
Data source: Department of the (US) Treasury

By broadening its investor base and diversifying its funding sources in this way, he expected the Treasury to be able to reduce its costs over time. He had previously been critical of analysis that purported to demonstrate that debt financed through the TIPS programme had proved more expensive than could have been achieved through issuance solely of nominal securities (see Chapter 4), arguing that it was too early to pass

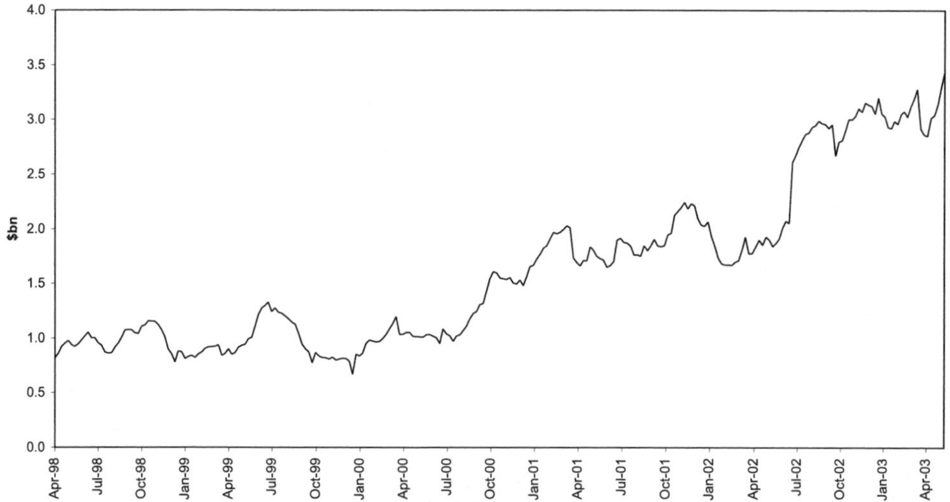

Figure 6.35 Average daily dealer transactions in Treasury Inflation-Indexed Securities (TIIS) (three-month moving average)
Data source: Federal Reserve Bank of New York

judgement, reasoning that "cost-effectiveness should only be determined after a product has been through an entire interest rate cycle."[177]

In the same speech, Deputy Assistant Secretary Bitsberger also discussed the relative liquidity of the conventional and inflation-indexed Treasury markets. While conceding that TIIS might never trade with the same market depth as their nominal counterparts, he claimed that liquidity was good when measured against any other standard and, moreover, was likely to get better. Indeed, secondary market trading of TIPS has significantly increased recently, with average daily volumes of $3.4bn recorded by the end of May 2003 which represented an 87% increase on the previous year (see Figure 6.35).[178] Sack and Elsasser (2002) report that, while the weekly turnover rate[179] for TIIS is significantly lower than that for benchmark nominal Treasury issues, it is in fact fairly close to that for nominal off-the-run Treasuries – although bid–offer spreads for the latter are still somewhat narrower (see Table 6.14).

Early in the life of the TIIS market it had been anticipated that the launch of exchange-traded futures and options contracts based on these securities would help improve the liquidity of the underlying bond market. On 3 July 1997 the CBOT introduced futures and options contracts on both medium- and long-term Treasury inflation-indexed notes,[180] and these were joined by comparable contracts on inflation-indexed bonds from 2 April 1998. These derivatives were designed to allow traders to

[177] See Bitsberger (2002).

[178] Note: over this period the nominal size of the TIIS market grew by less than 5%.

[179] The weekly turnover rate is defined to be the total weekly trading volume as a percentage of outstanding debt.

[180] Although these were the first futures contracts on US indexed securities, between 1985 and 1987 the New York Coffee, Sugar and Cocoa Exchange traded futures contracts on the CPI, though these were not a great success (see Horrigan, 1987). For the medium-term contract, deliverable Treasury indexed notes had an original maturity of up to five years and three months and a residual maturity of at least four years and three months. In the case of the long-term contract, the deliverable basket included any Treasury indexed note with residual maturity of between six and a half and ten years. The contract specifications appear in Chicago Board of Trade (1997a, b).

Table 6.14 Typical bid–offer spreads for US Treasury securities (in $\frac{1}{32}$nds of price)

	Maturities of five years or less	Maturities greater than five years
On-the-run nominal securities	$\frac{1}{4}$	$\frac{1}{4}$ to $\frac{1}{2}$
Off-the-run nominal securities	$\frac{1}{4}$ to $\frac{1}{2}$	$\frac{1}{4}$ to 1
Inflation-indexed securities	1 to 2	2 to 6

Reproduced from Sack and Elsasser (2002) by permission of Brian Sack. These spreads are for moderate-sized trades and are quoted in units of \$$\frac{1}{32}$ per \$100 notional as is the convention in the US Treasury bond market. Data are based on an informal survey of dealers by the Federal Reserve Bank of New York taken in early 2002.

take a position or to hedge movements either in real yields or in the CPI and were thereby expected to enhance overall liquidity. The Chicago Board of Trade (1997c) reports that the US Treasury "provided valuable input into the research needed to develop the contract", emphasised when Roger Anderson (then Deputy Assistant Secretary for Federal Finance at the Treasury) rang the opening bell at the Exchange on the day of their launch.

However, Richard Sandor (Second Vice Chairman of CBOT) sounded a note of caution at the time, warning that trading volume in the futures contracts might prove to be limited until investor interest built up. This was borne out by the first day's trading which saw a three-point bid–offer spread develop: buyers were prepared to pay \$94-00, while sellers sought \$97-00.[181] By the end of August 1997 only 14 contracts had traded on the 10-year indexed note and none on the 5-year note, compared with 4 million and 2 million, respectively, on the corresponding nominal Treasury contracts. Continued lack of interest led CBOT to withdraw the 10-year TIIS contract in March 1998, and the 5- and 30-year contracts met the same fate in June 2000. It is possible to conclude that these contracts were introduced too early in the life of the TIIS market and that perhaps they would prove more successful if launched today. An interesting development in June 2003 was the launch by Deutsche Bank and Goldman Sachs of monthly auctions of options and forwards on the level of CPI-U. This followed the successful launch of similar contracts on Euro-HICP ex-tobacco in May 2003 and should aid hedging in the TIPS market. More detail on these contracts is provided in Chapter 8.

The design of US Treasury inflation-indexed securities is based on that of Canada's RRBs. Like the Canadian bonds, TIIS are semi-annual CIBs with a three-month indexation lag (full details of the indexation and the price–yield relationship appear in Appendix 6.6). The only difference between the Canadian and American instruments is the "deflation floor" inherent in the latter, as the US Treasury guarantees that the nominal redemption payment of all its securities will not be less than the par value at issue (i.e., the government protects the nominal value of the principal should deflation occur over the life of the bond).[182] Details of the 10 US Treasury inflation-indexed

[181] See Bloomberg (1997a).

[182] Note that the same protection does not apply to the coupon payments. For full details of the terms and conditions of the US securities readers should refer to Department of the (US) Treasury (1997a).

Table 6.15 US Treasury Inflation-Indexed Securities (TIIS)

Coupon (%)	Maturity date	Date of first issue	Nominal amount outstanding ($mn)[a]	Uplifted nominal amount ($mn)
$3\frac{3}{8}$	15 Jan 2007	6 Feb 1997	15,758	18,069
$3\frac{5}{8}$	15 Jan 2008	15 Jan 1998	16,812	18,905
$3\frac{7}{8}$	15 Jan 2009	15 Jan 1999	15,902	17,616
$4\frac{1}{4}$	15 Jan 2010	18 Jan 2000	11,321	12,225
$3\frac{1}{2}$	15 Jan 2011	16 Jan 2001	11,001	11,483
$3\frac{3}{8}$	15 Jan 2012	15 Jan 2002	6,004	6,143
3	15 Jul 2012	15 Jul 2002	23,018	23,258
$3\frac{5}{8}$	15 Apr 2028	15 Apr 1998	16,808	18,852
$3\frac{7}{8}$	15 Apr 2029	15 Apr 1999	19,722	21,546
$3\frac{3}{8}$	15 Apr 2032	15 Oct 2001	5,012	5,130

Data source: Department of the (US) Treasury (2003b) (figures as at 31 March 2003). *Note:* there are some slight discrepancies between the amounts outstanding in this table and those in Table 6.13. This is because the figures in Table 6.13 were obtained from the US Treasury's auction results press releases, which do not necessarily reflect the full non-comp allocation of stock – regulations stipulate that to be accepted, postal non-competitive bids must be postmarked by midnight the day before an auction but can be received as late as the issue date. In addition to reflecting the full allocation of stock at each auction, Table 6.15 also reflects the buy-back operation that took place in April 2002.

[a] Includes stock awarded to the Federal Reserve Banks for their own account in exchange for maturing securities, as well as stock sold to foreign official institutions.

securities in issue at the end of March 2003 appear in Table 6.15. At that time the nominal size of the TIIS market stood at $141.4bn or $153.2bn when the inflation uplift was added, the latter valuation representing 4.6% of total marketable public debt as illustrated in Figure 6.36. In its May 2003 Quarterly Refunding Statement the Treasury announced its intention to return to the quarterly pattern of auctions last witnessed in 1999, with new 10-year indexed notes to be auctioned each January and July followed by a single reopening three months later, in April and October, respectively.[183]

All TIPS have been eligible for stripping into separate indexed cash flows since the outset of the market, although initially coupon strips from two different securities were not fungible. In its January 1997 document setting out the terms and conditions for its indexed securities the Treasury explained that "the Department is evaluating alternative methodologies for creating fungible stripped interest components from inflation-indexed securities. However, we are not yet in a position to adopt a methodology that would permit fungibility".[184] The rules that govern bond reconstitution were published in June 1998,[185] but did not take effect until 31 March 1999, in order to allow potential investors sufficient time to prepare. Grieves and Sunner (1999) explain the difficulties in making TIIS strips fungible and how the Treasury solved these problems. The first strip transaction took place in November 2000, and at the end of March

[183] See Department of the (US) Treasury (2003c).
[184] Department of the (US) Treasury (1997a, p. 14).
[185] See Department of the (US) Treasury (1998a).

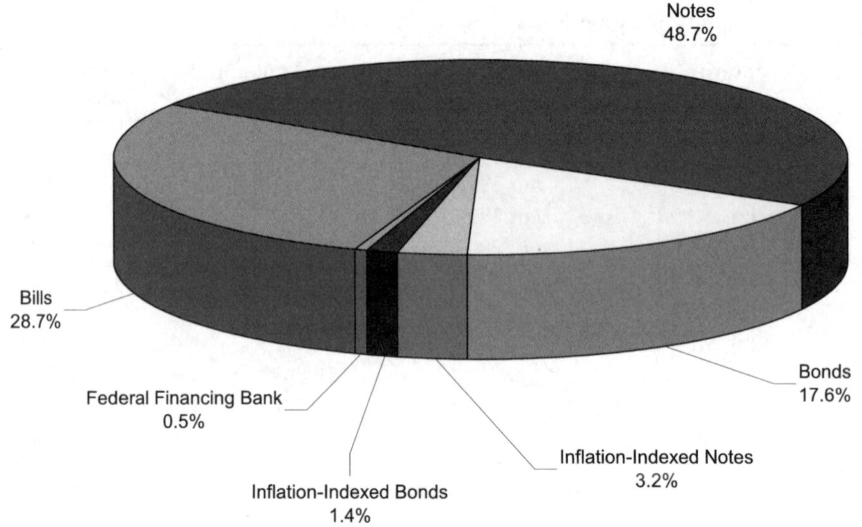

Figure 6.36 Composition of US marketable public debt (as at 31 March 2003). *Note*: amounts for inflation-indexed securities are quoted in terms of uplifted nominal
Data source: Department of the (US) Treasury.

2003 small amounts of three TIIS were held in stripped form: 0.59% of the 2008 TIIS, 0.03% of the 2028 TIIS and 0.64% of the 2029 TIIS.[186]

The increase due to inflation in the value of the principal of US indexed securities is treated as current income for tax purposes. Tax on this uplift is therefore levied on an annual basis, even though the uplift payment itself is not made until maturity. As discussed in Chapter 2, this feature may limit demand for these instruments to that from tax-exempt investors and those taxpayers with tax-deferred accounts. For this reason the Treasury launched non-marketable inflation-indexed savings bonds in September 1998 (referred to as *Series I Bonds*), aimed specifically at small investors.[187] Interest on I-Bonds accrues monthly, compounds semi-annually and is payable at redemption, but income tax is deferred until the securities are cashed in or until they stop earning interest after the full 30-years.

The earnings rate on I-Bonds is the combination of two rates: a fixed rate of return that remains constant over the life of the bond; and a rate of inflation that is adjusted every six months in line with movements in the CPI-U. The Treasury sets the fixed rate for new I-Bonds each May and November; the semi-annual inflation rate for all May cash flows is announced that month and is a measure of inflation over the six-month period from October to March immediately preceding the payment date. Likewise the inflation rate announced each November represents inflation over the period from the previous April to September. For example, on 1 May 2003 the Treasury announced that I-Bonds sold between May and October 2003 would have an earnings rate of 4.66% for the first six months of their life.[188] This earnings rate consisted of a 1.10% fixed rate of

[186] Source: Department of the (US) Treasury (2003b).
[187] See Department of the (US) Treasury (1998b).
[188] See Department of the (US) Treasury (2003d).

Figure 6.37 Specimen $1,000 US Series I Savings Bond
Reproduced by permission of the Department of the (US) Treasury

return and a 3.54% annualised rate of CPI-U inflation (since the CPI-U increased from 181.0 to 184.2 from September 2002 to March 2003, a six-month increase of 1.77%).[189] Like TIIS, I-Bonds are also issued with deflation protection but in the form of a guarantee that the earnings rate will never fall below zero.

I-Bonds are sold at face value in small denominations,[190] and individual investors can purchase up to $30,000 each calendar year. The bonds pay interest for as long as 30-years, but cannot be redeemed within the first year of issue, and investors who redeem their bonds after less than five years are required to forfeit the most recent three months' interest on the bond. Each I-Bond denomination features a prominent figure from a range of backgrounds and disciplines. For example, Dr Martin Luther King, Jr, appears on the $100 bond and Albert Einstein on the $1,000 bond – see Figure 6.37. By the end of March 2003 the nominal amount of I-Bonds outstanding was significant, standing at around $15bn. For more details on I-Bonds see Department of the (US) Treasury (2003a).

A number of government agencies, corporations and municipal issuers have issued inflation-indexed securities since the Treasury's inaugural launch in 1997. Swaps have played an important role in this process, since most issuers have proved unwilling to bear the inflation risk inherent in the instruments and so have used the derivatives market to swap CPI risk for nominal interest rate risk. It is unlikely to be a coincidence that the majority of non-Treasury issues have been IIBs, a structure that is much better suited for this activity compared with that of the Treasury's indexed notes. A large proportion of this issuance occurred immediately after the first TIPS auction, and it has been suggested that much of it represented an opportunistic effort to generate swaps

[189] More precisely, in the case of the example, the earnings rate was calculated as:

$$200 \times \left[\left(1 + \frac{1.10}{200}\right)\left(\frac{184.2}{181.0}\right) - 1\right]$$

[190] I-Bonds are currently sold in denominations of $50, $75, $100, $200, $500, $1,000, $5,000 and $10,000.

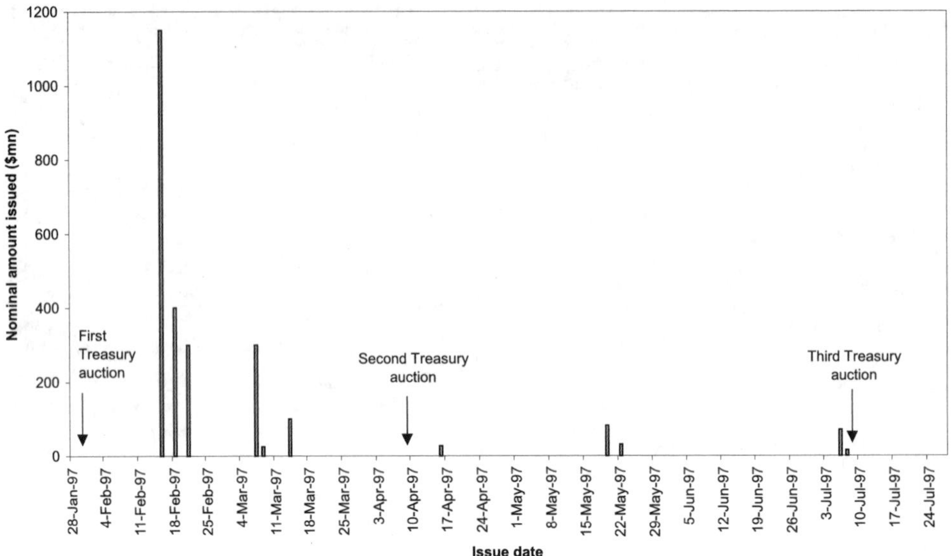

Figure 6.38 Issuance of US non-Treasury Inflation-Indexed Securities (end-January 1997 to end-July)
Data source: Bloomberg

business as opposed to being a true reflection of fundamental interest in the product – see Harper (1997). Figure 6.38 emphasises the concentration of non-government issues brought in February and March 1997, with subsequent activity that year being both smaller and less frequent.

Table 6.16 provides details of all non-Treasury inflation-indexed securities issued before the end of March 2003, at which point the size of the market stood at over $2.5bn. There has only been a handful of issues since 1997, as Table 6.16 illustrates, perhaps vindicating those who argued at the time that there would be only limited demand for corporate indexed issues, on the grounds that such risk-averse investors would demand an instrument that removes credit as well as inflation risks (for example, see Pesek, 1997).

Hammond (2002) suggests two reasons for the recent increase in interest in the TIIS market, one transient and the other more fundamental. The first relates to the strong recent performance of indexed securities relative to other asset classes (in particular, equities), as illustrated by Table 6.17. The second and more fundamental reason is a growing appreciation of the benefits of indexed securities among US investors, along with an increased acceptance that they constitute a distinct asset class in their own right. Hammond reports that at least seven US mutual funds have been created whose assets are primarily or exclusively invested in indexed bonds and that many major endowment portfolios invest between 5% and 10% of their funds in inflation-indexed securities. This, he argues, demonstrates that indexed bonds are at last beginning to play a significant role in asset allocation and retirement savings decisions in the USA.

Table 6.16 Non-government inflation-indexed securities in the USA (January 1997–March 2003)

Issuer	Issue date	Bond type	Nominal amount issued (US$mn)	Maturity (years)	Coupon
Federal Farm Credit Banks & Funding Company	14 Feb 1997	IIB	100.0	5.0	CPI+300bp
Federal Home Loan Bank	14 Feb 1997	IIB	300.0	5.0	CPI+315bp
JP Morgan & Company	14 Feb 1997	IIB	200.0	15.0	CPI+400bp
Salomon Inc.	14 Feb 1997	CIB	450.0	5.0	3.650
Toyota Motor Credit Corporation	14 Feb 1997	IIB	100.0	5.0	CPI+320bp
Nationsbank Corporation	18 Feb 1997	IIB	100.0	5.0	CPI+325bp
Tennessee Valley Authority	18 Feb 1997	CIB	300.0	9.9	3.375
Federal Home Loan Bank	20 Feb 1997	IIB	100.0	10.0	CPI+337.5bp
Student Loan Marketing Association	20 Feb 1997	IIB	200.0	3.0	CPI+290bp
Korea Development Bank	6 Mar 1997	IIB	300.0	5.0	CPI+340bp
Merrill Lynch	7 Mar 1997	IIB	25.0	5.0	CPI+300bp
Federal National Mortgage Association	13 Mar 1997	IIB	100.0	5.0	CPI+314bp
City of Orlando Waste Water System	16 Apr 1997	IIB	27.0	18.5	CPI+125bp
City of Gulf Breeze	20 May 1997	IIB	81.5	20.5	CPI+180bp
Illinois Development Finance Authority	22 May 1997	IIB	31.0	21.6	CPI+210bp
Delaware Valley Regional Finance Authority	7 Jul 1997	IIB	70.0	30.0	CPI+188bp
Sarasota County Public Hospital Board, Florida	8 Jul 1997	IIB	15.0	24.2	CPI+205bp
JP Morgan Chase	20 Mar 2001	IZCB	15.0	8.8	0
Connecticut State	28 Jun 2001	IIB	20.0	11.0	CPI+143bp
Florida State Muncipal Power Agency	30 Apr 2002	IIB	85.0	10.4	CPI+140bp
New York City Municipal Water Finance Authority	9 Jul 2002	IIB	20.0	10.9	CPI+153bp
Detroit Water Supply System	30 Jan 2003	IIB	18.5	11.4	CPI+136bp
Massachusetts State	12 Mar 2003	IIB	97.5	11.7	CPI+181bp

Data source: Bloomberg
IIB = Interest Indexed Bond; CIB = Capital Indexed Bond; IZCB = Indexed Zero-Coupon Bond; bp = basis points.

Table 6.17 Returns of different US asset classes (1997–2002)

	Lehman Index of Corporate & Government Bonds (%)	10-year nominal Treasury note (%)	10-year Treasury indexed note (%)	S&P 500 Index with dividends (%)
2002 returns	12.0	14.9	16.4	−22.1
Average annualised return	8.3	8.9	7.5	3.3
Monthly volatility	1.3	1.9	1.1	5.4
Annual volatility	5.7	8.2	6.1	22.0

Data source: Barclays Capital

6

Appendices to Chapter 6

The appendices that follow provide details on how indexed bond cash flows are computed in the bond markets described in Chapter 6. For each of these markets the price–yield equation is also given. In markets where bonds are issued on a real yield basis the formula provided is the official one used to compute the settlement price at issue. In the case of markets where bonds are issued on a price basis the equation given is the official method of computing real redemption yields for analytical and reporting purposes. The official price–yield formula for most markets is based on Equation (5.8), which is not dependent on an inflation assumption. For the UK market the formula is based on Equation (5.7).

In order to enable readers to readily compare the indexation approaches employed in these different markets the authors have standardised the terminology and notation used.

A6.1 CASH FLOW CALCULATIONS FOR AUSTRALIAN CAPITAL INDEXED BONDS (CIBs)[191]

A6.1.1 Calculation of interest payments

The quarterly interest payments I_t are calculated as:

$$I_t = \frac{c}{4} \times \frac{K_t}{100}$$

where: c = Annual real coupon rate (%).

K_t = Nominal value of the principal at the date of the next interest payment

$$= K_{t-1}\left[1 + \frac{i}{100}\right]$$

K_{t-1} = Nominal value of the principal at the date of the previous interest payment. If there is no previous interest payment $K_{t-1} = 100$ (the face value of the bond). K_t and K_{t-1} are rounded to two decimal places.

i = The average percentage change in the CPI over the two quarters ending in the quarter that is two quarters prior to that in which the next interest payment falls. For example, if the next interest payment is in November 1995, i is based on the average movement in the CPI between December 1994 and June 1995:

[191] For full details see The Treasury (Australia) (1994b).

$$= \frac{100}{2}\left[\frac{CPI_t}{CPI_{t-2}} - 1\right]$$

CPI_t = The CPI for the second quarter of the relevant two-quarter period.

CPI_{t-2} = The CPI for the quarter immediately prior to the relevant two-quarter period.

Interest payments derived using this formula are rounded to the nearest cent.

Note 1 No interest payment is based on a nominal value of less than Aus$100. If the nominal value of the principal falls to below Aus$100, then the interest payment would be based on a nominal value of Aus$100. Subsequent interest and/or principal payments will in such cases be reduced by the difference between the fixed interest payment that was paid in the period and the payment that would have been made under the above formula except for this provision.

Note 2 The Treasury guarantees that the final redemption value shall be no less than Aus$100 face value irrespective of the movements in the CPI over the life of the bond.

A6.1.2 Calculation of the settlement price

Australian CIBs are auctioned on a real yield basis. The settlement price, per Aus$100 face value, is calculated on the basis of the formula:

$$\text{Price per Aus\$100 face value} = w^{f/d}\left[\frac{c}{4}\left(x + \sum_{j=1}^{n} w^j\right) + 100w^n\right]\left\{\frac{K_t}{100}\left(1 + \frac{i}{100}\right)^{-f/d}\right\}$$

where: r = Annual real yield (decimal) (e.g., $r = 0.03$ for a real yield of 3%).

$$w = \left(\frac{1}{1 + r/4}\right)$$

$$x = \begin{cases} 1 & \text{if there is an interest payment at the next payment date,} \\ 0 & \text{if there is no interest payment at the next payment date.} \end{cases}$$

f = The number of days from the settlement date to the next interest payment date.

d = The number of days in the quarter ending on the next interest payment date.

n = The number of full quarters between the next interest payment date and the maturity date.

c, K_t and i are as above.

Note 1 The settlement price is calculated to nine decimal places, while settlement proceeds are rounded to the nearest cent.

Note 2 There is an ex-dividend period of seven calendar days in the Australian CIB market.

A6.2 CASH FLOW CALCULATIONS FOR CANADIAN REAL RETURN BONDS (RRBs)[192]

A6.2.1 Indexing process

An index ratio is applied to calculate the coupon payments, the redemption payment (i.e., the uplifted principal) and the accrued interest. The index ratio for a given settlement date is defined as the ratio of the reference CPI applicable to the settlement date ("Ref $\text{CPI}_{\text{Set date}}$") divided by the reference CPI applicable to the original issue date of the bond ("Ref $\text{CPI}_{\text{First issue date}}$"):

$$\text{Index ratio}_{\text{Set date}} = \left[\frac{\text{Ref CPI}_{\text{Set date}}}{\text{Ref CPI}_{\text{First issue date}}}\right]$$

The reference CPI for the first day of any calendar month is the CPI for the calendar month falling three months earlier, so the reference CPI for 1 June corresponds to the CPI for March, the reference CPI for 1 July corresponds to the CPI for April, etc. The reference CPI for any other day in the month is calculated by linear interpolation between the reference CPI applicable to the first day of the month in which the day falls and the reference CPI applicable to the first day of the month immediately following. Interpolated values for Ref $\text{CPI}_{\text{Set date}}$ are rounded to the nearest fifth decimal place, as are values for Index $\text{ratio}_{\text{Set date}}$.

The formula used to calculate Ref $\text{CPI}_{\text{Set date}}$ can be expressed as follows:

$$\text{Ref CPI}_{\text{Set date}} = \text{Ref CPI}_M + \left(\frac{t-1}{D}\right)[\text{Ref CPI}_{M+1} - \text{Ref CPI}_M]$$

where: D = The number of days in the calendar month in which the settlement date falls.

t = The calendar day corresponding to the settlement date.

Ref CPI_M = Reference CPI for the first day of the calendar month in which the settlement date falls.

Ref CPI_{M+1} = Reference CPI for the first day of the calendar month immediately following the settlement date.

For example, the reference CPI for 20 July 1996 is calculated as follows:

$$\begin{aligned}\text{Ref CPI}_{\text{20 July 1996}} &= \text{Ref CPI}_{\text{1 July 1996}} + \left(\frac{19}{31}\right)[\text{Ref CPI}_{\text{1 August 1996}} - \text{Ref CPI}_{\text{1 July 1996}}]\\ &= \text{CPI}_{\text{April 1996}} + \left(\frac{19}{31}\right)[\text{CPI}_{\text{May 1996}} - \text{CPI}_{\text{April 1996}}]\end{aligned}$$

where: $D = 31$ and $t = 20$.

[192] For full details see Bank of Canada (1994).

The Ref $\text{CPI}_{\text{First issue date}}$ for a given bond is calculated and rounded in exactly the same way as Ref $\text{CPI}_{\text{Set date}}$, although unlike Ref $\text{CPI}_{\text{Set date}}$ it will remain constant over a bond's life (except in the event that the index itself is rebased). However, different bonds may have different values for Ref $\text{CPI}_{\text{First issue date}}$ (depending on the value of the CPI when they were first issued).

Note For these calculations the original issue date for the 2021 RRB is 10 December 1991, for the 2026 RRB is 7 December 1995, for the 2031 RRB is 8 March 1999 and for the 2036 RRB is 9 June 2003.

A6.2.2 Calculation of interest payments

For an RRB the inflation uplift or inflation compensation accrued to a particular date ("Inflation $\text{Compensation}_{\text{Set date}}$") is defined as the product of the Principal and the Index Ratio for that date minus the Principal:

$$\text{Inflation Compensation}_{\text{Set date}} = \{[\text{Principal} \times \text{Index ratio}_{\text{Set date}}] - \text{Principal}\}$$

The semi-annual interest payments are calculated as:

$$\text{Interest payment}_{\text{Div date}} = \frac{c}{200} \times [\text{Principal} + \text{Inflation compensation}_{\text{Div date}}]$$

where: c = Annual real coupon rate (%).

For example, the interest payment due on 1 December 1994 for 4.25% RRB 2021 was calculated as:

$$\text{Interest payment}_{\text{1 Dec 1994}} = \frac{4.25}{200} \times [\text{Principal} + \text{Inflation compensation}_{\text{1 Dec 1994}}]$$

A6.2.3 Calculation of the redemption payment

The redemption payment is calculated as:

$$\text{Redemption Payment} = [\text{Principal} + \text{Inflation compensation}_{\text{Maturity date}}]$$

A6.2.4 Calculation of the settlement price

Canadian RRBs are auctioned on a real yield basis. Where the bond is settling before the *first* coupon date the settlement price, per Can$100 face value, is calculated on the basis of the formula:

$$\begin{aligned}&\text{(Nominal) price per \$100 face value}\\&\quad = (\text{Real price} \times \text{Index ratio}_{\text{Set date}}) + (RAI_b \times \text{Index ratio}_{\text{Set date}})\end{aligned}$$

and

$$\text{Real price} = w^{f/d}\left[D_1 + \frac{c}{2}\sum_{j=1}^{n} w^j + 100w^n\right] - RAI_a$$

where: r = Annual real yield (decimal) (e.g., $r = 0.03$ for a real yield of 3%).

$w = \left(\frac{1}{1 + r/2}\right)$

c = Annual real coupon rate (%)

D_1 = The *first* dividend payment

$= \frac{c}{2} \times \frac{e}{d}$

e = The number of days from the initial issue date to the *first* interest payment date.

f = The number of days from the settlement date to the first interest payment date.

d = The number of days in the regular semi-annual coupon period ending on the first interest payment date.

n = The number of full semi-annual coupon periods between the first interest payment date and the maturity date.

RAI_a = Real accrued interest (for real price calculation) $= \frac{c}{2} \times \frac{(e - f)}{d}$

and, when calculating the settlement proceeds for an auction:

$e = f$ for the initial issuance of a bond.

$e > f$ for any reopening prior to the first coupon payment.

RAI_a = Real accrued interest (for settlement purposes) $= \frac{c}{2} \times \frac{(e - f)}{182.5}$

Where the bond is settling after the *first* coupon date the settlement price, per Can$100 face value, is calculated on the basis of the formula:

(Nominal) price per $100 face value

$$= (\text{Real price} \times \text{Index ratio}_{\text{Set date}}) + (RAI_b \times \text{Index ratio}_{\text{Set date}})$$

and

$$\text{Real price} = w^{f/d}\left[\frac{c}{2}\sum_{j=0}^{n} w^j + 100w^n\right] - RAI_a$$

where: r, c and w are as above.

f = The number of days from the settlement date to the next interest payment date.

d = The number of days in the regular semi-annual coupon period ending on the next interest payment date.

n = The number of full semi-annual coupon periods between the next interest payment date and the maturity date.

RAI_a = Real accrued interest (for real price calculation) $= \frac{c}{2} \times \frac{(d - f)}{d}$

RAI_b = Real accrued interest (for settlement purposes) $= \frac{c}{2} \times \frac{(d - f)}{182.5}$

Note 1 Once the real price is derived using the formulae above it is rounded to the nearest third decimal place.

Note 2 There is no ex-dividend period in the Canadian RRB market.

A6.3 CASH FLOW CALCULATIONS FOR FRENCH OAT*i* AND OAT€*i* BONDS[193]

The formulae in this appendix apply to both OAT*i* and OAT€*i* bonds, the only difference being that the index referred to as the CPI in what follows is French CPI ex-tobacco in the case of OAT*i* bonds and Euro-HICP ex-tobacco in the case of OAT€*i* bonds.

A6.3.1 Indexing process

An index ratio is applied to calculate the coupon payments, the redemption payment (i.e., the uplifted principal) and the accrued interest. The index ratio for a given settlement date is defined as the ratio of the reference CPI applicable to the settlement date ("Ref $\text{CPI}_{\text{Set date}}$") divided by the base CPI ("Base CPI"):

$$\text{Index ratio}_{\text{Set date}} = \left[\frac{\text{Ref CPI}_{\text{Set date}}}{\text{Base CPI}}\right]$$

The reference CPI for the first day of any calendar month is the CPI for the calendar month falling three months earlier, so the reference CPI for 1 June corresponds to the CPI for March, the reference CPI for 1 July corresponds to the CPI for April, etc. The reference CPI for any other day in the month is calculated by linear interpolation between the reference CPI applicable to the first day of the month in which the day falls and the reference CPI applicable to the first day of the month immediately following. Interpolated values for Ref $\text{CPI}_{\text{Set date}}$ are rounded to the nearest fifth decimal place, as are values for Index $\text{ratio}_{\text{Set date}}$.

The formula used to calculate Ref $\text{CPI}_{\text{Set date}}$ can be expressed as follows:

$$\text{Ref CPI}_{\text{Set date}} = \text{Ref CPI}_M + \left(\frac{t-1}{D}\right)[\text{Ref CPI}_{M+1} - \text{Ref CPI}_M]$$

where: D = The number of days in the calendar month in which the settlement date falls.

t = The calendar day corresponding to the settlement date.

Ref CPI_M = Reference CPI for the first day of the calendar month in which the settlement date falls.

Ref CPI_{M+1} = Reference CPI for the first day of the calendar month immediately following the settlement date.

[193] Source: Agence France Trésor (2002a).

Table A6.1 Indexation details of French OAT*i* and OAT€*i* bonds

Bond	Date of first sale	Settlement date	Accrual date	Base index
3.00% OAT*i* 2009	15 Sep 1998	29 Sep 1998	25 Jul 1998	100.17406[a]
3.00% OAT€*i* 2012	25 Oct 2001	31 Oct 2001	25 Jul 2001	108.98710
2.50% OAT*i* 2013	6 Feb 2003	11 Feb 2003	25 Jul 2002	105.55484
3.40% OAT*i* 2029	21 Sep 1999	1 Oct 1999	25 Jul 1999	100.60000
3.15% OAT€*i* 2032	24 Oct 2002	31 Oct 2002	25 Jul 2002	111.15484

Data source: Agence France Trésor (figures as at 31 March 2003).
[a] In 1998 INSEE rebased the French CPI ex-tobacco index. The December 1998 CPI was rebased from 114.9 ("base 1990" CPI) to 100 ("base 1998" CPI). As a result, the base index for 3% OAT*i* 2009 changed from 115.10000 to 115.1 × (100/114.9) (i.e., 100.1740644038... INSEE = French National Institute of Statistics and Economic Studies; CPI = Consumer Price Index.

For example, the reference CPI for 20 July 1996 is calculated as follows:

$$\begin{aligned}\text{Ref CPI}_{20\text{ July 1996}} &= \text{Ref CPI}_{1\text{ July 1996}} + \left(\frac{19}{31}\right)[\text{Ref CPI}_{1\text{ August 1996}} - \text{Ref CPI}_{1\text{ July 1996}}] \\ &= \text{CPI}_{\text{April 1996}} + \left(\frac{19}{31}\right)[\text{CPI}_{\text{May 1996}} - \text{CPI}_{\text{April 1996}}]\end{aligned}$$

where: $D = 31$ and $t = 20$.

The Base CPI for a given bond is determined as the interpolated value of the CPI that would have applied on the quasi-coupon date prior to the original issue date of the bond. All indexed OATs have annual quasi-coupon dates of 25 July. The Base CPI is calculated in exactly the same way as Ref $\text{CPI}_{\text{Set date}}$ and should be rounded to the nearest fifth decimal place. However, unlike Ref $\text{CPI}_{\text{Set date}}$, it will remain constant over a bond's life (except in the event that the index itself is rebased). Different bonds may have different values for Base CPI (depending on the value of the CPI when they were first issued). Table A6.1 provides the date from which inflation accrues for each indexed OAT outstanding at 31 March 2003, along with the corresponding Base CPI value.

Note As inflation accrues from the quasi-coupon date prior to the issue date, rather than from three months before the issue date (the approach used in the other markets that employ the Canadian methodology) some bonds will be issued with far more accrued inflation than others. For instance, while for the 2009 OAT*i* the inflation accrual began two months before it was issued, in the case of the 2013 OAT*i* inflation accrued from seven months before it was issued.[194] One consequence of this is that, for bonds with a long period of inflation accrual prior to issue, the deflation floor will have less value than for bonds with a shorter period – assuming positive inflation during this period.

[194] The length of this period is partly a product of the convention of annual rather than semi-annual coupons in France.

A6.3.2 Calculation of interest payments

For an indexed OAT the annual interest payments per €N nominal are calculated as:

$$\text{Interest payment}_{\text{Div Date}} = \left(\frac{c}{100}\right) \times \text{Index ratio}_{\text{Div date}} \times N$$

where: c = Annual real coupon rate (%).

N = The face value of the bond (€).

A6.3.3 Calculation of the redemption payment

The redemption payment per €N nominal is calculated as:

$$\text{Redemption payment} = N \times \text{Max}\{\text{Index ratio}_{\text{Maturity date}}, 1\}$$

A6.3.4 Calculation of the settlement price

French inflation-indexed OATs are sold on a real price basis in both the primary and secondary markets, and so a price–yield equation is not necessary for calculating settlement proceeds. The official method of computing real redemption yields from prices for indexed OATs for analytical and reporting purposes is as follows:

$$\text{(Nominal) price per €100 face value} = \text{Inflation-adjusted price} + \text{Inflation-adjusted accrued interest}$$

and

$$\text{Inflation-adjusted price} = \text{Real price} \times \text{Index ratio}_{\text{Set date}}$$

$$\text{Real price} = w^{f/d}\left[c + c\sum_{j=1}^{n} w^{j} + 100w^{n}\right] - RAI$$

$$\text{Inflation-adjusted accrued interest} = RAI \times \text{Index ratio}_{\text{Set date}}$$

where: r = Annual real yield (decimal) (e.g., $r = 0.03$ for a real yield of 3%).

$w = \left(\frac{1}{1+r}\right)$

RAI = Unadjusted (or real) Accrued interest $= c \times \frac{(d-f)}{d}$ rounded to the nearest third decimal place.

f = The number of days from the settlement date to the next interest payment date.

d = The number of days in the regular annual coupon period ending on the next interest payment date.

n = The number of full annual coupon periods between the next interest payment date and the maturity date.

and c is as above

Note There is no ex-dividend period in the French indexed OAT market.

A6.4: CASH FLOW CALCULATIONS FOR SWEDISH INDEX-LINKED TREASURY BONDS[195]

A6.4.1 Indexing process

An index ratio is applied to calculate the coupon payments (for coupon bonds), the redemption payment (i.e., the uplifted principal) and the accrued interest (for coupon bonds). The index ratio for a given settlement date is defined as the ratio of the reference CPI applicable to the settlement date ("Ref $\text{CPI}_{\text{Set date}}$") divided by the base CPI ("Base CPI"):

$$\text{Index ratio}_{\text{Set date}} = \left[\frac{\text{Ref CPI}_{\text{Set date}}}{\text{Base CPI}}\right]$$

The reference CPI for the first day of any calendar month is the CPI for the calendar month falling three months earlier, so the reference CPI for 1 June corresponds to the CPI for March, the reference CPI for 1 July corresponds to the CPI for April, etc. The reference CPI for any other day in the month is calculated by linear interpolation between the reference CPI applicable to the first day of the month in which the day falls and the reference CPI applicable to the first day of the month immediately following. For the purposes of interpolation, each month is deemed to have 30 days.

The formula used to calculate Ref $\text{CPI}_{\text{Set date}}$ can be expressed as follows:

$$\text{Ref CPI}_{\text{Set date}} = \text{Ref CPI}_M + \left(\frac{t-1}{D}\right)[\text{Ref CPI}_{M+1} - \text{Ref CPI}_M]$$

where: $t =$ The calendar day corresponding to the settlement date (for 31-day months t should be set to 30 rather than 31).

Ref $\text{CPI}_M =$ Reference CPI for the first day of the calendar month in which the settlement date falls.

Ref $\text{CPI}_{M+1} =$ Reference CPI for the first day of the calendar month immediately following the settlement date.

For example, the reference CPI for 20 July 1996 is calculated as follows:

$$\begin{aligned}\text{Ref CPI}_{\text{20 July 1996}} &= \text{Ref CPI}_{\text{1 July 1996}} + \left(\frac{19}{30}\right)[\text{Ref CPI}_{\text{1 August 1996}} - \text{Ref CPI}_{\text{1 July 1996}}]\\ &= \text{CPI}_{\text{April 1996}} + \left(\frac{19}{30}\right)[\text{CPI}_{\text{May 1996}} - \text{CPI}_{\text{April 1996}}]\end{aligned}$$

where: $t = 20$.

For all Swedish indexed bonds first issued prior to April 1999 the same Base CPI is used (245.1). This value was determined by the first Swedish indexed bond, which was issued in April 1994. Although this bond was actually issued on 19 April, the Swedish authorities use the figure for January 1994 as the base (without interpolating) – in effect assuming that it was issued on 1 April 1994.

[195] For full details see Swedish National Debt Office (1994, 1996, 2000).

For the two bonds that were issued in April 1999 (loan numbers 3104 and 3105) the Base CPI is 256.2 – the official CPI for January 1999.

Note The SNDO employs essentially the same indexing process used for Canada's RRBs. The differences are that: (1) all Swedish bonds first issued prior to April 1999 use the same base CPI; (2) the base CPI used is not the "true" interpolated value; (3) the interpolation assumes 30-day months; (4) new issues from April 1999 feature a deflation floor; and (5) Ref $\text{CPI}_{\text{Set date}}$ and Index $\text{ratio}_{\text{Set date}}$ are not rounded.

A6.4.2 Calculation of interest payments (for coupon-bearing bonds)

For coupon-bearing indexed bonds the nominal coupon per SEK 100 face value is calculated each year as the product of the real coupon per SEK 100 face value and the index ratio for the dividend date. The resulting figure is then rounded to the nearest fifth decimal place:

$$\text{Nominal coupon}_{\text{Div date}} = \text{Real coupon} \times \text{Index ratio}_{\text{Div date}}$$

The interest payment per SEK N face value is then calculated as the product of this nominal coupon and the face value:

$$\text{Interest payment}_{\text{Div date}} = \frac{\text{Nominal coupon}_{\text{Div date}}}{100} \times N$$

where: N = The face value of the bond (SEK).

A6.4.3 Calculation of the redemption payment

For inflation-linked bonds without the deflation floor (bonds 3001, 3002, 3101, 3102 and 3103):

$$\text{Redemption payment} = N \times \text{Index ratio}_{\text{Maturity date}}$$

For inflation-linked bonds with the deflation floor (bonds 3104 and 3105):

$$\text{Redemption payment} = N \times \text{Max}\{\text{Index ratio}_{\text{Maturity date}}, 1\}$$

where: N is as above.

A6.4.4 Calculation of the settlement price

Zero-coupon bonds

Swedish index-linked Treasury zero-coupon bonds are auctioned on a real yield basis. The settlement price for a zero-coupon bond, per SEK N face value, is calculated on the basis of the formula:

$$\text{Price per SEK } N \text{ face value} = w^{f/d} \times N \times \text{Index ratio}_{\text{Set date}}$$

(The result of this calculation is rounded to the nearest SEK) where: N is as above.

$r =$ Annual real yield (decimal) (e.g., $r = 0.03$ for a real yield of 3%).

$$w = \left(\frac{1}{1+r}\right)$$

$f =$ The number of days from the settlement date to the *maturity* date (computed on a 30E/360 day basis).

$d = 360.$

Note For the purposes of discounting, a year is assumed to consist of 360 days.

Coupon-bearing bonds

Swedish index-linked Treasury coupon-bearing bonds are auctioned on a real yield basis. The settlement price for a coupon-bearing bond, per SEK N face value, is calculated on the basis of the formula:

$$\text{Price per SEK } N \text{ face value} = \frac{(\text{Price per SEK } 100 \times N)}{100} + \text{Accrued interest}_{\text{Set date}}$$

(the result of this calculation is rounded to the nearest SEK), and:

Price per 100 SEK (which is rounded to the nearest third decimal place)

$$= \left[\left(\sum_{i=1}^{n+1} cw^{f_i/d} + 100w^{f_{n+1}/d}\right) \times \text{Index ratio}_{\text{Set date}}\right] - \left[c\left(1 - \frac{f_1}{d}\right) \times \text{Index ratio}_{\text{Set date}}\right]$$

$$\text{Accrued interest}_{\text{Set date}} = c\left(1 - \frac{f_1}{d}\right) \times \text{Index ratio}_{\text{Set date}} \times \frac{N}{100}$$

where: N is as above.

$r =$ Annual real yield (decimal) (e.g., $r = 0.03$ for a real yield of 3%).

$$w = \left(\frac{1}{1+r}\right)$$

$c =$ Annual real coupon rate (%)

$f_i =$ The number of days from the settlement date to the date of the ith remaining coupon (computed on a 30E/360 day basis).

$d = 360.$

$n =$ The number of remaining coupon payments after the next coupon payment.

Note 1 Unlike Canadian RRBs, Swedish coupon-bearing bonds pay annual coupons.

Note 2 As there is an ex-dividend period of five business days in the Swedish market, for secondary market trades settling ex-dividend the price–yield formulae above will need to be adjusted accordingly.

Note 3 Examples of the calculations described in this appendix appear in Swedish National Debt Office (2000) and on the SNDO website: www.rgk.se

A6.5 CASH FLOW CALCULATIONS FOR UK INDEX-LINKED GILTS (IGs)[196]

A6.5.1 Indexing process

Capital and interest values are adjusted by the ratio to the base RPI of the RPI eight months prior to the month in which the cash flow is paid; the base RPI being the RPI level for the month that is eight months prior to the month in which the bond was first issued.

A6.5.2 Calculation of interest payments

(1) Standard dividend periods

$$\text{Dividend per £100 nominal} = \frac{c}{2} \times \frac{RPID}{RPIB}$$

(rounded using the convention detailed on p. 172)

where: c = Annual real coupon per £100 nominal of the gilt.

$RPID$ = The RPI that fixes the next dividend payment for the gilt (i.e., the RPI scheduled to be published seven months prior to the month of the next dividend payment and relating to the month before that prior month): for example, if the next dividend payment on the gilt will be in November, then the RPI that fixes its value is the RPI for March of that year.

$RPIB$ = The base RPI for the gilt (i.e., the RPI scheduled to be published seven months prior to the month of issue of the gilt and relating to the month before that prior month): for example, if the gilt is issued in November, then its base RPI is the RPI for March of that year.

(2) Short first dividend periods

$$\text{Dividend per £100 nominal} = \frac{f}{d} \times \frac{c}{2} \times \frac{RPID}{RPIB}$$

(rounded using the convention detailed on p. 172)

where: $RPID$ = The RPI that fixes the *first* dividend payment for the gilt (i.e., the RPI scheduled to be published seven months prior to the month of the first

[196] For full details see UK Debt Management Office (2002b).

dividend payment and relating to the month before that prior month): for example, if the first dividend payment on the gilt will be in November, then the RPI that fixes its value is the RPI for March of that year.

d = The number of days in the full quasi-coupon period in which the settlement date occurs.

f = The number of days from the *issue* date to the next (short) coupon date.

c and $RPIB$ are as defined in Subsection (1).

(3) Long first dividend periods

$$\text{Dividend per £100 nominal} = \left(\frac{f_1}{d_1} + 1\right) \times \frac{c}{2} \times \frac{RPID}{RPIB}$$

(rounded using the convention detailed below)

where: d_1 = The number of days in the full quasi-coupon period in which the *issue* date occurs.

f_1 = The number of days from the *issue* date to the next quasi-coupon date.

c, $RPID$ and $RPIB$ are as defined in Subsection (2).

A6.5.3 Calculation of the redemption payment

$$\text{Redemption payment per £100 nominal}(R) = 100 \times \frac{RPIR}{RPIB}$$

(rounded using the convention detailed below)

where: $RPIR$ = The RPI that fixes the redemption payment for the gilt (i.e., the RPI scheduled to be published seven months prior to the month of the redemption payment and relating to the month before that prior month): for example, if the redemption payment on the gilt will be in November, then the RPI that fixes its value is the RPI for March of that year.

$RPIB$ is as defined above.

Rounding conventions

Interest and redemption payments for the first three index-linked issues (namely, 2% Index-linked Treasury Stock 1996, 2% Index-linked Treasury Stock 2006 and $2\frac{1}{2}$% Index-linked Treasury Stock 2011) are rounded *down* to two decimal places per £100 nominal. For all other index-linked gilts with first issue dates before 2002 the payments are rounded *down* to four decimal places per £100 nominal. For index-linked gilts with first issue dates of 2002 onward, the interest and redemption payments are rounded to the nearest sixth decimal place per £100 nominal.

A6.5.4 Calculation of accrued interest

(1) Standard dividend periods

$$AI = \begin{cases} \dfrac{t}{d} D_1 & \text{if the settlement date occurs on or before the ex-dividend date} \\ \left(\dfrac{t}{d} - 1\right) D_1 & \text{if the settlement date occurs after the ex-dividend date} \end{cases}$$

where: AI = Accrued interest per £100 nominal of the gilt.

D_1 = Next dividend per £100 nominal of the gilt relative to the settlement date.

t = The number of days from the previous dividend date to the settlement date.

d = The number of days in the full quasi-coupon period in which the settlement date occurs.

(2) Short first dividend periods

$$AI = \begin{cases} \dfrac{t^*}{d} \times \dfrac{c}{2} \times \dfrac{RPID}{RPIB} & \text{if the settlement date occurs on or before the ex-dividend date} \\ \left(\dfrac{t^* - f}{d}\right) \times \dfrac{c}{2} \times \dfrac{RPID}{RPIB} & \text{if the settlement date occurs after the ex-dividend date} \end{cases}$$

where: AI = Accrued interest per £100 nominal of the gilt.

c = Real coupon per £100 nominal of the gilt.

t^* = The number of days from the *issue* date to the settlement date.

d = The number of days in the full quasi-coupon period in which the settlement date occurs.

f = The number of days from the *issue* date to the next (short) coupon date.

$RPID$ = The RPI that fixes the first dividend payment for the gilt (i.e., the RPI scheduled to be published seven months prior to the month of the first dividend payment and relating to the month before that prior month): for example, if the first dividend payment on the gilt will be in November, then the RPI that fixes its value is the RPI for March of that year.

$RPIB$ = The base RPI for the gilt (i.e., the RPI scheduled to be published seven months prior to the month of first issue of the gilt and relating to the month before that prior month): for example, if the gilt is first issued in November then its base RPI is the RPI for March of that year.

(3) Long first dividend periods

$$AI = \begin{cases} \dfrac{t}{d_1} \times \dfrac{c}{2} \times \dfrac{RPID}{RPIB} & \text{If the settlement date occurs during the first coupon period} \\[2ex] \left(\dfrac{f_1}{d_1} + \dfrac{f_2}{d_2}\right) \times \dfrac{c}{2} \times \dfrac{RPID}{RPIB} & \text{if the settlement date occurs during the second period and on or before the ex-dividend date} \\[2ex] \left(\dfrac{f_2}{d_2} - 1\right) \times \dfrac{c}{2} \times \dfrac{RPID}{RPIB} & \text{if the settlement date occurs during the second coupon period and after the ex-dividend date} \end{cases}$$

where: t = The number of days from the *issue* date to the settlement date in the first quasi-coupon period (this term only applies if the gilt settles in the first quasi-coupon period).

d_1 = The number of days in the full quasi-coupon period in which the *issue* date occurs.

d_2 = The number of days in the full quasi-coupon period after the quasi-coupon period in which the *issue* date occurs.

f_1 = The number of days from the issue date to the next quasi-coupon date.

f_2 = The number of days from the quasi-coupon date after the *issue* date to the settlement date in the quasi-coupon period after the quasi-coupon period in which the *issue* date occurs (this term only applies if the gilt settles in the second quasi-coupon period).

c, AI, $RPID$ and $RPIB$ are as defined in Subsection (2).

Note 1 The ex-dividend period is seven business days for all index-linked gilts.

Note 2 Examples of accrued interest and first dividend calculations for an index-linked gilt with a long first dividend period appear in UK Debt Management Office (2002c), which is available on the DMO website: www.dmo.gov.uk

A6.5.5 Calculation of real yields

Although index-linked gilts are issued and generally trade on a price basis, *in theory* they could be traded on a yield basis. Since the latter is at best a rare event the price–yield formula below is generally used to compute real yields from the prices of index-linked gilts rather than *vice versa*:[197]

[197] This price–yield formula is used for calculating yields for all index-linked gilts except those that are close to redemption. Index-linked gilts for which all remaining cash flows are known in nominal terms (i.e., the RPI determining the nominal value of the redemption cash flow has been published) are effectively nominal bonds, and so a nominal rather than a real yield is calculated. The price–yield formulae for index-linked gilts near to redemption appear in UK Debt Management Office (2002b).

$$\text{Price per £100 face value} = (uw)^{f/d}\left[D_1 + D_2uw + \frac{c}{2}\alpha\sum_{j=2}^{n} w^j + 100\alpha w^n\right]$$

where: D_1 = Cash flow due on next quasi-coupon date per £100 nominal of the gilt (this may be zero if the gilt has a long first dividend period or if the gilt is settling in its ex-dividend period; or may be greater or less than $c/2$ times the RPI ratio during long or short first dividend periods, respectively).

D_2 = Cash flow due on next but one quasi-coupon date after the settlement date per £100 nominal of the gilt (may be greater than $c/2$ times the RPI ratio during long first dividend periods).

For standard dividend periods this is calculated as:

$$D_2 = \begin{cases} \dfrac{RPID_2}{RPIB}\dfrac{c}{2} & \text{if } RPID_2 \text{ is known} \\ \dfrac{\alpha}{u}\dfrac{c}{2} & \text{if } RPID_2 \text{ is not known} \end{cases}$$

where: $RPIB$ = The base RPI for the gilt (defined earlier).

$RPIL$ = The latest published RPI at the time of settlement.

$RPID_2$ = RPI defining the dividend D_2.

r = Real yield (decimal) (e.g., $r = 0.03$ for a real yield of 3%).

$$w = \left(\frac{1}{1 + r/2}\right)$$

$\bar{\pi}^e$ = Assumed average annual inflation rate (decimal).

$$u = \left(\frac{1}{1 + \bar{\pi}^e}\right)^{1/2}$$

$$\alpha = \frac{RPIL}{RPIB}u^{k/6}$$

k = The number of months between the month of the RPI that defines the dividend due (or would ordinarily be due, in the case of a long first dividend or a gilt settling in its ex-dividend period) on the next quasi-coupon date and the month of the latest published RPI at the time of settlement. For example, if the RPI for January is the RPI that defines the dividend due (or would ordinarily be due, in the case of a long first dividend or a gilt settling in its ex-dividend period) on the next quasi-coupon date and the latest published RPI at the time of settlement is the RPI for April, then $k = 3$.

f = The number of days from the settlement date to the next quasi-coupon date.

d = The number of days in the full coupon period in which the settlement date occurs (i.e., between the prior quasi-coupon date and the following quasi-coupon date).

n = The number of full semi-annual coupon periods between the first/next quasi-coupon date and the maturity date.

Note 1 The current market convention in the index-linked gilt market is to use a 3% inflation assumption (i.e., $\bar{\pi}^e = 0.03$).

Note 2 The daycount convention in the UK gilt market for calculating accrued interest and redemption yields was changed in November 1998 from Actual/365 to Actual/Actual. Details on the price–yield formulae employed prior to November 1998 can be found in Bank of England (1997). This document also explains the adjustment that had to be made in the past to the price–yield formulae when gilts were issued in partly paid form. The last partly paid issue of an index-linked gilt was in September 1992.

A6.6 CASH FLOW CALCULATIONS FOR US TREASURY INFLATION-INDEXED SECURITIES (TIIS)[198]

A6.6.1 Indexing process

An index ratio is applied to calculate the coupon payments, the redemption payment (i.e., the uplifted principal) and the accrued interest. The index ratio for a given settlement date is defined as the ratio of the reference CPI applicable to the settlement date ("Ref $\text{CPI}_{\text{Set date}}$") divided by the reference CPI applicable to the original issue date of the bond ("Ref $\text{CPI}_{\text{First issue date}}$"):

$$\text{Index ratio}_{\text{Set date}} = \left[\frac{\text{Ref CPI}_{\text{Set date}}}{\text{Ref CPI}_{\text{First issue date}}}\right]$$

The reference CPI for the first day of any calendar month is the CPI for the calendar month falling three months earlier, so the reference CPI for 1 June corresponds to the CPI for March, the reference CPI for 1 July corresponds to the CPI for April, etc. The reference CPI for any other day in the month is calculated by linear interpolation between the reference CPI applicable to the first day of the month in which the day falls and the reference CPI applicable to the first day of the month immediately following. Interpolated values for Ref $\text{CPI}_{\text{Set date}}$ are rounded to the nearest fifth decimal place, as are values for Index $\text{ratio}_{\text{Set date}}$.

The formula used to calculate Ref $\text{CPI}_{\text{Set date}}$ can be expressed as follows:

$$\text{Ref CPI}_{\text{Set date}} = \text{Ref CPI}_M + \left(\frac{t-1}{D}\right)[\text{Ref CPI}_{M+1} - \text{Ref CPI}_M]$$

where: D = The number of days in the calendar month in which the settlement date falls.

t = The calendar day corresponding to the settlement date.

[198] For full details, including examples, see Department of the (US) Treasury (1997a).

Ref CPI_M = Reference CPI for the first day of the calendar month in which the settlement date falls.

Ref CPI_{M+1} = Reference CPI for the first day of the calendar month immediately following the settlement date.

For example, the reference CPI for 20 July 1996 is calculated as follows:

$$\text{Ref CPI}_{20\text{ July }1996} = \text{Ref CPI}_{1\text{ July }1996} + \left(\frac{19}{31}\right)[\text{Ref CPI}_{1\text{ August }1996} - \text{Ref CPI}_{1\text{ July }1996}]$$

$$= \text{CPI}_{\text{April }1996} + \left(\frac{19}{31}\right)[\text{CPI}_{\text{May }1996} - \text{CPI}_{\text{April }1996}]$$

where: $D = 31$ and $t = 20$.

The $\text{Ref CPI}_{\text{First issue date}}$ for a given bond remains constant over its life although different bonds may have different values for $\text{Ref CPI}_{\text{First issue date}}$ (depending on the value of the CPI when they were first issued).

Note The original issue date for the 10-year (2007) indexed note is assumed to be 15 January 1997 (the date on which it was originally intended to be issued), rather than the actual issue or settlement date of 6 February 1997.

A6.6.2 Calculation of interest payments

For a TIIS the semi-annual interest payments per $\$N$ nominal are calculated as:

$$\text{Interest payment}_{\text{Div date}} = \left(\frac{c}{200}\right) \times \text{Index ratio}_{\text{Div date}} \times N$$

where: c = Annual real coupon rate (%).

N = The face value of the bond ($).

A6.6.3 Calculation of the redemption payment

The redemption payment per $\$N$ nominal is calculated as:

$$\text{Redemption payment} = N \times \text{Max}\{\text{Index ratio}_{\text{Maturity date}}, 1\}$$

Note The Treasury guarantees that the final redemption value shall be no less than $100 per $100 nominal holding, irrespective of the movements in the CPI over the life of the bond.

A6.6.4 Calculation of the settlement price

The US Treasury price–yield formula for an inflation-indexed security is given by:

$$\text{(Nominal) Price per \$100 face value} = \text{Inflation-adjusted price} + \text{Inflation-adjusted accrued interest}$$

and

$$\text{Inflation-adjusted price} = \text{Real price} \times \text{Index ratio}_{\text{Set date}}$$

$$\text{Real price} = \left(\frac{1}{1+\frac{f}{d}\frac{r}{2}}\right)\left[\frac{c}{2}+\frac{c}{2}\sum_{j=1}^{n} w^{j} + 100w^{n}\right] - RAI$$

$$\text{Inflation-adjusted accrued interest} = RAI \times \text{Index ratio}_{\text{Set date}}$$

where: r = Annual real yield (decimal) (e.g., $r = 0.03$ for a real yield of 3%).

$$w = \left(\frac{1}{1+r/2}\right)$$

RAI = Unadjusted (or real) accrued interest $= \frac{c}{2} \times \frac{(d-f)}{d}$

f = The number of days from the settlement date to the next interest payment date.

d = The number of days in the regular semi-annual coupon period ending on the next interest payment date.

n = The number of full semi-annual coupon periods between the next interest payment date and the maturity date.

Note 1 This method uses simple rather than compound interest for discounting cash flows during the current coupon period. Although this is the method employed by the Treasury to compute settlement proceeds at auction, it differs from the "street" formula used by traders in the secondary market to compute yield from price – in the case of the latter, compound interest is used for discounting cash flows during the current coupon period.

Note 2 There is no ex-dividend period in the US TIIS market.

7
Other Indexed Bond Markets

Chapter 6 detailed some of the larger international markets for inflation-indexed securities, though in reality the product is far more widespread. The purpose of this chapter is therefore to outline the structure of indexed bond markets – past and present – in other countries, both to give a brief overview of their sometimes very different origins and to demonstrate the pervasiveness of the asset class globally.[1]

By way of illustration, Table 7.1 lists those countries whose governments have outstanding inflation-indexed bonds as of September 2003.

Table 7.1 Governments with outstanding inflation-indexed securities (as of September 2003)

Country	First issue date	Index currently used
Australia	1985	Consumer prices
Austria	2003	Euro-zone consumer prices
		US consumer prices
Bolivia	2002	Consumer prices
Brazil	1964	General market prices
	2002	Consumer prices
Canada	1991	Consumer prices
Chile	1967	Consumer prices
Colombia	1967	Consumer prices
France	1998	Domestic consumer prices
	2001	Euro-zone consumer prices
Greece	1997	Domestic consumer prices
	2003	Euro-zone consumer prices
Hungary	1995	Consumer prices
Iceland	1964	Consumer prices
Israel	1955	Consumer prices
Italy	2003	Euro-zone consumer prices
Kazakhstan	1999	Consumer prices
Mexico	1989	Consumer prices
New Zealand	1977	Consumer prices
Poland	1992	Consumer prices
South Africa	2000	Consumer prices
Sweden	1994	Consumer prices
Turkey	1997	Consumer prices
UK	1981	Consumer prices
USA	1997	Consumer prices

[1] Appendix 7.5 provides a table of exchange rates as of 30 June 2003 for reference.

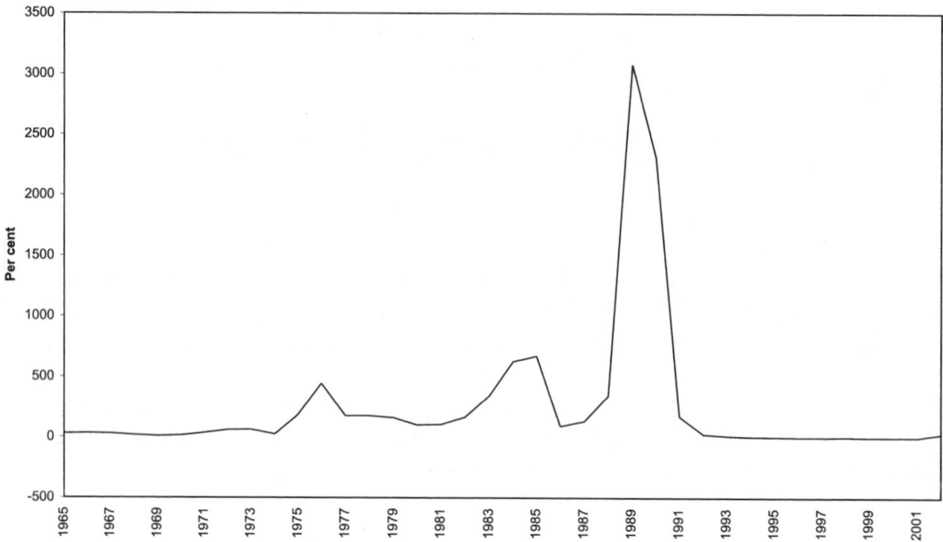

Figure 7.1 Annual percentage change in the Argentine Consumer Price Index (CPI)
Data source: International Financial Statistics.

7.1 ARGENTINA

Hyperinflation in Argentina in the early 1970s (see Figure 7.1) meant that the government found it increasingly hard to sell long-term public debt, with investor demand being for financial instruments that would protect the purchasing power of their capital. The problem was exacerbated by the fact that most financial instruments had government-imposed interest rate "caps", which would often lag behind the rate of inflation and so lead to negative real rates of interest. For example, Jud (1978) reports that, while inflation in December 1975 was running at in excess of 400% per annum, the rate of interest being paid by commercial banks on passbook savings accounts was capped at just 40%.

As a means to both meet this demand and prevent the collapse of its long-term capital markets, the Argentine government began issuing medium- and long-term peso-denominated marketable inflation-indexed bonds in November 1972. These first indexed bonds were referred to as *Valores Nacionales Ajustables* (VNAs) and were linked to non-agricultural wholesale prices.[2] VNAs paid a real coupon rate of 7% and their interest and principal payments were all indexed and exempt from tax (as were all government securities in Argentina at the time). In January 1975 the government extended the asset class by beginning to issue non-marketable General Adjustable Savings Bonds – *Bonos Generales de Ahorro Ajustable* – alongside VNAs. These had the same structure (they too were peso-denominated, had a 7% real coupon and were linked to wholesale prices excluding agricultural products), but typically had longer

[2] VNAs were traded on the Buenos Aires Stock Exchange.

Table 7.2 Transactions on the Buenos Aires Stock Exchange (breakdown of turnover by asset class)

Year	Public securities (indexed) (%)	Public securities (non-indexed) (%)	Private securities (%)
1971	12.5	55.2	32.3
1972	19.8	55.1	25.1
1973	28.5	50.6	20.8
1974	53.7	36.7	9.6
1975	96.7	1.9	1.4
1976[a]	86.6	0.2	13.3

Data source: Banco Central de la República Argentina (1976).
[a] Figures up to October 1976.

maturities (up to 30 years). Inflation adjustment on both types was on a quarterly basis, though on later series of indexed bonds this was reduced to monthly.

The rapid acceleration of inflation during 1975 led to a massive increase in demand for indexed bonds. Jud (1978) reports that during this period many executives were drawing only 15% of their monthly salary in cash and were using the rest to purchase indexed government bonds that they would then sell off as needed to meet expenses. Table 7.2 illustrates how clearly index-linked securities became the financial instrument of choice in this macroeconomic environment.[3] In 1975, transactions of indexed government bonds accounted for 96.7% of the total value of all transactions on the Buenos Aires Stock Exchange. By that same year, VNAs and General Adjustable Savings Bonds constituted 27.4% and 2.4%, respectively, of the public's financial assets. Interestingly, this rapid rise in inflation during the early 1970s did not stimulate the development of a private sector-indexed bond market in Argentina.[4]

During the 1970s and 1980s the Argentine government issued numerous different types of indexed bonds, such as *VAVIS* (most of which were linked to construction costs) and BARRA (which were tied to consumer prices), among others.[5] In 1982, in a move that apparently surprised investors,[6] the government bought back all of the outstanding VNAs (though other forms of indexed bonds continued to be issued) as part of a package of financial reforms. By the end of the 1980s hyperinflation[7] led the government to take more drastic monetary policy action: in December 1989 all outstanding domestic debt (indexed and non-indexed) was converted into a US dollar-denominated 10-year bond. In April 1991 the Argentine government passed the Convertibility Law, which prohibited all forms of indexation and tied the Argentine peso to the US dollar at an exchange rate of one-to-one. It remains to be seen whether the breaking of the dollar peg in 2002 rekindles interest in domestic inflation-indexed securities.

[3] The figures in Table 7.2 include foreign currency-indexed bonds as well as inflation-indexed bonds.
[4] While there were some private sector indexed issues, these were rare.
[5] Price (1997) provides more details on these instruments.
[6] See Boschen and Newman (1987).
[7] Inflation in Argentina peaked at over 3000% p.a. in 1989, see Figure 7.1.

7.2 AUSTRIA

Until 2003 Austria had seen only one public-sector indexed bond, issued by the Austrian Electricity Authority in 1953 and indexed to the price of a kilowatt hour of electricity. Since this was the first post-war issue in Austria, indexation was employed in order to help ensure its success. In April 1995 Immo-Bank AG, a privately owned institution, launched a 40 million schilling (approximately US$10mn) convertible bond maturing in 2010[8] indexed to the Austrian Consumer Price Index (CPI). It was to be another eight years before the Austrian government began issuing inflation-indexed bonds. In February 2003 it launched two indexed Euro MTNs – one a $75 million eight year MTN indexed to the US CPI-U and the other a €50 million 10 year MTN indexed to Euro-zone HICP excluding tobacco. A second dollar denominated indexed MTN, this time with a 10 year maturity, was launched in April 2003.

7.3 BOLIVIA

Indexation in Bolivia is a relatively recent phenomenon, particularly in light of the history of other South American markets. In December 2001 the Bolivian authorities introduced an inflation-linked unit of value defined in terms of the CPI, the *Unidad de Fomento de Vivienda* (UFV),[9] providing the impetus for financial institutions in Bolivia to begin offering inflation-indexed loans and investments. In April 2002 the Central Bank of Bolivia began issuing one-year Treasury bills denominated in UFVs. These are zero-coupon instruments that pay CPI-indexed redemption proceeds and by June 2002 represented 0.2% of total government debt (approximately US$2.4mn).

7.4 BRAZIL

7.4.1 1964–1986 Readjustable National Treasury Obligations (ORTNs)

The military government that took control in Brazil in 1964 inherited a large budget deficit and high inflation (see Figure 7.2), and general indexation was introduced in an attempt to finance the deficit in a non-inflationary manner at the same time as promoting the development of capital markets. At the time, the government envisaged that indexation would be only a temporary measure, the need for which would disappear once inflation had been brought under control. As part of this indexation programme the first indexed government bonds – *Readjustable National Treasury Obligations* (ORTNs) – were introduced during July 1964.

The government stipulated by decree[10] that ORTNs should be issued with original maturities of between three and twenty years and real coupon rates of up to 6%. Initially they were linked to the wholesale price index on a quarterly basis with a three-month lag in indexation, though this was soon reduced to a one-month adjustment with a one-month lag following the deceleration in inflation that occurred in 1965.[11] One- and two-year ORTNs were introduced in 1967 (with coupon rates of

[8] The option here is to convert the bond into share certificates.

[9] More details on the UFV can be found on the Central Bank of Bolivia's website: www.bcb.gov.bo

[10] Government of Brazil Decree Number 54.252/64.

[11] Despite this deceleration, because of the lag in indexation the government was still paying out the earlier higher rate of inflation in the form of the inflation adjustment on its bonds. Since it was felt that this in itself could cause an increase in inflation the government reduced the lag.

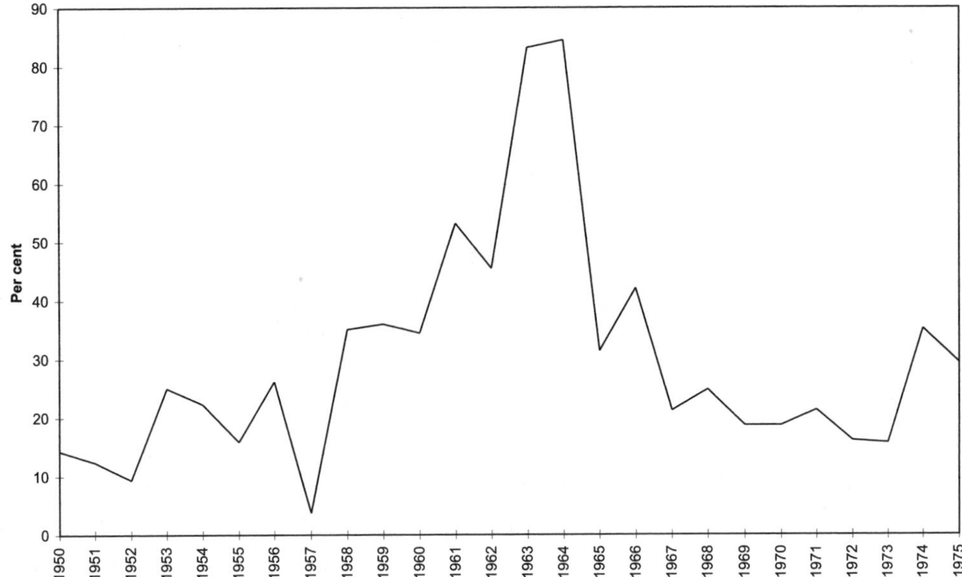

Figure 7.2 Annual percentage change in the Brazilian Wholesale Price Index (WPI) (December to December)
Data source: Getúlio Vargas Foundation (1976)

4% and 5%, respectively), while the coupon rate on new five-year ORTNs was increased to 7%. Jud (1978) reports that early issues of ORTNs were unpopular with investors, owing primarily to a lack of confidence in the government, and as a result the inflation adjustment on all bonds was respecified for a time to be the rate of increase of the wholesale price index or the price of the US dollar, whichever was the higher. This greatly increased the popularity of the bonds, and by the late 1960s they represented a significant proportion of government debt, though Baer and Beckerman (1980) note that this rapid development can at least partly be attributed to the fact that some institutions (such as insurance companies and the National Housing Bank) were compelled by law to hold ORTNs.

Driven by concerns that the inflation lag was causing "feedback" into price inflation in the broader economy, in 1972 the government further revised the indexing method for ORTNs. Under the new method (which remained in use until 1974) the inflation adjustment consisted of two equally weighted components – one reflecting past inflation and the other the government's forecast of future inflation. This was the first in what turned out to be a series of revisions to the indexation methodology. In August 1975 the government declared that indexation rules should exclude the effects of supply shocks, and so henceforth it would edit "accidental" sectoral price shifts out of the wholesale price index. Baer and Beckerman (1980) report that the authorities used the *Acidentalidade* or accident correction to exclude the prices of certain food items that had been affected by adverse weather conditions. In 1976 the government once again changed the indexation mechanism for ORTNs – this time defining the inflation adjustment to be the weighted average of past inflation (with an 80% weight) and a fixed rate of 15% (with a 20% weight). This system therefore undercompensated bondholders when inflation was above 15% and overcompensated them when it was below 15%. In May 1978 a regulation[12] was introduced which defined new coupon rates of 6% and 8%, respectively, for new issues of two- and five-year ORTNs.

The accident correction was again employed in September 1979, when petroleum-derivative prices were permanently removed from the price index. According to Simonsen (1983) the combination of this latest change to the formula introduced in 1976 meant that the ORTN adjustment was by now 30 percentage points lower than the "true" inflation adjustment. In 1980 the inflation compensation for ORTNs was capped at 54%, less than half the realised rate of inflation at the time. The final change to ORTNs came in 1985 when the coupon rates for new issues of all maturities were standardised at 6%. At the same time, issuance of ORTNs of over five-year maturity ceased. Not surprisingly, such a series of changes did little to instil investor confidence in the market.

7.4.2 1986–today National Treasury Obligations (OTNs), Treasury Bonds (BTNs) and National Treasury Notes (NTNs)

Between 1986 and 1991 the Brazilian government launched a series of unsuccessful economic stabilisation plans. In February 1986 ORTNs were replaced by National Treasury Obligations (OTNs) as part of the "Cruzado Plan", and in turn these were replaced by Treasury Bonds (BTNs) following the "Summer Plan" introduced in January 1989. BTNs were issued with maturities of between two and five years and paid semi-annual coupons linked to the CPI. Following the implementation of the "Collor I Plan" in March 1990 issuance of BTNs ceased, to be succeeded by National Treasury Notes[13] (NTN-Cs). Small quantities of these new indexed bonds were issued during 1991 and 1992. In 1993 inflation had peaked at an annual rate of over 2,700%, and as a result the government introduced the "Real Plan" in July 1994, which produced a substantial and lasting reduction in inflation – see Figure 7.3. Following the introduction of the Real Plan, issuance of NTN-Cs was suspended.

The strong de-indexation programme that was pursued in the first few years of economic stabilisation that followed the launch of the Real Plan proved to be unsustainable in the long run, as emerging market economies faced a period of turbulence beginning with the 1997 Asian Crisis. As a result, since December 1999 the government has resumed sales of NTN-C bonds. Bonds in the current series are issued by monthly uniform price auctions with original maturities of 3, 5, 6, 7, 10, 15, 20 and 30 years. Their cash flows are linked to the Index of General Market Prices (the IGP-M[14]) and all NTN-Cs pay semi-annual real coupons of 6% per annum.[15] Since the resumption of NTN-C sales in 1999 the proportion of public debt in the form of inflation-indexed bonds has gradually risen and by July 2002 stood at around 10%.[16] Figure 7.4 illustrates the maturity distribution of outstanding NTN-Cs as at 1 July 2002.

Since 1999 the National Treasury has committed to increase further the proportion of inflation-indexed bonds in its debt portfolio over time for two reasons: to reduce the

[12] This regulation is known as *Portaria 229*.
[13] *Notas do Tesouro Nacional.*
[14] The IGP-M is constructed as a weighted average of the consumer, wholesale and construction price indices.
[15] Except the 30-year bonds, which pay coupons of 12% per annum.
[16] This includes securitised public debt, most of which is inflation-indexed.

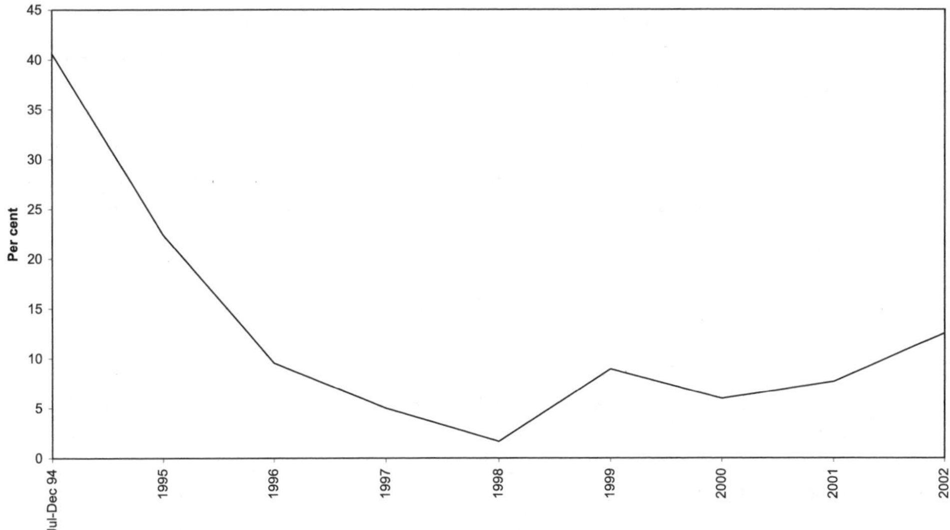

Figure 7.3 Annual percentage change in the Brazilian Consumer Price Index (IPCA)
Data source: Banco Central do Brasil.

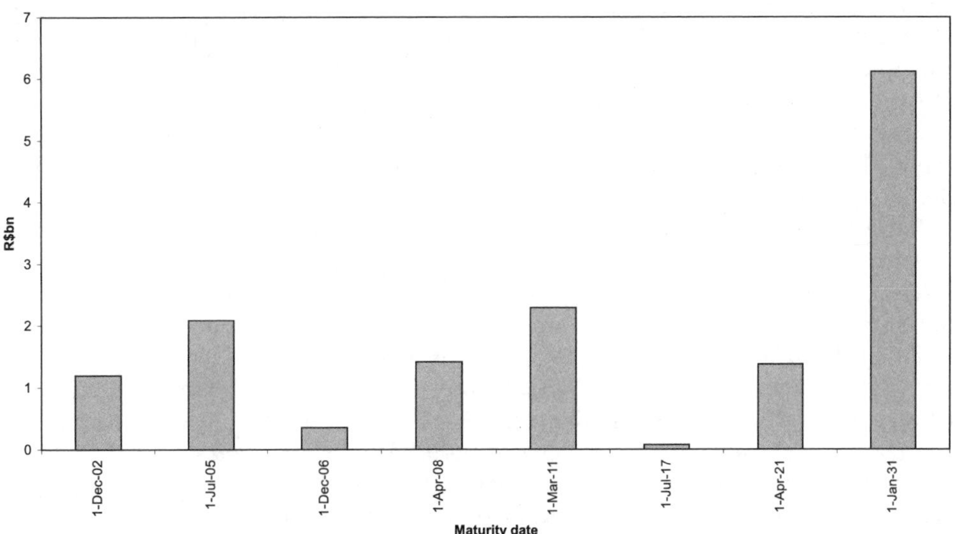

Figure 7.4 Maturity distribution of Brazilian NTN-C bonds (as at 1 July 2002)
Data source: National Treasury, Brazil

current mismatch between central government's inflation-indexed assets and liabilities,[17] and to aid the government in its desire to extend the average maturity of Brazilian public debt. To this end, in March 2002 the Treasury introduced a new series of inflation-indexed bonds, NTN-Bs, while continuing to issue NTN-Cs. Both

[17] At end January 2002 central government's inflation-indexed assets stood at R$223bn, while its inflation-indexed liabilities stood at R$53bn, giving rise to a mismatch of around R$170bn. Source: Brazilian National Treasury and Central Bank of Brazil.

series pay 6% real coupons on a semi-annual basis, but differ in the index used to define cash flows: NTN-Bs are indexed to the consumer price index (IPCA)[18] in contrast to the general price index used to index NTN-Cs. Like NTN-Cs, NTN-Bs are issued by uniform price auction.

In addition to government issues of inflation-indexed bonds there is also an established corporate market for these instruments in Brazil, with issuers including chemical companies, building and construction companies and hospitals. Several of these issues are perpetual bonds indexed to the IGP-M.

7.5 CHILE

Persistent inflation in Chile meant that until the early 1950s no real market existed there for long-term debt, and as a result most long-term investment projects had to be financed through the continued renewal of short-term obligations. However, 1953 saw the creation of the State Bank, with powers to issue bonds linked to the US dollar in order to finance medium- and long-term agricultural and construction projects. The first such bond was issued in 1956 to finance the *Antofagasta* water plant.

In 1967 the Chilean authorities introduced bonds indexed to the newly established *Unidad de Fomento* (UF) unit of account – representing an exchange rate between Chilean pesos and an index number linked to the CPI – with an indexation lag of approximately one month.[19] Since its introduction, indexation to the UF has become widespread in both the financial markets and the real economy: for instance, the prices of cars and real estate are typically set in UFs. Price (1997) reports that, by the end of 1995, about 60% of private financial assets, 71% of banks' loans and over 98% of central bank paper was indexed. Chile's experience of using the UF is discussed by Shiller (1997).

Jud (1978) argues that, without widespread indexation, it is unlikely that the financial system in Chile could have continued to function during the early 1970s when inflation rates exceeded 300% per annum. Indeed, Price (1997) notes that Chile is sometimes hailed as the country in which comprehensive indexation has done the best job of isolating the economy from the real effects of high and variable inflation. However, for several years now, Chile has gradually been de-indexing its economy as part of its drive toward greater price stability, on the basis that indexation will no longer be necessary, should inflation be sustainably reduced to a level typical of industrialised countries. Figure 7.5 illustrates how inflation in Chile has reduced over the last 20-years. In August 2001, as a demonstration of its commitment to de-index the economy, the Central Bank of Chile began to use a nominal (rather than a real) interest rate as its monetary policy instrument.

The Central Bank of Chile issues inflation-indexed bonds for the sole purpose of conducting its monetary policy operations in the market, as opposed to financing government deficits. Until recently two types of inflation-indexed securities were issued: *Pagarés Reajustables del Banco Central* (PRBCs) and *Pagarés Reajustables Pago Cupones* (PRCs).[20] Though the Central Bank retains the option to issue

[18] The government defines its inflation target in terms of the IPCA.

[19] Mendoza and Fernández (1994) provide more details on the construction of the UF.

[20] Between June 1987 and July 1988 a third type of inflation-indexed bond was issued, referred to as *Pagarés con Tasa de interés Flotante* or PTF.

Figure 7.5 Annual percentage change in the Chilean Consumer Price Index (CPI) (December to December)
Data source: Instituto Nacional de Estadísticas (INE)

PRBCs, at the time of writing none have been issued since April 2002. They are indexed discount securities and have been issued with maturities of one to five years. PRCs are coupon-paying indexed bonds (making semi-annual payments of both interest and principal) and, like PRBCs, are denominated in UFs. They have been issued with maturities of anything up to 20 years, although the latest issues were at 8 and 20-year maturities. In recent years the Central Bank of Chile has offered holders of PRCs a facility for stripping their bonds – each resulting zero-coupon bond replicating the combined (interest and principal) cash flow on the underlying PRC.

Following its switch in August 2001 to use a nominal interest rate as its monetary policy instrument, the Central Bank increased the range of maturities for its series of nominal discount securities – *Pagarés Descontables del Banco Central* (PDBCs). Previously, only 90-day and 1-year nominal PDBCs had been issued, but in August 2001 30-day and 2-year maturities were added. This change was part of the Bank's strategy for increasing the proportion of outstanding Central Bank debt represented by nominal securities. As a result of this strategy, by December 2001 PDBCs represented 32.1% of outstanding central bank debt, up from 15.8% 12 months earlier.

In August 2002 the Central Bank announced a series of new measures to reduce further the proportion of debt issued in the form of inflation-indexed securities and to redesign its financial instruments in line with international practice.[21] The new types of instrument launched since this programme was implemented on 3 September 2002 pay semi-annual coupons and have "bullet" maturities – with the principal repayment made in full at maturity, rather than amortised over the life of the bonds (the situation with PRCs). As part of this set of changes, issuance of 2-year (nominal) PDBCs has been replaced by issuance of 2 and 5-year (nominal) *Bonos Banco Central en Pesos*

[21] See (Chile) Ministry of Finance (2002).

(BCPs), while issuance of 8 and 20-year (inflation-indexed) PRCs has been replaced by issuance of 5, 10 and 20-year (inflation-indexed) *Bonos Banco Central en UF* (BCUs).

The Central Bank of Chile has employed two methods for issuing its real rate bonds: single price (electronic) auctions and "taps" through their discount window. Two types of auction format have been employed: "traditional" and "interactive". In a "traditional" auction, participants submit their bids and are informed of the results once the auction is closed. However, when submitting a bid in an "interactive" auction, participants are immediately informed whether or not their bid is successful and thus have the right to resubmit a higher or lower bid before the auction closes. When selling bonds through its discount window the Central Bank sets the discount rate (price) at which it is willing to issue debt, with interested parties specifying the quantity required at the set price.

7.6 COLOMBIA

Historically, the use of indexation in Colombia has been much more selective than in other Latin American countries, such as Argentina, Brazil and Chile. Indexation was first applied to the foreign exchange market in 1967 with the adoption of a crawling peg system for the currency. In 1972 indexation was extended to the market for housing finance with the introduction of a new type of savings instrument, the unit of constant purchasing power or UPAC (*Unidad de Poder Adquisitivo Constante*). In both cases the intention was to aid the acceleration of economic development rather than to deal with the effects of inflation.

The Colombian government first issued indexed bonds in 1967, which paid a real interest rate of 6% plus inflation compensation amounting to 70% of the annual change in the wholesale price index. Sales were boosted by a government requirement that the National Social Security Institute invest any increase in its reserves in these bonds.

In June 1995 the Colombian Government introduced interest indexed bonds tied to the CPI[22] – TES-IPC[23] bonds – both as an alternative source of funding and as a means by which it could offer investors a long-term asset that would maintain its real value. The first issue was of 5-year maturity and had a coupon equal to the CPI plus 10%,[24] though subsequent issues were of 3, 5 or 7-year maturities. TES-IPC bonds were either underwritten or sold by single yield auction.

In May 1999 the Ministry of Finance launched a new type of security – TES-UVR bonds – denominated in the UVR (Real Value Unit). The UVR is a daily index based on the standard monthly CPI produced by Colombia's national statistics agency, DANE (Departamento Administrativo Nacional de Estadísticas). The base date for the UVR is 15 May 1999, and its value is adjusted on a daily basis according to the previous month's inflation rate.[25] At present TES-IPC and TES-UVR bonds co-exist, although the former are no longer issued. TES-UVR bonds pay interest annually and

[22] The bonds' cash flows are determined by the CPI-60 index, which was first introduced in 1988.
[23] Here, TES denotes Treasury Notes and IPC the Index of Consumer Prices.
[24] Later issues paid a lower margin over the CPI.
[25] The formula used to derive the UVR can be found on the Colombian Ministry of Finance and Public Credit's website: www.minhacienda.gov.co

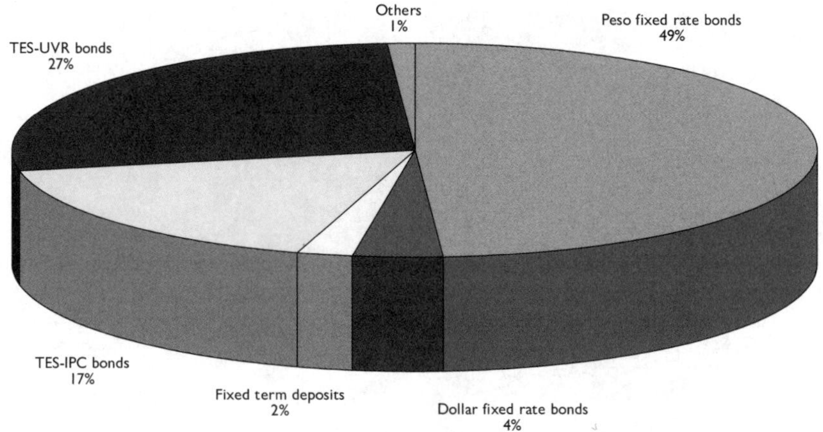

Figure 7.6 Composition of the Colombian government's domestic debt portfolio (as at 30 June 2002)

Data source: Ministry of Finance and Public Credit, Republic of Colombia. TES-UVR = Treasury Notes-Real Value Unit; TES-IPC = Treasury Notes-Index of Consumer Prices

Table 7.3 Amount outstanding of Colombian TES-UVR bonds

End year	Amount outstanding (Colombian peso mn)
1999	1,800,427
2000	5,400,632
2001	7,406,920
June 2002	10,364,818

Data source: Ministry of Finance and Public Credit, Republic of Colombia.

are currently auctioned at 5, 7 and 10-year maturities.[26] Table 7.3 illustrates the rapid growth in issuance of TES-UVR bonds since their introduction, so much so that by June 2002 they represented 27% of the gross domestic government debt in Colombia (Figure 7.6).

Inflation-indexed bonds have also been issued by a range of private sector organisations in Colombia, including television and utility companies. These bonds are indexed to consumer prices and have typically been issued with maturities of 5, 7 or 10-years.

7.7 CZECH REPUBLIC

The Czech Republic has issued inflation-indexed bonds on only one occasion, in August 1997, as part of the programme to aid flood victims in Moravia and Eastern Bohemia. Although the debt management policy of the Ministry of Finance only allowed for

[26] The formula used to convert yields bid at auction into prices is reproduced in Appendix 7.1.

Figure 7.7 Specimen CZK 10,000 certificate for the first line of the Czech Republic inflation-indexed bond

Reproduced by permission of the Ministry of Finance, Czech Republic

issuance of fixed rate bonds, on this occasion an exception was made based on the intention to market these "flood bonds" directly to households.

Three lines of flood bonds were issued, each with an initial maturity of 5 years and each paying a fixed nominal rate of 12.5% for the first year, followed by coupons in subsequent years of 2.5% plus compensation for the change in the domestic CPI over the year.[27] The first line, totalling CZK 1.0bn,[28] was issued on 1 August 1997 (at par, through a network of domestic commercial banks), and its bond certificates were deliberately kept to low denominations (CZK 1,000 or CZK 10,000) in order to increase the security's appeal to individual investors. The second and third lines were subsequently issued in the same manner on 29 August: an issue of CZK 1.2bn issued in physical form (i.e., identical to the first) and an issue of CZK 2.8bn issued in dematerialised form[29] and aimed primarily at institutions. Figures 7.7 and 7.8 illustrate specimen certificates for the two physical issues.

These bonds all matured in August 2002, and the Ministry of Finance has stated that it currently has no intention of issuing inflation-indexed bonds again in the future.

---

[27] The coupon payments were paid each August and were determined from the annual inflation rate from the preceding June. For example, the coupon payment in August 1998 would have been determined from the change in the CPI between June 1997 and June 1998.

[28] Equivalent at the time of issue to approximately US$30mn.

[29] A *dematerialised* security is one for which there are no physical certificates or paper – proof of ownership is electronic.

Figure 7.8 Specimen CZK 10,000 certificate for the second line of the Czech Republic inflation-indexed bond

Reproduced by permission of the Ministry of Finance, Czech Republic

7.8 DENMARK

The first broadly marketed index-linked investment in Denmark became available in 1956 with the introduction of savings schemes operated by private sector banks that paid indexed supplements from the Danish government. However, by 1971 these schemes had proven so popular that the government decided to terminate access to new indexation contracts. At the end of 1997 the balance of such accounts at Danish banks totalled DKr 16.8bn (equivalent to approximately 1.4% of GDP).

On 1 April 1982, following several years of debate, the *Folketing* (Danish parliament) granted permission for mortgage credit institutions to issue inflation-indexed bonds. Parliament was enthusiastic about their introduction because it wished to reduce both its current expenditure on subsidised housing and starting rent levels for non-profit housing. At the time inflation was fairly high (running at approximately 10% per year), as were nominal bond yields (approximately 19%). Traditional financing, based on ordinary annuity loans with constant nominal repayments until redemption, meant that a large proportion of central government expenditure for interest subsidies would be paid during the first few years of the loan's life. However, using index-linked bonds to finance this expenditure meant that nominal repayments would increase over the life of the loan in line with inflation.[30]

[30] Most of the description of the Danish market for index-linked securities that follows is taken from the very comprehensive article by Andersen and Gyntelberg (1999).

The *Folketing* approved the issuance of index-linked mortgage credit bonds[31] to finance several different types of building project, resulting in three different types of index-linked bond being introduced in 1982. *IS bonds* were reserved for directly subsidised housing (eligible for subsidies under the Act on Residential Construction, such as non-profit residential construction), co-operative housing, youth housing and public housing for the elderly. Initially, IS bonds were issued with a maximum maturity of $35\frac{1}{2}$ years and semi-annual payments of 2.4% of the original index-linked loan amount, though the revision of the Mortgage Credit Act (adopted in connection with the 1990 Finance Act) extended the maximum maturity of IS bonds at issue to 50-years and reduced the semi-annual payments to 1.4%. In the event of inflation the increase in the net Retail Prices Index (RPI) is compared with that of the hourly wage index and the lower of the two is used to compute nominal payments (the "real wage clause"). The outstanding debt is uplifted in line with the change in the index while instalments are adjusted at 75% of the increase (the so-called "waltz time scheme"). Any outstanding debt after the maximum loan period will fall due at that time.

Also introduced in the same year were *IE bonds*, reserved for the financing of newly constructed owner-occupied housing and issued with a maturity of $25\frac{1}{2}$ years. IE bonds were also subject to the real wage clause – indexation using the lower of the increases in the net retail price and hourly wage indices – but differed from IS bonds in having a fixed redemption date. All series of IE bonds were closed for further issues in 1989.

The third type of index-linked bond introduced in 1982 was the *I bond*, initially intended to finance business lending and leased properties. However, in May 1983 the rules were extended so that it became possible to issue this type of bond to finance newly constructed owner-occupied homes. Subsequently, following the revision of the Mortgage Credit Act in 1989, I bonds completely superseded IE bonds and thus became the sole index-linked vehicle available to finance this type of property. I bonds are fundamentally different from the IS and IE bonds, since the debtor compensates the investor for the full change in the net RPI. The loans are amortised as serial loans and as such are fully repaid on the fixed redemption date.

The government revised its rules further in 1986 to allow issuance of index-linked bonds for three additional purposes: for loans to the agricultural sector (*IJ* bonds), to finance renewable energy systems (*AI* bonds) and the development of shipyards (*SI* bonds). In order to assist the depressed agricultural sector, "farming" loans (IJ bonds) were introduced in 1986. They have maturities of 30-years and are always fully redeemed on the stipulated redemption date. Such farming loans must be refinanced on change of ownership and are thus the only callable index-linked mortgage credit loans. Since 1990 it has also been possible to issue a 10-year IJ loan which at maturity is refinanced with a 20-year fixed rate mortgage credit loan.[32]

In 1986 it also became possible to finance renewable energy systems by issuing AI bonds, index-linked annuities with maturity at issue of 20-years. The shipyard package in the autumn of 1986 introduced the third new type of index-linked financing – SI bonds – issued exclusively by the Danish Ship Credit Fund with a maximum maturity of $14\frac{1}{2}$ years, a coupon rate of 2.5% or 4% and a deferred payment structure. SI loans

[31] As is the case with all mortgage bonds in Denmark, index-linked or otherwise, each bond is secured on a specific property or group of properties.

[32] Such non-callable loans do not require refinancing in the case of a change in ownership of the underlying property.

also included an inflation guarantee for debtors, that the indexation and interest rate together may not exceed $5\frac{1}{2}\%$ per annum of the principal – effectively a payment "cap". The last loan funded by an SI bond was granted in 1995.

By the end of March 2003 the total market value of the Danish index-linked bond market was DKr 143bn, which represented around 6% of the total bond market.[33] Issuers of index-linked bonds have included mortgage institutions, such as the Agricultural Mortgage Bank and KommuneKredit. The Ship Credit Fund also issued index-linked bonds at one point, but ceased following the abolition of the special ship credit subsidy schemes in 1995.

One of the most important factors in the development of this market was the exemption of index-linked bonds from real interest tax. However, this exemption was removed as part of the 1999 Finance Act on the grounds that:

> *In view of the significant decrease in both inflation and real interest rates in recent years the basis for providing interest subsidies via tax exemption has been reduced considerably. In addition, transparency in the area of subsidies is enhanced by defraying investment subsidies to the expenditure budget rather than by granting less transparent subsidies on the basis of the tax exemption.*

These reforms also favoured financing with traditional, nominal mortgage credit loans rather than index-linked loans. As a result there is no longer a primary market for index-linked bonds and trading is limited to those outstanding bonds that remain exempt from real interest tax.

The Danish government has not issued index-linked bonds and is not expected to do so in the foreseeable future.

7.9 FINLAND

In Finland, financial market indexation was introduced immediately after the Second World War as part of a stabilisation programme. Government index-linked bonds were first issued in 1945 and were tied to the wholesale price index. These bonds took the form of 10-year amortised loans and were primarily issued to fund indemnity payments to evacuees from territories turned over to the Soviet Union following the war. Bonds were issued in indexed form since high inflation was anticipated. The first private sector index-linked bonds were issued in 1953, with cash flows typically linked to the dollar exchange rate or to import, export or output prices.

By the 1960s indexation in Finland had become widespread throughout the economy – in addition to bonds, indexation was also applied to wages, pensions, rents and bank accounts. This was actively encouraged by the authorities, with interest being tax-free[34] on index-linked government bonds and indexed bank accounts, and the policy was successful – by 1967 almost 75% of outstanding bonds and 35% of deposits were indexed. However, following the devaluation of the Finnish markka in 1967, the authorities began to express serious concerns that higher import prices combined with extensive indexation would create further price pressures and potentially lead to an inflationary spiral. This led the government to pass the Economic Special Powers Act in

[33] Source: Copenhagen Stock Exchange.
[34] Tax-free status for fully indexed bank accounts was introduced in 1964.

1968, which prohibited the use of index clauses in both financial and labour market contracts.

Since 1968 successive governments have continued to restrict indexation through the use of fixed term legislation, although in recent years this legislation has become increasingly relaxed. The current legislation, adopted in 1994 and referred to as "The Act on the Limitations on the Use of Index Clauses", has only a two-year rolling term and so has to be periodically renewed.[35] Although the Act places restrictions on indexation in certain contractual relationships, it does not apply to such financial securities as bonds or shares, and so – theoretically at least – index-linked bond issuance in Finland is legally acceptable. But, in spite of this, inflation-indexed securities are rarely issued in the Finnish financial markets and the government itself has not issued any since the loosening of those restrictions first imposed in 1968.

7.10 GERMANY

In Germany there has traditionally been a strong aversion to all types of indexation, stemming from the memory of the hyperinflation experienced there in the 1920s and 1930s. A prohibition on indexation was enshrined in the Federal Republic's Constitution of 1949, and, although in theory financial market practitioners could seek dispensation from the Bundesbank, Lindh and Ohlsson (1992) report that this was never forthcoming.

When Germany entered EMU in 1999 this indexation ban ceased to be valid.[36] As the government's debt manager, the Bundesbank had opposed the issuance of indexed bonds on the grounds that their existence might increase "the risk of fuelling inflation" – see Deutsche Bundesbank (1998, p. 27). The German Finance Agency (*Bundesrepublik Deutschland – Finanzagentur GmbH*) has since taken over responsibility for the operation of Federal debt management and has indicated that it might consider issuing indexed bonds in the future.[37]

Although the German government has yet to issue indexed bonds, a regional Landesbank – Landesbank Baden-Württemberg – launched an indexed bond in July 2002. This 6-year bond is denominated in euros and is indexed to harmonised Euro-zone CPI (Euro-HICP). The Federal State of Saxony-Anhalt has also issued euro-denominated indexed bonds – a 7-year in September 2002 and a 5-year in June 2003. Both of these bonds are indexed to Euro-HICP excluding tobacco.

7.11 GREECE

Following a period of consultation with potential investors and other interested parties, the Greek Ministry of Finance issued its first inflation-indexed bonds – referred to as *State Bonds Index Linked* (SBIL) – on 19 May 1997. Two bonds were issued in this first round – with 5 and 10-year maturities – and both pay a fixed margin of 4% above the

[35] This is renewable on 31 December 2003, 31 December 2005, etc.
[36] See *Investors Chronicle* (1998).
[37] For example, see Bundesrepublik Deutschland – Finanzagentur GmbH (2003, p. 1).

national CPI. The CPI was chosen by the Ministry of Finance because it was considered to be the most widely accepted measure of inflation and familiar to investors. The Ministry sold more than 70bn drachmas (US $277mn) of the bonds on the 19 May and issued two new five and 10-year bonds on 11 August; again, both had 4% real coupons. All four bonds were issued by public subscription.

The SBILs' design is based on that of Canadian Real Return Bonds (RRBs), but with the addition of a deflation floor. Interest is paid annually and is taxable on receipt to domestic investors, but the inflation uplift on the principal, which would normally also be considered to be an interest payment under Greek tax law, is exempt from tax.

Due to the rapid fall in inflation in Greece in recent years, the Ministry of Finance stopped issuing SBILs and even began accepting the bonds as an alternative form of payment in auctions of fixed rate nominal bonds.[38] By the end of May 2002 the total amount outstanding of the three remaining inflation-indexed bonds was around 51bn drachmas.

However, in March 2003 the Finance Ministry issued a new indexed bond, linked to a different index from that used for the SBILs. The new bond is based on the design of the French OAT€*i* securities,[39] with precisely the same inflation index (Euro-HICP excluding tobacco) to increase the attractiveness of the security to investors already familiar with the French bonds. Sale was via a syndicate of three lead managers – JP Morgan, the National Bank of Greece and UBS. The bond matures in July 2025[40] (i.e., just over 22 years to maturity at issue) and pays a real coupon of 2.9%. The Ministry initially intended to issue between €700mn and €1,000mn, but demand in the tender process was strong enough for the size to be increased to 1,250mn. The Greek authorities have made it clear that they issued this security in part due to the perceived strength of demand and, although they intend to build this issue to "benchmark" size (expected to be at least €2bn) in the near future, at this point they have no plans to construct a curve of Greek government Euro-HICP indexed bonds. Analysis on how to assess the relative value between the Greek bond and its French counterparts can be found in JP Morgan (2003).

7.12 HUNGARY

The Hungarian government first issued indexed bonds in May 1995 as a means of extending the maturity of its outstanding debt in the face of high inflation. It first issued a 2-year bond (designated the 1997/O series) which was followed by a 5-year bond (the 2000/C series) in August 1995, with both bonds being sold by public offering. The Hungarian Debt Management Agency (ÁKK) held its first auction of indexed bonds on 10 October 1996 for a new 7-year bond, maturing in September 2003 and referred to as the 2003/F series. The auction was carried out on a multiple price basis with a minimum acceptable price of Hungarian forint (Huf) 99. In addition, auction participants were offered the option of trading in their holdings of the 1996/K series

[38] For more information on the government bond market in Greece readers should refer to Hellenic Republic Ministry of Finance Public Debt Division (2000).
[39] Described in detail in Chapter 6.
[40] Coupon dates are aligned with the French OAT€*i*s.

conventional government bond (which was due to mature on 23 November) as payment for the new bond. Following the auction (at which Huf 9.625bn of the bond was sold) a further Huf 0.736bn was sold by public offering to foreign investors and Hungarian private investors between 14 and 18 October at Huf 102.42, a margin of Huf 0.20 above the average accepted price at auction. The 2003/F bond was reopened at several subsequent auctions and public offerings, and further new bonds were launched in March 1997 (a 7-year indexed bond, the 2004/F series) and July 1997 (a 6.7-year indexed bond, the 2004/G series).

All the Hungarian indexed bonds discussed above are IIBs with annual cash flows equal to the growth in the CPI plus a margin (2% in the case of the 1997/O series, 3.5% in the case of the 2000/C series and 3% in all other cases). Although interest is payable on an annual basis for these bonds, it is calculated as the arithmetic sum of the interest amounts determined for the two (six monthly) interest periods that make up the year. The amount of interest payable for a given (six monthly) interest period is calculated as the pro rata amount of annual interest (rounded to two decimal places), determined as the percentage of the principal based on the actual number of days between the two interest payment days (with the exception of 29 February) and a 365-day calendar year. The annual rate of inflation used for the determination of a given (six monthly) interest payment is defined as the growth in the CPI to the month preceding the coupon date from the same month in the previous year, representing a very short indexation "lag" relative to the design of bonds in the major markets. For example, consider the case of 2003/F, which pays annual coupons on 24 September each year. Interest for this bond is calculated twice yearly, on 20 March and 20 September. The interest for 20 March 2003 will be calculated using the growth in CPI from February 2002 to February 2003, while the interest for 20 September 2003 will be calculated using the growth in CPI from August 2002 to August 2003. For a more detailed explanation of this calculation readers should refer to Hungarian State Treasury (1996).

In May 1998 the ÁKK launched a 7-year inflation-indexed bond of a new design. While the earlier series of indexed bonds were CPI floaters, the new security was a Capital Indexed Bond (CIB) with a structure based on that of Canadian RRBs (see Chapter 6) with some minor differences, which are discussed below. It is referred to as the 2005/D series, has a real coupon of 4%, pays interest on an annual basis and matures on 12 March 2005. Both the coupons and the capital repayment are linked to the CPI with a lag of two months. During the year *real* interest accrues on an actual/365 basis, with the exception that in a leap year no interest is accrued on 29 February (in line with accrual for the CPI floaters described earlier). Nominal accrued interest is then calculated by multiplying real accrued interest by an inflation factor – as is the case for Canadian RRBs or US Treasury Inflation-Protection Securities (TIPS) – but this daily inflation factor is calculated in a slightly different way from its counterpart in the Canadian or US markets. Its calculation is complicated by the fact that there is no single official CPI index in Hungary of the type usually employed in other countries. As a consequence, there is no equivalent to the base CPI index reference level used for inflation-linked bonds elsewhere. Instead of a single inflation measure, the Hungarian Statistical Office publishes two CPI series: the first based on a year ago (=100) and the second based on the previous month (=100), thus giving year-on-year or month-on-month inflation. For the inflation adjustment of the 2005/D bond the month-on-month inflation index is used. The following extract from Barclays

Table 7.4 Hungarian government indexed bonds

Bond series	Bond structure	Coupon (%)	Maturity date	Date of first issue	Nominal amount outstanding (Huf bn)
2003/F	IIB	3.0	24 Sep 2003	17 Oct 1996	49.21
2004/F	IIB	3.0	12 Mar 2004	18 Mar 1997	25.65
2004/G	IIB	3.0	24 Mar 2004	7 Jul 1997	42.20
2005/D	CIB	4.0	12 Mar 2005	14 May 1998	26.40

Data source: Hungarian Debt Management Agency website: www.allampapir.hu (figures as at 30 April 2003). IIB = Interest Indexed Bond; CIB = Capital Indexed Bond.

Capital *Global Inflation-linked Monthly* from June 1998 illustrates how the inflation adjustment is calculated:

> *Interest starts accruing from the [issue date of] 14th May [1998] so a trade settling on the 24th May will have 10 days accrued interest. The reference CPI for this date is the month-on-month CPI for two months earlier. In this case the March CPI of 101.3 implies that monthly inflation was 1.3% in March. So the inflation accrual is 1.3% × 10/31 or 0.42%. The percentage inflation accrual is always rounded to 2 decimal places. The corresponding figure for the 31st May is 0.71% again rounded to 2 decimal places giving an indexation factor (equivalent to US) figure of 1.0071. This is then used as the starting point for June. For example, in June the relevant CPI is the figure for April, 101.0, implying inflation of 1% so on 14th June the inflation accrual in June will be 1.0% × 14/30 = 0.47% which on top of the inflation accrual in May gives an indexation factor of 1.0118. The result would be essentially identical to the US linking methodology if it were not for the rounding to two decimal places at the end of each month. This introduces a chain-linking element where we need to know the previous end-month indexation factor as a base value before we can calculate the values for this month.*

Demand for the 2005/D bond at the May 1998 auction was about double the Huf 5bn (US$23.7mn) on offer. The bond was reopened later in 1998 and then again in February 1999, although demand at this auction was poor. Bids were submitted for Huf 3.1bn and, although Huf 3bn of the bond was on offer, just Huf 2.25bn was allotted, with the ÁKK retaining a further Huf 450mn. Following this auction the ÁKK decided to cease issuing indexed bonds. It reported that institutional demand for the asset class had declined due to a variety of reasons including accounting difficulties and both poor returns and liquidity relative to conventional bonds. As a result, aside from one large insurance company, the only investors that continued to demand the product were from the retail sector. Another reason behind the ÁKK's decision to halt the programme was its desire to make its market simpler by reducing the range of securities that it offered. Table 7.4 provides details of the four Hungarian government indexed bonds currently outstanding.

Aside from government issuance there has been some interest in private sector indexed bonds in Hungary. *Euroweek* (1997) reports that in February 1997 a Hungarian mobile telephone company, Pannon GSM, brought the largest corporate bond issue in Hungary's post-communist era. The issue totalled over Huf 24bn (US$138mn) and consisted of three indexed bonds of 3, 4 and 5-year maturities (each being about

Huf 8bn in size), of a design based on that of the government's CPI floaters, with interest payments determined by the annual CPI growth rate plus 3%.

7.13 ICELAND

Financial indexation in Iceland has a long history. Long-term loans granted by the State Housing Fund to homebuyers have been partially indexed since 1955, while fully indexed government bonds have been issued on a regular basis since 1964. During the 1970s other Investment Credit Funds (ICFs) began indexing their long-term loans to industrial borrowers, as well as issuing indexed or partially indexed securities, which were typically bought by pension funds. Financial indexation was introduced as a means by which the authorities could maintain positive real interest rates to investors during periods of high and variable inflation. More recently, as price stability has begun to take hold in Iceland, the government has gradually limited the scope of financial indexation.

While recognising the benefits that financial indexation has provided in the past, in recent years the authorities have increased the issuance of non-indexed bonds aimed at international investors and hence broaden the appeal of Iceland's capital market. In 1995 the Central Bank of Iceland published new rules on the indexation of deposits and loans which stipulated that from 1998 the minimum permitted maturity of indexed deposits in banking institutions would be increased from 1 to 3 years, while that for indexed loans would be increased from 3 to 5 years. These minimum permitted maturities were extended again in 2000, to 7 years in the case of both deposits and loans.

The inflation index used for Icelandic bonds has changed several times.[41] Prior to 1979 indexed bonds were tied to the Building Cost Index (BCI);[42] however, in June that year a new index referred to as the Credit Terms Index (CTI) was established, a blend of the Cost of Living Index (CLI) with two-thirds weighting and the BCI (one-third weighting). All inflation-indexed bonds issued since 1980 have been linked to the CTI, though the definition of the CTI itself has changed twice. In the first instance, a decline in real wages during the 1980s adversely affected homeowners – due to the fact that mortgages are indexed in Iceland – which led to political pressure to change the index. As a result, in February 1989 the composition of the CTI was changed to include the Wage Index (WI) in addition to the CLI and BCI, with each being given equal weight. Price (1997) reports that the effect of this rebasing was significant, with the revised CTI rising by 7% less than the old index over the period from 1980 to early 1995.

In 1995 the authorities succumbed to further pressure to revise the index – this time in order to minimise the effect of anticipated real wage increases on the debt-servicing burden of households and firms. The wage and building components were both dropped from the CTI, which was then renamed the Consumer Price Index. The government justified this redefinition by observing that the use of a CPI for financial

[41] In addition to inflation-indexed bonds the authorities in Iceland have also issued bonds indexed to the SDR (Special Drawing Right from the IMF) and ECU currency indices.

[42] This index measured the cost of building a "standard" house.

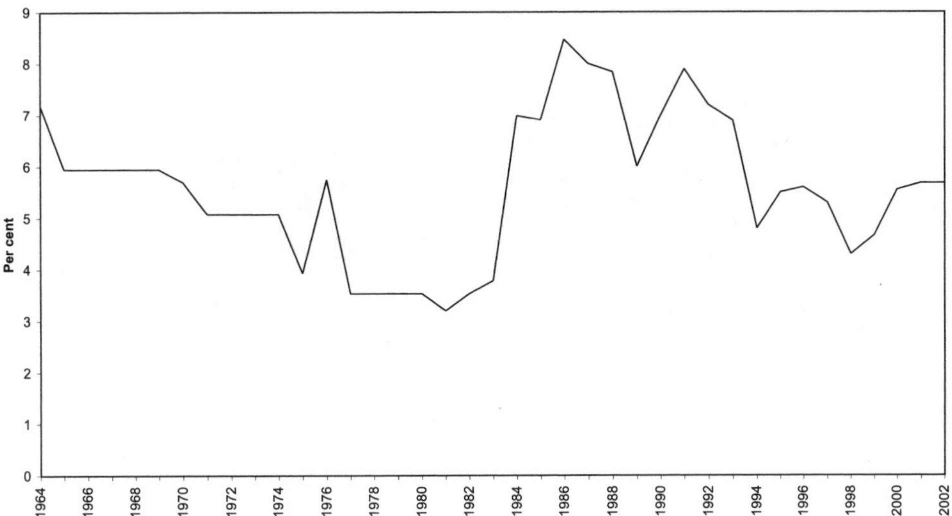

Figure 7.9 Real yield on 10-year Icelandic Treasury Indexed Bonds (annual data, 1964–March 2002)

Data source: National Debt Management Agency, Republic of Iceland

indexation was consistent with the practice in other countries and so would appear more permanent and credible – see Central Bank of Iceland (1995).

Since 1992 the Icelandic government has issued indexed bonds on a monthly basis by multiple yield auctions; prior to that bonds were issued by tap or special agreement. *Treasury bonds* are non-callable CPI indexed bonds with maturities of up to 15 years. These bonds are issued by the National Debt Management Agency (NDMA) and tend to be reopened at auctions for several years after the initial issue in order to establish them as liquid benchmarks. At the end of June 2002 there were five Treasury bonds in issue, two of which were listed as benchmarks on the Iceland Stock Exchange – RIKS 05 0410 and RIKS 15 1001, maturing on 10 April 2005 and 1 October 2015, respectively. As part of its strategy for reducing the proportion of indexed debt in its portfolio the NDMA has actively bought back its indexed bonds. The majority of Treasury bonds accumulate interest until redemption – they pay a single cash flow at redemption consisting of interest and principal components, both of which are adjusted for inflation. More recently Indexed Zero-Coupon Bonds (IZCBs) have also been issued – RIKS 15 1001 is one such bond. Details on the indexation methodology used to compute cash flows for Treasury bonds can be found in Appendix 7.2. Figure 7.9 illustrates the real yield history for 10-year Icelandic Treasury bonds.

Treasury notes are non-indexed, non-callable coupon-bearing or zero-coupon securities issued by the NDMA. At the end of June 2002 there were three issues listed as benchmarks on the Iceland Stock Exchange – RIKB 03 1010, RIKB 07 0209 and RIKB 13 0517, maturing in 2003, 2007 and 2013, respectively. In addition to Treasury notes and bonds there are two further types of government bond – Housing Bonds and Housing Authority Bonds. Both categories of bond are issued by the Housing Financing Fund, which was established on 1 January 1999 and took over all the assets and obligations of its predecessor, the State Housing Board. The Fund's

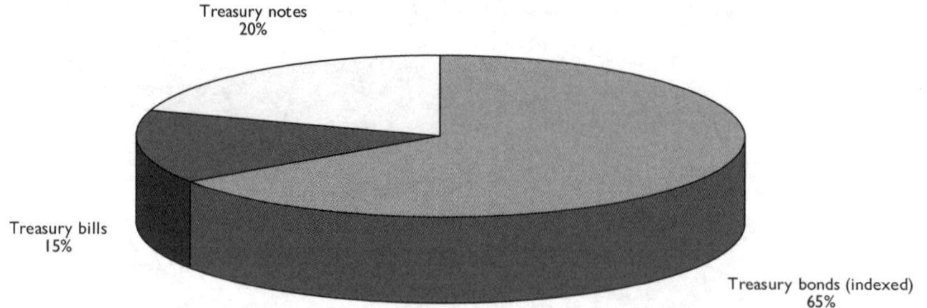

Figure 7.10 Composition of the Icelandic Treasury securities market by market value (as at 31 March 2002)

Data source: National Debt Management Agency, Republic of Iceland

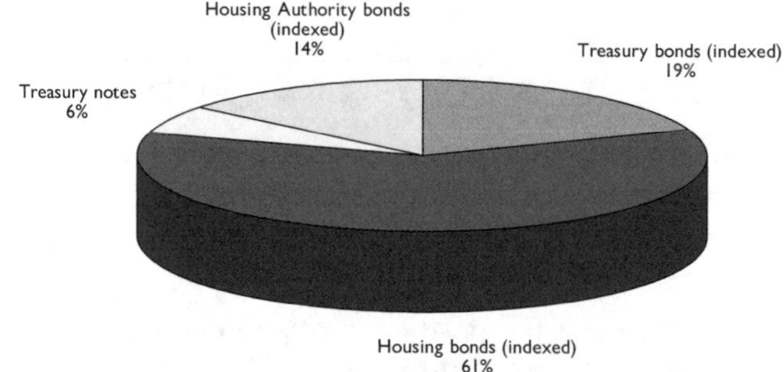

Figure 7.11 Composition of the Icelandic government long-term bond market by market value (as at 31 March 2002)

Data sources: National Debt Management Agency and Iceland Stock Exchange

purpose is to arrange loans to individuals, local authorities, companies and non-governmental organisations with respect to their acquisition of private dwellings, whether for their own use or for leasing out. All bonds issued by the Fund carry an explicit government guarantee, and so can be considered as part of Iceland's government bond market.

Housing Bonds are issued and delivered in exchange for a mortgage loan taken out by the builder or the owner of a property. The bonds are callable CPI indexed annuities and are currently issued with maturities of 25 or 40-years. *Housing Authority Bonds* are non-callable annuities, are indexed to the CPI and are currently issued with maturities of 24 or 42 years.

Despite the ongoing programme to reduce the prevalence of indexation in Iceland's economy, the government bond market is still dominated by indexed bonds. As Figure 7.10 shows, indexed Treasury bonds represented 65% of the total domestic government debt market by market value at the end of March 2002.[43] Considering only long-term government securities,[44] the total market value of indexed bonds outstanding in March 2002 was IKr 340.1bn or 94% of the market – Figure 7.11 provides a

[43] Source: National Debt Management Agency, Republic of Iceland (2001).

[44] Excluding money market instruments, but including the government-guaranteed bonds issued by the Housing Financing Fund.

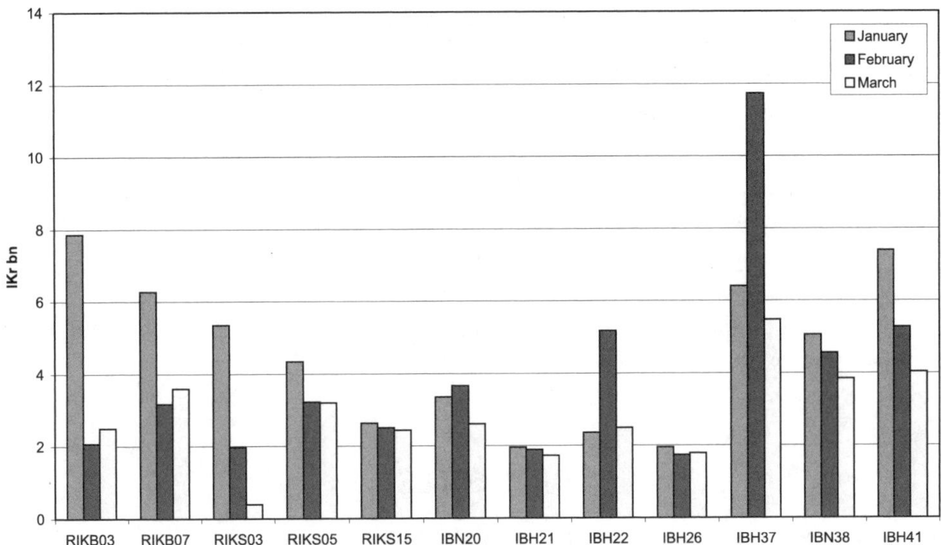

Figure 7.12 Turnover in Icelandic benchmark government bonds (Q1 2002). *Note*: RIKB are non-indexed, all other types of bond are indexed
Data source: Kaupthing Bank

full breakdown. Figure 7.12 provides an indication of relative liquidity between the four different types of government bond.[45]

7.14 INDIA

During the 1990s the authorities in India experimented with issuing a variety of different types of financial instruments, including zero-coupon bonds, partly paid bonds, floating rate bonds and a single inflation-indexed bond. The latter was issued in December 1997 and was indexed to wholesale prices. It had a CIB structure, paid a real coupon of 6% and was issued with a 5-year maturity. At the time of writing this is the only inflation-indexed bond that has been issued by the Indian government.

7.15 IRELAND

Although the Irish government has not itself issued indexed bonds, they have been issued in Ireland by the Housing Finance Agency (HFA) – a state-sponsored company that operates as a funding agency for local authority mortgages.[46] Of the three indexed bonds issued by the HFA, details of the two still outstanding as of June 2003 can be found in Table 7.5 (the third bond, which paid a 2% coupon, matured in 1993).

[45] Here the code RIKB is used to denote Treasury notes, RIKS is used for Treasury bonds, IBN is used for Housing Authority Bonds and IBH is used for Housing Bonds. The numeric part of each code indicates the year of maturity.
[46] For more details about the HFA visit the website www.hfa.ie

Table 7.5 Irish Housing Finance Agency indexed bonds

Coupon (%)	Maturity date	Date of first issue	Nominal amount outstanding (€mn)
2.0	27 Jan 2008	21 Jan 1983	107.9
4.0	3 Apr 2015	3 Apr 1985	95.2

Data source: Housing Finance Agency plc (2003) (figures as at 31 December 2002).

Both the coupon payments and the redemption value of the HFA indexed bonds are adjusted by growth in the CPI with a 6-month lag.[47]

7.16 ISRAEL

For much of its life the Israeli bond market has operated under the shadow of high and volatile inflation. Indexed bonds were first issued by the Israeli government in 1948 as a means of enabling the bond market to function properly under such conditions. Although these bonds were initially linked to the dollar exchange rate, the link was changed to the CPI when devaluations became common after 1955.[48] The early 1950s also saw the establishment of a private sector-indexed bond market in Israel. These private issues were usually indexed to the output prices of the companies concerned, with issuers including those engaged in land development (bringing bonds indexed to the price of land), cement production, orange grove sales and apartment construction (indexed to the price of apartments). During the 1960s and 1970s CPI indexed bonds increasingly dominated the government debt portfolio such that by the mid-1980s almost 100% of government debt was indexed to either the CPI or the US dollar exchange rate.[49]

Throughout the 1970s the annual inflation rate in Israel averaged around 40%, but in the early 1980s this rose to over 100% and peaked above 400% in 1984. As a result the Israeli government embarked on an economic stabilisation programme in July 1985, the main elements of which were a freeze on all shekel aggregates (wages, prices, the exchange rate and credit), a reduction in the domestic budget deficit by cutting subsidies on goods and services and by raising taxes, and the passage of an amendment to the Bank of Israel Law, thereby prohibiting the government from borrowing from the central bank. Implementation of the stabilisation programme had an immediate (and dramatic) impact on inflation, as illustrated by Figure 7.13.

Once the stabilisation programme had begun to take effect the authorities reformed the capital market, the main objective being to reduce the government's involvement.[50] Since the reforms the Israeli bond market has undergone major changes, one of the most significant being a rapid increase in the quantity of non-indexed bonds being

[47] For more information on these bonds see Housing Finance Agency plc (1983).
[48] High inflation continued through the 1950s. For instance, between 1950 and 1955 the price level rose by 130%.
[49] Dollar-indexed debt issuance having resumed by then.
[50] Since its inception the Israeli capital market had experienced a particularly high level of government involvement. Details of the reforms can be found in Battley (1997).

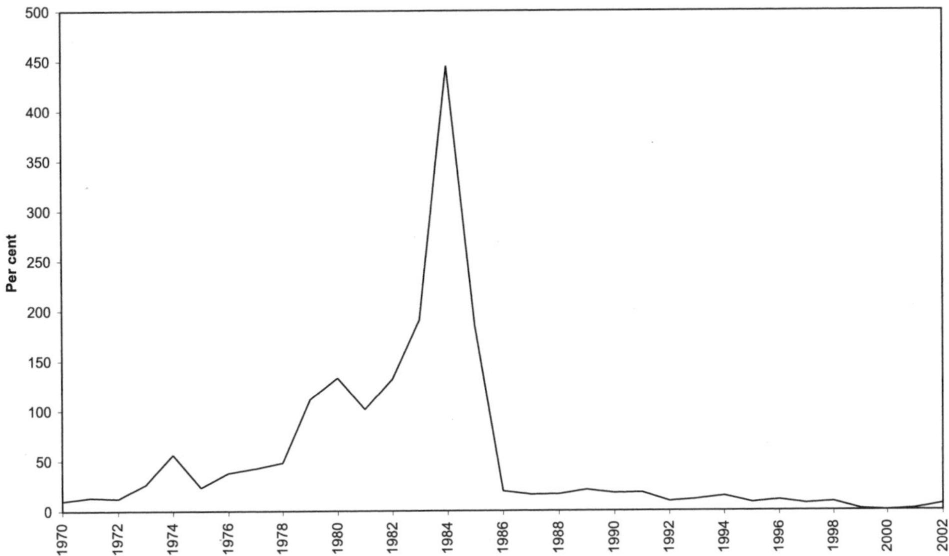

Figure 7.13 Annual Consumer Price Index (CPI) inflation rates in Israel
Data source: Central Bureau of Statistics, Israel

issued. For instance, while non-indexed bonds constituted just 3% of government issuance in 1992, this figure had risen to 88% in 2000[51] before falling off slightly in 2001 and 2002. This move has been part of an ongoing and wide-ranging policy to reduce the role of indexation in the economy and has been aided by exchanges of CPI-linked bonds for nominal bonds. Yariv (1997) suggests that one reason for this policy is to enlarge the lobby against inflation, thereby encouraging the government and the central bank to take a tougher inflationary stance. The development of a nominal bond market has also enabled the Israeli authorities to derive estimates of the markets' expectations of inflation – see Yariv (1994). Figure 7.14 shows the paths of real yields on 2 and 10-year Israeli inflation-indexed bonds over the period from 1985 to 2002.

All debt issued by the Israeli government is currently sold by multiple price auction,[52] and takes the form of either marketable or non-marketable bonds. All non-marketable bonds are indexed to the CPI and predominantly held by pension and insurance funds. Short-term marketable bonds (those with remaining maturities of less than two years) tend to be held by mutual funds specialising in short-term investments and by stock exchange companies; medium-term bonds (2–7 years) tend to be held by mutual funds and by banks that use them for 2–4-year saving schemes; and long-term bonds tend to be held by provident funds, insurance companies and mutual funds. Figure 7.15 illustrates the composition of outstanding marketable government debt at the end of March 2003 and shows that, despite the strong shift toward issuance of

[51] Dollar-indexed bonds are grouped in with CPI indexed bonds for this comparison. Over this period the percentage of issuance in the form of CPI indexed bonds fell from 80% to 11%.

[52] The Bank of Israel switched to a multiple price format for its auctions in the late 1980s – prior to that bonds were sold by single price auction.

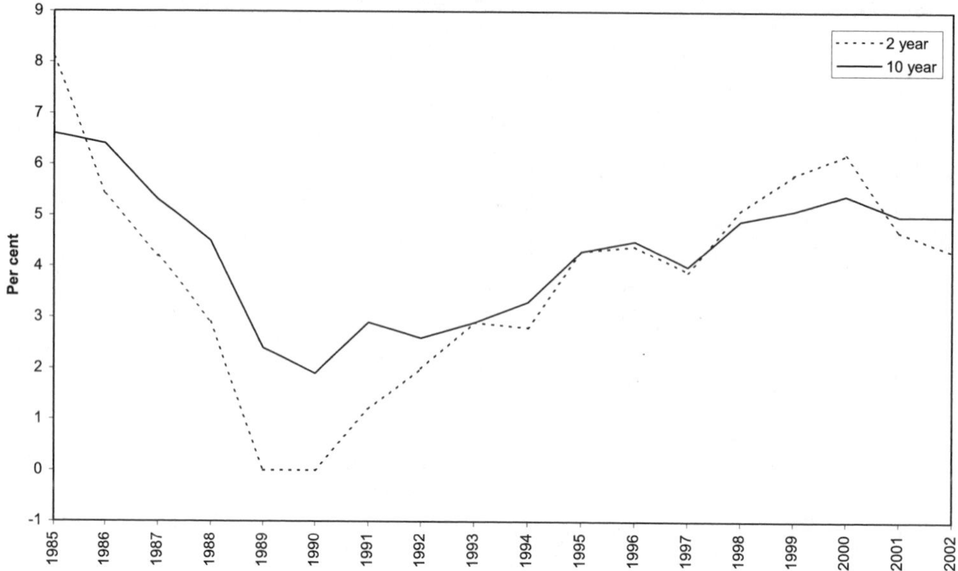

Figure 7.14 Real yields on Israeli (Sagi and Galil) inflation-indexed government bonds (annual average rates, 1985–2002)
Data source: Bank of Israel

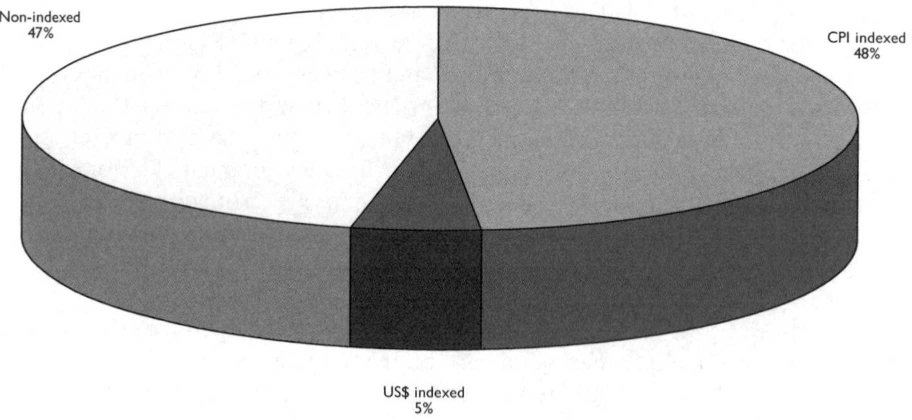

Figure 7.15 Breakdown of Israeli marketable government debt (as at 31 March 2003)
Data source: Bank of Israel

nominal fixed rate bonds, bonds indexed to the CPI still constitute close to half of the debt portfolio.

At present there are four types of marketable indexed government bonds in existence: *Sagi, Galil, Kfir* and *Gilboa.* As in other markets each new bond tends to be reopened over a period of several months.

Sagi and *Galil* are both CPI CIBs that pay annual coupons. The first Sagi bonds were issued in December 1984 and have been issued with maturities of between 5 and

6 years. The fixed coupon rate on these bonds was set by the Ministry of Finance and has ranged from 0% to 8% per annum. The last Sagi bond was issued in November 1997. The first Galil bond was also issued in December 1984 and, though in general they can be issued with between two and thirty years to maturity, in practice they have been issued with maturities between seven and twenty years. The coupon rate on Galil bonds is determined to be the higher of 1% and the weighted average yield of all fixed interest CPI indexed bonds of corresponding maturity. Galil bonds are still being issued, although several changes were made to their terms in November 1998.

Kfir bonds were introduced in September 1990 and are floating rate bonds with cash-flows indexed to the CPI. The original Kfir bonds paid semi-annual coupons and were issued with maturities of between 7 and 12 years (although in theory the authorities were permitted to issue Kfir with maturities of between 4 and 25 years). Kfir bonds are structured differently from the floating rate indexed bond designs discussed in Chapter 2. Whereas the real coupons on IIBs and current pay bonds are fixed, the real rate floats on Kfir bonds and is set according to the secondary market real yield on tradable 3–5-year fixed rate CPI indexed bonds. Both principal and interest payments are indexed, and the principal uplift is paid at redemption.[53] In February 1998 Kfir bonds were superseded by *New Kfir* bonds. Although structurally similar to their predecessors, these new bonds paid quarterly coupons and were issued as 6-year instruments (although New Kfir bonds with maturities of anything between 1 and 25 years could have been issued should the authorities have chosen to do so). The interest is calculated once every three months for the subsequent quarter in the following manner: the annual rate of interest is calculated as the weighted average of the gross yields in the secondary market of marketable, fixed rate, CPI indexed government bonds with a term to maturity of between 2 and 5 years,[54] during the two calendar months preceding the month during which the interest was set. The last New Kfir bond was issued in November 1999.

Sagi, Galil and Kfir bonds are all indexed to the CPI with a lag of one month. Although all CPI-linked bonds currently outstanding are fully indexed, in the 1970s partially indexed bonds were issued, providing only 80% or 90% inflation compensation. Figure 7.16 illustrates how the annual issuance of CPI indexed bonds has been split between Sagi, Galil and Kfir since 1996.

Gilboa are dollar-linked floating rate bonds with semi-annual coupon payments based on six-month LIBOR (London Inter Bank Offer Rate) rates and were issued with maturities of either 4–5 years or 10-years. The last Gilboa bond was issued in January 2000.

The Israeli government currently issues two types of nominal bonds: *Shahar* (fixed rate) and *New Gilon* (floating rate), which were introduced in August 1995 and April 1999, respectively.[55] Figure 7.17 graphically illustrates how the introduction of nominal bonds in 1992 has changed the composition of the government's debt issuance profile.

[53] The price-yield equations for Sagi, Galil and Kfir bonds appear in Appendix 7.3.
[54] The gross yields are weighted by market value.
[55] In fact, *New Gilon* bonds superseded *Gilon* bonds in April 1999. Gilon bonds were originally introduced in July 1992.

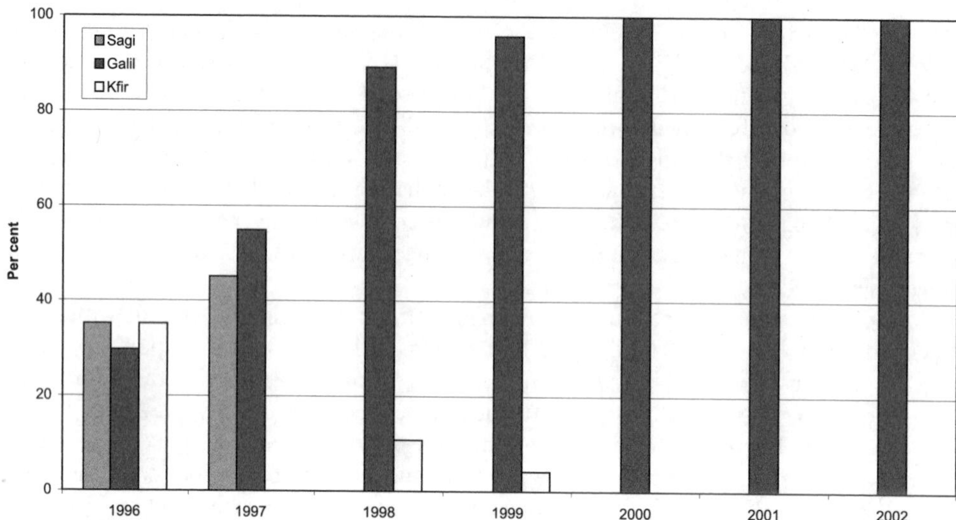

Figure 7.16 Breakdown of Israeli marketable government CPI indexed bond issuance (1996–2002)

Data source: Bank of Israel

Figure 7.17 Breakdown of Israeli marketable government debt issuance by market value (1988–2002)

Data sources: Bank of Israel and the Ministry of Finance, Israel

7.17 ITALY

The idea of issuing index-linked government bonds in Italy can be traced back to the Baffi Commission's "Report on the Defence of Savings from Inflation" of 1981[56] and the subsequent report of the Monti Commission in 1982.[57] However, to date, the Italian Treasury has issued only two inflation-indexed securities. The first was a 10-year bond issued in August 1983 and was known as a *Certificato del Tesoro Reali*[58] or CTR. The CTR paid coupons annually, and both coupons and principal were adjusted for the change in inflation. The government decided to issue CTRs to extend the maturity of government debt, enhance monetary policy credibility and lower the cost of borrowing. During the early 1980s the Italian government also introduced other new types of securities, such as floating rate notes and ECU-denominated bonds as part of its strategy of lengthening the average life of government debt.

However, the 1983 issue was not the success that had been hoped for. The Treasury offered several explanations for this in its public debt report of 1988:[59]

> *The failure is to be attributed more to the timing and method of making the issue than to a lack of interest on the part of investors. The issue was made suddenly, without investors being adequately informed, during the August holiday period. In addition, the real interest rate offered, 2.5%, was too low in comparison with market rates.*

As a result the market initially repriced the CTR to provide a real yield of between 3% and 4%, and later, as the bond approached maturity, it was priced to bring its nominal yield into line with that of conventional securities. Foresi *et al.* (1997) suggest several further possible reasons for the failure of the issue: it was too small to be liquid (lira 1,000bn – approximately US$630mn);[60] the indexation lag of a year was too long; and there was a general lack of familiarity with the chosen price index (the deflator of GDP at factor cost[61]).

Despite the problems outlined above, the CTR does appear to have produced cost savings for the Italian government. Foresi *et al.* (1997) compare the cash flow cost of the CTR over its life with three alternative borrowing strategies: issuing a single floating rate bond, rolling over one-year Treasury bills, or issuing a basket of securities with characteristics similar to the outstanding debt. Relative to the total debt-servicing costs of the government over this 10-year period, their analysis suggests that the savings from issuing the CTR were between 12% and 20%. The authors qualify these results by noting that inflation declined unexpectedly during the life of the bond and that there was probably a large liquidity premium attached to the privately placed issue so the selling price may have been artificially high. However, although these factors may have biased upward their estimate of the total savings, the authors are convinced that the bonds did produce a genuine cost reduction for the Italian government.

---

[56] See Ministero del Tesoro (1981).

[57] See Ministero del Tesoro (1982).

[58] Real Treasury Certificate.

[59] See Ministero del Tesoro – Direzione Generale del Debito Pubblico (1988, vol. 1, p. 80).

[60] The small size of the bond was partly due to the fact that it was seen as an experimental issue rather than as part of a committed programme.

[61] The Italian government chose this index in preference to the CPI because of concerns that using the latter could lead to the "import" of inflation. That is to say, if the currency was to fall the CPI would increase as the cost of importing goods would rise.

Although the introduction of the CTR in 1983 was not a great success, support for the idea of issuing government index-linked bonds in Italy remained. The *Report on Financial Wealth, the Public Debt and Monetary Policy* published in 1987 by the Sarcinelli Commission recommended greater and more regular issuance of CTRs, and in its 1988 public debt report the Treasury suggested that "the Italian domestic market would express a demand for such a bond, especially if it were issued with a longish maturity."

More recently, the University of Rome hosted a conference in October 1995 entitled "Index-linked Bonds in Theory and Practice". At the conference Barone and Masera (1997) discussed possible design features for a new type of CTR, including indexation to the CPI, a 15-day indexation lag and quarterly reopening of the bond in order to help establish liquidity. The potential for cost savings that could be made from the issuance of indexed bonds was also discussed at the conference (Foresi *et al.*, 1997).

In December 2002 the Treasury announced that during 2003–04 it would evaluate whether to launch an inflation-indexed bond programme.[62] Following the successful completion of this exercise, in September 2003 the Treasury launched a 5-year BTP[63] indexed to Euro-HICP excluding tobacco. The bond, which has a 1.65% real coupon and matures in September 2008, was sold through a syndicate with lead managers Banca IMI, MCC-Capitalia and Morgan Stanley.[64] Although the market had initially expected the size of the issue to be between €2–3bn, stronger than anticipated demand enabled the Treasury to sell €7bn nominal, the largest ever syndication of a single inflation-linked bond. The issue attracted over €11bn in orders from more than 220 investors and sold at a price of €99.79, equivalent to a real yield of 1.694%. The bond shares the same instrument design as the French OAT€*i* bonds although coupons for the BTP€*i* are paid semi-annually.

Despite the relative lack of Treasury issuance, there has been a reasonable amount of issuance of indexed bonds by other Italian financial institutions. The Istituto Italiano di Credito Fondiario[65] has issued several CPI indexed bonds, the first issue taking place in April 1982 (over a year before the Treasury issue) and the most recent in January 1992. At end-March 2003 there were two Istituto Italiano di Credito Fondiario CPI indexed bonds outstanding: both bonds were originally issued as 15-year bonds, have sinking funds and offer only partial inflation protection – the indexation adjustment representing 75% of the change in the CPI. In 1998 the commercial bank Monte dei Paschi di Siena issued a 10-year bond indexed to Euro-HICP which has the feature of deflation floors on both the principal and the annual coupon payments.

Another bank, Banco Ambrosiano issued an indexed bond in January 2001 with a novel cash flow structure: this 10-year bond paid a fixed nominal coupon on its first coupon date (5 January 2002) and then annual coupons linked to Euro-HICP until 5 January 2006, the date on which it could be called. Coupon payments for the final 5 years of the bond's life are based on the 12-month EURIBOR (i.e., nominal) money market rate. While there was only limited inflation-indexed issuance between 1982 and 2001, during 2002 and 2003 a significant number of new issues have been launched. The

[62] Department of the (Italian) Treasury (2002).
[63] Buoni Poliennali del Tesoro. The inflation-indexed BTP is often referred to as a BTP€*i*.
[64] The inclusion of two Italian banks in the syndicate reflected the attraction such securities held for domestic retail investors at the time. See Chapters 8 and 9 for more details.
[65] The Italian Institute of Mortgage (Landed) Credit is a financial services company specialising in Italian mortgage loans.

majority of bonds are issued by banks and have five-year maturities, with indexation to either Euro-HICP or Euro-HICP excluding tobacco. Many are equity-linked notes aimed at the retail sector, and the volume of such issuance has helped the development of the Euro-HICP inflation swap market – see Chapter 8.

7.18 JAPAN

Although no legal restriction on indexation exists in Japan, the government has yet to issue indexed bonds. However, in September 2002 the Ministry of Finance announced that it has plans to do so, their stated intention being to provide a vehicle to appeal to investors who might be concerned that inflation will erode the value of nominal bond payments.[66] In the past, the Bank of Japan has also expressed an interest in the introduction of indexed bonds because of the information that they can provide to monetary policy makers.[67]

In its planned issuance programme for the 2003/04 financial year the Ministry of Finance indicated that it anticipates issuing 100 billion yen of index-linked government bonds during the year.[68] It has subsequently reaffirmed this intention and has indicated that its first indexed JGB (Japanese Government Bond) will be launched sometime between January and March 2004. The first bond will have a 10-year maturity and will be linked to the core CPI with a 3-month lag. Perhaps surprisingly, the Ministry of Finance decided that such bonds will not feature a deflation floor for the principal payment, particularly interesting in the light of Japan's recent and prolonged experience of CPI deflation (see Figure 7.18).

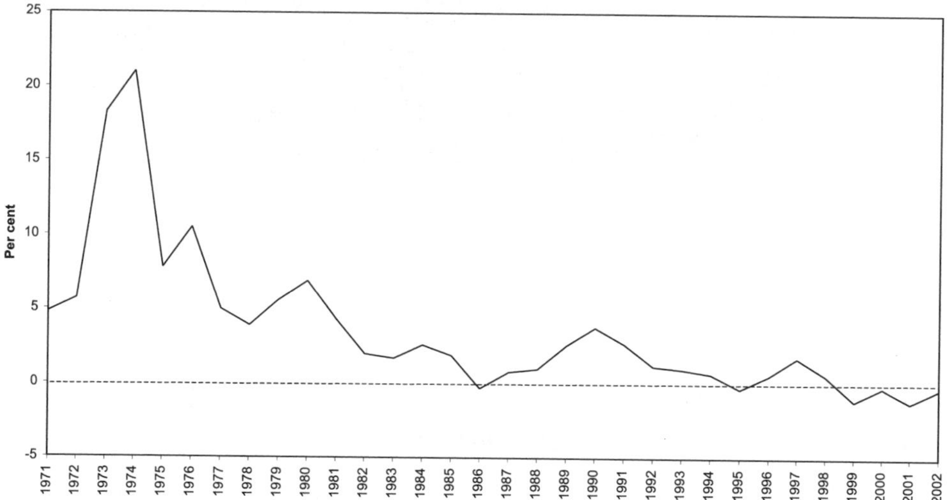

Figure 7.18 Annual percentage change in the Japanese Consumer Price Index (CPI) (December to December)

Data source: Statistics Bureau, Japan

[66] See Bloomberg (2002).
[67] See Kitamura (1997).
[68] See Ministry of Finance, Japan (2002).

7.19 KAZAKHSTAN

The Ministry of Finance in Kazakhstan has been issuing *Inflation-Indexed Treasury Securities* (IITS) on a monthly basis since 1999, although in practice it is the National Bank of Kazakhstan that is actually responsible for auctioning and redeeming all government bonds, as part of its role as a financial agent of the Finance Ministry. Participation at these auctions is limited to primary dealers as approved by the Finance Ministry.

IITS are indexed to consumer prices and have a floating real coupon rate, which is refixed annually. Cash flows on these bonds are paid on a quarterly basis and consist of both interest and principal components. As of 13 August 2002 the size of the IITS market was 8,554mn tenge (equivalent at the time to around US$55.4mn) and represented approximately 10% of the domestic government debt market. The Ministry of Finance has issued IITS at a range of maturities ranging from 9 months to 7 years, although the 9-month bonds have now matured. Figure 7.19 illustrates the breakdown of the IITS market by time to maturity at issue.

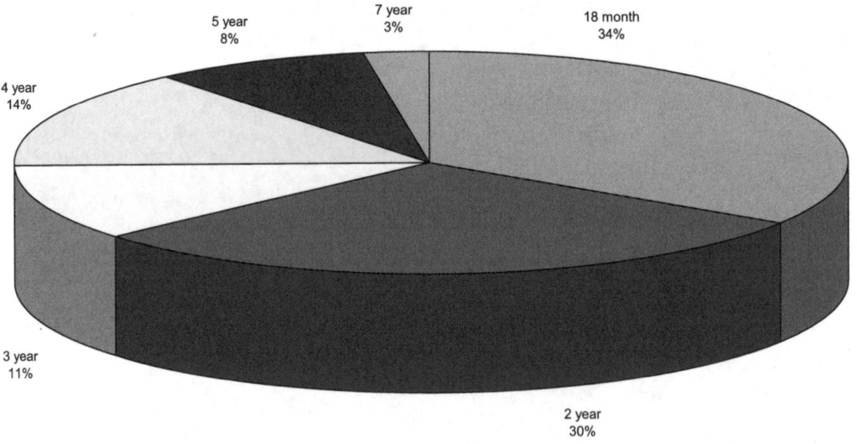

Figure 7.19 Breakdown of Kazakhstan's Inflation-Indexed Treasury Securities (IITS) market by maturity at issue (as at 13 August 2002)
Data source: National Bank of Kazakhstan

7.20 MEXICO

Mexico's indexed bond market dates back at least as far as the late 1970s and the petrobond issues of the State Development Corporation, Nafinsa. These bonds were issued with a 3-year maturity and paid a return linked to the increase in the oil price. Today there exists a large number of indexed corporate bonds, with issue maturities ranging from under 2 years to almost 30 years. The Mexican government introduced indexed bonds in July 1989 as part of its financial market reforms aimed at transforming government financing from direct bank credit to marketable public debt. In addition to *ajustabonos* (*Bonos Ajustables del Gobierno Federal*), linked to the National Consumer Price Index (NCPI), the government also introduced *tesobonos* tied to the dollar exchange rate. Although initially only issued as three-year instruments, in November 1990 the Mexican government began to offer 5-year ajustabonos – with both lines structured as CIBs that paid coupons on a quarterly basis. High inflation in the past had led the government to publish the NCPI bimonthly,[69] enabling ajustabonos to employ an indexation lag as short as two weeks.

In 1994 recurrent pressures on the peso and the maintenance of an exchange rate band led the Mexican authorities to encourage investors to switch their peso-denominated government bonds (including ajustabonos) into dollar-denominated tesobonos. However, although this may have helped stabilise the financial markets in the short run, by the end of the year the authorities were forced to abandon the exchange rate band and the peso depreciated by 63%. All tesobonos were redeemed as part of the subsequent macroeconomic stabilisation programme, while the Ministry of Finance and Public Credit ceased issuing inflation-indexed ajustabonos in January 1995.

On 30 May 1996 the government introduced a new form of inflation-linked security in place of ajustabonos – *Bonos de Unidades de Inversión* or *udibonos* (Federal Government Development Bonds denominated in Investment Units). These are CIBs that pay semi-annual coupons linked to the *Unidad de Inversión* (UDI), an inflation-linked unit of value defined in terms of the CPI. They were issued to help extend the maturity of public debt, to lower the cost of funding and to increase the range of public financing instruments.[70] Initially, all udibonos had maturities of three years, but as the instrument became more established the authorities gradually lengthened the maturities of new issues as a means of extending the average maturity of its debt. On 20 February 1997 the first 5-year bond was issued, while issuance of 3-year udibonos ceased on 20 August 1998. Subsequently, the authorities launched the first 10-year udibono on 14 October 1999 and issued the last 5-year udibono on 14 September 2000. Currently only 10-year udibonos are issued, although some of the 5-year bonds have yet to mature. Real coupons have varied from 6% to 8.4%.

The Ministry of Finance and Public Credit preannounces its quarterly auction calendar toward the end of the preceding quarter. Udibonos are auctioned on a multiple price basis every six weeks to brokers, banks, finance and insurance companies as well as to investment funds. Retail clients cannot bid at auction, but instead can purchase bonds through brokers. As Figure 7.20 shows, at the end of March 2003 udibonos constituted 9.4% of the total uplifted nominal amount of outstanding domestic government securities. In addition to udibonos there are three other types of peso-denominated government securities issued by the Mexican government: *cetes* (short-term fixed rate securities), *bondes* (FRNs) and *bonos* (long-term fixed rate securities). Now that the authorities have successfully established the market for long-term fixed rate government bonds they are no longer as reliant on the issuance of inflation-indexed bonds to extend the maturity of the debt profile, and so the share of udibonos in the government debt portfolio has gradually been falling.

[69] The index number for the first 15 days of the month is announced on the 25th of each month and the index figure for the latter 15 days of the month is released on the 10th of the following month.
[70] Ministry of Finance and Public Credit, Mexico (1996).

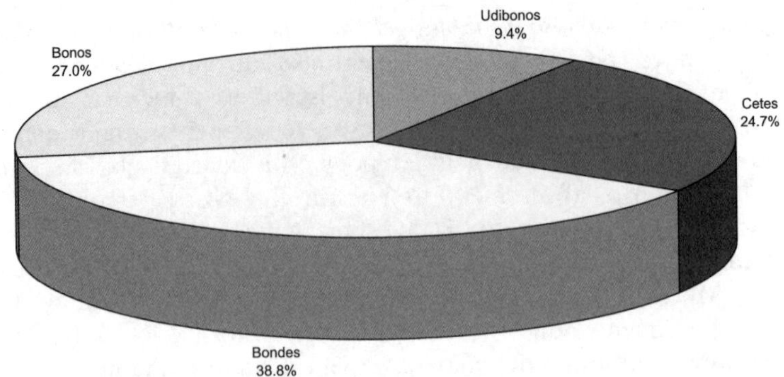

Figure 7.20 Composition of outstanding Mexican government peso-denominated debt (as a percentage of uplifted nominal amount as at 31 March 2003)
Data source: Minstry of Finance and Public Credit, Mexico (2003)

Demand for such securities is also now being met by the private sector, and the promotion of the non-government-indexed bond market was another factor behind the government's decision to reduce issuance of udibonos, as announced in July 2000.[71] The issuance of UDI-indexed bonds by issuers other than the Ministry of Finance and Public Credit – mostly large corporations – has thus become an important source of supply in recent years. While the majority of bonds in this market have maturities shorter than 15 years there are some exceptions: for instance, Highway *Indemnization* Bonds (which carry a Federal Government guarantee) have been issued with maturities as long as 30 years.

7.21 NETHERLANDS

In the Netherlands the issuance of indexed bonds was prohibited until November 1990, when the ban was lifted as part of a more general liberalisation of the capital market. However, an indexed bond market has failed to develop. Although large insurance companies have indicated an interest in purchasing such bonds, there have been few private sector issues and the government has clearly stated that it has no intention of stimulating the market.[72] The main reason for this lack of government interest seems to be a concern that indexed bond issuance could prove costly should an unanticipated acceleration of inflation occur, as this would give rise to increased (nominal) interest costs.[73] The handful of private sector indexed bonds that have been issued to date have maturities of between two and ten years and are indexed to Euro-zone CPI.

7.22 NEW ZEALAND

The New Zealand government first issued inflation-indexed bonds in 1977, to emphasise the government's commitment to controlling inflation and to provide a means by which

[71] See Ministry of Finance and Public Credit, Mexico (2000).
[72] See Lindh and Ohlsson (1992).
[73] See Hallsten (1993).

the authorities could fund its deficit without locking into what they viewed to be the excessively high nominal yields demanded by the market for conventional debt at the time. Between 1977 and 1984 the government issued two main types of CPI indexed bonds.[74] *Inflation Adjusted Savings Bonds* (IASBs) were non-marketable bonds sold to the retail market on a tap basis. These bonds were particularly popular with those individuals facing high marginal tax rates, since the inflation uplift on the principal was tax-free.[75] This tax treatment, coupled with the fact that the bonds had no fixed maturity date, meant that they were expensive for the government and they were all redeemed in 1994. The total amount outstanding of IASBs peaked at NZ$933mn in 1983, equivalent to 8.7% of total domestic government debt.

Index Linked New Zealand Government Stocks (ILNZGSs) were introduced in December 1983. These were issued to the wholesale market through tenders to primary dealers and had maturities ranging from just over three years to just over eighteen years. At the peak in 1986/87, the total amount outstanding stood at NZ$1,878mn, equivalent to 11% of total domestic government debt. However, all of these bonds have now either matured or been repurchased by the government and cancelled.[76]

ILNZGSs were IIBs that paid semi-annual coupons. The inflation adjustment was calculated as the percentage change in the "All Groups" CPI for the 6 months ending in the quarter immediately prior to the coupon payment, provided that this amount was greater than zero. If the relevant 6-monthly change in the CPI was negative, then the inflation adjustment was set to equal zero – in other words, a deflation "floor" was applied for each 6-month period. The bonds were fully taxable – both the coupon and any capital gain on the principal were taxed. ILNZGSs could be stripped to separate the inflation (CPI) element of the coupon from the fixed part of the coupon – something that proved popular according to Potter (1995).

On 20 December 1994 Bill Birch, then Minister of Finance, announced that the Treasury was designing a new type of inflation-indexed bond for the wholesale market. Support for New Zealand's return to index-linked issuance came from Donald Brash, the Governor of the Reserve Bank of New Zealand. In a speech made to the Society of Actuaries in April 1995 Brash stated:[77]

> *I am convinced that issuing inflation-adjusted bonds has great benefit to the ordinary New Zealand saver. To put this in context, it is worth recalling that inflation is a process, sanctioned by the Government and the central bank, which enables borrowers to steal from savers... Issuing inflation-adjusted bonds is the best way of saying that, even if some future Government decides to sanction theft-through-inflation, the present Government does not approve of such theft, and is willing to provide a means by which savers can protect themselves against it.*

Governor Brash put forward further reasons why he thought that the issuance of index-linked bonds would be beneficial: it would enable the government to reduce the real cost of borrowing *vis-à-vis* nominal debt, help the Reserve Bank to maintain price stability and provide a measure of inflation expectations.

---

[74] In addition, a third type – "New Zealand Government Our New Zealand Bonds" – were sold to the retail sector. Issuance of all three types of bond ceased in 1984.
[75] In the late 1970s marginal income tax rates in New Zealand were as high as 60%.
[76] The last bond matured in 2001.
[77] See Brash (1995).

Table 7.6 New Zealand Treasury inflation-indexed bond auction results

Auction date	Amount issued (NZ$mn)	Bid-to-cover ratio	Allocation yield (%)
23 Nov 1995	75	5.9	5.0
29 Feb 1996	48	1.3	5.6
16 May 1996	75	3.2	6.0
27 Jun 1996	76	2.2	6.1
25 Jul 1996	50	2.0	5.9
26 Sep 1996	50	5.9	5.8
28 Nov 1996	49	3.6	4.9
13 Feb 1997	50	2.2	4.8
3 Apr 1997	50	1.7	5.4
5 Jun 1997	50	3.4	5.2
21 Aug 1997	50	5.2	5.3
9 Oct 1997	50	4.8	5.0
20 Nov 1997	50	5.0	5.0
22 Jan 1998	50	3.5	5.2
2 Apr 1998	50	3.5	5.3
21 May 1998	50	3.7	5.0
27 Aug 1998	50	2.1	4.8
22 Oct 1998	48	2.3	4.6
26 Nov 1998	50	1.3	4.8
25 Feb 1999	50	3.1	4.9
25 Mar 1999	50	1.9	5.0
27 May 1999	50	3.6	4.7

Data source: The New Zealand Debt Management Office.

From the Treasury's perspective the main benefit was to enable the government to diversify its funding base, and in June 1995[78] it confirmed its intention of issuing a new inflation-indexed bond during the 1995/96 fiscal year. Full details of the new security, referred to as an *Inflation-Indexed Bond*, were announced in October:[79] a real coupon of $4\frac{1}{2}$% and a maturity date of 15 February 2016. The first auction occurred on 23 November 1995, though the bond has since been reopened many times (see Table 7.6). The bond has always been issued by single yield auction, with the highest accepted real yield (the yield at which all bonds are allocated) being converted into a settlement price using a standard formula published by the Debt Management Office (DMO).[80] As the Inflation-Indexed Bond trades on a real yield basis in the secondary market this formula is also used to settle trades.

The structure of the Inflation-Indexed Bond is based on that of Australia's CIBs, with both the quarterly interest payments and the principal adjusted by the average quarterly percentage change in the "All Groups" CPI over the 6-month period ending two quarters prior to that in which the next interest payment falls. For example, the coupon paid in February 1997 was calculated using an adjustment based on the average

[78] See New Zealand Debt Management Office (1995a).
[79] See New Zealand Debt Management Office (1995b).
[80] The price-yield formula is given in Appendix 7.4.

quarterly movement in the CPI over the two-quarter period ending in September 1996.[81] The tax treatment of the bond is the same as that for conventional New Zealand government bonds, with inflation uplift on both coupons and principal being subject to income tax.

Although the bond is sold primarily to the wholesale market, it is eligible to be broken down into smaller parcels for retail investors. It is also eligible for stripping into three components: the unadjusted principal, the principal uplift and the set of adjusted nominal coupon payments.[82] Holders of the set of coupon payments (i.e., an annuity) can apply to separate further the individual coupons. Despite some initial interest in stripping the Inflation-Indexed Bond, none had taken place by the end of April 2002.

Initial response to the Inflation-Indexed Bond was poor. This was partly due to the fact that a number of major institutional investors were unsure of how to classify the instrument within their internal asset allocations. In addition it has been suggested that investor confidence in the strength of the government's monetary policy framework was such that indexed bonds served little purpose, though doubts over the DMO's commitment to increase the liquidity of the issue also appear to have contributed to the bond's poor reception. Following the first few auctions interest in the bond increased, reflected in both an increase in the bid-to-cover ratio and a reduction in the real yields achieved at auction. However, more recently demand again waned and since the 1999/2000 financial year the DMO has suspended issuance of its indexed bond – partly due to the reduced demand but also reflecting cost considerations, the spread relative to nominal bonds having declined substantially from that achieved when the bond was first introduced.

Liquidity of the Inflation-Indexed Bond in the secondary market is poor compared with nominal bonds, partly due to its relatively small issue size (currently NZ$1,171mn, compared with nominal bonds that typically have sizes in excess of NZ$3,500mn). During 1999 average turnover for the bond was around NZ$75mn per month compared with NZ$19,000mn per month for nominal bonds.[83] Inflation-indexed bond turnover represented around 0.5% of total bond turnover while representing 6.3% of the total bonds in the market. Approximately half the bond is held offshore, with the majority of the remainder being held by domestic institutions. Domestic fund managers still do not appear to treat inflation-indexed bonds as an asset class in their own right, and this would seem to have further hampered demand for the product. Perhaps unsurprisingly, a corporate indexed bond market has not developed. More information on the New Zealand inflation-indexed bond market appears in Reddell and Watt (1997).

7.23 NORWAY

The Norwegian government has issued indexed bonds on only two occasions – in January and May 1982. These bonds – referred to as *Verdi-Spar* – were designed to

[81] See Appendix 7.4 for further details on the indexation technique.

[82] The New Zealand indexed strip market is unique in allowing the principal uplift to be separated from the unadjusted principal in this way.

[83] There were eight nominal government bonds outstanding as of December 1999, representing a total nominal amount of NZ$26.0bn.

be a retail savings vehicle linked to the CPI and were issued with a maturity of 5 years.[84] According to Price (1997), issuance was abandoned as falling inflation and a reduction in tax rates made them less attractive to domestic investors. Although there have not been any further issues from the government, some CPI indexed bonds were issued by financial institutions and regional government bodies in the 1990s. The maturities of these bonds range from 9 to 20 years, with the most recent having been issued in December 1998 by Industrifinans Naeringseiendom Asa, a real estate investment trust.

7.24 PERU

Private sector bonds indexed to inflation were first issued in Peru in 1994. These bonds are linked to the *Valor Adquisitivo Constante* or VAC, an index based on consumer prices. Their maturities at issue range from 4 to 6 years and some are callable. Although the Peruvian government has not itself issued inflation-indexed bonds, they have been issued by a public agency – the Corporación Financiera de Desarrollo SA (COFIDE). COFIDE began issuing CPI indexed bonds in 1999, and by end March 2002 the total amount outstanding had grown to 281mn soles, equivalent to 14% of the public sector bond market. COFIDE has issued several bonds, with maturities of between 5 and 10 years. Figure 7.21 provides a breakdown of the Peruvian bond market as at end March 2002.

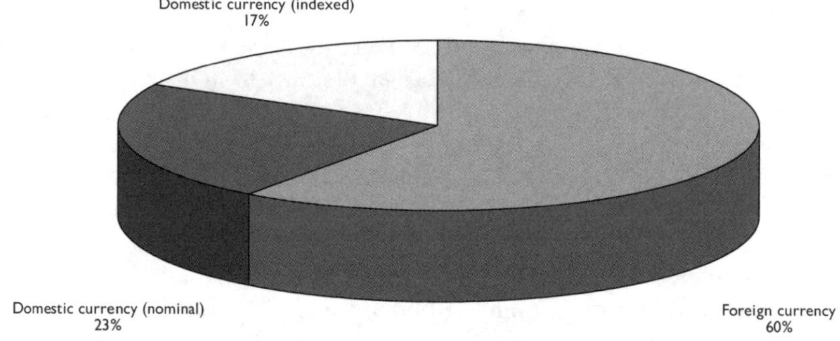

Figure 7.21 Composition of the Peruvian bond market (as at 31 March 2002)
Dat source: Central Reserve Bank of Peru

7.25 POLAND

In 1989 Poland's transition from a centrally planned economy to a market-based one led to the implementation of important political, economic and financial reforms. The financial reforms included reopening the Warsaw Stock Exchange – which had been closed since 1939 – and the establishment of the National Depository for Securities to provide clearing and settlement services. Until 1991 the state had met its financing needs

[84] For more details on these bonds see Royal Ministry of Finance and Customs, Norway (1982).

by borrowing directly from the National Bank of Poland. However, since then the government's main source of financing has come from the issuance of Treasury bills and bonds by the Ministry of Finance.

The Ministry of Finance began issuing 1-year index-linked bonds in May 1992, motivated by the high and variable price inflation experienced at the time. Initially these bonds were in the form of *PPJ* bonds – a new bond being introduced every three months that could be purchased either before the beginning of each quarter at auction, or by public sale at any time up to the end of the quarter.[85] Interest on PPJs was paid at maturity and was calculated as the growth in the CPI plus a margin of 5%. This annual CPI growth factor was computed as the product of the 12 monthly growth factors, lagged by two months (an example later in this section clarifies how the indexation worked). PPJ bonds were available for public sale until the end of May 1994 and the last one matured in March 1995.

In May 1994 the Ministry of Finance auctioned its first index-linked *IR* bond. Although these had the same design as PPJ bonds, some of the rules of sale were different. For instance, while the ownership of PPJ bonds had been limited to domestic investors, foreign investors were also eligible to purchase IR bonds. Also, in addition to the established auction and public sale methods, from June 1995 IR bonds could be purchased by subscription. In this context, subscription means that revenues received from a maturing IR bond could be reinvested directly in a new bond. From May 1996 IR bonds were issued with a reduced interest rate margin of 3%.

Since the structure of IR (and PPJ) bonds was somewhat unique, it is worth outlining an example to illustrate how the interest on an IR bond was determined.[86] On 1 September 1994 the Ministry of Finance issued an IR bond that matured on 2 September 1995. The bond paid interest at a margin of 5% over the CPI growth rate. The amount of interest due was determined in September 1995, based on the compounded growth in the price index for the period 1 July 1994 to 30 June 1995. Table 7.7 illustrates the monthly inflation growth rates.

The annual CPI growth rate could then be calculated as the geometric average of the monthly rates:

$$(1.015 \times 1.017 \times 1.045 \times 1.029 \times 1.018 \times 1.019 \times 1.039 \\ \times 1.021 \times 1.017 \times 1.023 \times 1.018 \times 1.010) - 1 = 0.3066$$

The nominal interest rate on the bond was therefore:

$$(0.3066 \times 100\%) + 5\% = 35.66\%$$

In May 1996 a new type of index-linked bond became available – the *RP* bond – issued alongside the IR bonds. This new instrument was again of one-year maturity and employed the same CPI linkage as the IR bonds. However, RP bonds were zero-coupon instruments and so paid no margin above the CPI growth rate (i.e., they were issued at a discount to par). RP bonds were sold exclusively by auction, with each issue usually being auctioned twice prior to the start of secondary market trading. Like IR bonds, a new RP bond was introduced every 3 months. With the introduction

[85] For example, the first PPJ bond could be bought at auction in the second half of May, but was also available for public sale from 1 June 1992 to 31 August 1992.

[86] Source: Republic of Poland Ministry of Finance Public Debt Department (1996, p. 15).

Table 7.7 Polish month-on-month Consumer Price Index (CPI) growth rates from July 1994 to June 1995

Month no.	Price index		Month of bond life
	Month	Price growth (%)	
1	Jul 1994	1.5	Sep 1994
2	Aug 1994	1.7	Oct 1994
3	Sep 1994	4.5	Nov 1994
4	Oct 1994	2.9	Dec 1994
5	Nov 1994	1.8	Jan 1995
6	Dec 1994	1.9	Feb 1995
7	Jan 1995	3.9	Mar 1995
8	Feb 1995	2.1	Apr 1995
9	Mar 1995	1.7	May 1995
10	Apr 1995	2.3	Jun 1995
11	May 1995	1.8	Jul 1995
12	Jun 1995	1.0	Aug 1995

Data source: Republic of Poland Ministry of Finance Public Debt Department (1996, p. 15).

of RP bonds, IR bonds ceased to be issued by auction, reflecting the different markets at which the products were targeted: RPs at the wholesale sector and IRs at the retail sector. By the end of March 1997 the size of the Polish index-linked bond market had grown to 3.929bn zlotys (approximately US$1.3bn), representing just over 5% of the total amount of outstanding government debt.[87]

The last RP bond was auctioned in February 1998. The Ministry of Finance decided to cease issuance of RP bonds because by 1998 inflation had dropped below 10% for the first time and, as a result, it concluded that issuance of 1-year nominal (rather than real) bonds would provide a cheaper cost of funding. In 1999, as part of the Ministry's policy to extend the maturity of its debt, issuance of IR bonds was superseded by that of *COI* bonds – 4-year CPI indexed Treasury savings bonds. These bonds were designed to be safe medium-term savings vehicles for retail investors and are sold through a network of around 550 Customer Service Outlets (CSOs). COI bonds are non-marketable and so are not quoted on any regulated market, although it is permitted for individuals to trade them under civil law regulations.

Although interest on COI bonds is paid at redemption it is calculated on an annual basis. The interest rate for a given year is calculated as the sum of the annual inflation rate for the preceding year and the additive spread fixed for each issue. As this structure incorporates an indexation lag of one year (as opposed to two months for the earlier types of bond) the precise nominal amount of interest on this bond will be known after three years of its four-year lifetime. While early issues featured a margin of 4.5%, this was increased to 5.5% in May 2000 and again to 7.0% in July 2000.[88] COI bonds also include a put option that enables the holder to redeem their bond early. This can be exercised at any time except during the first 3 months following the purchase date, or

[87] Source: Republic of Poland Ministry of Finance Public Debt Department (1997).
[88] See Ministry of Finance, Poland (2000, p. 46).

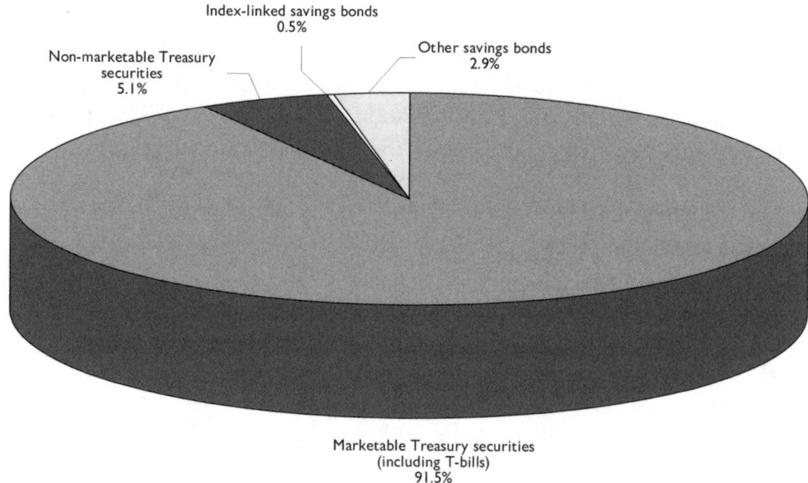

Figure 7.22 Composition of Poland's Treasury securities market (by nominal value, as at 30 June 2002)
Data source: National Bank of Poland

during the 2 months prior to the redemption date. At the end of June 2002 the nominal value of all Treasury securities was 203.8bn zlotys, equivalent to approximately 90% of Poland's domestic debt, of which COI bonds accounted for around 0.5% (1,005.5mn zlotys), as Figure 7.22 shows.

7.26 PORTUGAL

There are just a handful of inflation-indexed bonds in Portugal, all but one having been issued by banks. The exception is an issue brought in 1998 by Brisa-Auto Estradas de Portugal SA (BRISA), a firm responsible for constructing, maintaining and operating motorways. Since toll charges form the main source of its income,[89] BRISA might be thought of as a "natural" issuer of indexed bonds.

While many indexed bonds issued during the 1990s were indexed to domestic inflation, recently issues have been more typically linked to Euro-zone CPI.

7.27 SOUTH AFRICA

Index-linked corporate debt, in the form of CPI indexed leases, has existed in South Africa for some time. Also, more recently, several CPI indexed bonds have been issued to finance toll roads under concession agreements.[90] These bonds have been privately placed and, at the time of issue, have had maturities of between 18 and 25 years.

[89] Toll charges accounted for 97% of BRISA's income in 2000.
[90] By May 2002 there were four such issues with a combined uplifted nominal value of approximately R3bn outstanding.

It was against this backdrop that the South African government began issuing inflation-indexed bonds in 2000. On 6 January 2000 the Department of Finance announced that, having consulted with market practitioners and foreign treasuries, it intended to introduce its first inflation-indexed bonds in March of that year. Although the announcement coincided with a bull run in bonds, officials emphasised that the government was keen not to rush into issuing indexed bonds because of the poor reception that such bonds had received in some other markets.[91] Two weeks later, Standard Corporate and Merchant Bank (SCMB) was appointed to provide advice on marketing the inflation-indexed bonds as well as technical assistance to the Department regarding the structure and pricing conventions of the new product.

On 7 March 2000, details were revealed of the first auction of *Republic of South African (RSA) government inflation-linked bonds* – or *SAIL* bonds as they have been dubbed by some in the market – along with some of the government's reasoning for issuing such securities.[92] Based on its view that inflation would fall over the medium-term, the government viewed the issuance of inflation-indexed bonds as a means by which it could reduce the real cost of servicing its debt. Also, given the large and well-developed funded pension system in South Africa, the government was confident that there would be demand for the product. From the outset the Department of Finance made it clear that its intention was to develop an inflation-indexed yield curve from 10 to 30-years. It also announced that initially the new product would be issued mainly into market demand, with the long-term aim of increasing the proportion of inflation-indexed debt to 10% of total debt. The first auction was held on a single price–yield basis to enable market practitioners to adjust to the new product, before changing to a multiple price–yield basis for subsequent auctions.[93] The Department has in fact adopted a similar approach with subsequent issues of new indexed bonds, with the aim of aiding price discovery.

The price index used for RSA indexed bonds is the "CPI – All items for metropolitan areas". The securities are semi-annual CIBs, with a structure based on that of Canada's RRBs (see Chapter 6). However, the lag for the South African instruments is four months, in contrast to the 3-month period more often used by other governments that have adopted the Canadian design, and is required due to the 6-week lag in the announcement of the monthly CPI in South Africa. RSA indexed bonds also feature a deflation floor, as implemented in the design of US Treasury inflation-indexed securities.[94]

South African inflation-indexed bonds are subject to the same tax treatment as indexed bonds in Canada, New Zealand and the USA. As such, all interest payments (including the inflation uplift) and the increase in the redemption value of the principal due to the inflation adjustment are taxable on an annual basis.[95]

On 15 March 2000 the Department of Finance held the first RSA inflation-indexed bond auction. The bond, referred to by its serial code R189, has a $6\frac{1}{4}$% coupon and matures in March 2013. Although the auction of R1bn of the bond (US$140mn) was

[91] See Sanghera (2000).
[92] See Republic of South Africa Ministry of Finance (2000a).
[93] Greenwood (2000) reports that during the government's consultation exercise, investors had indicated that they would require real yields ranging from 3% to 10%!
[94] For the full terms and conditions of issue, readers should refer to Republic of South Africa Department of Finance (2000b).
[95] For more details on the taxation of inflation-indexed bonds see Republic of South Africa Department of Finance (2000a).

oversubscribed (bids for R1.675bn were received), bids ranged from a real yield of 5% to 10% and so the Department chose to set a real yield cut-off of 6.5%, resulting in just R495mn of the bond being issued on this occasion. After the auction the authorities noted that although all BESA[96] registered market participants could have taken part in the auction, the majority of bids were submitted through the primary dealers, suggesting to them that many in the investment community were unsure about the mechanics of the new product.[97]

The 2013 bond was reopened in September 2000. This second auction was a lot smaller than the first (R250mn as opposed to R1bn) and bids were much more competitive, ranging from 6% to 7%. The auction was 3.7 times covered and the bond was allotted at an average real yield of 6.255%. Further reopenings of the R189 bond occurred on roughly a monthly basis. After the October 2000 auction the South African authorities reported that there was a significant increase in the number of independent bidders at this auction, suggesting a wider understanding of the mechanics of the product and greater acceptance of its role within a diversified asset portfolio. As well as continuing to build up the size of the R189 bond through outright auction, in March 2001 the South African authorities sought to further boost its size by initiating several switch auctions into it from nominal bonds. Table 7.8 provides a full list of inflation-indexed bond auctions held up to June 2003.

In the light of the good performance of the 2013 bond during the 2000/01 fiscal year and given the difficulties faced by investors wanting to match their liabilities using this single bond, in February 2001 the National Treasury[98] announced that it would issue a new longer maturity inflation-indexed bond. The new bond – 5.5% 2023 (code R197) – was first auctioned on 25 May 2001 and, like the R189, its issue size has been built up at subsequent auctions. In November 2001 the gap in the government yield curve between the two bonds was bridged when the Trans-Caledon Tunnel Authority (TCTA) issued a government-guaranteed 5% 2018 CPI indexed bond.[99] The TCTA issued this bond as part of a package to finance the Lesotho Highlands Water Project – a scheme to provide additional water to the Vaal River System in the RSA and to generate hydro-electric power in Lesotho. The bond shares its instrument design with the Treasury bonds and is also listed on BESA. Although the initial issue amount was R700mn the placing document allowed for further issuance, subject to a maximum total nominal amount in issue of R2.5bn,[100] and the bond was reopened in both February and April 2002, taking the issue size to R1.35bn. However, its liquidity remained poor when compared with Treasury bonds, even accounting for its smaller issue size, as discussed in a research article published in April that year by Rand Merchant Bank (RMB)[101] and illustrated in Table 7.9.

In April 2002 the National Treasury launched a new inflation-indexed bond maturing in 2008, bond R198. As with previous issues, the first auction was conducted on a uniform yield basis and R500mn was sold. Included in the terms and conditions of this bond is a reference to the National Treasury's intention to allow the bond to be

[96] The Bond Exchange of South Africa.
[97] See Republic of South Africa Ministry of Finance (2000b).
[98] The Department of Finance was merged with another government department in 2000 to form the National Treasury.
[99] This bond has the instrument code WS05.
[100] See Trans-Caledon Tunnel Authority (2001).
[101] See Baker and Greenwood (2002a).

Table 7.8 Auctions of South African index-linked Treasury bonds

Auction date	Auction type	Bond(s) issued	Nominal amount issued (Rand)	Average yield (%)
15 Mar 00	Outright	R189	495,000,000	6.500
7 Sep 00	Outright	R189	250,000,000	6.255
27 Oct 00	Outright	R189	350,000,000	6.284
17 Nov 00	Outright	R189	350,000,000	6.283
15 Dec 00	Outright	R189	350,000,000	6.240
12 Jan 01	Outright	R189	500,000,000	6.225
26 Jan 01	Outright	R189	200,000,000	6.195
12 Feb 01	Outright	R189	300,000,000	6.028
23 Mar 01	Switch	R189	446,731,905	5.822
25 May 01	Outright	R197	400,000,000	5.629
7 Jun 01	Outright	R197	250,000,000	5.691
29 Jun 01	Outright	R197	300,000,000	5.383
6 Jul 01	Outright	R189	500,000,000	5.455
14 Sep 01	Outright	R189	1000,000,000	5.386
1 Oct 01	Outright	R189	500,000,000	4.400
12 Oct 01	Switch	R189	4539,950,048	5.321
		R197	141,000,017	5.229
26 Oct 01	Outright	R197	500,000,000	5.140
2 Nov 01	Outright	R189	200,000,000	5.150
		R197	300,000,000	5.050
7 Dec 01	Outright	R197	300,000,000	4.887
8 Feb 02	Switch	R189	3172,388,507	4.679
15 Mar 02	Outright	R197	1000,000,000	4.364
5 Apr 02	Outright	R197	500,000,000	4.334
19 Apr 02	Outright	R197	500,000,000	4.132
26 Apr 02	Outright	R198	500,000,000	4.050
24 May 02	Outright	R197	200,000,000	4.034
		R198	300,000,000	3.826
21 Jun 02	Outright	R197	300,000,000	3.999
		R198	95,000,000	3.787
5 Jul 02	Outright	R189	250,000,000	4.130
		R197	250,000,000	4.010
26 Jul 02	Switch	R189	7,403,600	4.120
6 Sep 02	Outright	R197	200,000,000	3.985
		R198	200,000,000	3.767
27 Sep 02	Outright	R197	135,000,000	3.676
11 Oct 02	Outright	R197	300,000,000	3.718
6 Dec 02	Outright	R197	400,000,000	3.989
7 Mar 03	Outright	R198	500,000,000	3.844
20 Mar 03	Outright	R197	500,000,000	3.948
11 Apr 03	Outright	R197	400,000,000	3.920

Data sources: Republic of South Africa National Treasury, and Rand Merchant Bank (figures as at 30 June 2003).

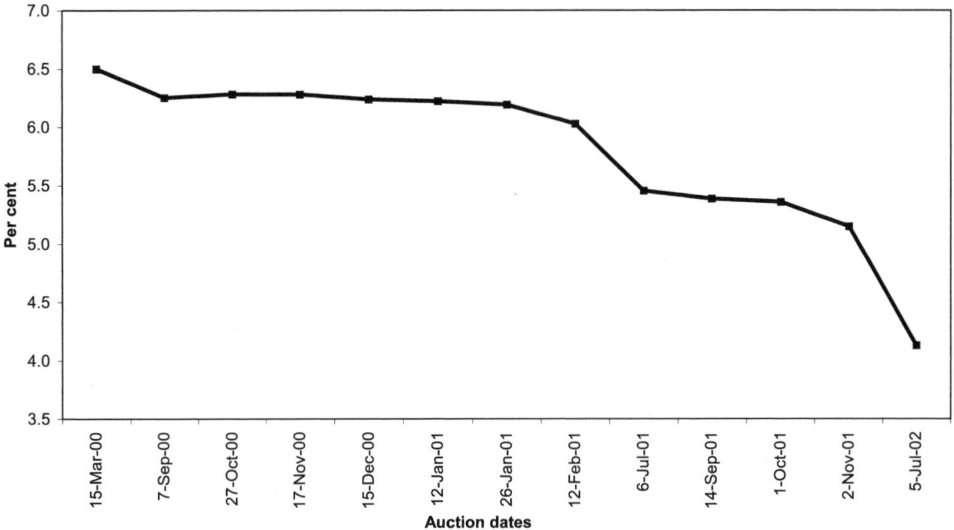

Figure 7.23 South African government bond R189 (6.25% 2013): average accepted real yield at auction

Data source: National Treasury, Republic of South Africa.

Table 7.9 Turnover in South African index-linked bonds*

Bond code	Turnover in 3 months to 16 April 2002 (R, mn)	Weighted average issue size (R, mn)	Turnover as a percentage of issue size (%)
R189	1,607	12,718	13
R197	832	2,798	30
WS05	0.88	872	0.1

* Reproduced by permission of the Rand Merchant Bank (based on BESA [Bond Exchange of South Africa] market daily statistics, excluding turnover on the day of an auction).

stripped in the future.[102] The coupon on this bond was fixed at 3.8%, significantly lower than the coupons on the earlier bonds reflecting the progressive fall in real yields in South Africa since the inception of the inflation-indexed bond programme. Figure 7.23 plots the average allotted yields at each of the auctions of the original R189 (March 2013) issue and illustrates how this decline in real yields began to accelerate throughout 2001 and 2002 – reflecting a combination of factors, but in particular the strong demand for CPI-indexed paper and investor concerns regarding the possibility of higher inflation.

[102] See Republic of South Africa National Treasury (2002). In fact, once the market for stripping nominal bonds is established the National Treasury envisages making all its CPI indexed bonds strippable.

Table 7.10 South African index-linked government bonds

Issuer	Bond code	Coupon (%)	Maturity date	Date of first issue	Nominal amount outstanding (R, bn)
RSA	R198	3.80	31 Mar 2008	2 May 2002	1.60
RSA	R189	6.25	31 Mar 2013	20 Mar 2000	13.41
TCTA	WS05	5.00	1 Aug 2018	15 Nov 2001	1.35
RSA	R197	5.50	7 Dec 2023	30 May 2001	6.88

Data sources: Republic of South Africa National Treasury and Rand Merchant Bank (figures as at 30 June 2003). Although not issued by the National Treasury, the TCTA (Trans-Caledon Tunnel Authority) bond carries an explicit government guarantee.

Ahead of the R198 auction in April 2002, Baker and Greenwood (2002b) noted that in the previous 11 CPI indexed Treasury auctions the real yield declined on the day of the auction relative to the previous day's close, a further indication of the strength of demand for these bonds. The primary reason for issuing such a short maturity indexed bond was to meet the demand from the retail banks to hedge their CPI-linked structured/synthetic products. However, the bond would also have appealed to institutional investors wanting inflation protection but a shorter duration exposure than that offered by the two existing Treasury bonds.

June 2002 saw the first inflation-linked swap in the South African market, as the National Roads Agency swapped R500mn of its fixed rate bonds into inflation-indexed instruments in order to match better its assets and liabilities. Though the agency has sold concessions for some of its toll roads to the private sector, it still runs several toll roads itself that generate revenues, which are expected to rise with inflation.

The second half of 2002 saw reduced inflation-indexed issuance by the Treasury as a result of a lower than expected funding requirement due to tax revenues exceeding government projections. Despite this, all three of the existing RSA indexed bonds were reopened, and there was also a further switch auction into the R189 bond, although the result of the latter was poor with just R7.4mn nominal being created. Table 7.10 provides a summary of the three current Treasury bonds along with the TCTA issue.

7.28 SPAIN

Although the Spanish government has not issued index-linked bonds, they are not completely unknown in Spain. The electrical utility Fuerza Eléctrica de Cataluña has issued four bonds indexed to the Spanish CPI, the first two in the mid-1960s with maturities of approximately 35 years, while the other two were issued in 1988 with maturities of approximately 12 years. These semi-annual IIBs were callable, and all were redeemed early in August 1997. In March 2000 the international electrical group Endesa issued a 20-year bond which is indexed to the Spanish CPI and callable in March 2010.

7.29 SWITZERLAND

In September 1990 two Swiss banks, Berner Kantonalbank and Luzerner Kantonalbank, both issued 10-year bonds that paid floating nominal coupon payments (with a 5% floor and 10% cap) for the first 7 years and then CPI-indexed coupons for the remaining 3 years. Both these bonds have since matured and remain the only inflation-indexed securities issued in Switzerland by either the government or private sector organisations. However, the Swiss Finance Ministry is known to be considering whether it should introduce indexed bonds – see Bloomberg (2003).

7.30 TURKEY

The Turkish government began issuing 1 and 2-year inflation-indexed bonds in July 1994 as a means of reducing its funding costs. These IIBs were linked to the Wholesale Price Index (WPI) and paid a coupon of WPI plus a margin. Although the margin (or real coupon) on some issues was as high as 25%, later bonds typically paid WPI+6%. Coupon payments were made semi-annually and issuance was by tap.

Due to weak demand for these WPI bonds, in March 1997 the Turkish authorities launched a new type of bond indexed to the CPI. These securities were of 2-year maturity and paid interest quarterly. Their structure was based on the current pay format (discussed in Chapter 2), and they were sold by single yield auction, with the coupon on each issue being set at the auction. Unlike the earlier bonds, the CPI indexed securities paid inflation-adjusted coupons – an important difference given Turkey's inflationary environment. Initially, at least, these bonds proved much more popular than the WPI indexed bonds that they replaced. An interesting design feature of the 2-year CPI indexed bonds was the method used to index the cash flows. Instead of scaling each cash flow by a 3-month inflation growth rate, the index ratio was calculated by taking the fourth root of an annual rate. For example, consider a bond issued in April 1997 that paid its first coupon in July 1997: the nominal value of this first coupon was determined by the fourth root of the increase in the CPI between March 1996 and March 1997,[103] as opposed to the increase in the CPI between December 1996 and March 1997 (i.e., using the more common indexation methodology employed in many other markets). The rationale behind this design feature was to lessen the impact of seasonality of inflation on the cash flows, in order to reduce the variability of the nominal cash flows. It was felt that this would make the bonds more attractive to investors, as well as providing the Turkish authorities with a more stable liability profile. The Turkish Treasury has calculated that its choice of index ratio did indeed reduce the volatility of the nominal cash flows – over the period from April 1994 to January 1997 the standard deviation of its index ratio was approximately one-third that of the "standard" index ratio.[104]

The Turkish Treasury auctioned its last 2-year CPI indexed bonds in December 1997, replacing them with issuance of 1-year CPI indexed bonds from January 1998. This move was an attempt by the Treasury to improve liquidity in the market by issuing bonds that the market would find easier to price – apart from shorter maturity, the

[103] Turkey uses a 4-month indexation lag.

[104] Source: The Treasury (Turkey) (1997). Over this period the average index ratio was the same for both indexation methods.

1-year bond series had a simpler design than its predecessors, with both interest and principal paid at redemption. The Treasury had also hoped that the abolition of withholding tax in 1998 would boost liquidity since it would enable bonds to be reopened. In September 1998 the maturity of new indexed bonds was increased from 1 year to 14 months. However, demand for the securities continued to be poor and the final auction was held in June 1999. The Treasury can still issue small quantities of indexed bonds directly to potential purchasers, but these are seldom traded in the secondary market.

7
Appendices

A7.1 CALCULATION OF THE SETTLEMENT PRICE FOR COLOMBIAN TES-UVR BONDS[105]

A7.1.1 Calculation of the settlement price

TES-UVR bonds are auctioned on a yield basis. The settlement price per 100 UVR face value is calculated on the basis of the formula:

$$\text{Price per 100 UVR face value} = c\sum_{j=1}^{n} w^{N_j/d} + 100w^{N_n/d}$$

where: r = Annual real yield (decimal) (e.g., $r = 0.05$ for a yield of 5%).

$$w = \left(\frac{1}{1+r}\right)$$

c = Annual real coupon rate (%).

N_j = The number of days from the settlement date to the date of the jth interest payment, calculated on a 365-day basis for all years (including leap years).

$d = 365$.

n = The number of remaining interest payments.

A7.1.2 Price calculation example

Auction date: 20 May 1999
Settlement date: 25 May 1999
Maturity date: 20 May 2002
Coupon: 5% per annum
Yield: 5.5% per annum

[105] Source: Ministry of Finance and Public Credit, Republic of Colombia.

Parameters:

$$r = 0.055$$
$$w = 0.947\,867\,3$$
$$c = 5$$
$$N_1 = 360$$
$$N_2 = 725$$
$$N_3 = 1090$$
$$d = 365$$
$$n = 3$$

So

$$\begin{aligned}\text{Price} &= 5 \times \left\{0.947\,867\,3^{\frac{360}{365}} + 0.947\,867\,3^{\frac{725}{365}} + 0.947\,867\,3^{\frac{1090}{365}}\right\} + 100 \times 0.947\,867\,3^{\frac{1090}{365}} \\ &= 98.723\ \text{UVR}\end{aligned}$$

A7.2 CALCULATION OF THE SETTLEMENT PRICE FOR ICELANDIC TREASURY BONDS[106]

A7.2.1 Indexing process

An index ratio is applied to calculate the redemption payment and coupon payment (in the case of coupon-bearing bonds). The index ratio for a given settlement date is defined as the ratio of the reference CPI applicable to the settlement date ("Ref $\text{CPI}_{\text{Set date}}$") divided by the base CPI ("Base CPI"):

$$\text{Index ratio}_{\text{Set date}} = \left[\frac{\text{Ref CPI}_{\text{Set date}}}{\text{Base CPI}}\right]$$

where Ref $\text{CPI}_{\text{Set date}}$ is the calculated daily value of the CPI for the settlement date $= CPI_{i-1} \times (1+\pi)^{x/d}$

When the next value of the CPI is known (usually from the 12th day of each month):

$$\pi = \left(\frac{CPI_i}{CPI_{i-1}}\right)^{12} - 1$$

Otherwise:

$$\pi = \text{latest (annualised) central bank inflation forecast}$$

where:
π = The intra-month prediction of the CPI.
x = The number of days from the beginning of the month.
d = 360.
CPI_i = Most current issued value of the CPI.
CPI_{i-1} = Value of the CPI for the month.

[106] Source: National Debt Management Agency, Republic of Iceland (2001).

A7.2.2 Calculation of the settlement price

Icelandic Treasury bonds are auctioned on a real yield basis. The settlement price per 100 Icelandic krona (IKr) face value is calculated on the basis of the formula:

$$\text{Price per 100 IKr face value} = \left(\frac{I}{N}\right) \times w^{f/d} \times \text{Index ratio}_{\text{Set date}}$$

where: N = The face value of the bond (IKr).
I = The principal and coupon at maturity.
r = Annual real yield (decimal) (e.g., $r = 0.03$ for a real yield of 3%).

$$w = \left(\frac{1}{1+r}\right)$$

f = The number of days from the settlement date to the *maturity* date (computed on a 30E/360 day basis).

Note For the purposes of discounting, a year is assumed to consist of 360 days.

A7.2.3 Price calculation example

Bond code: RIKS 15 1001
Settlement date: 30 October 2001
Issue date: 29 September 1995
Maturity date: 1 October 2015
Coupon: 0% per annum

Parameters:

$$CPI_i = 217.7$$

$$CPI_{i-1} = 216.3$$

$$CPI_{\text{base}} = 173.5$$

$$x = 29$$

$$N = 1 \text{ (in cases where the nominal interest rate is 0)}$$

$$I = 100$$

$$r = 0.052$$

$$w = \left(\frac{1}{1+r}\right) = 0.950\,570\,342$$

$$f = 5011$$

So

$$\pi = \left(\frac{217.7}{216.3}\right)^{12} - 1 = 0.080\,495\,38$$

$$\Rightarrow \text{Ref CPI}_{\text{Set date}} = 216.3 \times \left[(1 + 0.080\,495\,38)^{\frac{29}{360}}\right] = 217.653\,187\,7$$

So

Price per 100 IKr face value

$$= 100 \times (0.950\,570\,342)^{\frac{5011}{360}} \times \left(\frac{217.653\,187\,7}{173.5}\right) = 61.946\,772\,73$$

For further examples see the website: www.bonds.is which is hosted by the National Debt Management Agency.

A7.3 CALCULATION OF REAL YIELDS FOR ISRAELI INFLATION-INDEXED BONDS[107]

Israeli indexed bonds are sold on a price basis and so there is no need to have a price formula for settlement purposes.

A7.3.1 Sagi and Galil bonds

The formula that is used to calculate the real yield from the price of either a Sagi or Galil bond is:

$$\text{Price per 100 shekel face value} = \left\{ w^{f/d} \left[c \sum_{j=0}^{n} w^j + 100w^n \right] \right\} \times \text{Index ratio}$$

where: r = Annual real yield (decimal) (e.g., $r = 0.03$ for a real yield of 3%).

$$w = \left(\frac{1}{1+r}\right)$$

c = Annual real coupon rate (%).
f = The number of days from the settlement date to the first or next interest payment date.
d = 365.
n = The number of full annual coupon periods between the first or next interest payment date and the maturity date.

$$\text{Index ratio} = \left[\frac{\text{Latest CPI}}{\text{Base CPI}}\right]$$

A7.3.2 Kfir bonds

The formula that is used to calculate the real yield from the price of a Kfir bond is:

$$\text{Price per 100 shekel face value} = \left\{ w^{f/d} \left[D_1^* + c^* \sum_{j=1}^{n} w^{j/2} + 100w^{n/2} \right] \right\} \times \text{Index ratio}$$

where: r = Annual real yield (decimal) (e.g., $r = 0.03$ for a real yield of 3%).

[107] Source: Battley (1997).

$$w = \left(\frac{1}{1+r}\right)$$

D_1 = Next known annual coupon

$D_1^* =$ Next known semi-annual coupon $= 100\left\{\left(1+\frac{D_1}{100}\right)^{1/2} - 1\right\}$

c = Variable interest rate, as published by the Bank of Israel (%).

$c^* =$ Forecast semi-annual coupon $= 100\left\{\left(1+\frac{c}{100}\right)^{1/2} - 1\right\}$

f = The number of days from the settlement date to the first or next interest payment date.

$d = 365$.

n = The number of full semi-annual coupon periods between the first or next interest payment date and the maturity date.

$$\text{Index ratio} = \left[\frac{\text{Latest CPI}}{\text{Base CPI}}\right]$$

A7.4 CASH FLOW CALCULATIONS FOR NEW ZEALAND TREASURY INFLATION-INDEXED BONDS[108]

A7.4.1 Calculation of interest payments

The quarterly interest payments I_t are calculated as:

$$I_t = \frac{c}{4} \times \frac{K_t}{100}$$

where c = Annual real coupon rate (%).

K_t = Nominal value of the principal at the date of the next interest payment

$$= K_{t-1}\left[1 + \frac{i}{100}\right]$$

K_{t-1} = Nominal value of the principal at the date of the previous interest payment. If there is no previous interest payment $K_{t-1} = 100$ (the face value of the bond), K_t and K_{t-1} are rounded to two decimal places.

i = The average percentage change in the CPI over the two quarters ending in the quarter that is two quarters prior to that in which the next interest payment falls. For example, if the next interest payment is in November 1995, i is based on the average movement in the CPI between December 1994 and June 1995.

$$i = \frac{100}{2}\left[\frac{\text{CPI}_t}{\text{CPI}_{t-2}} - 1\right]$$

CPI_t = The CPI for the second quarter of the relevant two-quarter period.

[108] For full details see New Zealand Debt Management Office (1995c).

CPI_{t-2} = The CPI for the quarter immediately prior to the relevant two-quarter period.

Note Although this is the same methodology that is employed to compute the cash flows for Australian CIBs, in the case of the New Zealand bonds there are no clauses preventing the nominal value used in the calculation of interest payments from falling below NZ$100. Also, the redemption payment could fall below NZ$100 face value.

A7.4.2 Calculation of the settlement price

New Zealand inflation-indexed bonds are auctioned on a real yield basis. The settlement price per N New Zealand dollars face value is calculated on the basis of the formula:

Price per NZ$$N$ face value

$$= \left\{ w^{f/d}\left[\frac{c}{400}\left(x + \sum_{j=1}^{n} w^j\right) + w^n\right]\right\}\left\{\frac{K_t}{100}\left(1+\frac{i}{100}\right)^{-f/d}\right\} \times N$$

where: N = The face value of the bond (NZ$).

r = Annual real yield (decimal) (e.g., $r = 0.03$ for a real yield of 3%).

$$w = \left(\frac{1}{1 + r/4}\right)$$

$$x = \begin{cases} 0 & \text{if the settlement date is after the record date and up to but not including, the next interest payment date;} \\ 1 & \text{otherwise.} \end{cases}$$

f = The number of days from the settlement date to the next interest payment date.

d = The number of days in the quarter ending on the next interest payment date.

n = The number of full quarters between the next interest payment date and the maturity date.

The settlement price is rounded to the nearest cent.

Note This is the same methodology that is employed to compute the settlement price for Australian CIBs, the only difference being that the New Zealand formula is expressed as a price per NZ$$N$ face value rather than a price per NZ$100 face value.

A7.5 EXCHANGE RATES

Table A7.1 shows exchange rates for each of the countries featured in Chapter 7, as of 30 June 2003:

Table A7.1 Exchange rates as of 30 June 2003

			Exchange rate versus		
Subsection	Country	Currency	US dollar	Euro	UK pound
1	Argentina	Peso	2.798	3.212	4.624
2	Austria†	Schilling	11.983	13.760	19.806
3	Bolivia	Boliviano	7.611	8.739	12.579
4	Brazil	Real	2.863	3.287	4.731
5	Chile	Peso	698.5	802.0	1,154.4
6	Colombia	Peso	2,817.0	3,234.8	4,655.9
7	Czech Republic	Koruna	27.481	31.556	45.421
8	Denmark	Krona	6.469	7.428	10.692
9	Finland†	Markka	5.178	5.946	8.558
10	Germany†	Deutsche Mark	1.703	1.956	2.815
11	Greece†	Drachma	296.74	340.75	490.46
12	Hungary	Forint	231.57	265.91	382.74
13	Iceland	Krona	76.280	87.592	126.076
14	India	Rupee	46.164	53.010	76.299
15	Ireland†	Pound	0.686	0.788	1.134
16	Israel	Shekel	4.323	4.964	7.144
17	Italy†	Lira	1,686.2	1,936.3	2,787.0
18	Japan	Yen	120.10	137.91	198.50
19	Kazakhstan	Tenge	147.04	168.85	243.03
20	Mexico	Peso	10.482	12.037	17.325
21	Netherlands†	Guilder	1.919	2.204	3.172
22	New Zealand	Dollar	1.706	1.959	2.820
23	Norway	Krona	7.233	8.306	11.955
24	Peru	Sol	3.471	3.986	5.737
25	Poland	Zloty	3.895	4.473	6.438
26	Portugal†	Escudos	174.59	200.48	288.56
27	South Africa	Rand	7.484	8.594	12.369
28	Spain†	Peseta	144.90	166.39	239.49
29	Switzerland	Franc	1.353	1.554	2.237
30	Turkey	Lira	1,418,500	1,628,864	2,344,497

Data source: Bloomberg.

† These countries now use the euro as their official currency. The exchange rates reported here reflect the fixings of the legacy currencies at the creation of the euro on 1 January 1999.

8

Inflation-linked Derivatives: Market Description

8.1 OVERVIEW

8.1.1 Introduction

Inflation-linked (IL) derivatives are financial products used by entities, such as sovereigns, state and local governments, financial institutions and corporations, to manage the risks associated with variable rates of inflation. Although the majority of IL derivative contracts are inflation swaps of various "flavours", there is growing demand from market participants and end-users for increasingly complex option structures to satisfy demanding risk management requirements and to construct ever more sophisticated exposures to the future path of inflation.

IL derivatives provide additional sources and destinations for IL flows; their existence helps to lower barriers of entry to the index-linked market and thereby expands the universe of market participants beyond those who invest in or who issue inflation-indexed bonds alone. Over time this has enhanced liquidity and made the underlying sovereign and corporate inflation-indexed bond markets more efficient.

This chapter tracks the development of the IL derivatives market since its inception in the early 1990s,[1] describes its current state and some likely trends, and introduces a number of important examples of widely utilised structures (drawn from the UK and continental Europe) to illustrate the practical implementation of derivatives in the marketplace. The end-users in these examples fall into two broad categories of *payers* and *receivers* of IL flows, analogous to issuers and investors in IL bonds, respectively.

Today, in mid-2003, the IL derivatives market has grown sufficiently to merit a full and separate treatment in its own right alongside any analysis of IL bonds. In the same way that Interest Rate Swaps (IRSs) and other interest rate derivatives complement the markets for conventional bonds, the development of IL derivatives has likewise added flexibility to the underlying inflation-indexed bond markets and opened up opportunities to achieve financial objectives unavailable through the use of indexed bonds in isolation. Although derivatives still represent a relatively small fraction of the whole index-linked universe, the exponential growth experienced since the year 2000 points to a development similar to that of the IRS market in the early 1980s, with the potential to open up a global market bigger than that of the underlying cash bonds.[2] Even though

---

[1] Although a number of deals in the UK market were transacted as early as 1993, the major deal flow did not begin in earnest until 1999.

[2] For example, by March 2003 the monthly total notional size traded in Euro-zone Harmonised Index of Consumer Prices (Euro-HICP)-linked derivatives had risen to more than 25% of the corresponding volume of underlying OAT€*is* traded in the secondary market.

such an outcome is still distant, developments in 2002 and 2003 have firmly established IL derivatives as one of the major growth areas in the world of derivatives, as monthly trade volumes over €3bn become increasingly common.

8.1.2 Why Inflation-linked (IL) derivatives?

Derivatives in the inflation market offer many opportunities to market participants: to transfer risk, access increased liquidity, optimise market timing, meet portfolio hedging requirements, customise cash flows, effect market arbitrage and create hybrid structures (e.g., inflation-protected equity or credit-linked bonds), to name but a few. Their existence therefore facilitates the execution of strategies that are cheaper and more efficient than those available using just the bond market and helps participants to meet needs that the bond market is unable to satisfy. Interest rate derivatives have been used extensively to convert between fixed and floating rates, to accommodate changes in profile and maturity, and in the construction of many other structured finance products. The addition of a third variable, the real interest rate, opens up possibilities to expand still further the range of available debt-financing solutions. This section provides brief details of some examples to illustrate the universe of opportunities provided by the use of IL derivatives.

When investor interests and issuer needs cannot be fully matched, IL derivatives can be used to bridge mismatches in *maturity*, *timing*, *index*, *profile* and *size*. For example, a financial intermediary can synthetically convert an issuer's 10-year bond into a 15-year maturity issue by swapping out the issuer's cash flows and thereby assuming the maturity mismatch risk, thus delivering to the investor the desired *maturity*. Pension fund demand for corporate index-linked issues in the UK, for example, is mainly for securities with maturities of 15 years or greater, with little or no interest in shorter dated issues. Similarly, a floating rate issue can be combined with a (fixed) real rate versus LIBOR (the London Inter Bank Offer Rate, a floating rate) swap to achieve the desired index-linked maturity for an issuer. For example, demand for short-dated index-linked corporate bonds can be weak in the UK, particularly in relation to other forms of debt from the same issuer. A corporate borrower can exploit any such mismatch through the combination of a short-dated Floating Rate Note (FRN) with a real versus LIBOR swap, for example, to achieve its desired index-linked maturity.

An attractive break-even inflation rate can be "locked in" by an issuer through the use of a real versus fixed (nominal) rate swap to help optimise *timing*. In many markets, break-even inflation rates have tended to display a mean-reverting pattern over time: for example, trading around a mid-range of 2% in the case of Euro-zone indexed bonds (in-line with the ceiling of the current European Central Bank (ECB) inflation target) and 2.5% in the case of Retail Prices Index (RPI)-linked bonds in the UK (consistent with the Bank of England's current target). A borrower may wish to take advantage of perceived market distortions and lock in wide break-even inflation rates through the use of a real versus fixed rate swap and subsequently issue an underlying security as and when it is convenient to do so.[3] Moreover, a corporate issuer with exposure to the price

[3] Such a strategy will result in a reduced effective real rate on the bond should break-even rates fall between the execution of this "rate lock" and the subsequent issue date.

index of a single European country can tap the more liquid Euro-zone inflation-indexed market through a swap from one *index* into another.

Many liability structures tend to resemble a constant real annuity and so most closely reflect the *profile* of an amortising bond. However, investors are often more interested in standard bullet issues, for which pricing and secondary market trading is more straightforward. Again, IL swaps can be employed to swap out an issuer's bullet index-linked issue and so convert the debt profile to an annuity structure, thereby more closely matching the issuer's expected cash flows.

Finally, an issuer may fall short of the amount it wishes to raise through a particular index-linked bond issue. For example, there may be limited interest in its long-dated inflation-indexed bond issues due to investor preferences for holding a diverse set of issuers by name and by industry group.[4] In such cases an issuer might cover the shortfall by selling a fixed nominal rate bond (thereby tapping the wider group of traditional bond investors) and use the overlay of a real-fixed swap to effectively achieve the desired *size* of exposure to real rates.

8.1.3 The Inflation-linked (IL) derivatives markets in 2003

The previous examples are more than merely theoretical conjecture. In 2002 more than €4bn notional of Euro-zone IL swaps (ILSs) traded through the broker market, followed by another €8bn in the first quarter of 2003 (see Figure 8.1). In the month of May 2003 alone over €3bn notional of ILSs traded through the brokers, an amount that excludes swaps between market-making banks and their "end-user" clients,[5] breaking the previous monthly records set successively in January and February of 2003.

By 2003 more than 15 major market-making banks and a similar number of smaller regional financial institutions in Europe were involved in this market, building up trading capabilities to meet the increase in demand from their client base for structured IL products. This activity is complemented by the involvement of at least seven brokerage firms,[6] each of which is able to charge significantly higher brokerage fees than for comparable vanilla swaps in nominal interest rates. Until recently this was seen as a "trade by appointment" market, but this is clearly no longer the case.[7]

Central banks and other monetary authorities have begun to use the inflation derivatives market as another "barometer" of expectations for future inflation rates. Additionally, sovereign debt issuers have considered the use of IL derivatives to complement to their issuance programmes.[8] The Bank of England, with a long history of using measures of inflation expectations derived from index-linked gilt prices (see Chapter 5), first commented on inflation swaps in its spring 2001 *Quarterly Bulletin* and has since considered their more rigorous inclusion in such analysis (see Scholtes,

[4] In the UK market, for example, most unswapped non-sovereign inflation-indexed bonds have either been issued by water companies or are AAA-rated, insurance-wrapped amortising securities to finance hospital projects (see below).
[5] No data are collated for such contracts, and so the volumes in question are much harder to estimate than those traded through the broker markets.
[6] Garban-Intercapital, Cantor Fitzgerald, Tradition, Tullet & Tokyo, Eurobrokers, Prebon and HPC are all involved in the IL derivatives markets globally.
[7] Richard Grey, broker at Garban-Intercapital, quoted in the *Financial Times* (see Skorecki, 2003).
[8] The narrowing spreads between swap break-evens and bond break-evens in December 2002 indicated the emergence of more payers of inflation in the swap market – see Barclays Capital (2003a). Since then, there have been strong rumours that this was due to a sovereign issuer paying in the swap market.

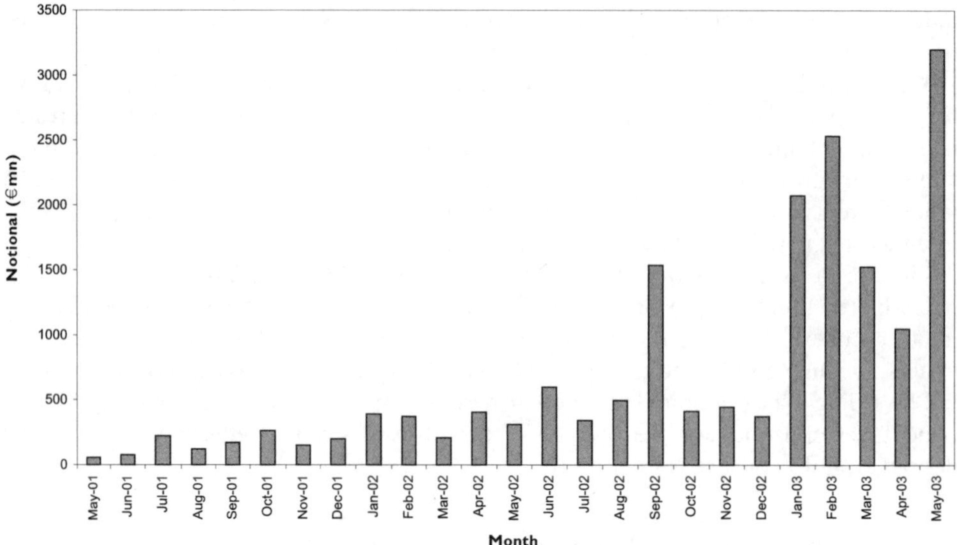

Figure 8.1 Monthly volumes of index-linked swaps traded through the broker market
Reproduced by permission of Garban-Intercapital

2002). The Federal Reserve has also expressed an interest in inflation swaps,[9] as has the Agence France Trésor (AFT), which regularly consults with swap market participants ahead of new index-linked bond issues.[10]

Once consigned to the occasional mention in the technical pages of monthly or weekly trade publications, such as *Risk Magazine*, *International Financing Review (IFR)*, *Financial Products* and *Derivatives Week*, the mention of inflation derivatives is now more frequent in the mainstream financial press, such as the *Financial Times*.[11] As more sovereigns begin to issue inflation-indexed debt, so investors and borrowers alike are starting to become more aware of the benefits of the asset class. The UK already has approximately 25% of all government debt in the form of index-linked issues, France has made clear its intention to reach similar levels, while the US Treasury continues to reiterate its commitment to the product.[12] Furthermore, this continual increase in government issuance around the globe has encouraged a significant increase in corporate indexed debt issuance. Current IL derivatives volumes of approximately \$5bn notional per month equate to just under 1% of the nominal rate derivatives market.[13] As the ratio of indexed debt to nominal debt grows to 10% or more for major sovereign issuers and as more corporate issuers enter the market, one can expect the ratio of IL derivative trade volumes relative to the much larger nominal market to grow in a similar fashion. If this indeed came to pass it would represent a 10-fold

[9] Initial consultations were held privately with a number of market participants in June 2003.
[10] Private consultations with inflation swap houses began as early as January 2001.
[11] For example, see "Inflation Derivatives on the Rise" which featured as the main article in the "Capital Markets" section of the *Financial Times* on 2 April 2003 (Skorecki, 2003).
[12] See Chapter 6 for more information on the major government issuers of indexed bonds.
[13] Data available from the International Swaps and Derivatives Association (ISDA) indicate that, on average, \$6,250bn notional of swaps, options and currency swaps were dealt per year in the period 1987–2002, equating to \$521bn per month. Source: www.isda.org

increase in volumes for IL derivatives from the current record monthly volumes set in the first half of 2003. The IL market may very soon begin to challenge credit as the main growth area in the derivatives business.

8.2 A BRIEF HISTORY OF INFLATION-LINKED DERIVATIVES MARKETS

8.2.1 Early history

To trace the brief history of ILSs, it is instructive to first look at the development of the now ubiquitous IRS market in the early 1980s. The two share a number of similarities that can help explain the ILS market's development thus far and help chart its likely future course. The IRS market started in 1981. Initially, only a few companies and banks were involved, and banks running swap books did so on a "matched" basis whereby each bank acted as an intermediary taking counterparty credit risk. Over time, the market has moved toward a "mismatched book" approach whereby, instead of matching swaps immediately, dealers choose to "warehouse" risk until swaps can be matched at a later date. In the meantime the banks hedge their portfolios with available exchange-traded instruments, such as futures and government bonds – see Decovny (1998).

The ILS market has so far developed in a similar fashion. However, because of the well-established experience gained in the IRS market over more than two decades, the ILS market's development is being pushed along at a vastly accelerated pace. A move toward the existence of large unmatched books would normally necessitate the existence of tradable instruments with similar risk characteristics, and so it was that the UK market was the first to take the step as it had the earliest and most developed market for government-issued IL bonds. Moreover, the existence of a real rate "curve" across a wide range of maturities means that the banks running inflation swap books need incur very little duration-related basis risk. Instead, the bond-swap spreads, resets, repo spreads, etc., became the focus of risk management for ILS books in the UK – just as they had for nominal IRS books previously.

The existence of tradable instruments linked to inflation, such as sovereign-issued IL bonds, typically results from the response of an issuer to a need in the market for such investment vehicles. Their presence in itself indicates a clear awareness among investors of the usefulness and attractiveness of the asset class, while also reflecting the desire of the issuers to establish such exposure. An ILS market is likely to thrive in such circumstances, not just because the underlying bonds can be used to construct a real curve but more importantly because the existence of the index-linked bond market in itself implies an existing two-way interest in such products – paying (issuer) and receiving (investor) interest is already clearly established.

The UK ILS market is a prime example of one that has been built on already established two-way interests: the pension industry is the major investor in indexed bonds and the government, though increasingly accompanied by many corporations, is the issuer. The key for the long-term sustainability of any derivatives market is the existence of balanced, two-way interest. In ILS markets where this is indeed the case, break-even inflation rates tend to trade at levels roughly in line with market consensus expectations for future inflation. The US Treasury Inflation-Protection Securities (TIPS) market, on the other hand, has long suffered from lacklustre demand for the product which, until recently, has resulted in relatively high real yields and therefore low break-even inflation rates – averaging around 1.5% in the period from 2001 through to mid-2003 for TIPS with 10 years or less to maturity. This level of break-evens is significantly below realised inflation rates as well as below consensus long-term inflation estimates,[14] which means that to pay on IL swaps or straight index-linked issuance is relatively unattractive to potential issuers. Not surprisingly, therefore, the size of the US CPI swap market is a fraction of those in the UK and in the Euro-zone, despite the fact that in July 2000 the total market capitalisation of TIPS overtook that of index-linked gilts to become the largest government inflation-indexed bond market.

8.2.2 The UK market

The index-linked bond market in the UK exists in tandem with a regulatory regime that encourages certain pension liabilities to be hedged with index-linked securities (see Section 6.5). The main issuer remains the government, through HM Treasury's Debt Management Office (DMO), while the main groups of investors are pension funds and life insurance companies. In addition, many gas, water and electricity rate increases are regulated and explicitly linked to changes in the Retail Prices Index (RPI),[15] while 20–25% of payment streams for public–private partnership infrastructure projects (e.g., under the Private Finance Initiative, or PFI) are explicitly linked to the RPI.[16] Furthermore, many housing associations have rental increase targets explicitly linked to the RPI, as are many property lease agreements. Thus there are more payers (issuers) of index-linked flows than simply the DMO. The existence of such a diverse range of interests has created a situation with a varied and balanced mix of both payers and receivers of inflation-indexed flows, which has proven to be very conducive to the development of a healthy and sustainable two-way inflation-indexed derivatives market.

Under the PFI in the UK, the government contracts out to the private sector the construction and maintenance of infrastructure projects or new buildings, in return for a guaranteed income stream for a fixed period of time (usually between 20 and 30 years). The onus to raise capital for the project's construction phase is therefore squarely with the private sector firms involved. Since more than 10% of PFI contracts have specified that the income stream paid by the government will be inflation-indexed, such agreements have proved to be a large and steady source of flows to the index-linked market – either through direct bond issuance or through the combination of bank borrowing and an IL derivative hedge.

The introduction of the gilt repo market in 1996 was an important development for the derivatives industry in the UK, since it enables participants to borrow both nominal and index-linked gilts and so more efficiently hedge both nominal and inflation-indexed swaps. In November 1999 the first inflation-indexed swap traded through the inter-dealer broker market. This took the shape of a stream of interest-indexed cash flows on

[14] For example, see Sack (2000), Shen and Corning (2002) and Craig (2003).
[15] See Section 6.5.
[16] Barclays Capital estimate.

Table 8.1 UK Retail Prices Index (RPI)-linked swapped AAA-rated issues

Issue date	ISIN	Size (£ million)	AAA-rated Issuer	Lead manager	Coupon (%)	Maturity date	Launch spread[a]	Benchmark IL gilt
9 Aug 00	XS0116389023	100.00	IBRD	RBS	2.505	22 Jul 2030	[b]	$4\frac{1}{8}$% IL 2030
15 Aug 00	XS0116636217	178.00	EBRD	Barclays	2.746	17 Jul 2024	0.95%	$2\frac{1}{2}$% IL 2024
15 Aug 00	XS0116636134	120.00	NIB	Barclays	2.805	17 Jul 2024	1.01%	$2\frac{1}{2}$% IL 2024
16 Aug 00	XS0116772665	50.00	CDC	Barclays	2.551	22 Jul 2030	0.86%	$4\frac{1}{8}$% IL 2030
23 Aug 00	XS0117016393	50.00	RFF	Barclays	2.504	22 Jul 2030	0.79%	$4\frac{1}{8}$% IL 2030
1 Sep 00	XS0117430214	100.00	NIB	RBS	2.954	16 Apr 2020	[b]	$2\frac{1}{2}$% IL 2020
18 Oct 00	XS0119565488	350.00	EIB	MSDW, RBS	2.650	16 Apr 2020	0.61%	$2\frac{1}{2}$% IL 2020
31 Jan 01	XS0124499418	50.00	EBRD	RBS	2.380	16 Apr 2020	0.37%	$2\frac{1}{2}$% IL 2020
20 Feb 01	XS0125447408	100.00	CDC	Barclays	2.493	16 Apr 2020	0.50%	$2\frac{1}{2}$% IL 2020
23 Jul 01	XS0132108704	50.00	EIB	Barclays	2.400	22 Jul 2030	0.30%	$4\frac{1}{8}$% IL 2030
9 Dec 02	XS0159818813	120.00	EIB	RBS	2.600	16 Aug 2013	0.24%	$2\frac{1}{2}$% IL 2013

Total Issuance: £1,265.00 million

Reproduced by permission of Barclays Capital. IBRD: International Bank for Reconstruction and Development; EBRD: European Bank of Reconstruction and Development; NIB: Nordic Investment Bank; CDC: Caisse des Dépôts et Consignations; RFF: Réseau Ferré de France; RBS: Royal Bank of Scotland; Barclays: Barclays Capital; MSDW: Morgan Stanley Dean Whitter; EIB: European Investment Bank.

[a] The difference between the yield of the bond at issue and the underlying benchmark gilt yield.

[b] Not available.

one leg (similar to the payments on an Interest Indexed Bond [IIB] – see Section 2.2) versus a floating nominal interest rate, 6-month sterling LIBOR (London Inter Bank Offer Rate), on the other.[17] The notional size was £10mn and the maturity was 25 years (see Exhibit A8.6 on p. 265 for an example of a similar structure). This transaction represented a watershed in the inflation-indexed swap market, opening the way for what has since become a market in which swaps totalling multiple billions of sterling are transacted each month and where deals of £50mn to £100mn have become the norm at long-dated maturities (15 years and over). This increase in flows between dealers has served to improve price transparency, idea sharing and efficient risk transfer and has led ultimately to a liquid and efficient inflation-indexed swap market in the UK.

In the second half of 2000 a large number of so-called "supranational", AAA-rated issuers such as the IBRD (International Bank for Reconstruction and Development) EBRD (European Bank for Reconstruction and Development), EIB (European Investment Bank), NIB (Nordic Investment Bank), RFF (Réseau Ferré de France), CDC (Caisse des Dépôts et Consignations), and others entered the index-linked market in the UK for the first time, encouraged by the strong investor demand from the UK pension and life insurance sectors for "eligible" RPI-linked bonds offering higher real yields than corresponding index-linked gilts – see Table 8.1. These new bonds were all swapped, since the issuers were ultimately interested only in floating rate (LIBOR) funding, with Barclays Capital and the Royal Bank of continental Scotland as the

[17] The swap was in fact structured as year-on-year inflation versus a *fixed* nominal rate, but this is equivalent to the inflation versus *floating* rate design described here coupled with a standard nominal IRS.

principal swap counterparts, although a number of continental European and US banks were also involved.

These swapped AAA issues have proved to be a simple but effective way for pension funds and insurance companies to gain exposure to higher yielding instruments than the traditional sovereign-issued index-linked gilts. The structure was particularly popular in 2000 when UK gilt swap spreads were at all-time highs, and so swapped issues were priced at yields of 0.60% to 1.00% above index-linked gilt real yields despite some aggressive issuer funding targets.[18]

However, 2001 saw swap spreads fall and a corresponding decline in AAA issuance (as illustrated by Table 8.1), and so pension funds and insurance companies began to explore alternative means by which they could receive index-linked cash flows. Although demand for highly rated non-sovereign index-linked bonds was strong, it was not met with sufficient supply from corporate issuers, who more typically preferred to have nominal debt. However, the development of the ILS market has enabled investors to purchase *synthetic* index-linked corporate bonds, by investing in nominal corporate bonds combined with derivative contracts which swap the fixed coupons for IL cash flows. Indeed, this concept can be extended to translate the coupons from a *portfolio* of fixed rate bonds into IL flows that more closely match a fund's liability profile (see Section 8.4 for more details). Since 2002, such swaps have become an increasingly acceptable way of gaining exposure to IL credit – see Procter and Williams (2003).

8.2.3 The French and Euro-zone markets

The first ILS activity in the French market began in 1998 and coincided with the French Trésor's introduction of its 2009 OAT*i* bond. However, the market remained small and illiquid, confined predominantly to French financial institutions, until the launch in 1999 of further bonds linked to French inflation (see Section 6.3). Bonds of six different maturities now exist, albeit some less liquid than others,[19] and so a reasonable "curve" can be constructed from 2006 out to 2029 to provide a basis on which ILSs can be valued. More recently, both cash flow-matching swaps and swapped inflation-indexed Medium Term Notes (MTNs) intended for purchase by pension funds have been transacted, similar to the structures first developed in the UK market in the late 1990s, and recent activity in the broker market indicates that this is set to become an increasingly liquid market.

The Euro-HICP ILS market started trading in May 2001, several months before the Trésor issued its first bond linked to this particular inflation index (the OAT€*i* 2012), in response to the introduction of retail inflation-protected equity products issued by the Italian Post Office and others (see Section 8.4). The issuers' need to hedge their inflation

[18] The "swap spread" of a bond is usually defined to be the spread to LIBOR on the floating rate leg of a swap whose fixed rate cash flows are identical to those of the underlying security. Issuers who sell such a security and enter into a LIBOR-based swap to receive the same fixed rate cash flows will therefore pay a floating interest rate on their loan of LIBOR plus (or minus) the bond's swap spread. In 2000, such supranational entities were able to issue both conventional and index-linked bonds in this fashion at very attractive floating rates due to such strong demand for the securities.

[19] At mid-year 2003 there were three OAT*i* bonds and three bonds issued by Caisse d'Amortissement de la Dette Sociale (CADES) that were linked to the French Consumer Price Index (CPI) ex-tobacco. There were also other bonds issued by public entities, such as CNA (Caisse Nationale des Autoroutes) and RFF (Réseau Ferré de France), but these were smaller in size – see Section 6.3 for more details on these bonds.

exposure was the catalyst for activity in the inter-bank and brokered Euro-zone ILS markets, which have both seen a steadily increasing uptrend in volumes (see Figure 8.1). In turn, a market to swap cash flows linked to Euro-zone inflation for those linked to indices for specific zones has developed and is supported in particular by investors who want to express views regarding convergence (or divergence) within the Euro-zone – see Borgy and Couzineau (2001). To date, the volume of ILSs transacted with pension funds or corporate issuers has still not reached levels seen in the UK, although some transactions in structures designed to hedge infrastructure cash flows have taken place.

The Dutch are "world leaders in pension assets per capita".[20] With a large proportion of their liabilities implicitly linked to inflation, Dutch pension funds have been significant investors in the French OAT*i* and OAT€*i* bonds. Indeed, as a group they are regularly seen to be significant participants in the Trésor's indexed bond auctions. In addition, many Dutch rental property contracts specify rents and leases linked to price indices, an exposure that can be hedged by the property companies through either issuance of IL debt or the transaction of an IL derivative. Either way, IL cash flows need to be paid for the entities to be hedged to the variability of their rental income, and so, combined with pension fund demand, a market with two-way interest has been created and a limited swap market has also developed. It might be expected that these products will evolve alongside those linked to pan-European HICP inflation in much the same way as has occurred in France. Nevertheless, this development will be handicapped without the issuance of liquid sovereign debt indexed to Dutch inflation, and the pricing in the derivatives market is therefore likely to remain relatively opaque.

In Spain, several inflation-indexed swap transactions have taken place, initiated in particular by corporations involved in the construction of highways and toll roads, as well as by property companies with rental streams linked to the Spanish CPI. A number of pension fund managers have also been involved in this market as receivers of indexed cash flows. However, the divergence of domestic CPI indices from their Euro-zone counterparts implies a significant basis risk, which has reduced the relative attraction of Euro-zone HICP-linked derivatives to receivers (investors) in Spain. For this reason the market for derivatives linked to domestic inflation has developed further than is the case in many other European countries, even without the existence of government index-linked bonds.

The Italian pension system is a combination of different schemes, the three most important of which are the private sector employers fund, the public sector employers schemes and the self-employed schemes. Together they cover a total of approximately 20 million active workers and 16 million pensioners, and the pension benefits provided by each are all inflation-indexed, primarily to the Italian CPI. A pool of indexed liabilities of this magnitude naturally leads to strong demand for assets linked to Italian consumer prices and is one of the major factors why the government has begun to issue index-linked bonds – see Section 7.17. A number of corporations have come to realize that exposure to inflation is desirable and have entered into inflation-indexed swaps.[21] This realisation, coupled with the investor demand noted above,

[20] See the Ambachtsheer Letter (2000).

[21] For example, the debt of Snam Rete Gas was restructured in the second quarter of 2002, including a €500mn inflation-linked swap overlay of an existing fixed coupon bond (see Snam Rete Gas, 2002).

should make the issuance of index-linked debt an attractive option for more Italian corporations.

Italy has also proven to be the primary source of demand for retail products linked to pan-European inflation indices. In the two years since its initial issue in May 2001 the Italian Post Office alone has sold more than €2bn of such structures, see Section 8.4. This demand accelerated further in 2003, in which the first two quarters alone each saw more than €2bn of swapped issuance targeted primarily at retail investors. This also highlights the fact that Euro-zone price indices are seen as valid substitutes for the national index in Italy, which enables the liquid Euro-HICP-linked market to be tapped – especially useful when large volumes are required. This trend is likely to be continued across Europe as issuers and investors alike appreciate that the basis risk between domestic and pan-European measures of inflation is at least partially offset by the superior liquidity available for the latter, and that over time the individual inflation measures are likely to converge further. As discussed in Section 7.17 the decision by the Tesoro to issue the BTP€*i* 2008 in early September 2003 was very much linked to this retail demand – both directly and indirectly: €2.5bn of the €7bn issued was allocated for retail distribution, and a large proportion is likely to have been absorbed by swap houses intermediating retail issues.

Nevertheless, as France has demonstrated, some of the larger European countries are likely to be able to sustain parallel markets for products linked to *both* the pan-European and national price indices, although a prerequisite would appear to be a programme of committed sovereign issuance of securities linked to the national price index. Demand is such in Germany, Italy and Spain that markets for IL government bonds in those countries are likely to find similar success to that in France, if and when the relevant authorities decide to pursue such a course.[22] In the long run, however, it is reasonable to expect that economic convergence and increased labour mobility in the Euro-zone, coupled with standardisation and reforms in the pensions arena, will cause such issuance to be concentrated in products linked to pan-European indices, such as the OAT€*i* issuance programme already undertaken by the AFT. Indeed, the successful Italian Treasury issuance of the €7bn BTP€*i* in early September 2003 is evidence of such a trend.

8.2.4 The Swedish market

After a number of limited and curtailed efforts, the Swedish government launched the current index-linked bond market in 1994 (see Section 6.4), and swap market activity started shortly thereafter (see Alaton, 1997b). However, the market remains relatively illiquid and limited mainly to local interest, and SEK-denominated swap transactions do not feature regularly in the inter-dealer broker market.

8.2.5 Non-European markets

A healthy ILS market has existed for many years in Australia (see Carmody and Glover, 1998). More recently, following the introduction of indexed government

[22] Traded inflation-indexed swaps linked to Spanish and Italian inflation, as well as interest shown in Germany, are good indicators of such demand.

bonds, a small but fast-growing ILS market has developed in South Africa where demand from pension funds is met by issuance linked to infrastructure projects as well as some limited corporate-paying interest.

With the largest market in sovereign inflation-indexed bonds, the US ILS market has potential to develop, and indeed an expansion would appear likely in the near future. As briefly mentioned in Chapter 6, several corporate IL bonds were issued shortly after the issue of the first US Treasury inflation-indexed note in January 1997. Each issuer swapped the cash flows back to floating rate, and the majority of the bonds were of a non-standard year-on-year inflation coupon variety (unlike most sovereign indexed bonds which have a Capital Indexed Bond [CIB] structure). The US corporate market has remained largely dormant since this initial flurry of activity.[23] Low break-even inflation rates (relative to consensus expectations of future inflation) and a lack of product knowledge have combined to discourage potential issuers or payers from entering the market. Realised inflation has been consistently above the break-even inflation rates of most TIPS, which in turn results in negative "carry" for payers of inflation-indexed flows (or issuers of index-linked debt) due to the downward slope of the forward inflation curve, and has proved to be an additional obstacle to issuance for agency and corporate payers.[24] Finally, a number of accounting rules applicable in the USA can complicate matters for a potential issuer. While interest payments on bonds are usually treated precisely as debt interest by accounting rules, many derivative contracts have to be "marked-to-market" on a continuous basis even if the derivatives have been specifically designed to swap the bond's cash flows from one form to another. Such rules can generate material swings in reported profit and loss accounts which do not accurately reflect the underlying financial situation of the company and, as such, can prove to be a material barrier to the use of such products.

However, with increased interest in inflation-indexed bonds from a large group of dealers and from a variety of investors,[25] coupled with the potential for lower expected future inflation rates, break-even inflation rates would appear likely to reach more palatable levels for corporate issuers to enter the market. Should such two-way interest materialise it seems reasonable to expect an active ILS market to develop in a similar form to those in the UK and in parts of continental Europe. The vast majority of inflation-indexed derivative transactions in these countries have been undertaken to hedge real exposures, and so it would appear likely that in time the accounting obstacles in the USA can be overcome as such contracts come to be seen as products that mitigate risk rather than risky financial instruments.

The explosion in IL retail investment products in Europe in the first quarter of 2003 has proved to be a catalyst for several swapped issues linked to the US CPI,

[23] Table 6.16 illustrates how the initial burst of corporate activity in 1997 was not sustained.

[24] The concept of "carry" is widely used to illustrate the nature of short term cash flows, should the evolution of inflation and interest rates remain perfectly static at current levels, as opposed to following the paths priced into the market. In this instance, the issuer of an inflation-indexed bond who has opted to swap its coupon payments for fixed nominal cash flows faces "negative carry" – simply because the initial nominal coupons that the issuer will receive on the IL leg of the swap are smaller than the corresponding fixed nominal rates which must be paid.

[25] The Bond Market Association of America held a TIPS Conference in New York at the end of June 2003 which was sponsored by several major dealers on Wall Street, including some European banks, and attended by over 150 participants.

and by mid-2003 these totalled over $400mn.[26] However, these products have mostly been sold outside the USA and to date have not been balanced by a similar volume of offsetting flows from natural payers, which means that the financial intermediaries have so far had to "warehouse" the risk. Ultimately, as elsewhere, the viability of the IL derivatives market in the USA will be strongly dependent on the development of such two-way interest, and so it seems unlikely that swapped issuance can be sustained without the emergence of payers (issuers) other than the US Treasury. However, the recent developments in Euro-zone inflation derivatives vividly demonstrate that a multi-billion market can grow from nothing in a matter of a few months, with a direct and measurable impact on the underlying sovereign indexed bond markets. Therefore, although transactions in the US CPI derivatives market are still very much "by appointment only" as of mid-2003, this situation could change very rapidly in the near future.

8.3 INFLATION PAYERS (ISSUERS)

As in any market, the set of available instruments is determined by a combination of investor (or receiver) demand and issuer (or payer) need for such exposure, combined with the ability and willingness of financial intermediaries to take basis risk in order to bring the two sides together. This section considers how debt issuers can utilise the IL derivatives markets to modify or complement existing bond issuance, and the following subsections provide examples of three classes of derivative solutions for inflation payers which serve to illustrate the significant features of the vast majority of IL derivative structures transacted to date.

The simplest option open to issuers is to sell standard "bullet" profile bonds. Payers of index-linked cash flows typically have a net exposure to an IL income stream. Very often this exposure is a steady stream of future cash flows (as is the case in the vast majority of rental or lease agreements) which are constant in real terms and, as such, resemble a *real rate annuity*. In such cases it is often appropriate to hedge this steady stream of future inflation-indexed cash flows with a structure to pay index-linked flows to the market. Arguably, all index-linked income streams or earnings are of this form (including the tax receipts of sovereigns, as described in Section 4.1) and can be managed through the issuance of a series of bullet structures to cover the full range of exposed maturities.

Nevertheless, in many cases such structures do not perfectly match the issuer's expected cash flows, and so this section begins with a discussion of the various derivative solutions appropriate in these situations. The concepts introduced are also applicable to non-bullet issues, although amortising and other more "bespoke" bond designs are described separately here based on practical applications related to examples drawn from the UK market, in which infrastructure project-related IL structures have become commonplace. The UK government's Project Finance Initiative has been widely applied with over £35bn of capital-spending projects already approved, and similar initiatives have been implemented or are under consideration in other countries. Finally, property lease and rental-related income structures are considered, in which

[26] Source: www.mtn-i.com

the annual increases in lease or rental payments are often implicitly or explicitly linked to inflation.

8.3.1 Standard derivative solutions for Inflation-linked (IL) issuers

As was discussed in Section 8.2, whenever issuer and investor interests are not aligned due to mismatches in *maturity*, *timing*, *index*, *profile* or *size*, derivatives can be employed to bridge these gaps. The following examples illustrate a number of practical applications.

Consider an issuer who simply wants to issue a 20-year bullet index-linked bond. The standard solution is to bring a new issue targeted explicitly at a series of investors – typically with an investment bank as lead manager for the issue, or through a group of banks acting as "co-leads", as illustrated in Figure 8.2.

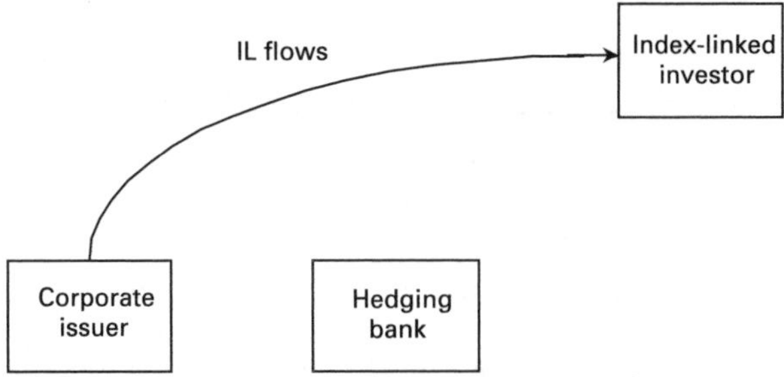

Figure 8.2 Index-linked bond issuance – standard approach

Now consider the scenario in which investors have only a limited appetite for bonds from a particular issuer, perhaps due to credit exposure considerations. For example, index-linked investors may already be "overweight" bonds issued by a particular corporate entity or industry (relative to their benchmark index, perhaps), or they might be more generally constrained with respect to securities with the same credit rating. An issuer with inflation-indexed future income may be able to tap the wider market for conventional or floating rate bonds to satisfy its immediate funding requirements, although it would still fall short of its desired index-linked exposure. However, through the additional overlay of a real versus nominal (fixed or floating) swap the issuer can effectively transform its nominal bond into an IL liability and thereby synthetically create an index-linked issue to achieve its full objective. This concept is illustrated in Figure 8.3.

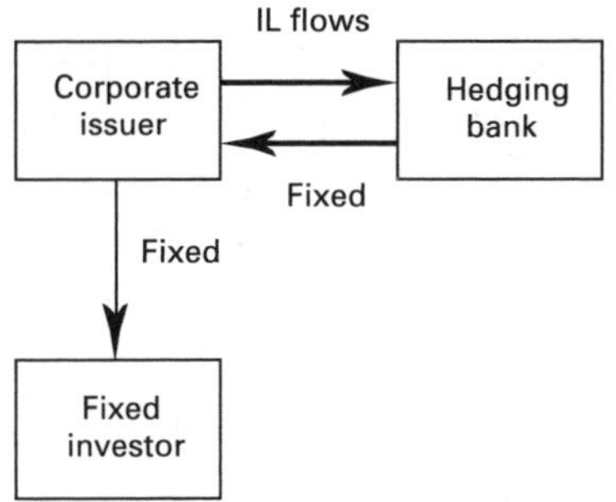

Figure 8.3 Synthetic index-linked bond issuance – fixed plus overlay

A variation on this theme is provided by the example of a frequent issuer, such as one of the AAA-rated supranational bodies (such as EBRD, EIB, IBRD, KfW (Kreditanstalt für Wiederaufbau), etc.), who may seek to exploit investor demand for AAA-rated index-linked paper. As discussed above (and illustrated in Table 8.1) this situation has been prevalent in the UK where over £1bn of such issues have been swapped and sold to investors since 2000, usually purchased by pension funds and insurance companies managing pensions linked to the RPI. Figure 8.4 schematically shows the cash flow profile of these swapped issues.

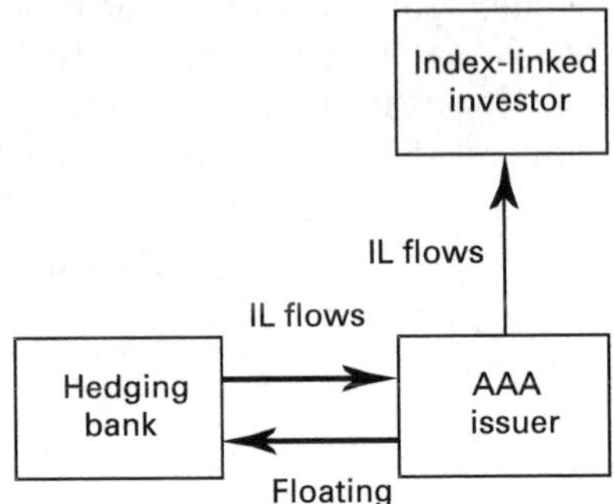

Figure 8.4 Swapped index-linked bond issuance

The stream of cash flows paid and received by the financial intermediary (usually an investment bank) are similar in each of the examples above. The combination of Figures 8.3 and 8.4 illustrates how, by entering into both swaps, the bank can neutralise its index-linked exposure. All that remains is to hedge the remaining fixed versus floating risk by entering into a vanilla Interest Rate Swap (IRS), and the whole package is illustrated in Figure 8.5.

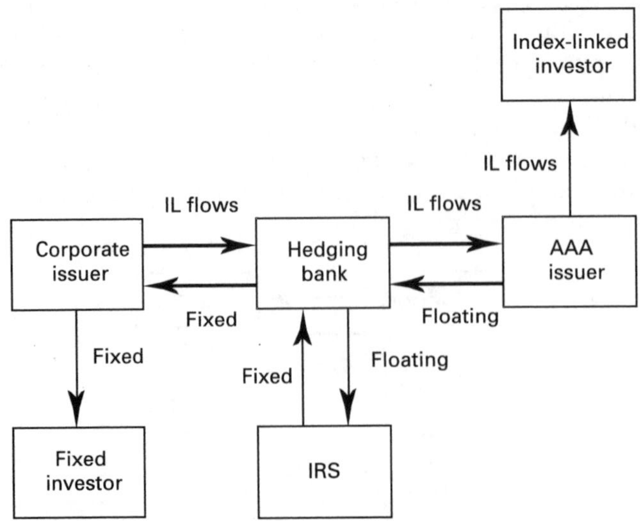

Figure 8.5 Combined matched hedging
IRS = Interest Rate Swap

The set of issuers, investors and investment banks shown in Figure 8.5, along with the streams of cash flows between them, represent the ideal scenario in which the notional amounts, roll dates and maturities perfectly match, and so leave the intermediary bank with very little to do except to manage any small difference in the real coupons on the two opposing swaps.[27] In reality, the *maturity*, *timing* and notional *size* are rarely matched exactly, so the investment bank is required to warehouse some or all of the risks associated with such discrepancies. For example, all the AAA-swapped bonds placed in the UK by the supranationals have adopted maturities and roll dates of existing UK index-linked gilts, as illustrated by the "Benchmark IL gilt" column in Table 8.1. In doing so they have helped to minimise "timing" risk for any swap counterparties comfortable hedging their RPI exposure through the use of an index-linked gilt position – although such a choice means the swap counterparty is exposed to swap spread risk, a form of basis risk. On the other hand, new issues by utilities have maturities that are dictated by the issuer's funding horizons and these in general will not match index-linked gilt maturities. An intermediary between such a utility and an AAA-rated issuer (as in Figure 8.5) can therefore remove the swap spread basis risk but only at the cost of the introduction of cash flow-timing risk.

Figure 8.5 illustrates the key features of a number of situations that exist in reality. For example, a utility or other corporate issuer may want to lock-in an advantageous level of break-even inflation rates available in the market *prior* to the proposed date of a formal debt sale. In the UK, for example, break-even inflation rates have typically varied around the 2.5% level, which is also the Bank of England's target for inflation.[28] This variation mostly reflects supply and demand conditions but also reflects the general state of the economy and other factors. A corporate treasurer who believes that this mean-reverting nature of break-even rates will continue is likely to perceive value inherent in issuing with break-even inflation rates above 2.5%, and the existence of inflation swaps allows these terms to be "locked" *prior* to actual issuance, should market conditions allow. The transaction of a real versus fixed swap will lock in any break-even level for any such issuer and can be unwound subsequently (if desired), when the indexed bond is brought to market. A variation on the same theme occurs when an issuer wishes to embark on a programme to reconstitute its existing debt portfolio and, for example, increase the proportion of its debt that is indexed to inflation. The traditional approach would be to redeem existing fixed rate bonds and simultaneously issue IL securities, but this can be both disruptive and expensive. Alternatively, by entering into fixed (or floating) nominal versus real swaps to match the maturities and coupons of existing fixed (or floating) bonds, the issuer can synthetically achieve the same result.

Several variations can also take place on the investor side of the structures shown in Figure 8.5. For example, an investor may wish to enter into a real versus fixed swap directly with the investment bank, rather than purchase a swapped issue. The investor thereby gains exposure to generic inflation risk and is left free to invest in fixed rate

[27] Typically, the difference in the credit rating of a corporate issuer and that of an AAA-rated issuer would mean that, for any given maturity, the real coupons paid by the corporate issuer would be higher than those paid to the AAA-issuer, reflecting the higher real borrowing costs faced by the corporate issuer compared with those of an AAA-rated supranational entity.

[28] As discussed in previous chapters, the Bank's target is currently defined in terms of the RPIX (RPI excluding mortgage interest) measure of inflation and looks likely to change to the UK HICP before the end of 2003, whereas index-linked gilts are linked to the headline RPI. However, the differences between these three indices are likely to be small over the long term – particularly when compared with the observed volatility of break-even inflation rates in the market.

nominal paper from a wider pool of issuers, including AAA issuers. Such an approach is often used to synthetically create an inflation-indexed bond from a particular corporation or other entity who themselves would not choose to issue such a security. Typically, the swaps between the hedging banks and the pension funds or insurance companies are covered by collateralisation agreements to reduce the credit exposure risk of both parties.

The earliest swaps between banks and UK pension funds/insurance companies are believed to have taken place in 1998, and the frequency and size of such deals have rapidly increased in the ensuing years. Developments in continental Europe – especially in France but also in Spain and in Italy – show that these solutions pioneered in the UK market are directly applicable elsewhere.

8.3.2 Private Finance Initiative (PFI) projects in the UK

The PFI in the UK was introduced in 1992 to attract private sector investment into major social infrastructure and public services projects, such as the construction of schools, hospitals and roads. Through the use of PFI deals the UK government has – to a degree – shifted its role away from one of an owner/operator of assets to that of a purchaser of cost-effective, high-quality services. It has also enabled the government to replace some "on balance sheet" capital spending with a stream of annual (and often indexed) expenses spread over several decades.

Typically, a Special Purpose Vehicle (SPV) is set up to build, operate and maintain a particular infrastructure asset, in return for a government or quasi-government obligation to pay a contractually agreed revenue stream over the term of the concession. The stream of revenues is usually determined during the bidding process for a project and is designed to be sufficient to meet the SPV's operating, debt service and maintenance costs and at the same time provide an acceptable post-tax return on equity to the SPV's owners. When the concession expires the private investors are contracted to return the infrastructure asset to the appropriate government department (or local authority) in good condition with a pre-agreed remaining useful life.

For example, in a PFI agreement typical of the health sector, a private sector consortium (e.g., consisting of a construction company, a bank, a facilities management contractor and consultants) will agree to finance and construct a new hospital for the National Health Service (NHS), the universal publicly funded health system in the UK. In return the local NHS Trust will agree to pay the consortium a regular fee for the use of the hospital, set to cover both the construction costs and rental of the facility.[29] The NHS typically employs some of the staff – primarily the medical staff, doctors and nurses – and agrees to rent the building and other facilities from the consortium for a significant period of time, usually at least 25 years.

One attraction of PFIs for the government is that the cost of building the infrastructure project does not appear as an immediate lump sum payment in public expenditure, but is instead spread over the lifetime of the agreement. Although some

[29] In addition, support services provided by the private sector are also paid for by the Trust, although this is not always part of the PFI agreement itself.

Table 8.2 UK Private Finance Initiative (PFI) projects

Department	Completed projects		Signed projects	
	No. of projects	Capital spend (£mn)	No. of projects	Capital spend (£mn)
Department for Culture Media and Sport	1	42.00	1	42.00
Department for Environment Food and Rural Affairs	6	373.50	11	999.50
Department for Education and Skills	21	855.50	44	1,725.00
Department of Health	18	1,052.90	37	2,798.31
Department of Trade and Industry	4	78.00	5	167.00
Department for Transport	19	3,522.20	32	19,675.58
Department for Work and Pensions	4	945.00	4	945.00
Cabinet Office	1	330.00	1	330.00
Foreign and Commonwealth Office	1	17.10	3	386.10
HM Customs and Excise	2	83.00	2	83.00
HM Treasury	1	141.00	1	141.00
Home Office	15	596.70	25	1,603.10
Inland Revenue	3	399.80	4	517.80
Lord Chancellor's Department	7	231.60	7	226.60
Ministry of Defence	29	2,048.02	34	2,579.80
Northern Ireland Office	4	100.80	7	177.50
Office of the Deputy Prime Minister	5	110.90	11	357.30
Scottish Executive	16	1,067.10	33	1,830.10
Welsh Assembly	6	323.40	8	454.50
Miscellaneous	1	37.00	1	37.00
Total	*164*	*12,355.50*	*271*	*35,076.20*

Reproduced by permission from the PPP Forum, as of 1 March 2003.

have argued that it "provides a very useful device by which the government can hide the true extent of government debt",[30] the PFI is still widely regarded as a way to harness the private sector's resources and experience in the funding, management and technology for the efficient delivery of social infrastructure and public services. The future viability of the PFI in the UK will depend on the outcome of such debates. Nevertheless, as of 1 March 2003 over £35bn of capital spending through PFI agreements has been authorised, of which over £12bn has already been completed (see Table 8.2), and this process seems set to continue at least for the near future. Of the PFI projects approved to date, 20–25% have RPI-linked cash flows, including all those for the Department of Health as well as many road, school and defence projects.

On the private sector side, the market for PFI projects is dominated by companies affiliated with the major construction groups,[31] many of whom have separate financial advisory groups set up specifically to structure the financing and hedging of the projects' cash flows. The construction phase of each project is financed either through bank borrowing or through bond issuance. Sterling PFI-backed bonds already represent a

[30] Lord Saatchi, in a debate in the House of Lords, on 12 February 2003 (see the United Kingdom Parliament, 2003).
[31] For example, Jarvis, Kier Group, Carillion, etc. (see Labour Research Department, 2001).

multibillion pound market. With few exceptions, each bond is "credit-wrapped" with a guarantee from one of the primary AAA-rated financial guaranty insurance companies[32] in order to maximise the bond's credit-rating and thereby help to minimise funding costs.

For those projects whose managers have opted to borrow directly from banks as opposed to accessing the capital markets and where the revenue stream is linked to the RPI, an inflation hedge is still required to effectively hedge future cash flows since banks typically lend on a floating rate basis. There are a number of approaches to this problem. If bank lending took the form of a real loan (i.e., an amortising real notional profile with real coupons and real principal paybacks, as illustrated in the first six columns of Table 8.3), the project would be hedged in precisely the same way as

Table 8.3 Example real annuity loan repayment schedule

i	Roll date	Real principal	Real interest	Real principal payback	Total real payment	Forward RPI	Discount factor	Nominal payment
0	1 Jul 03	50,000,000.00					1.000	
1	1 Jul 04	48,937,064.95	1,465,000.00	1,062,935.05	2,527,935.05	182.66	0.948	2,591,133.43
2	1 Jul 05	47,842,985.90	1,433,856.00	1,094,079.05	2,527,935.05	187.22	0.898	2,655,911.76
3	1 Jul 06	46,716,850.34	1,401,799.49	1,126,135.56	2,527,935.05	191.90	0.852	2,722,309.56
4	1 Jul 07	45,557,719.00	1,368,803.71	1,159,131.34	2,527,935.05	196.70	0.807	2,790,367.30
5	1 Jul 08	44,364,625.12	1,334,841.17	1,193,093.88	2,527,935.05	201.62	0.765	2,860,126.48
6	1 Jul 09	43,136,573.58	1,299,883.52	1,228,051.53	2,527,935.05	206.66	0.725	2,931,629.64
7	1 Jul 10	41,872,540.14	1,263,901.61	1,264,033.44	2,527,935.05	211.82	0.687	3,004,920.38
8	1 Jul 11	40,571,470.51	1,226,865.43	1,301,069.62	2,527,935.05	217.12	0.651	3,080,043.39
9	1 Jul 12	39,232,279.55	1,188,744.09	1,339,190.96	2,527,935.05	222.55	0.617	3,157,044.48
10	1 Jul 13	37,853,850.29	1,149,505.79	1,378,429.26	2,527,935.05	228.11	0.585	3,235,970.59
11	1 Jul 14	36,435,033.05	1,109,117.81	1,418,817.24	2,527,935.05	233.81	0.555	3,316,869.85
12	1 Jul 15	34,974,644.47	1,067,546.47	1,460,388.58	2,527,935.05	239.66	0.526	3,399,791.60
13	1 Jul 16	33,471,466.50	1,024,757.08	1,503,177.97	2,527,935.05	245.65	0.498	3,484,786.39
14	1 Jul 17	31,924,245.42	980,713.97	1,547,221.08	2,527,935.05	251.79	0.472	3,571,906.05
15	1 Jul 18	30,331,690.76	935,380.39	1,592,554.66	2,527,935.05	258.09	0.448	3,661,203.70
16	1 Jul 19	28,692,474.25	888,718.54	1,639,216.51	2,527,935.05	264.54	0.424	3,752,733.79
17	1 Jul 20	27,005,228.70	840,689.50	1,687,245.56	2,527,935.05	271.15	0.402	3,846,552.14
18	1 Jul 21	25,268,546.85	791,253.20	1,736,681.85	2,527,935.05	277.93	0.381	3,942,715.94
19	1 Jul 22	23,480,980.22	740,368.42	1,787,566.63	2,527,935.05	284.88	0.361	4,041,283.84
20	1 Jul 23	21,641,037.89	687,992.72	1,839,942.33	2,527,935.05	292.00	0.343	4,142,315.93
21	1 Jul 24	19,747,185.25	634,082.41	1,893,852.64	2,527,935.05	299.30	0.325	4,245,873.83
22	1 Jul 25	17,797,842.72	578,592.53	1,949,342.52	2,527,935.05	306.78	0.308	4,352,020.68
23	1 Jul 26	15,791,384.47	521,476.79	2,006,458.26	2,527,935.05	314.45	0.292	4,460,821.20
24	1 Jul 27	13,726,136.98	462,687.56	2,065,247.49	2,527,935.05	322.31	0.276	4,572,341.72
25	1 Jul 28	11,600,377.74	402,175.81	2,125,759.24	2,527,935.05	330.37	0.262	4,686,650.27
26	1 Jul 29	9,412,333.76	339,891.07	2,188,043.98	2,527,935.05	338.63	0.248	4,803,816.52
27	1 Jul 30	7,160,180.09	275,781.38	2,252,153.67	2,527,935.05	347.10	0.235	4,923,911.94
28	1 Jul 31	4,842,038.31	209,793.28	2,318,141.77	2,527,935.05	355.78	0.223	5,047,009.74
29	1 Jul 32	2,455,974.99	141,871.72	2,386,063.33	2,527,935.05	364.67	0.211	5,173,184.98
30	1 Jul 33	0.00	71,960.07	2,455,974.98	2,527,935.05	373.79	0.200	5,302,514.60

Real interest = Real principal × Real coupon
Real coupon = 2.93%
Break-even inflation rate = 2.50%
Nominal rate = [(1 + Real coupon) × (1 + Break-even inflation rate)] − 1 = 5.50%
Forward RPI = Base RPI × $(1 + \text{Break-even inflation rate})^i = 178.20 \times (1 + 2.50\%)^i$
Discount factor = $1/(1 + \text{Nominal rate})^i = 1/(1 + 5.50\%)^i$

[32] The major AAA guarantors – Ambac Inc., FSA Insurance Co. and MBIA Inc. – are often referred to as "monoline insurers", as they offer no other insurance products, such as property, casualty or life insurance.

had the managers opted to issue an index-linked bond. However, many lending banks do not have the capabilities to manage real cash flows, and so project companies have to resort to borrowing on a nominal profile (e.g., as shown by the nominal payments in Table 8.3) and execute additional hedge transactions with the market, typically in the form of a real annuity versus compounded fixed swap of the type depicted in Exhibit A8.4 on p. 264. The real annuity leg matches the sum of the real cash flows on each roll date[33] (and the unitary real payment which the project receives), while the compounded fixed leg matches the sum of the nominal payments on each roll date. PFI swaps are typically structured to have semi-annual, quarterly or monthly roll dates to exactly match their revenue stream but typically with annual rate resets (i.e., the example numbers shown in Exhibit A8.4 on p. 264 can be interpreted as total annual flows).

8.3.3 UK housing associations

Housing associations are the main providers of new social housing in the UK. There are over 2,000 housing associations in England alone, managing approximately 1.45 million homes and housing 3 million people.[34] The regulatory requirements covering rents specify that guideline limits to rate increases are to be set annually by the Housing Corporation. As shown in Table 8.4 the guideline limits for the last 5 years have all been explicitly linked to the RPI.

Housing associations in the UK therefore receive cash flows linked to the RPI in much the same way as inflation-indexed PFI projects, and likewise these cash flows represent a real annuity stream and are therefore best hedged through the use of real annuity swaps or bond issues. In practice the small scale of individual housing associations has meant that the latter route has yet to be taken. Instead, associations typically rely on bank borrowing, with RPI-linked cash flows hedged through the use of inflation swaps as deemed appropriate. The cash flows in these cases tend to be very similar to those of RPI-linked PFI projects, and so the derivative solutions detailed earlier are also applicable here.

Table 8.4 Housing Association rental increase guidelines in the UK

Year	Guideline limit	Year-on-year increase in RPI at the previous September	Guideline limit for rent increases
1 Apr 03 to 31 Mar 04	RPI + 0.5%	+1.7%	2.2%
1 Apr 02 to 31 Mar 03	RPI + 0.5%	+1.7%	2.2%
1 Apr 01 to 31 Mar 02	RPI + 1.0%	+3.3%	4.3%
1 Apr 00 to 31 Mar 01	RPI + 1.0%	+1.1%	2.1%
1 Apr 99 to 31 Mar 00	RPI + 1.0%	+3.2%	4.2%

Reproduced from the Housing Corporation Regulatory Circular, November 2002 with permission.

[33] This is typically the starting point for "sculpting" the amortisation profile: the unitary real payment that the project receives – typically a constant real amount per year – is matched against a real coupon plus real principal repayment. This real amount also equals the real annuity leg of the swap depicted in Exhibit A8.4 on p. 264.

[34] Source: The Housing Corporation website: www.housingcorp.gov.uk. The Housing Corporation is a Non-Departmental Public Body (NDPB), sponsored by the Office of the Deputy Prime Minister (ODPM).

8.3.4 Swap structures to mitigate credit exposure

Overlay swaps used to convert a fixed rate bond into a synthetic index-linked issue or to asset-swap a bullet index-linked bond both typically involve the transfer of a large cash amount at maturity – the redemption pickup – defined by the following formula:

$$RP(m) = \text{Notional}\left[\frac{\text{CPI}(m)}{\text{CPI}(s)} - 1\right] \tag{8.1}$$

where: $RP(m) =$ the redemption pickup at maturity.

$m =$ the maturity date.

$s =$ the start date.

The latter two are lagged appropriately using the standard convention applicable for the market in question. For long-dated swaps (e.g., a 30-year deal), the expected maturity payment may be greater than the swap notional, thus exposing one of the parties to a large default risk.[35] For many swap counterparties, putting in place a collateralisation agreement through a Credit Support Annex (CSA) agreement[36] is the obvious solution to this problem. In many situations, however, a CSA agreement may not be possible and other mechanisms need to be found to reduce the credit exposure where necessary.

One attractive solution is to break down $RP(m)$ into a sum of n annual amounts. Defining the start-to-date redemption pickup $RP(i)$ as:

$$RP(i) = \text{Notional}\left[\frac{\text{CPI}(s+\text{i})}{\text{CPI}(s)} - 1\right] \tag{8.2}$$

where: $i =$ the number of years from the start date.

It can be observed that:

$$RP(m) = \sum_{i=1}^{n}[RP(i) - RP(i-1)] \tag{8.3}$$

where: $RP(0) = 0$.

Making an "early" payment of $[RP(i) - RP(i-1)]$ at the end of each of the n years from start to maturity would reduce the credit exposure of the receiver of $RP(m)$. In the above transaction, the payer of the redemption pickup instead makes incremental early payments totalling the redemption pickup. In order to be compensated for the early payments, the appropriate interest rate is then charged for these early cash flows, typically LIBOR. This solution has no pricing or market risk implications for either party and is simply a structure that modifies the cash flow profile to mitigate the credit exposure inherent in the original swap.

---

[35] An average realised inflation rate of 2.5% compounded over 30 years results in a maturity payment of approximately 110% of the notional.

[36] A CSA describes the terms of the collateralised relationship between two parties. It includes legal, operational and credit provisions.

8.4 INFLATION RECEIVERS (INVESTORS)

This section considers the incentives of market participants who seek to receive IL flows – analogous to investors in the underlying index-linked bond market. Inflation derivatives can be used to modify or complement an existing investment and, again, available instruments reflect the intersection of investor demand and issuer supply. There have been two main sources of demand: from pension fund managers to hedge their inflation-indexed liabilities and from the retail sector attracted either by equity products with real principal guarantees or more recently by inflation plus fixed interest products.

8.4.1 The use of inflation swaps to hedge pension liabilities

Pension liabilities are typically linked, either explicitly or implicitly, to a cost of living index, such as the CPI. It is therefore no surprise that many pension funds worldwide have direct or indirect investments in indexed bonds, particularly since the introduction of sovereign indexed bond markets in the USA and continental Europe in 1997 and 1998, respectively (see Chapter 6). The UK has a mature private pension system with schemes that pay inflation-indexed benefits and a long history of the use of index-linked bond investments to match such RPI-linked liabilities (see Section 6.5). The UK's experience may therefore provide some indication as to the likely development of the US and European markets in the future.

The existence of inflation derivatives presents alternative strategies for fund managers than the straightforward purchase of indexed bonds to match IL pension liabilities. Mismatches in maturity, index, profile and size between assets and liabilities can be bridged with the use of derivatives. For example, to date, the existing sovereign-issued indexed bonds in the Euro-zone have only been linked to either French or Euro-zone price indices, whereas pension liabilities in individual European countries are typically linked to a domestic price index. Derivatives can be used to bridge this basis risk. Additionally, there is demand from pension funds for solutions that use inflation derivatives to preclude the need to continuously reinvest the coupon payments and principal redemptions inherent within an indexed bond portfolio. Finally, inflation derivatives can be used to allow the synthetic construction of higher yielding corporate index-linked debt instruments (see, for example, Procter and Williams (2003), as well as Section 8.3).

8.4.2 Inflation-guaranteed and Inflation-linked (IL) retail products

The biggest single category of demand in the Euro-zone inflation swap market to date has arisen from retail investors, and upward of 90% of such retail products sold in Europe in the 2 years since mid-2001 have been placed in Italy. The first Italian Post Office (Posta Vita) deals from 2001 (approx €2–3bn) were instrumental in the launch of the Euro-zone HICP swap market (several months *before* the French Trésor issued the first bond linked to that index in September 2001).[37] The early Italian retail issues

[37] Details of the first Posta Vita issue appear at www.poste.it/bancoposta/postevita/orizzonte.shtml

were inflation and capital-protected equity-linked notes: for example, 5 or 10-year investments which paid 50% of any appreciation in the specified stock index and with the real value of the principal payment guaranteed. These products proved popular in the equity bear market of the time – investors were still keen to buy equity-linked notes if downside protection was provided. The form of the payout on such securities is shown in Equation (8.4):

$$\text{Payout at maturity} = \text{Max}\left\{100\%, \frac{\text{HICP(maturity)}}{\text{HICP(start)}}\right\} + X\% \times \text{Max}\left\{0\%, \frac{\text{Equity index(maturity)}}{\text{Equity index(start)}} - 1\right\} \quad (8.4)$$

Such a security is often referred to as a *"sum of" hybrid* product wherein the different components can be valued independently and then aggregated to produce the final product price. The inflation component of the payout is similar to that of the "deflation floor" on US TIPS and French indexed OATs – see Sections 6.3 and 6.6, respectively. In addition, several *best of* inflation-equity products have been sold to retail investors, which at maturity pay the return of an equity index or the change in the price index over the life of the bond, whichever has been the greater. However, the valuation of such products poses certain difficulties, in particular an estimate of the correlation between equity returns and future inflation is required, as are estimates for the volatility of the two variables. Equity market volatilities can be implied from exchange-traded and Over The Counter (OTC) option prices, but the volatility of forward inflation is hard to estimate and particularly difficult to hedge.[38] Such structures have therefore often been viewed to be too expensive compared with the simpler "sum of" products.

Close to €2.25bn of swapped IL MTNs were issued in the first quarter of 2003 (see Table 8.5). This volume, coupled with the associated hedging activity in the ILS market, was significant enough to materially impact the underlying inflation-indexed bond market in Europe. In the first quarter of 2003 alone, swap activity through the brokers was more than double that for the whole of 2002, and the subsequent purchases required to hedge the inflation exposure noticeably changed the relative pricing of short-dated indexed bonds. Retail MTNs were all structured as IIBs (see Section 2.2), although some had one or two cash flows fixed in nominal terms. They were sold mostly in Italy through various retail-banking channels, despite the fact that roughly two-thirds were linked to the pan-European HICP (excluding tobacco), the same index used by the French Trésor for its OAT€*i* bonds. Very few MTNs were linked to domestic Italian inflation, with the remainder in fact indexed to French CPI.

Those countries in Europe that have historically experienced relatively high rates of inflation (almost regardless of current inflation levels) might be expected to provide most demand for inflation-protected assets of this nature, and indeed this partly explains the product's recent popularity not only in Italy but also in Spain and Portugal as well as the contrasting complete lack of penetration in the German market. Finally, the "simple" structure of the payout – a year-on-year inflation coupon plus a spread – is

[38] Often there are no instruments that can be used to delta-hedge the exact inflation exposure. Even when an approximate hedge is chosen, crossing bid–offer spreads for frequent rehedging of the delta can prove to be very costly.

Table 8.5 Issuance of Medium Term Notes (MTNs) linked to European price indices in Q1 2003*

Issuer	Notional (€ million)	Start date	Maturity date	Price index
Kreditanstalt für Wiederaufbau	125	21 Jan 03	21 Jan 11	HICPx
European Investment Bank	130	24 Jan 03	24 Jan 10	HICPx
Dexia Municipal Agency (Dexia)	53	7 Feb 03	7 Dec 15	FrCPIx
Dexia Credit Local de France	50	14 Feb 03	14 Feb 08	HICPx
Compagnie de Financement Foncier	185	17 Feb 03	17 Feb 15	FrCPIx
Republic of Austria	50	20 Feb 03	28 Feb 13	HICPx
European Investment Bank	150	24 Feb 03	24 Feb 11	HICPx
European Investment Bank	100	28 Feb 03	28 Jan 13	HICPx
Lehman Brothers Treasury Co BV[a]	80	28 Feb 03	28 Feb 10	ItCPIx
Eni Coordination Center SA	50	28 Feb 03	28 Feb 08	HICPx
International Bank for Reconstruction and Development	100	3 Mar 03	3 Mar 10	HICPx
France Telecom[b]	60	4 Mar 03	4 Mar 08	ItCPIx
Renault Credit International SA Banque	400	6 Mar 03	6 Jun 08	HICPx
Kreditanstalt für Wiederaufbau	50	10 Mar 03	10 Sep 09	HICPx
European Investment Bank	100	11 Mar 03	11 Mar 11	HICPx
European Investment Bank	70	11 Mar 03	11 Mar 11	HICPx
Volvo Treasury AB (Publ.)	32	11 Mar 03	11 Mar 10	HICPx
Compagnie de Financement Foncier	107	12 Mar 03	17 Feb 15	FrCPIx
European Investment Bank	100	20 Mar 03	20 Sep 11	HICPx
Compagnie de Financement Foncier	150	24 Mar 03	24 Mar 13	FrCPIx
European Investment Bank	100	27 Mar 03	27 Mar 15	HICPx
Total	*2,242*			

* *Note*: this table only includes swapped issues. Reproduced from www.mtn-i.com with permission. HICPx: Euro-zone Harmonised Index of Consumer Prices (excluding tobacco) (unrevised); FrCPIx: French Inflation CPI (excluding tobacco); ItCPIx: Italian Consumer Price Index (excluding tobacco).

[a] Lehman Brothers Treasury Co BV, a wholly owned subsidiary of Lehman Brothers Holdings, is a special purpose entity formed for the purpose of issuing notes.

[b] Section 8.4 provides a detailed description of the France Telecom issue.

easier to understand than the more traditional "real coupon plus redemption" form of inflation-indexed government bonds and thus makes the product easier to sell in retail markets.

As an example, consider the MTN in Table 8.5 issued by France Telecom in March 2003.[39] Exhibit A8.6 on p. 265 shows the general structure of inflation swaps used in conjunction with issuance of the MTNs aimed at the retail market, although in reality the retail products themselves have often had one or more of the initial annual coupons fixed and so the structure of the swap would need to be modified accordingly. The France Telecom issue is linked to Italian CPI, the first coupon was fixed at 5% nominal while subsequent coupons pay 2% plus the annual increase in the Italian CPI excluding tobacco, with a nominal floor of 2%.

[39] This bond has International Securities Identification Number (ISIN) XS0163325938.

8.5 INFLATION OPTIONS

8.5.1 Options embedded in bonds

The concept of embedded options in indexed bonds has become standard since the introduction of TIPS and OAT*i*s, with their "deflation floors", in the USA and France, respectively (the swap analogue of these floors trades in the broker markets and is illustrated in Exhibit A8.9 on p. 267). Although UK index-linked gilts do not have such a feature, the Limited Price Indexation (LPI) pension legislation (see Section 6.5) has spurred the issuance of LPI bonds by utilities and other corporations. For example, Glas Cymru issued an LPI bond in May 2001[40] and Tesco[41] issued a similar security the following October. Both are examples of securities that explicitly set out to provide pension funds with assets that are a more precise match for their LPI liabilities than are index-linked gilts.

The swapped retail MTNs issued in Europe in 2003 (see Table 8.5) all had 0% floors on the inflation payout of their coupons (as well as the principal) as illustrated in Exhibit A8.6 on p. 265. Similarly, other retail products, such as the inflation and capital-protected equity-linked notes more popular in 2001, have also featured embedded "deflation protection" options struck at 0%, in this case a par redemption guarantee similar to that on TIPS, OAT*i*s and OAT€*i*s.

8.5.2 Standalone inflation options in the Over The Counter (OTC) market

The launch of the retail products described above in 2001 necessarily introduced options into the fledgling inflation swap market at the same time. The issues swapped by the larger financial intermediaries who run their own "proprietary" inflation derivatives trading books have typically left unhedged the option component of the derivative structures. However, a large number of issues were swapped by banks that simply did not have the infrastructure to manage the risk and therefore sought to hedge it through the inflation derivatives broker market. Such option contracts, 0% year-on-year floors on inflation, have thus become a standard instrument in the derivatives market (e.g., see Exhibit A8.10 on p. 267) – not too surprising considering the volume of swapped issues of this kind already in existence.

In May 2003 Deutsche Bank and Goldman Sachs introduced auctions for options on the monthly Euro-HICP ex-tobacco releases, as part of their joint *Economic Derivatives programme*.[42] Auctions are held monthly, and each one lasts several hours during which time participants can enter bids for the contracts on offer, usually digital options struck at different levels for a future index setting. The contracts are intended to be tradable in a "grey market" through an inter-dealer broker, Garban-Intercapital, although as of end-June 2003 none had traded outside the monthly auction hours.

Using the basic digital option as a building block, simpler call and put options can also be traded, as can forward contracts. The latter are likely to prove the most useful for the ILS market since they will greatly help to manage price index reset risk. "In theory, the arrival of the three- and six-month inflation options could do for the short

[40] See Thomas (2001).
[41] See Royal Bank of Scotland (2001).
[42] See Deutsche Bank (2003). More details on these options can be found at www.economicderivatives.com

end of the inflation curve what short-dated interest rate futures did for the interest-rate swap market."[43] However, the liquidity and transparency that already exists for the Euro-HICP-linked swaps, through voice brokerage, perhaps points to a more likely source of liquid hedging instrument. The standard zero-coupon swap (Exhibit A8.7 on p. 266) is essentially a forward contract on the index level and, although more regularly traded with maturities of 2, 5 or 10 years, the standard contracts can easily be altered to reference monthly index fixings at any maturity, including those shorter than 1 year.

8.6 FUTURE TRENDS

8.6.1 Market standardisation

By mid-2003 there was already an estimated €20–30bn[44] notional of outstanding ILSs and options on the books of various market-making banks, other financial institutions and corporations. However, despite this large volume of existing transactions, ISDA had yet to incorporate standard definitions into its universally referenced swap documentation. In the absence of such ISDA standards, a number of public and private discussions have taken place between the major market participants with the aim of agreeing some standards to aid orderly execution in the market. For example, in November 2001, representatives from Agence France Trésor, traders from 17 market-making banks and 2 of the main inter-dealer brokers gathered in London to discuss various ways in which Euro-zone ILSs might be standardised.

As of mid-2003 it appears likely that ILSs and other derivatives will feature on ISDA's agenda for consideration during 2004. Such a step would provide a great boost to the market and would undoubtedly help the further development of inflation swaps and other derivatives.

8.6.2 Pension reforms in Europe

Pension reforms in Europe will be a significant factor driving the development of the Euro-zone market for inflation derivatives and for real assets in general. It seems likely that, as the European pension market reforms along the lines of the UK with more IL liabilities, so demand will increase for IL derivatives and real assets. The relative size of the Euro-zone, not to mention the liquidity of its capital markets, suggests that the inflation derivative market will likewise become more liquid and efficient than its UK counterpart. Although the business has so far tended to be dominated by that generated by retail demand, pension reforms of this nature are likely to switch this emphasis as demand for longer dated real assets and accompanying derivative solutions is boosted. An early indicator of this trend was the longest dated French IL MTN to date, a 20-year security issued by KfW in June 2003.[45]

[43] Source: Haggerty (2003).
[44] Barclays Capital estimate, June 2003.
[45] This was a €100mn swapped issue and had an ISIN code of DE0008879057.

8.6.3 The implications of changes to accounting standards

In 2005 the European Union will adopt accounting standards as set by the International Accounting Standards Board (IASB). When this change comes into effect, all public companies listed on exchanges anywhere within the European Union will have to prepare accounts in line with the International Accounting Standards (IASs). This change will have a widespread impact on the way companies report their financial statements. In particular, those companies with Defined Benefit (DB) pension schemes will be impacted by the application of the relevant standard IAS-19. In broad terms, this standard requires firms with DB pension schemes to reflect the fully marked-to-market valuation of such schemes in their financial statements.

A similar change is already under way in the UK, where the national Accounting Standards Board (ASB) published its FRS-17[46] standard to apply a similar regime to all companies publicly listed on the London Stock Exchange. Although they have their differences, the key element of both FRS-17 and IAS-19 is the same: pension liabilities should be measured on a projected cash flow basis (based on actuarial assumptions with regard to life expectancy) which are then present-valued using bond yields. Fixed income securities therefore form the asset class that provides the closest liability match. Fund managers who opt to hold a large fraction of their assets in other forms (such as equities or property) are likely to introduce significant volatility into the financial statements of their sponsor companies, as their asset valuations will move in line with their market prices while the present value of their liabilities will be impacted by the market prices of bonds.

The potential role here for IL derivatives is clear: if pension fund trustees opt to minimise the mark-to-market volatility of the funds under their management, they need to purchase assets that match their liabilities as closely as possible. To the extent that such liabilities are inflation-indexed, this will require the purchase of inflation-indexed bonds or IL derivative structures of the types discussed previously in this chapter. The growth of the LPI market in the UK (in response to different legislation, the Minimum Funding Requirement – see Section 6.5) is an example of how the IL derivative market can respond to such regulatory pressures. The introduction of IAS-19 in 2005 could result in similar growth of the Euro-HICP-linked market.

8.6.4 Further development of the inflation derivatives markets

Options (caps and floors), swaptions and other derivatives are likely to start trading alongside the ILS market on a more standardised basis but are likely to develop in line with the requirements of the users (in the same manner that LPI swaps with 0% floors and 5% caps are transacted in the UK market, and the 0% principal floor on HICP swaps in Europe) rather than simply by replicating products that already exist in the nominal interest rate market.

As the underlying markets in swaps and forwards become more liquid, with narrower bid–offer spreads, confidence in the ability to efficiently delta-hedge options would increase among market makers. In turn, this should allow tighter price quotes and spur increased interest from both buyers and sellers of options. In principle, this

[46] Financial Reporting Standard.

would become a virtuous cycle, whereby the market evolves gradually from historical volatility-based pricing to that based on implied volatilities – from observed market prices of more and more complex options – mimicking the development of markets for nominal interest rate volatility products during the course of the previous 20 years.

In the same vein, the existence of IL derivatives in principle enables the emergence of more sophisticated pension-hedging structures, such as those with embedded swaptions. In addition, it is easy to imagine the establishment of a real mortgage market, especially in those countries with a tradition of long-dated fixed nominal rate mortgages. The economic rationale for structuring mortgage index payments as a fixed real annuity (as opposed to a fixed nominal annuity) is clear: the loan repayments would tend to grow with future income growth, to the extent that nominal incomes grow in line with consumer prices.

In September 2003 it was reported that the Chicago Mercantile Exchange (CME) is likely to start trading CPI futures from early 2004.[47] The existence of such contracts will allow the direct pricing of forward real yields on TIPS and so could encourage the development of a TIPS options market, as well as enabling more efficient swap pricing and hedging. Because the inflation-linked swaps market in the USA is at a relatively early stage of development compared to that in Europe, such an innovation may well be the more natural progression. In Europe, where the OTC inflation derivative markets have been growing fast, it seems more likely that the evolution will mimic that of the nominal interest rate markets in which OTC structures became established before any exchange-traded contacts existed. In time, however, it seems likely that OTC and exchange-traded derivatives will co-exist in inflation markets globally.

Whatever the precise details of its future development, IL derivatives have already become established as an integral part of the broader market for inflation-indexed financial products, and in mid-2003 this role looks set to expand significantly.

[47] See de Teran (2003).

8
Appendix

A8.1 EXAMPLE SWAP AND OPTION STRUCTURES

A few typical swap structures are presented here in term sheet format to illustrate the various forms that are most commonly traded in the market.

A8.1.1 Capital Indexed Bond (CIB)-style swaps

By replicating the cash flows on the sovereign IL bonds on one leg of the swap, these flows can be matched against fixed or floating flows on the other in order to convert existing investments from fixed or floating nominal into real securities (Exhibit A8.1).

Exhibit A8.1 OAT€*i*-style versus EURIBOR flat rate or fixed rate

Amount:	€50mn (for example)
Start date:	[TBD]
End date:	[TBD]
Bank pays:	6 million EURIBOR flat rate, semi-annual act/360 *or* Fixed rate, annual 30/360
Bank receives:	Real coupon of $X\%$: $X\% * [\text{HICP}(p-3)/\text{HICP}(s-3)] * \text{Dayfrac} * \text{Notional}$, annual 30/360 Additionally, at maturity: $\text{Notional} * \text{Max}\{0\%, [\text{HICP}(m-3)/\text{HICP}(s-3) - 1]\}$ where p = payment date, s = start date and m = maturity date $\text{HICP(base)} = \text{HICP}(s-3)$ We use the standard 3-month lag for indexation

An alternative to the above structure results from splitting the coupons and redemption payment into two separate swaps (Exhibits A8.2 and A8.3). The zero-coupon-only swap is attractive to those wishing to purchase a single, inflation-protected cash flow.

The real-coupon-only swap has features that are attractive to those needing to hedge real annuity exposures.

Exhibit A8.2 Real coupon (only) versus EURIBOR flat rate or fixed rate

Amount: €50mn (for example)

Start date: [TBD]

End date: [TBD]

Bank pays: 6 million EURIBOR flat rate, semi-annual act/360
or
Fixed rate, annual 30/360

Bank receives: Real coupon of $X\%$:

$$X\% * [\text{HICP}(p-3)/\text{HICP}(s-3)] * \text{Dayfrac} * \text{Notional, annual 30/360}$$

where p = payment date, s = start date and m = maturity date
HICP(base) = HICP($s-3$)
We use the standard 3-month lag for indexation

Exhibit A8.3 Zero-coupon only versus upfront or EURIBOR flat rate – spread

Amount: €50mn (for example)

Start date: [TBD]

End date: [TBD]

Bank receives: Upfront premium
or
6 million EURIBOR flat rate – spread, semi-annual act/360

Bank pays: At maturity:

$$\text{Notional} * \text{Max}\{0\%, [\text{HICP}(m-3)/\text{HICP}(s-3)-1]\}$$

where s = start date and m = maturity date
HICP(base) = HICP($s-3$) = HICP(type in month and year)
= Type in value
We use the standard 3-month lag for indexation

A8.1.2 Real annuity swaps

Alternatively, the real annuity structure can be replicated in a different format in which compounded inflation flows are exchanged for compounded fixed flows (Exhibit A8.4). The zero-coupon alternative can be traded with an additional payment at maturity (Exhibit A8.5).

Exhibit A8.4 Real annuity versus compounded fixed rate

Amount:	€50mn (for example)
Start date:	[TBD]
End date:	[TBD]
Bank pays:	Compounded fixed annual payments each year t:
	Notional $*$ $(1 + X\%)^t$
Bank receives:	Real annuity paid annually:
	Notional $*$ $[\mathrm{HICP}(p-3)/\mathrm{HICP}(s-3)]$
	where p = payment date and s = start date HICP(base) = HICP($s - 3$) We use the standard 3-month lag for indexation

Exhibit A8.5 Zero-coupon plus fixed rate versus EURIBOR flat rate

Amount:	€50mn (for example)
Start date:	[TBD]
End date:	[TBD]
Bank pays:	6 million EURIBOR flat rate, semi-annual act/360
Bank receives:	At maturity:
	Notional $*$ $[\mathrm{Max}\{0\%, [\mathrm{HICP}(m-3)/\mathrm{HICP}(s-3) - 1]\} + X\%\}]$
	where s = start date and m = maturity date HICP(base) = HICP($s - 3$) We use the standard 3-month lag for indexation

A8.1.3 Interest Indexed Bond (IIB)-style swaps

The most commonly traded structure in 2003, with a year-on-year inflation coupon, can be structured as shown in Exhibit A8.6. This structure was the core component of the swapped Euro MTN programme detailed in Table 8.5.

Exhibit A8.6 Year-on-year inflation plus spread versus EURIBOR flat rate

Amount: €50mn (for example)

Start date: [TBD]

End date: [TBD]

Bank pays: 6 million EURIBOR flat rate, semi-annual act/360

Bank receives: Year-on-year inflation plus spread:

$$\{\mathrm{Max}[0\%, [\mathrm{HICP}(p-3)/\mathrm{HICP}(p-15)-1]] + X\%\} * \mathrm{Dayfrac} * \mathrm{Notional, annual\ 30/360}$$

or

$$\mathrm{Max}\{0\%, [\mathrm{HICP}(p-3)/\mathrm{HICP}(p-15)-1] + X\%\} * \mathrm{Dayfrac} * \mathrm{Notional, annual\ 30/360}$$

(keep one of the two alternatives: 0% floored inflation rate or 0% floored total coupon)

where p = payment date
HICP(base) = HICP($s-3$)
We use the standard 3-month lag for indexation

A8.1.4 Standard inter-dealer broker market structures

A number of the standard broker market swap structures are illustrated in Exhibits A8.7, A8.8, A8.9 and A8.10. These are designed to be simple, transparent and to reduce counterparty credit exposure. The first two form the building blocks of the zero-coupon and year-on-year end-user structures without any optionality, while the last two are versions of the same swaps but with the addition of 0% "deflation" floors.

Exhibit A8.7 Standard broker market swaps: zero-coupon swap

Amount: €50mn (for example)

Start date: [TBD]

End date: [TBD]

Bank pays: At maturity:

Notional $*$ {[HICP(m – 3)/HICP(s – 3) – 1]}

or

Notional $*$ {[HICP(m – 2)/HICP(s – 2) – 1]}

Bank receives: At maturity:

Notional $* [(1 + X\%)^t - 1]$

where s = start date, m = maturity date and t = number of years from start date to end date
The market typically uses a 2 or 3-month lag for indexation

Exhibit A8.8 Standard broker market swaps: year-on-year swap

Amount: €50mn (for example)

Start date: [TBD]

End date: [TBD]

Bank pays: Year-on-year inflation, paid annually unfloored:

[HICP(p – 2)/HICP(p – 14) – 1] $*$ Dayfrac $*$ Notional, annual 30/360 unadjusted

or

[HICP(p – 3)/HICP(p – 15) – 1] $*$ Dayfrac $*$ Notional, annual 30/360 unadjusted

Bank receives: Annual fixed coupon:

$X\%$ $*$ Dayfrac $*$ Notional, annual 30/360 unadjusted

where p = payment date
The market typically uses a 2 or 3-month lag for indexation

Exhibit A8.9	Standard broker market options: 0% floor on zero-coupon swap
Amount:	€50mn (for example)
Start date:	[TBD]
End date:	[TBD]
Bank pays:	At maturity: Notional $*$ Min{0%, [HICP($m-3$)/HICP($s-3$) − 1]} *or* Notional $*$ Min{0%, [HICP($m-2$)/HICP($s-2$) − 1]}
Bank receives:	Upfront premium where s = start date, m = maturity date and t = number of years from start date to end date The market typically uses a 2 or 3-month lag for indexation

Exhibit A8.10	Standard broker market swaps: 0% floor on a year-on-year swap
Amount:	€50mn (for example)
Start date:	[TBD]
End date:	[TBD]
Bank pays:	Max{0%, [1 − HICP($p-2$)/HICP($p-14$)]} $*$ Dayfrac $*$ Notional, annual 30/360 unadjusted *or* Max{0%, [1 − HICP($p-3$)/HICP($p-15$)]} $*$ Dayfrac $*$ Notional, annual 30/360 unadjusted
Bank receives:	Upfront premium where p = payment date The market typically uses a 2 or 3-month lag for indexation

9
Inflation-linked Derivatives: Pricing, Hedging and Other Technical Aspects

9.1 OUTLINE

Chapter 8 described a number of Inflation-linked (IL) derivative structures that have been developed in recent years to provide solutions for both investors and borrowers whose requirements cannot be met using index-linked bond markets in isolation. As is the case for many derivatives, these IL structures have their own individual idiosyncrasies that may not immediately be clear to the uninitiated. This chapter highlights some important approaches to the pricing of IL derivatives, outlines some specific model frameworks and their applicability to structures, such as those described in Chapter 8.

The most common IL derivative transacted to date is the inflation swap, and so this class of instruments forms the focus of the chapter. In addition, two options that are frequently found embedded within IL products are also described: the "deflation floor" found in many of the major sovereign index-linked bond markets and the "year-on-year inflation floor" built into many of the retail products issued in Italy and other parts of Europe since 2001.

First, the concept of "pricing" is discussed. The various IL bond and derivative markets around the world display widely varying degrees of development, which in turn means that very different approaches are required to price instruments in each. It is helpful to categorise these developmental stages, and each such definition is discussed in turn. The subsequent sections go on to describe some general aspects that are important to price any IL derivative contract and highlight distinctions between the different techniques required to both price and hedge instruments in each category of market.

Finally, the chapter concludes with an overview of some of the more important aspects of pricing options on inflation, in particular the estimation and properties of inflation volatility as well as some specific properties of the two forms of inflation floor that are frequently transacted in the market today.

9.2 PRICING APPROACHES

9.2.1 What is meant by "pricing"?

In general, the "pricing" of inflation-indexed bonds is typically confined to the identification of market levels at which supply meets demand,[1] to the translation of prices to

[1] For example, through a syndication process a particular new issue is "priced" at a spread over an appropriate reference bond, typically a sovereign bond with the same index, indicating where investor demand can absorb the full size of the issue.

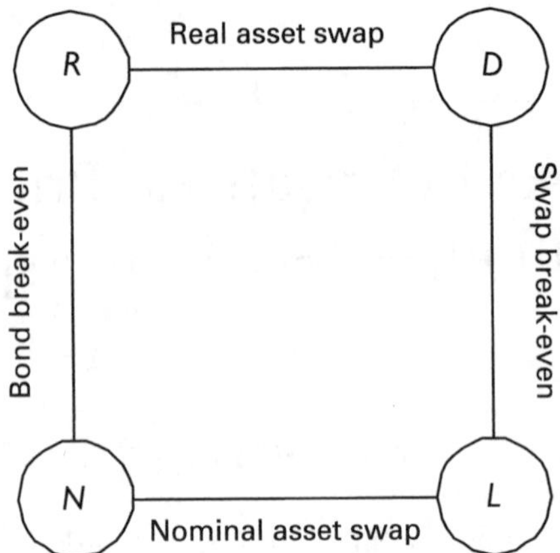

Figure 9.1 Connections between nominal and real bonds and swaps
N = nominal bond; R = real bond; L = IRS; D = inflation-linked swap.

real yields (and vice versa) and perhaps to the concept of "beta".[2] Market prices are simply determined by supply and demand and represent the level at which the two offset one another. In nominal markets, asset swap levels for sovereign bonds connect bond and swap prices where both instruments trade in large liquid markets. Similarly, in a near-complete market one would also expect inflation-indexed bonds and IL swaps (ILSs) to trade in a corresponding manner, with the real asset swap levels to form the connection. The concept of asset swap levels in the above context, however, is purely an observation mechanism and does not "price" one instrument relative to the other – the two sets of instruments are already trading in their own liquid markets and thus establish clearing valuations somewhat independently of one another.

The connection between nominal and real bonds, and between nominal interest rate and inflation-indexed swaps, is represented conceptually in Figure 9.1. Nominal bonds are represented by N, real bonds by R, nominal interest rate swaps (IRSs) that are LIBOR-indexed by L and ILSs by D. Nominal asset swaps connect N and L, real asset swaps link R and D, while break-even inflation rates in the bond and swap markets form the other connections.

At the time of writing, in most countries the markets for ILSs are less liquid relative to those of the underlying inflation-indexed bonds. These derivatives typically have payouts linked to the same index as the inflation-indexed bonds from which they are derived but may also involve other indices (such as LIBOR) that are linked to other, more liquid instruments. The traded prices for ILSs and other derivatives would therefore be expected to be consistent with those of the more actively traded instruments. Pricing models for inflation-indexed derivatives therefore take as inputs the traded levels or prices of the underlying instruments L, N, and R and thereby ensure self-consistency in pricing across the four assets.

[2] In this context, the term "beta" describes the price movement of inflation-indexed bonds relative to those of nominal bonds from the same issuer. See Chapter 5 for a more detailed description of the concept.

9.2.2 Four levels of pricing

Inflation swap markets can be broadly divided into four categories, corresponding to four levels of development, which will be called Levels I, II, III and IV. The divisions between these are sometimes blurred, but pricing and hedging approaches are sufficiently distinct to justify such a categorisation.

9.2.3 Level I

A Level I market is one in which there are no tradable market instruments linked to the index of interest. Swap prices are therefore made on the basis of matched trades, supply and demand and/or the taking of basis risk by using instruments from Level II or III markets as hedges. An example of a Level I market is the Spanish inflation swap market, where wide bid–offer spreads are common,[3] pricing and trading is typically driven by matched flows and often involves taking basis risk through the use of French or Euro-zone inflation swaps (or a combination of OAT*i*s/OAT€*i*s and nominal bonds) to hedge general inflation risk.

9.2.4 Level II

Level II markets are defined to be those with one or more tradable market instruments, again typically sovereign inflation-indexed bonds, which serve to "anchor" and bound a few points on the inflation or real yield curve. However, due to the scarcity of suitable candidates in the range of maturities of interest, supply and demand still drives prices at the "missing" points along the yield curve. Examples of Level II markets include the Euro-zone and the domestic French inflation swap markets. However, including the three CADES*i* (Caisse d'Amortissement de la Dette Sociale) issues in the latter category, along with the recently issued Greek Government Bond GGB€*i* 2025 and the Italian BTP€*i* 2008 bond in the former, both might be more correctly categorised as in transition between Levels II and III.

9.2.5 Level III

Level III markets are those where "many" tradable market instruments exist, and so a near complete and near arbitrage-free inflation or real swap curve can be constructed. In such cases swap reset risks, repo costs and convexity issues are the dominant factors that determine the swap rates relative to the more liquid securities along the yield curve. Specific supply and demand in the swap market then becomes a secondary issue that more finely defines the inflation swap prices within these bounds. The UK Retail Prices Index (RPI) swap market falls into this category, and the observed swap prices tend to adhere to these rules. Interestingly, the US Consumer Price Index (CPI) swap market should be similarly categorised due to the existence of a reasonably full and liquid Treasury Inflation-Protection Securities (TIPS) curve. However, as of mid-2003, this market was still at a very early stage of development (see Chapter 8).

[3] For example, a five-year Spanish inflation swap is typically quoted with a bid–offer spread of 40 basis points.

9.2.6 Level IV

Although the current state of the inflation-linked swap (ILS) markets around the world is such that each falls into one of the above three categories, a fourth level might reasonably be expected to emerge in the future. This hypothetical Level IV market is one that has reached a level of maturity, liquidity and stability analogous to the major nominal IRS markets, such that inflation-indexed swaps trade in their own right but side-by-side the inflation-indexed bonds. Under such conditions the ILSs would themselves be basic tradable market instruments and their prices set somewhat independently of any underlying sovereign or other index-linked bond market, and as a result the IL bond asset swap spreads would also be set independently of their nominal counterparts. Should such a Level IV ILS market exist, then pricing models of the form outlined above would not be required, as the market swap rates could be used to construct a self-consistent forward inflation or forward index curve in an analogous fashion to those for nominal swap markets and asset swap spreads. It would then be possible to view spreads between ILSs and indexed bonds in an analogous fashion to their nominal counterparts.

Paradoxically, the Euro-zone inflation-indexed swap market, which is only a Level II or Level III market by the above definitions, is now the most liquid inflation-indexed derivatives market in the world with certain characteristics of a Level IV market at particular maturities. Indeed, the liquidity relative to the underlying bonds (BTP€*i* 2008, OAT€*i* 2012, GGB€*i* 2025 and OAT€*i* 2032) is such that swap flows are now often seen to drive bond prices, an issue discussed in more detail in Section 9.8.

9.3 DERIVING A FORWARD CONSUMER PRICE INDEX (CPI) CURVE FOR LEVEL II AND III MARKETS

Consider a market for a particular index in which there are k tradable inflation-linked bonds. We know k different prices, one for each of these bonds, from observed levels in the market. If the forward price index series were known for all future settings related to the payouts on each of the k bonds, all future coupon and redemption flows on these securities would be known in nominal terms. For each of the k bonds the total present value of these flows, computed using the discount curve for instruments with the same credit rating (typically the corresponding nominal sovereign bonds), represents a fair market price for each security based on such a series of forward index settings. This set of "fair" prices only replicates those observed in the market if the series of forward index settings represents market expectations, and so this framework can be characterised as a k-degrees-of-freedom problem.

Recalling Equations (5.1) and (5.3):

$$P_N = \sum_{j=1}^{n} \frac{C_N}{(1+y_j)^j} + \frac{R_N}{(1+y_n)^n} \tag{9.1}$$

$$P_R = \sum_{j=1}^{n} \frac{C_R}{(1+r_j)^j} + \frac{R_R}{(1+r_n)^n} \tag{9.2}$$

where y_j represents the spot interest rate on a loan repayable at date j and, extending the notation, let k represent the number of tradable indexed bonds for a particular price index.[4] Using the nominal market discount curve, the present value of all future cash flows for each of the k inflation-indexed bonds can be calculated and the Nominal Dirty Price (NDP) of the k inflation-indexed bonds $P_{\mathrm{NDP}(i)}$ can be written out as:

$$P_{\mathrm{NDP}(i)} = \sum_{j=1}^{n(i)} \frac{C_{R(i)}}{(1+y_{j(i)})^j} \frac{\mathrm{CPI}_{j(i)}}{\mathrm{CPI}_{\mathrm{base}(i)}} + \frac{R_{R(i)}}{(1+y_{n(i)})^{n(i)}} \frac{\mathrm{CPI}_{n(i)}}{\mathrm{CPI}_{\mathrm{base}(i)}}, \qquad i = 1, 2, \ldots, k \quad (9.3)$$

Note that in the above set of equations the only unknowns are the series of future CPI settings and, generally, they represent a system of k equations with $\sum_{i=1}^{k} n(i)$ unknowns. Typically, however, roll dates for a system of k such bonds often coincide, and so the number of unknowns is reduced. Nevertheless, we have far fewer equations than the number of independent variables. To solve the above problem, a number of simplifying assumptions need to be made in order to reduce the number of variables to k. Since the k redemption amounts dominate the coupon flows, the problem lends itself to being reduced to a system of k equations with k unknowns. Two simple approaches to the above problem are now presented. They are all based on assuming a functional form for CPI(t) for each time segment $T_{i-1} < t < T_i$ for $i = 1, 2, \ldots, k$, where T_i, $i = 1, 2, \ldots, k$ are the dates for the publication of the CPI value that sets the redemption payment for each of the k bonds.

9.3.1 Piecewise linear continuous function in CPI space

Assume the following functional form for CPI(t):

$$\alpha_i = \frac{\mathrm{CPI}(T_i) - \mathrm{CPI}(T_{i-1})}{T_i - T_{i-1}}, \qquad i = 1, 2, \ldots, k \quad (9.4)$$

where T_0 is the date corresponding to the last known CPI number. Defining CPI(t) for all times $T_0 < t < T_k$:

$$\mathrm{CPI}(t) = \mathrm{CPI}(T_i) + \alpha_i (t - T_i), \qquad T_{i-1} \le t \le T_i, \quad i = 1, 2, \ldots, k \quad (9.5)$$

Equation (9.3) can thus be recast in terms of k unknown variables α_i, $i = 1, 2, \ldots, k$ to produce a set of k equations that can be solved sequentially, starting from i equals 1 to k.

The above methodology is relatively simple and will produce a forward CPI curve consistent with the prices of the traded inflation-indexed bonds. However, it has two particular drawbacks: it will in general produce an unrealistic discontinuous and "jumpy" forward inflation curve and it will ignore any seasonal patterns that are significant in the CPIs of many countries (as illustrated by Figure 2.1).

[4] For example, as of mid-2003, $k = 11$ for TIPS, 10 for index-linked gilts, 3 for OAT*i*s (linked to French CPI ex-tobacco) and 2 for OAT€*i*s (linked to the Euro-zone Harmonised Index of Consumer Prices [Euro-HICP] ex-tobacco index).

9.3.2 Piecewise linear continuous function in inflation space

An alternative approach is to impose a continuous functional form on the forward *inflation* curve, as opposed to the price index itself. Defining the year-on-year inflation rate at time t as $I(t)$:

$$I(t) = \frac{\text{CPI}(t)}{\text{CPI}(t-1)} - 1 \tag{9.6}$$

the model is built similarly to the piecewise linear continuous CPI model above, by first defining the k slopes φ_i of each line segment in the forward inflation curve:

$$\varphi_i = \frac{I(T_i) - I(T_{i-1})}{T_i - T_{i-1}}, \qquad i = 1, 2, \ldots, k \tag{9.7}$$

where T_i are as previously defined. Defining $I(t)$ for all times $T_0 < t < T_k$:

$$I(t) = I(T_i) + \varphi_i(t - T_i), \qquad T_{i-1} \leq t \leq T_i, \quad i = 1, 2, \ldots, k \tag{9.8}$$

$I(0)$ is defined using Equation (9.6), knowing CPI(0) and all previous CPI settings. For a given φ_1 all $I(t)$ are known for $T_0 \leq t \leq T_1$ and by again using Equation (9.6) all CPI(t) for $T_0 \leq t \leq T_1$ are also known, thus allowing the valuation of all the cash flows associated with $P_{\text{NDP}(1)}$ (i.e., one equation with one unknown can be cast and solved for φ_1).[5]

This method to fit the forward inflation curve has the advantage that it will maintain and propagate forward the seasonal pattern in the observed CPI. However, the form of the functional relationship between $I(t)$ and CPI(t) as illustrated by Equation (9.6) implies that the relative seasonal pattern of the latest 12 months of CPI data will be reflected throughout the forward CPI curve. This is clearly a distinct improvement over those models that assume month-on-month inflation to be constant in any given period but has the drawback that any unusual patterns observed in the past 12 months will be assumed to occur each and every subsequent year. For example, if a particular published level of the price index was unusually high due to a spike in oil prices caused by a one-off and non-seasonal event (such as a war or a strike, etc.), this feature will be incorrectly propagated forward as if it were a seasonal pattern. An improvement over the above would be to specify an "adjusted" set of seasonal factors for 12 months to represent an averaged seasonal pattern that excludes one-off events, such as those just described. The seasonality inherent in price indices is discussed further in Chapter 2.

Having derived a forward curve for the price index, ILS cash flows can be valued using the LIBOR or other appropriate discount curve. The inputs to the pricing of ILSs are therefore the LIBOR curve L, the nominal bond prices N and the real bond prices R. The three sets of inputs, L, N and R, are also the instruments with which ILSs are hedged. This is discussed in Section 9.7 in the context of the practical example: the hedging of a swapped new issue.

The impact of tax and accounting factors on the market prices for various securities are difficult to isolate. Nevertheless, such features are more of a concern in the context of inflation prediction and policy making (see Chapter 5) rather than for the pricing and hedging of IL derivatives. In most cases derivatives should be priced to be consistent

[5] A similar but simpler approach to that described here is one based on a piecewise constant year-on-year inflation assumption, as applied to the UK index-linked gilt market by Flavell (2002).

with the underlying hedge instruments, regardless of whether or not the latter are perceived to be distorted.

9.4 "LEVEL I" MARKETS IN EUROPE: INTRAREGIONAL EURO-ZONE INFLATION SPREADS

As described both above and in previous chapters, markets for indexed bonds linked to the French and Euro-zone price indices are well developed, and so the methods outlined in Section 9.3 can be employed to build forward index curves and thereby price various IL derivatives linked to those indices. Indeed, the inflation swap market for both these indices has developed some depth. However, in addition there is demand from both payers and receivers in the Euro-zone (outside France) for exposure to their respective domestic price indices, as described in Chapter 8.

Italy and Spain are particularly good examples of markets where transactions linked to the domestic price index have been structured and transacted. Prices in these markets are often quoted as spreads to the Euro-HICP ex-tobacco ILSs[6] and reflect market sentiments regarding the future prospects for inflation in these economies relative to the Euro-zone average. Bid–offer spreads tend to be relatively wide, sometimes as wide as 40 basis points,[7] reflecting not only a lack of liquidity but also the inherent uncertainty.

In the absence of any inflation-indexed securities (government-issued or otherwise) it is necessary to devise a more theoretical framework in which to price such derivatives.[8] However, for countries within EMU, it is reasonable to base such analysis on an assumption of medium-term price level convergence. It is useful to consider the macroeconomic factors that would help to explain the different inflation rates in the different Euro-zone countries but also to then employ such simple economic assumptions in order to put some bounds on possible values for inflation swap spreads at different maturities. For example, it would seem sensible to quote a price for the spread of Spanish inflation over the Euro-zone average that is in line both with the observed inflation data and with economic theory with regard to the convergence of prices across the monetary union.

Eurostat provides price indices for the individual EU member states that are computed using the same methodology as the Euro-HICP index (see, for example, Table 9.1). Given the level of the index in any particular country (that represents the price of the "standard" basket of goods in that country), the Euro-zone average for the same basket and an assumed time horizon in which the two price indices will converge, it is then possible to determine some reasonable bounds for the spread to the Euro-zone inflation swap at different maturities. The following simplified analysis shows how such price convergence can relate inflation rates in the Euro-zone $\pi_{\text{Euro-zone}}$, inflation spreads

[6] The Euro-HICP ex-tobacco index is most commonly used for this purpose, using the same unrevised series that is used to determine the cash flows of the OAT€*i* bonds.

[7] By comparison, "vanilla" Euro-HICP swaps are almost always quoted with bid–offer spreads of less than 10 basis points.

[8] The BTP€*i* 2008 issued by the Italian Treasury in September 2003, like the French OAT€*i* bonds, is linked to Euro-HICP (excluding tobacco). As such, therefore, there are still no actively traded securities that are linked to a domestic Italian price index.

Table 9.1 European Union price level indices in year 2000

Country	France = 100	EU15 = 100
Austria	95	98
Belgium	98	101
Denmark	119	122
Finland	113	117
France	100	103
Germany	98	101
Greece	78	80
Ireland	106	109
Italy	83	86
Luxembourg	93	96
Netherlands	96	99
Portugal	70	72
Spain	81	84
Sweden	125	129
UK	115	119

Data source: Eurostat.

$\pi_{\text{Spread},i}$ and starting price levels $P_i(0)$ in Euro-zone member country i, given an assumed time to convergence of n years:

$$\begin{aligned} P_i(t) &= P_i(0) \prod_{j=1}^{t} [1 + \pi_{\text{Euro-zone}}(j) + \pi_{\text{Spread},i}(j)] \\ &= P_i(0)[1 + \bar{\pi}_{\text{Euro-zone}} + \bar{\pi}_{\text{Spread},i}]^t \end{aligned} \tag{9.9}$$

$$\begin{aligned} & P_i(n) = P_{\text{Euro-zone}}(n) \\ \Rightarrow \quad & P_i(0)[1 + \bar{\pi}_{\text{Euro-zone}} + \bar{\pi}_{\text{Spread},i}]^n = P_{\text{Euro-zone}}(0)[1 + \bar{\pi}_{\text{Euro-zone}}]^n \\ \Rightarrow \quad & \bar{\pi}_{\text{Spread},i} = \left[\left(\frac{P_{\text{Euro-zone}}(0)}{P_i(0)}\right)^{1/n} - 1\right](1 + \bar{\pi}_{\text{Euro-zone}}) \end{aligned} \tag{9.10}$$

For example, a country with a price index of 80 relative to the Euro-zone average of 100 would require an inflation spread of 1.14% if it were to converge to the Euro-zone average in 20 years, assuming that Euro-zone inflation averages 2% over this period. By varying the expected average Euro-HICP inflation rate as well as the convergence horizon, a "sensitivity analysis" can be carried out to determine sensible bounds for this spread.

This analysis can be expanded by taking a portfolio approach to value Euro-zone domestic inflation-indexed swaps. Equation (9.11) describes how the HICP basket for the Euro-zone is a weighted sum of the individual baskets for each of the current 12 Euro-zone countries:

$$P_{\text{Euro-zone}} = \sum_{i=1}^{12} w_i P_i \tag{9.11}$$

Similarly, a portfolio of appropriately weighted inflation swaps for the individual domestic indices can be treated as being similar to a single Euro-zone swap and can therefore be hedged using either a combination of OAT€*i*s and nominal OATs or Euro-zone inflation-indexed swaps (or any appropriate combination of the two).[9]

In practice, gaining exposure to *all* Euro-zone price indices in the appropriate weightings may not be practical. Nevertheless, a portfolio with exposure to the larger economies is highly correlated with the full Euro-zone basket. For example, a portfolio of German, Italian and Spanish inflation swaps can be used to construct a proxy for pan-Euro-zone inflation: a mixture of low (Germany and France[10]), medium (Italy) and high (Spain) inflation countries constructed with the same weightings as the Euro-zone basket. This portfolio to proxy a Euro-zone inflation swap can then be hedged with bond break-evens (using a combination of OAT€*i*s and nominal OATs). Although useful in many situations, such an approach is impractical if the portfolio contains large exposures to smaller Euro-zone countries. Indeed, the difficulty in applying this approach is inversely proportional to the relative size of the economy in question within the Euro-zone. For example, a portfolio containing a large exposure to an index that represents 5% of the Euro-HICP basket would require an additional portfolio of swaps that is an order of magnitude larger than the original exposure to hedge in this manner. In such cases this portfolio approach may be expensive to implement, or require transactions that are simply too large to execute in the market.

9.5 ALTERNATIVE APPROACHES TO THE CONSTRUCTION OF INFLATION CURVES

Section 9.3 describes a number of "bootstrap" techniques to construct estimates of forward price indices, and Chapter 5 detailed a number of other methods to produce term structures of forward inflation rates from observed bond prices.[11] This section reviews a number of further techniques that have specific application to the pricing of IL derivatives.

One straightforward approach is to apply the bootstrap techniques to the market prices of asset swaps. As shown in Figure 9.1, nominal bond and swap prices are connected at different maturities by swap spreads – in effect, a term structure of nominal swap spreads is directly observable. A starting point for building a forward price index curve is to assume that the term structure of (nominal) swap spreads for IL bonds is identical to that of their nominal counterparts. Analogous to the techniques of Section 9.3, a series of assumptions are required to cast the problem as one with the same number of unknowns as observable swap spreads. Beginning with the shortest maturity index-linked bond a set of forward index levels is chosen such that the bond's swap spread is in line with those of similar duration nominal bonds, and the forward inflation or index curve between the remaining bonds is then "bootstrapped" iteratively along the curve (using the appropriate counterpart to either Equation (9.3) or (9.5)). With reference to Figure 9.1, this approach sets the real asset swap spread linking R and

[9] Following the introduction of the Greek GGB€*i* 2025 and Italian BTP€*i* 2008 bonds during 2003, coupled with increasing prospects of issuance by other European governments, it is perhaps more appropriate to refer to €*i* bonds – without specific reference to the OAT issues.

[10] Exposure to domestic French inflation can be achieved using either swaps or a combination of OAT*i*s and nominal OATs.

[11] Other, similar approaches are outlined by Das (2001).

D to be identical to the nominal asset swap spread linking N and L. When using the prices of nominal bonds to estimate future inflation rates there is always a risk that the results are distorted by idiosyncrasies of individual securities, such as differing liquidity at different points along the curve.[12] Using swap spreads helps to sidestep such distortions, since nominal interest rate swap curves are typically much less affected by such issues. When using this approach, care should be taken when the nominal swap spread curve is not flat, since the duration of an index-linked bond is typically longer than that of its conventional counterpart with similar maturity.[13]

Kazziha (1999) provides some useful analysis for pricing IL derivatives, including options. In particular, she considers the pricing of year-on-year inflation swaps and recognizes a required drift adjustment that, based on market prices observed in brokered inter-bank markets, is seemingly often ignored. In essence it is a recasting of the effect of Jensen's inequality (see Chapter 5): to correctly price the pay-off for coupons on year-on-year inflation swaps the expectation of the *reciprocal* of each forward index is required, as well as the usual expectation of the forward index itself:

$$\exp\left[\frac{\text{CPI}(t)}{\text{CPI}(t-1)} - 1\right] \tag{9.12}$$

Expressed naïvely (and incorrectly, see Equations (5.14) and (5.16)), one may be tempted to recast the above as:

$$\frac{\exp[\text{CPI}(t)]}{\exp[\text{CPI}(t-1)]} - 1 \tag{9.13}$$

Kazziha derives the adjustment to the "drift" term required in most interest rate term structure models to correct Equation (9.13). Her results indicate that, for given estimates of inflation and interest rate volatility (and a correlation between the two), prices for year-on-year inflation swaps can deviate significantly from those based on the "naïve" Equation (9.13). This is especially true for swaps with maturities of 20 years or longer, where such convexity effects are larger and deviations can be as large as 30 basis points per annum.

A recent paper by Jarrow and Yildirim (2003) presents a more comprehensive solution to the problem. The authors appeal to an analogy with the pricing of exchange rates: real yields corresponding to foreign prices, nominal yields to domestic prices and the inflation rate to the spot exchange rate. This insight provides a consistent framework within which standard models for pricing foreign exchange rate and interest rate derivatives can be applied to inflation-linked bonds and derivatives.

The interest rate parity equation, which links the forward exchange rate to the spot exchange rate, can be written as:[14]

$$F = Se^{(r-r_f)(T-t)} \tag{9.14}$$

[12] Chapter 5 described a number of studies that used other approaches to mitigate any such effects.
[13] This issue is discussed in Chapter 5.
[14] Following Hull (1993).

where: S = the spot rate.

F = the forward rate.

r = the domestic currency interest rate.

r_f = the foreign currency interest rate.

t and T = the start and end dates, respectively.

The above (continuously compounded) interest rate formula can be recast in discrete time and using the annual real r and nominal n yields with the CPI index in place of the exchange rate:

$$\text{CPI}(T - t) = \text{CPI}(t) \times \left(\frac{1+n}{1+r}\right)^{(T-t)} \tag{9.15}$$

Although the three-factor Heath, Jarrow and Morton (HJM) model proposed by Jarrow and Yildirim (2003) is hard to calibrate, especially as applied to real rates and inflation, the general theoretical framework is consistent with modern option-pricing theory. The increasingly liquid inflation-indexed swap market in the Euro-zone is likely to be the first to allow tighter option pricing based on lower cost delta-hedging scenarios. In time, as the markets for various inflation derivatives develop, a broader range of option prices are likely to become available to better calibrate such models and thereby make them more applicable in practice.

9.6 ASSET SWAPS – CONNECTING SWAP AND BOND PRICES

The existence of balanced two-way swap flows requires a mature, advanced market with active and knowledgeable issuers and investors. As detailed in previous chapters this state of affairs has typically evolved gradually, initiated by the expansion of the set of sovereign bonds in response to an increase in demand for such new issues (e.g., from the pensions industry, individual investors, etc.). In turn this encourages corporate and supranational issuance alongside the sovereign bonds as the demand for non-sovereign securities is met. Such a situation currently exists in a number of inflation-linked bond markets, in particular that of the UK and those initiated by the French government linked to the French CPI and the Euro-HICP indices. Under such conditions real rates do not tend to move away from "fair value" for persistent periods of time, as market participants arbitrage away any anomalies. Additionally, since 2002 cross-market trading of real yields and break-even inflation rates has increased significantly, acting as a further force to correct market anomalies.

Such development of established and "self-correcting" sovereign and corporate inflation-indexed bond curves forms the basis for corporate and supranational involvement in the ILS market. For example, the strong demand for retail products linked to Euro-zone and French inflation during 2002 and 2003 (detailed in Chapter 8) has led to a situation where receivers of inflation have dominated the swap market. In many cases this demand has been met by proprietary risk takers (hedge funds and other investors, investment banks who warehouse the risk, etc.) paying inflation through swaps to arbitrage "overbought" forward inflation levels. If the inflation curve is deemed to be too high at a particular maturity, an investor may be tempted to enter into an asset swap whereby he purchases a sovereign inflation-indexed bond, which typically can be funded at a floating "repo" rate below LIBOR[15], and at the same time enters a swap through which he pays inflation-indexed flows that are identical to those of the bond and in return receives a floating rate plus a fixed spread. If the inflation forward curve is high enough, it may be possible for a hedging bank to pay a floating rate of interest at LIBOR flat or even LIBOR plus a margin in return for the inflation-indexed flows. The investor has a bond from which he receives inflation but pays floating repo rates, coupled with a swap contract through which he pays the same inflation flows and receives LIBOR plus a margin, a package which in sum corresponds to a fixed annuity over the life of the bond paying annual cash flows of (LIBOR + Spread − Repo rate).

These concepts are often observable in reality in the markets for OAT*i*, OAT€*i*, BTP€*i* and CADES*i* bonds and their associated inflation-indexed swaps. As of mid-2003 the 10-year maturity points are well established in both markets, due to the existence of the OAT*i* 2013 and the OAT€*i* 2012 bonds. At shorter maturities French inflation-indexed swaps cannot trade too far from levels consistent with reasonable asset swap levels for shorter dated bonds such as the OAT*i* 2009 and the CADES*i* issues. However, before the issuance of the BTP€*i* in September 2003, shorter dated Euro-zone inflation-indexed swaps could not rely on such corrective mechanisms since there were no such bonds at maturities shorter than 2012, and so prices were mostly driven by supply and demand. The high volume of swapped Medium Term Notes (MTNs) sold in the first half of 2003 was such that the flows in the five-year area of the Euro-HICP curve were primarily driven by receivers of inflation and resulted in inflation swap rates significantly higher than consensus expectations for this period at the time. Figure 9.2 illustrates this role that inflation swaps play to "plug" holes in the maturity spectrum of sovereign issues and indicates were shorter dated OAT€*i* bonds may trade in break-even inflation rate terms, other things being equal, if and when they appear in the market. The successful BTP€*i* 2008 issue reflected the high demand for an €*i* bond in the five-year maturity and served to "plug" this hole.

Table 9.2 illustrates asset swap levels for several European inflation-indexed bonds as of September 2003 and compares them with the nominal market asset swap levels.

Figure 9.1 suggests that, as a first estimate of fair value, real and nominal asset swap prices should be similar, which in turn implies that bond and swap break-evens are also similar. However, supply and demand can skew such relationships within an "arbitrage boundary"[16]. For example, a "rich" swap curve relative to bonds simply reflects a supply and demand imbalance, a misvaluation that can increase to a level at which asset swaps become attractive. For such a structure to be viable for an asset swap investor, the improvement over the nominal market levels must be at least sufficient

[15] A "repo" or repurchase transaction is a standard technique used by investment banks and other leveraged investors to finance purchases of financial instruments. For example, an investor may purchase a government bond and simultaneously borrow the money required through a repo transaction for which the investor puts up the same bond as collateral. As such the interest rate on the collateralised loan is likely to be lower than LIBOR, which itself represents uncollateralised borrowing rates.

[16] Observations from the European bond and swap markets as of 2003 suggest that such an "arbitrage boundary" might be as wide as ten basis points, or 0.10%.

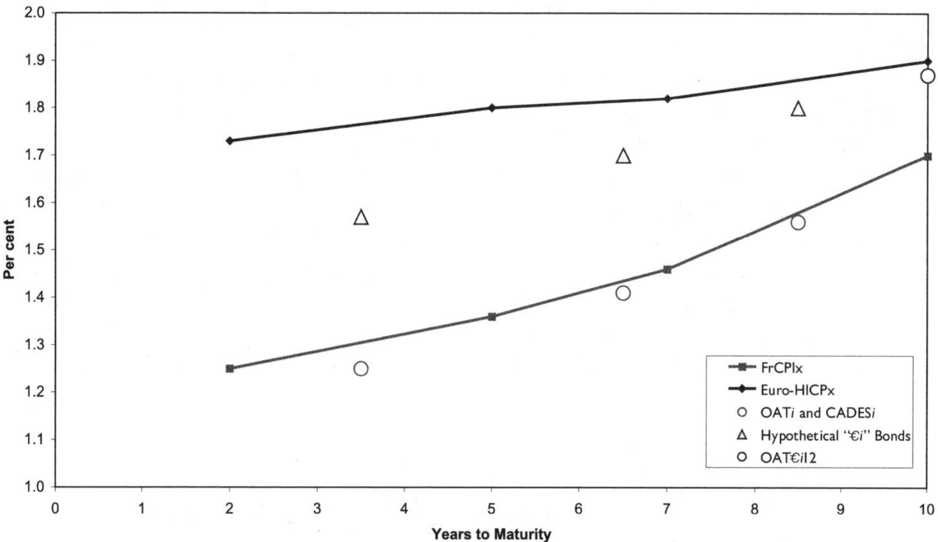

Figure 9.2 Comparison of the French and Euro-zone inflation swap curves with the break-even inflation rates for underlying Sovereign Bonds

Table 9.2 Example asset swap levels for Euro-zone index-linked bond and swap relative value analysis

	Asset swap levels (%)		Inflation swaps (%)	
Bond	Real	Nominal	Cheap	Rich
BTP€*i*08	0.065	−0.035		0.100
OAT*i*09	−0.005	−0.105		0.100
OAT€*i*12	−0.005	−0.075		0.080
OAT*i*13	−0.075	−0.080		0.005
OAT*i*29	−0.095	−0.025	−0.070	
OAT€*i*32	−0.080	−0.035	−0.045	

Reproduced by permission of Barclays Capital (market estimates as of 24 September 2003)

to cover transaction costs (e.g., to cross bid–offer spreads to buy the bonds and hedge with swaps) in order to generate the flows to offset the supply–demand imbalance.

9.7 HEDGING A SWAPPED NEW ISSUE

Chapter 8 outlined a number of IL derivative solutions: for a new corporate issue to be structured as a fixed coupon bond plus a fixed versus real swap overlay and for an issuer of an inflation-indexed bond who did not want the inflation exposure (such as the issuers of the AAA-rated bonds in the UK shown in Table 8.1). It is of course possible to transact the above two structures simultaneously whereby the hedging bank takes minimal inflation risk, since the IL derivative requirement is essentially equal and opposite in each case. In reality, however, an exact match (with respect to maturity, timing and size) for a swap transaction is hard to achieve, and without one an alternative hedging strategy is required that uses other financial instruments. The example below illustrates such a solution for a swapped new issue.

Consider a new AAA-rated inflation-indexed security issued in the UK, with coupon and maturity dates that match those of an existing index-linked gilt, $2\frac{1}{2}$% IL 2024. Investors would expect the new issue to be priced close to par, with a real yield equal to that on the corresponding government bond (R) plus a margin to reflect the credit spread between the issuer and the government: the *issuer Real Spread* (RS). The issuer typically has a targeted floating rate funding level, expressed as a spread to LIBOR: the *issuer LIBOR Spread* (LS): for example, three-month LIBOR minus 0.15%.

9.7.1 A simple "interim" hedge

An investment bank faced with such a transaction as the one described above will typically look first for a simple "interim" hedge, to neutralise its core risk as quickly and cheaply as possible. In this example the bank has committed to pay inflation to the issuer who in turn receives inflation to hedge the index-linked payments on its new 2024 AAA-rated bond. The simplest solution for the investment bank is to purchase $2\frac{1}{2}$% IL 2024 and sell short a nominal gilt of a similar maturity (for the purposes of this example 5% Treasury 2025), thereby "locking-in" the break-even inflation rate for the index-linked gilt. The inflation-indexed redemption date is perfectly matched in this case, as both the maturity date and the indexation lag for the $2\frac{1}{2}$% IL 2024 and the new AAA-rated bond are identical. A nominal IRS is also required to balance the floating rate (LIBOR-indexed) flows paid by the issuer versus the fixed flows to be paid out through the short 5% Treasury 2025 position. Ideally the cash flow dates on the IRS will match the coupon dates and maturity of the nominal gilt. These flows are shown schematically in Figure 9.3.

As illustrated in Figure 9.3, the real yield on the new issue R^* can be approximated by the following expression:

$$\begin{aligned} R^* &= R + \mathrm{RS} \\ &= R + \mathrm{SS} \pm \mathrm{LS} - \mathrm{FC} \\ &= R + \mathrm{IRS} - N \pm \mathrm{LS} - \mathrm{FC} \end{aligned} \tag{9.16}$$

where: FC = the net funding cost[17] associated with holding $2\frac{1}{2}$% IL 2024 versus a short position in 5% Treasury 2025.

N = the nominal gilt yield.

IRS = the swap rate for the same maturity.

SS = the swap spread, equal to IRS $-N$.

and R, RS and LS are as defined earlier

[17] The funding cost for this position is the spread between the "repo" interest rate charged to finance the long position in $2\frac{1}{2}$% IL 2024 and the "reverse repo" rate earned on the proceeds of the 5% Treasury 2025 sale (a loan collateralised with the same bond).

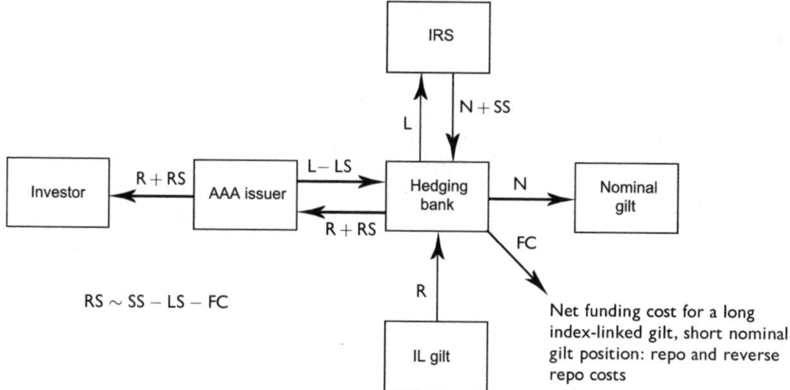

Figure 9.3 Swapped new issue showing hedged cash flows
IRS = Interest Rate Swap; L = LIBOR; R = Index-linked gilt real yield; N = nominal gilt yield; SS = Swap Spread; LS = issuer LIBOR Spread; RS = issuer Real Spread; FC = net Funding Cost

The expression in Equation (9.16) is necessarily approximate because a number of simplifying assumptions have been made. In the special case where the issuer LIBOR spread is equal to the swap spread (i.e., LS = SS), the real and nominal sovereign issues are both priced at par (i.e., with real and nominal yields matching the respective coupons); then the above approximation becomes exact, with Equation (9.16) simplifying to:

$$R^* = R - \text{FC} \tag{9.17}$$

9.7.2 A more precise hedge

The use of a forward inflation curve as described in Section 9.3 to value the cash flows on the swap between the hedging bank and the issuer allows a more precise hedge to be derived for this transaction. Given a set of nominal and real hedging instruments, the combination that best matches the inflation risk of the new bond can be determined using this method. For example, Tables 9.3a and 9.3b illustrate the portfolios of nominal and index-linked gilts that best hedge the inflation risk of the hypothetical AAA-rated 2024 new issue described above.

In cases where the coupon and redemption date for the swapped issue do not match those of an existing sovereign inflation-linked bond an additional basis risk is introduced, particularly as it relates to the reset risks associated with the mismatched redemptions of the swapped issue and any hedge. For example, a new issue in the UK with a maturity date in 2027 would require positions in both $2\frac{1}{2}$% IL 2024 and $4\frac{1}{8}$% IL 2030 as an effective hedge.[18] In terms of the daily valuation of the swap (for "mark-to-market" purposes) such a hedge should prove to be stable, especially if the long-term nominal and real yield curves both maintain smooth slopes close to the 2027 maturity date. Nevertheless, some dynamic hedging may be necessary as swap spreads and break-even inflation rates along the curve change over time. In the extreme, as $2\frac{1}{2}$% IL 2024 approaches maturity and the RPI level for its redemption payment has been set, a three-year bond will be hedged with a combination of an eight-month nominal

[18] See Section 6.5 for details of bonds in the UK index-linked gilt market.

Table 9.3a Index-linked gilt risk for swapped issue

Index-linked gilt	Price per £100 nominal	Real yield (%)	Risk (£mn)
$4\frac{3}{8}$% IL 2004	£137.25	0.791	0.0
2% IL 2006	£263.81	1.033	−0.1
$2\frac{1}{2}$% IL 2009	£239.43	1.457	0.0
$2\frac{1}{2}$% IL 2011	£253.59	1.687	−0.1
$2\frac{1}{2}$% IL 2013	£212.59	1.803	−0.2
$2\frac{1}{2}$% IL 2016	£231.63	1.963	−0.2
$2\frac{1}{2}$% IL 2020	£227.33	2.088	−0.4
$2\frac{1}{2}$% IL 2024	£194.00	2.127	52.7
$4\frac{1}{8}$% IL 2030	£186.19	2.116	0.0
2% IL 2035	£100.18	2.103	0.0

Reproduced by permission of Barclays Capital.

Table 9.3b Nominal gilt risk for swapped issue

Nominal gilt	Price per £100 nominal	Nominal yield (%)	Risk (£mn)
$6\frac{1}{2}$% 2003	£101.21	3.226	1.5
$6\frac{3}{4}$% 2004	£104.54	3.268	4.2
$7\frac{1}{2}$% 2006	£111.76	3.757	6.8
$5\frac{3}{4}$% 2009	£108.88	4.150	6.7
5% 2012	£104.42	4.379	9.4
8% 2015	£132.33	4.553	17.2
8% 2021	£139.83	4.685	−12.2
5% 2025	£103.58	4.733	−130.4
6% 2028	£118.53	4.737	0.0
$4\frac{1}{4}$% 2032	£92.27	4.744	0.0

Reproduced by permission of Barclays Capital.

bond and a six-year index-linked bond. Managing such exposure as the bonds approach maturity can potentially be a costly endeavour, a scenario that should be considered at the outset when pricing the original transaction.

9.7.3 A portfolio hedge for net outright inflation risk

A transaction such as that described above hedged in isolation typically involves potentially significant funding and dynamic hedging costs. A more efficient approach is to manage a portfolio of such deals together, with a reasonably balanced deal flow of payers and receivers of inflation. In this manner the outright inflation risk associated with any single derivative is managed with bonds for perhaps only a fraction of its life, until other swaps are transacted which provide a better hedge.

In this regard the inter-dealer market can prove valuable. Two investment banks may well have opposite inflation exposures: one particular bank may be more adept at placing swapped issues (which generate a receiving interest), for example, while another may have a client base that typically generates paying flows. Even if the exposures of the two banks are not perfectly offsetting – it is unlikely that the size, maturity and payment profiles match exactly – an ILS transaction of some sort is mutually beneficial, as it reduces the net outright inflation risk of both. The zero-coupon swap structure (shown in Exhibit A8.3 on p. 263) gives exposure to a single forward RPI setting and is therefore a convenient mechanism through which opposing risk positions can effectively be neutralised.

9.8 THE EVOLUTION OF THE EURO-ZONE HICP SWAP MARKET

The period from the end of 2002 to mid-2003 has proven to be a very important one in the evolution of the Euro-zone inflation swap market. Since the end of 2002 its behaviour has served to illustrate a number of important features of a developing IL derivatives market. Figure 9.4 illustrates the path taken by three Euro-HICP inflation zero-coupon swap rates (ZC2, ZC5 and ZC10 are the 2, 5 and 10-year inflation swap rates, respectively[19]), as well as the break-even inflation rate from the OAT€*i* 2012 bond, since October 2002 and so reflects a period that starts before the surge in

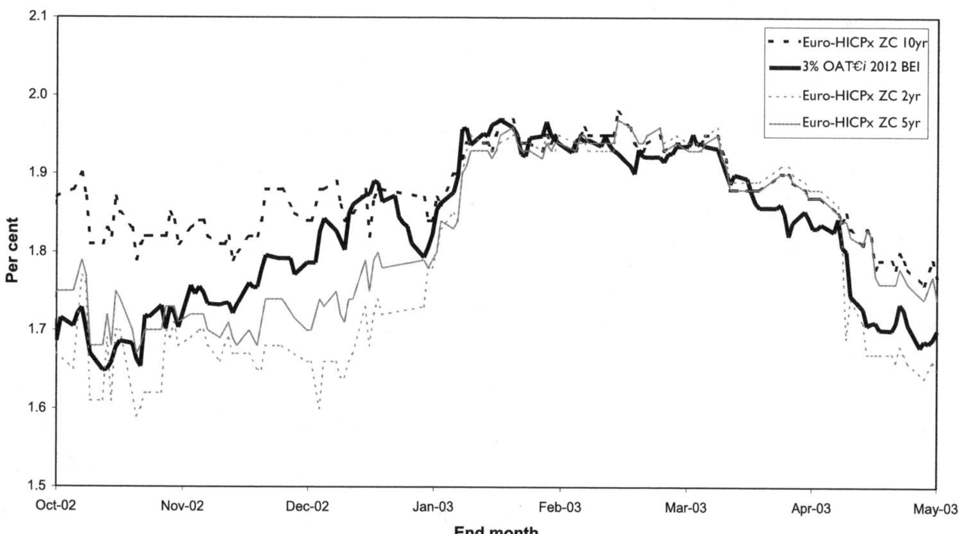

Figure 9.4 Comparison of 2, 5 and 10-year Euro-zone inflation zero-coupon swap rates with the break-even inflation rate on 3% OAT€*i* 2012
Reproduced by permission of Barclays Capital. Euro-HICP = Euro-zone Harmonised Index of Consumer Prices; OAT = Obligations assimilables du Trésor; BEI = Break-even inflation rate

[19] See Exhibit A8.7 on p. 266 for the standard definition of a zero-coupon inflation swap.

MTN issuance and related swap activity (see Figure 9.6 on p. 287) of early 2003. Section 9.8.1 highlights some of the crucial features of this particular period.

9.8.1 Seven lessons from seven months of Euro-zone inflation swap data

(1) *Inflation swap rates are higher than bond break-even inflation rates when the inflation curve is upward sloping.* From Figure 9.4 it is clear that an upward-sloping break-even inflation rate curve (i.e., long-dated higher than short-dated inflation rates) has tended to coincide with ZC10 inflation levels being higher than the 10-year bond break-even inflation rate. It is important to note that this is simply the result of a mathematical phenomenon; when the slope of a term structure of inflation or interest rates is rising, zero-coupon rates are above par rates. Without a short-dated OAT€*i* security the slope of the break-even curve is not directly observable using the bond market in isolation. However, using the shorter dated inflation swap rates it can be demonstrated that the apparent spread between the 10-year inflation swap rate and the bond break-even rate is often explained by this effect.

(2) *The swap market can often drive the bond market.* The surge in bond break-even inflation rates from mid-January until early February to levels sustained through to the end of the quarter coincided with the unprecedented volume of swapped inflation-indexed MTNs in early 2003. Since all the MTNs were swapped no new supply of inflation-paying flows was generated, and so the purchases flowed through the swap market to represent a net purchase of OAT*i*s and OAT€*i*s. The flow was so significant that break-even inflation rates rose even as nominal interest rates fell to historically low levels by the end of March, as illustrated in Figure 9.5.

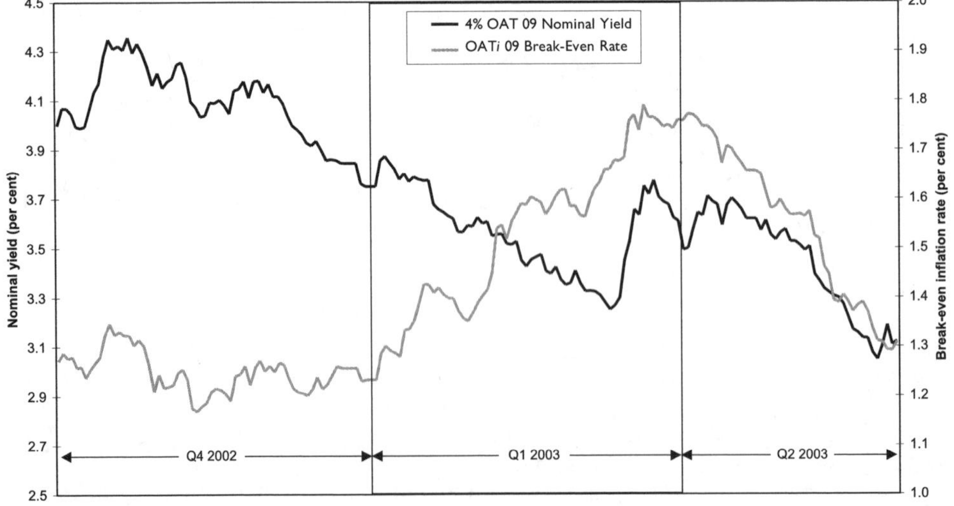

Figure 9.5 Nominal yield on 4% OAT 2009 compared with the break-even inflation rate for 3% OAT*i* 2009
Reproduced by permission of Barclays Capital. OAT = Obligations assimilables du Trésor

(3) *At maturities where liquid inflation-indexed bonds exist, discrepancies between swap and bond prices tend to be quickly corrected.* Any discrepancy of this kind that does become apparent represents an arbitrage opportunity that can easily be exploited by investors who have access to both bond and swap markets, through the execution of asset swap packages. In these circumstances inflation swap and bond break-even inflation rates tend to be close to one another, having adjusted for the zero versus par coupon effect described in (1), though the presence of significant transaction costs means that this arbitrage relationship in general will not hold precisely.

(4) *For maturities where no IL bonds exist, inflation swap rates are as likely to reflect supply and demand as to be consistent with bond break-evens at other maturities on the yield curve.* For example, the slope of the break-even curve flattened sharply (i.e., the difference between ZC5 and ZC10 narrowed) from approximately 0.15% down to 0.00% during January 2003. The relative move in ZC5 simply reflected the increase in demand to receive inflation flows in that sector arising from the MTN purchases. Without a liquid 5-year IL bond there was no pure arbitrage relationship for investors to exploit to bring any perceived misvaluation back into line. For example, the spread between 5 and 10-year OAT*i* break-even inflation rates was approximately 0.25% at the time (i.e., 0.10% wider than for the equivalent spread in the Euro-HICP swap market). Following the BTP€*i* 2008 issue in September 2003, this specific situation would appear to have been largely corrected: by late September the spread between French inflation-linked swaps in five and ten years was 0.08%, while the spread between Euro-HICP ex-tobacco swaps in the same maturities was 0.11%. Nevertheless, supply and demand imbalances can, and regularly do, still push the swaps above or below "fair value" – although usually within the "arbitrage boundary" as defined by asset swap valuations.

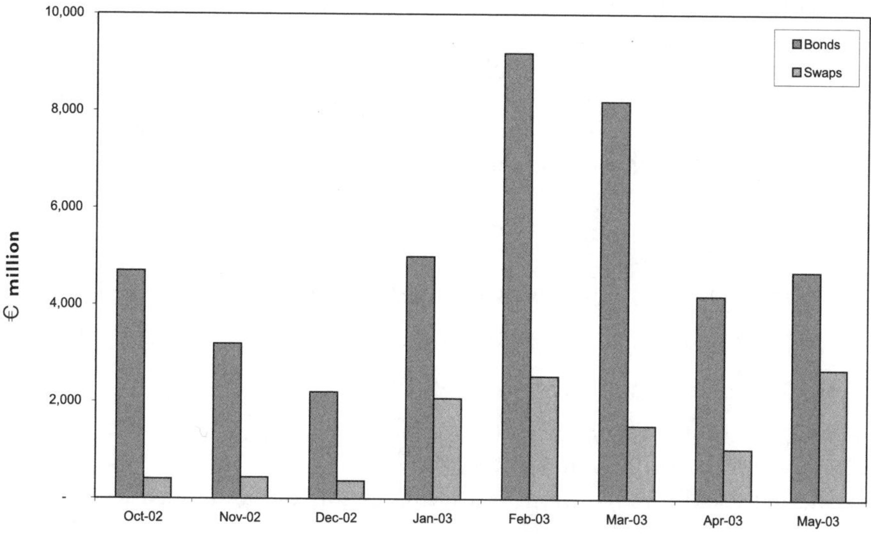

Figure 9.6 Monthly Euro-zone turnover of inflation swaps and indexed government bonds
Note: these figures represent the turnover between dealers – dealer to customer flows are excluded
Reproduced by permission of Barclays Capital and Garban-Intercapital

(5) *Inflation swap transaction volumes can impact bond market turnover.* Over and above relative pricing considerations, swap activity can also impact turnover in the bond market. In many instances, such as at the beginning of 2003, the link is straightforward: swap intermediaries turning to the bond market to hedge their inflation exposure. This is graphically illustrated in Figure 9.6, which demonstrates how government bond market turnover more than doubled in the first quarter of 2003 compared with the previous three months.

(6) *Inflation swap levels can be more "sticky" than bond break-even inflation rates.* Bond break-even inflation rates began to decline in mid-April, but it took a little while for each of ZC2, ZC5 and ZC10 to respond and begin to fall themselves.

(7) *The swap "tail" often wags the bond "dog".* Each of these examples is in effect a variation of the same point: the inflation-indexed swap and bond markets are interdependent. Moreover, it is not always the more mature bond market that determines the valuations of swaps – it can often be the other way around. The Euro-zone inflation bond market should no longer be analysed in isolation.

9.9 HISTORICAL ESTIMATION OF PRICE INDEX VOLATILITIES

The pricing of inflation options hinges crucially on appropriate measures of the volatility of the price index or of the inflation rate. In the absence of a liquid inflation-indexed options market, the estimation of the relevant volatility parameters requires assumptions based at least in part on analysis of historical data. The UK market is chosen to illustrate a number of useful techniques, with its full set of inflation-indexed bonds which have been in existence for a relatively long period (as illustrated by Figures 9.7 and 9.8).

The estimation of spot index volatility is a straightforward task as outlined in various standard option textbooks.[20] However, it is the volatility of the *forward* indices that is often required for pricing options on inflation-indexed cash flows. Since the forward indices are typically not traded assets they need to be indirectly estimated. One approximation is to use the break-even inflation rates from the gilt market and estimate the forward index using the following relation:[21]

$$\mathrm{RPI}\left(m-\frac{8}{12}\right)=\mathrm{RPI}\left(s-\frac{8}{12}\right)[(1+\mathrm{BEI})^{(m-s)}] \tag{9.18}$$

where: m = the maturity date for the relevant index-linked gilt.

s = the spot date.

BEI = the break-even inflation rate for the bond.

An 8-month lag is applied to the dates, in keeping with the index-linked gilt indexation convention. Break-even inflation rates can be obtained from historical prices of nominal and index-linked gilts using such techniques as those outlined in Chapter 5.

[20] See, for example, Hull (1993).

[21] For indexed zero-coupon bonds (IZCBs) this is an exact formula. For a perfectly "flat" break-even curve this approximation is also exact for coupon-paying bonds. However, in other circumstances, such as an upward-sloping curve, the effect of the coupon payouts distorts the relation to some extent.

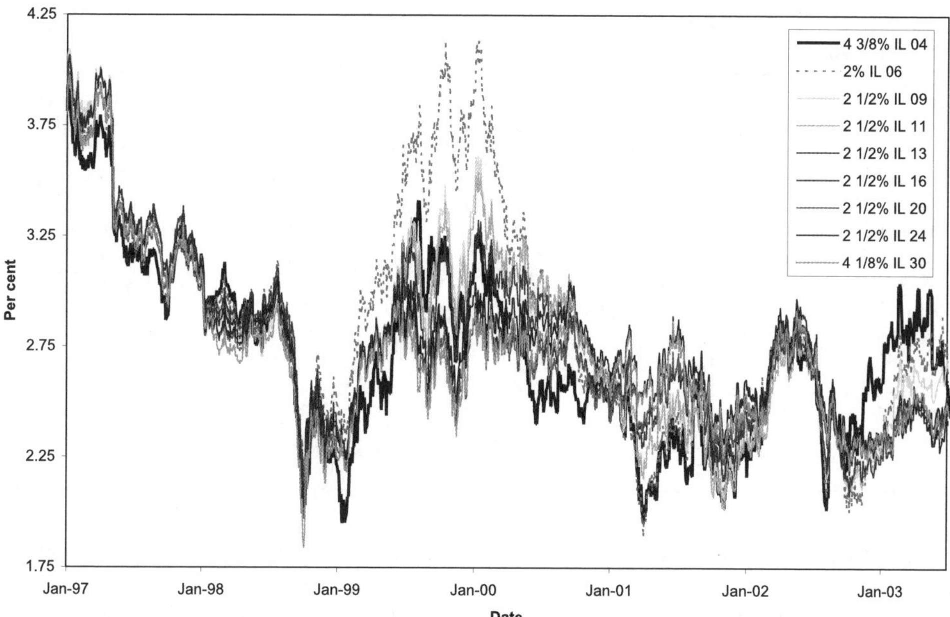

Figure 9.7 Break-even inflation rates for index-linked gilts (1 January 1997–30 June 2003)

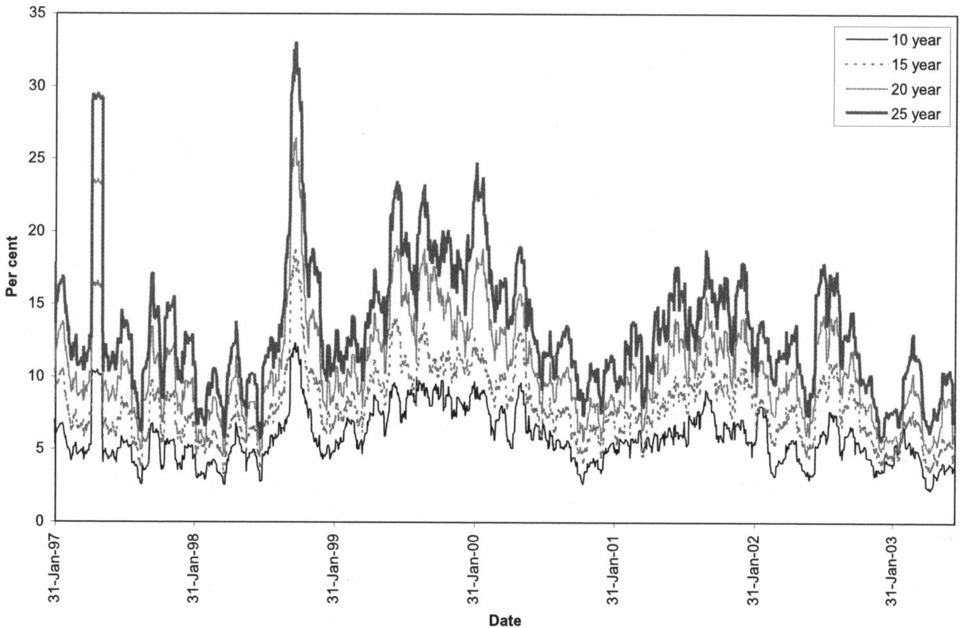

Figure 9.8 Historical volatilities for forward Retail Prices Index (RPI) of different maturities

Table 9.4 Estimates of forward UK Retail Prices Index (RPI) derived from index-linked gilt break-even inflation rates

Trade date	RPI value (10 years ahead)	RPI value (15 years ahead)	RPI value (20 years ahead)	RPI value (25 years ahead)
1 Jan 97	229.90	279.70	333.61	398.29
1 Feb 97	227.16	277.25	329.02	392.77
1 Mar 97	227.09	273.17	327.08	388.65
1 Apr 97	232.31	282.04	342.51	412.25
1 May 97	228.08	274.34	329.28	392.37
1 Jun 97	220.01	259.75	306.02	358.48
1 Jul 97	217.74	256.02	299.78	349.36
1 Aug 97	218.18	255.47	298.06	346.33
1 Sep 97	219.51	258.25	300.94	350.40
1 Oct 97	213.60	249.40	287.34	331.04
1 Nov 97	220.80	259.64	301.63	351.01
1 Dec 97	220.17	257.94	299.60	348.04

Having thereby obtained a time series of forward indices for the maturity indexation date of each bond, constant maturity forward indices for each future date can be obtained through interpolation. For example, estimates of 10, 15, 20 and 25-year forward indices derived in this manner are shown in Table 9.4 for a selected range of dates in the past.

More generally, the methods described in Section 9.3 can be employed to produce a forward RPI curve for every trading day. For a given maturity term T, CPI(T) can be obtained by direct observation from the forward curve. Performing the standard volatility calculation on the constant maturity forward indices thus derived, such as those shown in Table 9.4, historical estimates for the volatility of constant maturity 10, 15, 20 and 25-year forward indices can be obtained. Averaging these estimates for the period from January 1997 through to June 2003 the volatilities are seen to be roughly proportional to the maturity date of the index, as shown in Table 9.5.

A few observations and calculations can be made to explain and validate the above result. The volatilities of break-even rates appear to be similar for index-linked gilts with different maturities, as illustrated in Figure 9.8. Apart from the outperformance of the 2% IL 2006 break-even inflation rates during the 18-month period starting in January 1999, break-even rates for different maturities appear to move more or less in line and with similar variations. Indeed, the volatilities of the break-even inflation rates are all approximately 20% for the selected historical period. The notable exceptions are the two shorter dated issues, but, noting how the quoted real yields of short-dated index-linked gilts jump as the UK RPI is published each month,[22] this result is not altogether unexpected and the data for these two securities are ignored in what follows.

The historical results detailed above can be theoretically validated. Following standard conventions, the Stochastic Differential Equations (SDEs) to describe the CPI and

[22] Such "jumps" are associated with the convention for calculating real yields in the UK market. Yield calculations for all index-linked gilts are affected, but the impact is more pronounced for shorter maturity bonds where quoted real yields can sometimes move by 20–30 basis points when a new RPI figure is published without any corresponding movement in the price of the bond, as illustrated in Table 5.1. The formula used to compute UK index-linked gilt yields is given in Appendix 6.5.

Table 9.5 Estimates of forward inflation rate volatility in the UK

Horizon (years)	Forward volatility (%)
10	5.9
15	8.1
20	10.7
25	13.4

Estimates are based on nominal and index-linked gilt prices from January 1997 to June 2003.

break-even processes are shown below. For ease of notation, C is used to denote CPI, while Z is used to denote the zero-coupon or spot inflation rate (equivalent to the break-even inflation rate if the inflation curve is flat[23]):

$$dC = \mu_C C\,dt + \sigma_C C\,dW_C \tag{9.19}$$

$$dZ = \mu_Z Z\,dt + \sigma_Z Z\,dW_Z \tag{9.20}$$

where μ_C, σ_C and dW_C represent the mean, variance and "white noise" error term associated with the process for C, and similarly μ_Z, σ_Z and dW_Z for the process for Z. The relationship between the forward CPI process and the zero-coupon break-even process is defined by:

$$C = C_0(1+Z)^t \tag{9.21}$$

where: C_0 = is the spot CPI.

Differentiating and transposing Equation (9.21) results in the following derivation:

$$\begin{aligned} dC &= C_0 t(1+Z)^{t-1}\,dZ \\ &= C_0(1+Z)^t \frac{t}{1+Z}\,dZ \\ &= C\frac{t}{1+Z}\,dZ \end{aligned} \tag{9.22}$$

Substituting for dC and dZ from Equations (9.19) and (9.20), squaring both sides, ignoring second-order terms and rearranging, the volatility of the forward index σ_C is shown to relate to the volatility of the zero-coupon rate σ_Z as follows:

$$\sigma_C = \left(\frac{Z}{1+Z}\right) t\sigma_Z \tag{9.23}$$

The above derivation ignored the volatility of the spot index C_0. Including this would modify Equation (9.23) to:

$$\sigma_C = \sigma_{C_0} + \left(\frac{Z}{1+Z}\right) t\sigma_Z \tag{9.24}$$

[23] A more general approach would substitute $\prod_{j=1}^{t}(1+\pi_j)$ in place of $(1+Z)^t$, where π_j $(j = 1, 2, \ldots, t)$ are the forward inflation rates, and thereby extend the analysis to situations in which the forward inflation rate curve is not flat.

From the form of Equation (9.24) the following can be noted: (a) for zero volatility of break-even inflation rates, the forward index volatility will be the same as the spot index volatility; and (b) forward index volatilities are proportional to the time to maturity. For example, with $\sigma_Z \sim 20\%$, $\sigma_{C_0} \sim 0.49\%$ and taking z to be on average around 2.5% in the UK RPI market, σ_C takes the following functional form:

$$\sigma_C = 1.25\% + 0.49\% t \tag{9.25}$$

The above analysis is based on an assumption that the forward break-even inflation rate curve is flat; modifications to the conclusions would be necessary if this assumption was relaxed, and, furthermore, variations in the level of break-even rates would influence the volatility of $(1+z)$. Nevertheless, the essence of Equation (9.25) is that volatilities for forward indices will generally be proportional to the difference between the spot and forward dates measured in years. This is indeed borne out in the empirical results presented in Table 9.4, the data in which provide evidence for a slope of approximately 0.47% per year – encouragingly close to the analytical result in Equation (9.25).

Similar studies can be undertaken for other markets as more bonds are issued and more data become available as time passes. In particular, the US TIPS market is sufficiently large, with a relatively full curve and several years of traded prices, to allow a similar study in an environment where the break-even inflation rate curve has not typically been flat.

9.10 PRICING INFLATION OPTIONS[24]

In principle, options on inflation could take a wide variety of forms. However, to date, two structures stand out: the redemption floor inherent in many government index-linked bonds and the "year-on-year" inflation floors that form part of the many MTNs issued in Europe during 2002 and 2003.

It is not immediately obvious whether there exists a simple distributional form that is well suited to the inflation rate process. It has been well documented that inflation is positively autocorrelated.[25] Additionally, the recent experience of Japan indicates that once an economy experiences significant and sustained deflation it may prove difficult to reflate. Taken together, this may mean that a realistic forward distribution for the long-run inflation rate is bimodal or at least is a distribution that is more complex than the normal or log-normal one usually assumed in order to price options on other assets. Alternatively, it could be argued that a vigilant central bank, having learned from the Japanese experience, would act pre-emptively to ensure that any signs of potential deflation do not develop further. Moreover, estimates of forward index volatilities computed using historical data will not provide meaningful inputs into models that also include the possibility of sustained deflationary environments, since inflation has been overwhelmingly positive in most industrialised economies.

There is therefore great uncertainty surrounding how far historical data can be used

[24] The analysis in this section refers to a number of standard option-pricing techniques and associated mathematical results that are not reproduced here (for more details see Hull, 1993).

[25] For example, see Smith (1999), Das (2001) and Barclays Capital (2002e).

to proxy the future volatility of inflation. Furthermore, in an environment in which there is a possibility of sustained deflation, however small, it is likely that a complete market for inflation options would exhibit a significant "skew" – although the lack of liquidity in such structures means this is currently merely conjecture. Without a liquid market in inflation volatility and with a history of inflation that is only positive, further analysis is severely hampered. Notwithstanding these caveats, standard Black–Scholes analysis is presented below to help provide some intuition regarding this issue and to provide at least an approximate method to calibrate the value of inflation options.

9.10.1 Zero percent zero-coupon floors

The *zero percent zero-coupon floor* is the structure embedded in the majority of sovereign indexed bonds, such as those issued by the French and US governments, which is sometimes referred to as a "deflation floor". In most cases it takes a very simple form: that the nominal value of the redemption payment will never fall below its face value at issue.[26] What follows is a worked example to value a 0% floor on a 10-year zero-coupon inflation swap (see Exhibit A8.9 on p. 267).

Notwithstanding the issues discussed above, the assumption is made that the price index itself behaves like a "Black" asset. If the latest value of the index is 100 (normalising for ease of exposition) and the 10-year break-even inflation rate is 2.50%, then the forward value of the index is given by:

$$C(T) = C(0)(1 + Z_{10})^T \tag{9.26}$$

And so:

$$C(10) = 100(1 + 2.5\%)^{10} = 128.01 \tag{9.27}$$

The forward volatility is then estimated using Equation (9.25) to be 6.15%. To price the floor it is an estimate of the *average*, rather than the terminal, volatility that is required. Since the volatility of the index is proportional to time to maturity, as demonstrated in Section 9.9, the average forward volatility over the 10-year horizon is always significantly lower than the terminal forward volatility.[27] Using a nominal discount factor of 0.633 (corresponding to a 10-year interest rate of 4.68%) and the Black–Scholes formula, the value of the floor is calculated to be 0.018% per annum (or 1.2 basis points in yield). However, if the volatility is assumed to be just 10% higher than that estimated using historical data, the value of the floor increases and almost doubles to 0.29% per annum. The price of the option is demonstrably very sensitive to the volatility estimates, as illustrated in Figure 9.9. Moreover, any "skew" that may exist (for the reasons outlined above) is likely to amplify the volatility as the strike gets lower and thereby increase the value of the floor option.

9.10.2 Year-on-year inflation floors

Year-on-year (y/y) inflation floors have traded through the brokered inter-bank market for several years now. Recently, trading has become more frequent since each of the inflation-indexed swapped MTNs launched since January 2003 has been issued with an

---

[26] See, for example, Appendix 6.6 for a definition of the deflation floor on US TIPS.

[27] The average volatility is computed as the square root of the average instantaneous variance to the horizon in question.

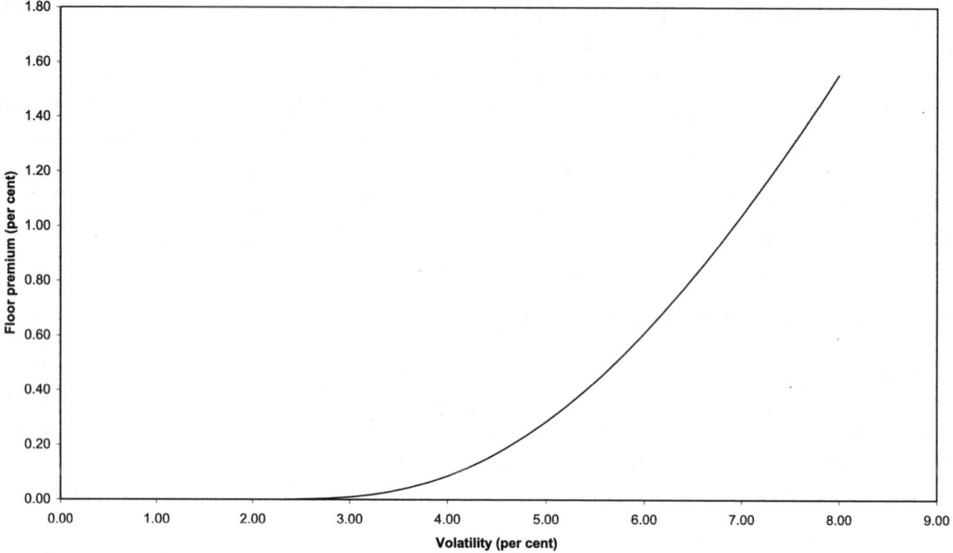

Figure 9.9 Sensitivity of 0% zero-coupon floor prices to volatility

embedded 0% y/y floor,[28] and the volume of such transactions meant it was necessary for many intermediary banks to find ways to offset this risk. Many have had little desire to warehouse any swap exposure and so would aggressively enter the market to hedge out all the risk, including the 0% y/y floor. As one trader has described the situation: "some clients will just bid outright for a 10-year, year-on-year floor,"[29] and so the price of such structures is often interpreted to be somewhat higher than "fair value".

Interest rates in the Euro-zone are driven primarily by the European Central Bank's (ECB's) interest rate decisions, which in turn are based on an inflation target with a ceiling of 2%. Since the official nominal rate set by the ECB is likely to be highly correlated with the level of inflation, it is reasonable to expect a nominal interest rate floor to provide a reasonable proxy hedge for a 0% y/y inflation floor. For example, if inflation is expected to remain at low levels for a sustained period of time, then in turn it might be reasonable to expect that the ECB would be likely to keep rates low too. The pricing of 0% y/y inflation floors for different maturities has mirrored that of interest rate floors to such an extent that the two sometimes trade as a spread. So, rather than valuing an inflation floor using solely the implied volatility of inflation for a given floor price, it can be equally instructive to observe the implied interest rate strike for any given price of a 0% y/y inflation floor. These implied strikes have ranged between 1.50% and 2.00% over the course of the 12 months since June 2002.[30]

The usefulness of such options to hedge y/y inflation floors depends to a large extent on how negative the inflation rate might reasonably be expected to go. For example, if it was felt it would not remain below −1.0% for a significant period of time, then a short

[28] See Section 8.4, and Table 8.5 in particular, for details of such issues brought in the first half of 2003. Exhibit A8.6 on p. 265 details the structure of the standard year-on-year inflation floor.
[29] See Patel (2003).
[30] Barclays Capital estimate.

y/y inflation floor position might be usefully hedged by the purchase of an interest rate floor at an implied strike of 2.00% or just below – since the ECB might reasonably be expected to cut rates significantly below 2% in such a period of mild but sustained deflation. However, in more extreme scenarios, the ECB cannot cut interest rates below 0%, whereas there is theoretically no limit to how fast prices can fall. The use of an interest rate floor alone to hedge a y/y inflation floor is therefore only effective in periods of moderate deflation.

A further problem arises when applying the analysis described in Section 9.9 to price a y/y inflation floor. It is possible to treat the level of the forward index as a standard "Black asset", estimate forward volatilities as described above and price options on the index in a standard Black–Scholes framework. However, this straightforward approach overlooks a number of additional issues that may complicate the analysis. For example, the framework based on Equations (9.19) and (9.20) explicitly assumes that the process for inflation follows a log-normal distribution. One implication is that the inflation rate is assumed to never be negative – not a desirable feature for a process used to value a 0% y/y inflation floor.

The pricing of IL options is clearly at an early stage of development. Many options embedded in bonds are practically ignored (e.g., LPI bonds in the UK – with 0% floors and 5% caps – often trade at a price equivalent to an RPI-linked bond without options[31]). Meanwhile, at the other extreme, prices on some options (such as the Euro-HICP y/y 0% floors described above) are demand-driven and appear to be expensive when compared with interest rate floors. Nevertheless, more sophisticated options are just beginning to appear on the horizon, driven mainly by client demand. As more market participants become familiar with these structures, price discovery can only improve and will provide a framework within which models such as the Jarrow–Yildirim model can be calibrated.

9.11 SUMMARY

Although the markets for ILSs and options have developed only relatively recently, participants have built on their experience with other derivatives and "standard" forms of IL structures already exist. At the time of writing, techniques for pricing inflation swaps are well established and each market trades reasonably efficiently within the bounds set by its relative level of development. Indeed, some have advanced to operate in a manner not too dissimilar to a "Level IV" market, in which models of the type described above are no longer required.

The issuance of the BTP€*i* 2008 by the Italian Treasury in September 2003 might well be described as a landmark event in the inflation-indexed market: expanding the yield curve of €*i* bonds, acting as a trigger for a further expansion of the inflation swap market, while notably making the Italian Treasury the fifth G7 government to actively issue inflation-linked bonds. The Euro-zone inflation swap market provides a textbook example of how derivatives can be the catalyst for the development of a government bond market, and going forward the two are likely to evolve to be dependent on one another.

[31] Smith (1999) and Huang and Cairns (2002) are rare examples of attempts to price LPI options.

However, as of September 2003 the markets for options on inflation are less developed. Many well-known financial techniques lend themselves readily, at least in part, to the modelling of the process of inflation necessary to efficiently price index-linked derivatives. Nevertheless, this chapter has highlighted a number of idiosyncrasies that imply that the straightforward application of nominal interest rate techniques is not wholly appropriate, not least because the market is not yet sufficiently developed to allow adequate calibration of many model parameters. However, it seems likely that, as the use of IL derivatives continues to expand, so the application of these techniques will be refined to enable the market to mature and more closely resemble its nominal counterpart.

10
Conclusion

The key attribute of inflation indexation is the concept of *real value certainty*. It is an aspect of finance that has been understood for centuries, as attested by the existence of indexed securities as far back as the 18th century and their sponsorship by many esteemed economists for the subsequent two hundred years or more.

At a theoretical level, the attraction of financial instruments that can provide such certainty is clear: in the final analysis, savers should be concerned only with the *real* purchasing power of their savings. The fact that securities and other savings arrangements have historically been transacted and quoted on a nominal basis serves only to provide a potential source of "money illusion". So, if individuals can be certain that deferred consumption is equivalent to more consumption, then that fact in itself should provide a powerful incentive to save. The parallel argument for corporations is also valid: to the extent that the future *real* value of their capital is increased, so too is their incentive to refrain from immediate investment.

The preponderance of nominal investment and savings vehicles through history has clouded this clarity. In such periods as the 19th century, when inflation was remarkably stable by modern standards, such concerns were somewhat academic in nature. Indeed, in the extreme scenario that the rate of inflation is known with certainty at all points in the future, real and nominal securities become equivalent. However, the experiences of the Western economies in the second half of the 20th century, not to mention those of many South American countries and (perhaps most spectacularly) pre-war Germany, to name but a few, have changed the world's view about the impact of nominal price instability in the real economy. It is at such times that savers find to their cost that the difference between real and nominal returns, and therefore between the real and nominal value of their deferred consumption, can be material.

It is also the occurrence of such periods that has led to the popular view that inflation is bad for savers and good for borrowers. While undoubtedly true, since inflation simply transfers *real* wealth from the former to the latter, it is also a serious over-simplification. Uncertainty surrounding the potential for future inflation encourages savers collectively to charge borrowers for assuming this risk, thereby raising the cost of capital higher the more uncertain the future for nominal prices. Such a state of affairs represents a welfare loss to the whole of society since, all else being equal, the higher real cost of capital will result in a slower real growth rate for the economy as a whole. It is precisely this phenomenon that has directly led to the elevation of the "inflation rate" to be one of the principal targets, if not the sole target, of monetary policy in many countries around the world. Moreover, this is also what makes inflation *uncertainty* a cost to borrowers. Indeed, as of mid-2003 the threat of *deflation* – falling prices for a prolonged period of time, and therefore a transfer of real wealth *to* savers *from* borrowers – has also become a matter of concern in Western economies and a fact in Japan.

Perhaps it is because inflationary events have occurred relatively recently in the history of the global economy that the concept of inflation-indexed savings and investment vehicles did not become more popular earlier. A number of governments around the world experimented with the indexation of their debt, the motivation of many being to bring credibility to their macroeconomic policies and therefore stability to their currencies. However, in the event many such episodes simply served to highlight the importance of market confidence – as soon as investors became sceptical and the currency suffered accordingly, so the inflationary pressures built and the governments invariably found themselves facing higher debt interest burdens when they could least afford them. The introduction of index-linked gilts by the UK authorities in 1981 marked one of the earliest attempts by a Western government to issue such securities, at a time when the UK itself was recovering from the effects of a period of historically high inflation. Shortly afterward a number of other industrialised countries followed suit, with Australia, Canada and Sweden all having issued index-linked bonds by the mid-1990s.

Up until this point it still appeared that the benefits offered by the product were outweighed by the practical difficulties in their design, implementation and sponsorship as well as by general investor apathy. In spite of some limited success in each of the countries where the securities were issued, it was not until the launch of index-linked bond programmes by the governments of the USA and France, in 1997 and 1998, respectively, that the shift from niche market to mainstream investment product began. Even then the transformation did not occur rapidly, and it took several years for these two markets to reach their critical mass. The US Treasury and France Trésor remained committed to their respective programmes: in 2000 the US Treasury Inflation-Indexed Securities (TIIS) market overtook that of the UK to become the largest government inflation-linked (IL) bond market by capitalisation, and the following year the French Government began to issue its OAT€*i* bonds linked to the Euro-zone Harmonised Index of Consumer Prices (Euro-HICP) excluding tobacco.

The combination of these two events helped the asset class to become established globally and, coupled with a return to public sector deficits in many industrialised countries in 2002, its growth has accelerated. When the first edition of this book was published in early 1998, total inflation-indexed bond issuance in the five largest markets (USA, UK, Canada, Sweden and Australia) totalled $150bn by market value. Just five years later, with the addition of the French securities and growth in the existing markets, this total had more than doubled to over $380bn (end of March 2003).

The appeal of the asset class is also beginning to widen. Initially, the bonds were perceived to be the preserve of pension funds and life assurance companies, for whom the securities proved a very efficient means to hedge long-dated IL liabilities. As the product has become more established it has also formed a basis for retail investments in a number of different guises: in the UK the preferential treatment given by tax regulations to the capital gains from index-linked gilts has made the short-dated securities very popular with individuals who seek tax-efficient investments. Although the reverse is in fact the case in the USA, where the tax rules can actually penalise taxpayers who own TIIS, the development of the less tax-disadvantaged "I-Bonds" has helped raise interest in the securities. Moreover, the three-year equity bear market since 2000 has helped the launch of index-linked bond mutual funds in the USA. Hammond (2002) notes that seven such funds had been created by September 2002, each of which invests primarily or exclusively in the asset class. In Europe, inflation-indexed bonds have also become attractive investment vehicles for individuals, albeit in a more indirect fashion. Since their introduction by the Italian Post Office in 2001, inflation and capital protected notes (equity-linked bonds with the real value of the initial investment guaranteed) have been a resounding success in Italy as well as in some other parts of the Euro-zone.

This latter interest has also proved to be the catalyst for a further major development in the index-linked market in the past few years, the explosion in the use of inflation derivatives. IL derivatives have their genesis in the UK in the early 1990s, driven in particular by the desire of pension funds and insurance companies to match more closely their assets to their IL liabilities. The continued increase in scale of the Private Finance Initiative (PFI) by the UK government has also served to generate interest in the requisite derivative structures. However, the introduction of retail products linked to European price indices, such as those first issued by the Italian Post Office in 2001, and the subsequent need of the products' creators to hedge their exposure to variable inflation rates, has taken the market to another level of liquidity. As the derivatives market develops and matures, so it offers both investors and borrowers alike a vastly expanded range of alternatives compared with those available using bonds in isolation.

This series of developments has led to the point where, in mid-2003, there exists a liquid, truly global market in inflation-indexed securities. The rapid evolution over the preceding five years or so can be put down to a wide range of factors, but three stand out as the most influential: the creation of government index-linked bond markets in the USA and France, the adoption of a de facto standard bond design based on that of Canadian Real Return Bonds (RRBs) and the near-exponential growth in the use of derivatives. Investors now have a distinct asset class into which they can diversify from more traditional investments, such as equities, nominal bonds and property. Moreover, just as bond managers and issuers alike have always been able to express views on the term structure of nominal interest rates both domestically and through the use of foreign currency-denominated bonds, so the real interest rate counterpart has developed.

The first edition of this book concluded in 1998 that "it [was] not beyond the realms of possibility that inflation-indexed securities could soon become as commonplace as conventional, non-indexed bonds." Although it is still too premature to claim that this has already occurred, the explosion of interest in the products over the past five years means that this state of affairs is significantly closer to becoming reality. There are still notable gaps in the global market that render it far from complete: to date, only four of the G7 governments have established liquid inflation-indexed bond markets, though, this could soon change. The Italian Treasury looks likely to become the fifth following the successful launch of its BTP€*i* programme in September 2003, the Japanese Ministry of Finance has announced plans to issue inflation-linked government bonds early in 2004 and the German Finance Agency has signalled that it too is studying the feasibility of such instruments. The lack of a meaningful inflation-linked derivatives market in the USA is also an oddity, particularly in the light of developments in the Euro-zone and the UK in recent years. Nonetheless, it would seem to be only a matter of time before these developments occur and the product matures to rival its nominal counterpart. Despite their flaws, inflation-indexed bonds form the asset class that comes closest to the most fundamental requirement of savers – knowledge of the *real* value of deferred consumption. To quote one respected analyst:[1]

> *There is a certain irony, recalling Oscar Wilde's quote, in knowing a nominal bond's yield to the third decimal place but only having the loosest perception of what it will be worth (in real terms) when it matures. If the market had invented inflation-linked bonds first, would they have bothered to invent nominals?*

[1] Mark Capleton, in Barclays Capital (2002b, p. 9). This is based on the quote "What is a cynic? A man who knows the price of everything and the value of nothing" from Oscar Wilde's *Lady Windermere's Fan*.

References

Abuhoff, N. and Malik, H. (1996) *Introducing Inflation-protected Bonds*. New York: JP Morgan Securities Inc. Fixed Income Research, 12 September.

Abuhoff, N. and Malik, H. (1997) *Inflation-protected Bonds: Answering Frequently Asked Questions*. New York: JP Morgan Securities Inc. Fixed Income Research, 24 January.

Adams, K. (1996) The gilt market and inflation expectations. *Index-Linked Debt – Papers Presented at the Bank of England Conference September 1995, August*, pp. 151–167.

Agence France Trésor (2001) *State Financing Programme for 2002* (technical communication, 17 December).

Agence France Trésor (2002a) *Investor's Guide: OAT€i*, October.

Agence France Trésor (2002b) *Indicative State Financing Programme for 2003* (press release, 12 December).

Agence France Trésor (2003) *Monthly Bulletin*, No. 155, April.

Alaton, P. (1997a) *Realräntederivat* (Skandinaviska Enskilda Banken mimeo, 27 October) [in Swedish].

Alaton, P. (1997b) Swap markets: A real rate swap. *Risk Magazine Nordic Markets Supplement*, 12–13 December.

Alston, R.M., Kearl, J.R. and Vaughan, M.B. (1992) Is there a consensus among economists in the 1990's? *American Economic Review*, Volume 82, No. 2 (May), 203–209.

Andersen, J.V. and Gyntelberg, J. (1999) Index-linked mortgage bonds. *Danmarks Nationalbank Monetary Review*, 1st quarter.

Anderson, N.L., Breedon, F.J., Deacon, M.P., Derry, A.J. and Murphy, G. (1996) *Estimating and Interpreting the Yield Curve*. Chichester: John Wiley & Sons.

Anderson, N.L. and Sleath, J. (2003) New estimates of the UK real and nominal yield curves. *Journal of Bond Trading and Management*, Volume 1, No. 3, 239–263.

Arak, M. and Kreicher, L. (1985) The real rate of interest: Inferences from the new UK indexed gilts. *International Economic Review*, Volume 26, No. 2 (June), 399–408.

Arora, A., Lindner, P. and Vankudre, P. (1997) *Treasury Inflation-Protection Securities: Opportunities and Risks*. New York: Lehman Brothers Fixed Income Research, January.

(Australian) Department of the Treasury (2002) *Review of the Commonwealth Government Securities Market* (discussion paper, 30 October).

(Australian) Department of the Treasury (2003) *Budget Strategy and Outlook 2003–04*, 13 May.

Australian Financial Markets Association (2002) *2002 Australian Financial Markets Report: Overview*.

Australian Office of Financial Management (2000a) *2000-01 Treasury Indexed Bond Programme* (public notice, 10 July).

Australian Office of Financial Management (2000b) *Annual Report 1999–2000*.

Australian Office of Financial Management (2002) *Planned Debt Management Activities in 2002-03* (press release, 9 July).

Aziz, A.R. and Prisman, E.Z. (2000) After-tax term structures of real interest rates: Inferences from the UK linked and non-linked gilt markets. *Journal of Banking and Finance*, Volume 24, 1433–1455.

Baer, W. and Beckerman, P. (1980) The trouble with index-linking: Reflections on the recent Brazilian experience. *World Development*, Volume 8, 677–703.

Baffi, P. (1979) Indicizzazione. In F. Cotula and P. De Stefani (eds), *La politica monetaria in Italia*. Bologna: Il Mulinom, pp. 691–699 [in Italian].

Baker, G. and Greenwood, M. (2002a) WS05 and R197 CPI-bond auctions. *Rand Merchant Bank*, 17 April.

Baker, G. and Greenwood, M. (2002b) R198 CPI-bond auction. *Rand Merchant Bank*, 24 April.

Banco Central de la República Argentina (1976) *Boletín Estadística*, October, 49.

Bank of Canada (1994) Canada Real Return Bonds. *Prospectus*, 25 November.

Bank of England (1983) Issue by tender of £1,000,000,000 $2\frac{1}{2}$% Index-linked Treasury Convertible Stock, 1999. *Prospectus*, 28 April.

Bank of England (1993) Chapter 5: Prospects for inflation. *Inflation Report*, May, 182–183.

Bank of England (1996) *Index-Linked Debt – Papers Presented at the Bank of England Conference September 1995, August*.

Bank of England (1997) *Stock Exchange Formulae for Calculating Gilt Prices from Yields* (mimeo, September).

Bank of England (1998) International real yields. *Quarterly Bulletin*, February, Volume 38, No. 1, 16–17.

Barclays Capital (1998a) The US 30-year auction. *The Global Inflation-linked Monthly*, April, 2–3.

Barclays Capital (1998b) *The Global Inflation-linked Monthly*, May.

Barclays Capital (1998c) Hungary launches an inflation-linked bond. *The Global Inflation-linked Monthly*, June, 8–9.

Barclays Capital (1998d) France. *The Global Inflation-linked Monthly*, October, 12–13.

Barclays Capital (1999) France. *The Global Inflation-linked Monthly*, November, 3.

Barclays Capital (2000) US: The CPI reconditioned. *The Global Inflation-linked Monthly, October*, 13.

Barclays Capital (2001a) The TIPS program. Speak out! *The Global Inflation-linked Monthly*, May, 4–7.

Barclays Capital (2001b) US: TIPS for curve flatteners. *The Global Inflation-linked Monthly*, November, 15.

Barclays Capital (2002a) France: An insurance play. *The Global Inflation-linked Monthly*, January, 6–7.

Barclays Capital (2002b) *Inflation-linked Bonds – A User's Guide*, September.

Barclays Capital (2002c) *Barclays Sterling Inflation-linked Bond Index Guide*, September.

Barclays Capital (2002d) Sweden: 2003 funding outlook. *The Global Inflation-linked Monthly*, December, 10–13.

Barclays Capital (2002e) Understanding the floor – Part 1. *The Global Inflation-linked Monthly*, 22 August, 4–7.

Barclays Capital (2003a) Europe: Real yields to fall further. *The Global Inflation-linked Monthly*, January, 5.

Barclays Capital (2003b) *Equity Gilt Study*, February.

Barone, E. and Masera, R.S. (1997) Index-linked bonds from an academic, market and policy-making standpoint. In: M. De Cecco, L. Pecchi and G. Piga (eds), *Managing Public Debt: Index-linked Bonds in Theory and Practice*. Cheltenham, UK: Edward Elgar, pp. 117–147.

Barro, R.J. (1994) *A Suggestion for Revising the Inflation Adjustment of Payments on Index-Linked Bonds* (mimeo, 24 August).

Barro, R.J. (1996) Optimal funding and indexed bonds. *Index-Linked Debt – Papers Presented at the Bank of England Conference September 1995*, August, pp. 39–44.

Basta, K.M., Douglas, N. and Islam, I. (1994) *Special Focus: Index-Linked Bonds – Prospects for Issuers and Investors. An Analysis of Index-Linked Bond Markets in: UK, Canada, Australia.* London: Merrill Lynch Global Fixed Income Research, 10 October.

Basta, K.M., Islam, I., Kan, W., Lucas, G., Quek, T. and Sowanick, T.J. (1996) *Understanding Treasury Inflation Protected Securities (TIPS): A Fundamental and Analytical Framework.* London: Merrill Lynch Global Fixed Income Research, 20 December.

Battley, N. (ed.) (1997) *The European Bond Markets* (6th edn). New York: McGraw-Hill.

Baxter, M. (ed.) (1998) *National Statistics: The Retail Prices Index Technical Manual* (1998 edn). London: HMSO.

Beaton, R. and Fisher, P.G. (1995) *The Construction of RPIY* (Bank of England Working Paper No. 28, February).

Bernstein, D. and Gardner, J. (1997) The United States: Second auction of inflation-indexed Bonds. *Bridgewater Daily Observations.* Westport, CT: Bridgewater Associates, 8 April.

Bitsberger, T.S. (2002) *Remarks to the Fixed Income Summit Palm Beach, Florida*, 5 December.

Bitsberger, T.S. (2003) *Presentation to the Bond Market Association's Inflation-Linked Securities Conference, New York*, 26 June.

Bloomberg (1997a) CBOT's US Treasury Inflation-indexed Notes Start Slowly. *Bloomberg News*, 3 July.

Bloomberg (1997b) US Five-year Inflation-indexed Notes Yield 3.744%. *Bloomberg News*, 9 July.

Bloomberg (1997c) Treasury's Summers Speaks on Inflation-indexed Bonds. *Bloomberg News*, 30 September.

Bloomberg (1998a) US 30-year Inflation-indexed Bonds Yield 3.740%. *Bloomberg News*, 8 April.

Bloomberg (1998b) US to Sell $8.0 Bln in $9\frac{1}{4}$-yr Inflation Notes. *Bloomberg News*, 29 September.

Bloomberg (1998c) Fed Purchases Inflation-linked Treasuries to Add Reserves. *Bloomberg News*, 23 November.

Bloomberg (2000) US to Auction $32 Bln, Reduce Sales, Start Buyback. *Bloomberg News*, 3 February.

Bloomberg (2001) US Treasury Leaks Decision to End 30-year Bond. *Bloomberg News*, 31 October.

Bloomberg (2002) Japan to Issue Inflation-linked Bonds, MoF Says. *Bloomberg News*, 3 September.

Bloomberg (2003) Switzerland May Decide on Inflation-linked Bond Sales This Year. *Bloomberg News*, 15 October.

Bodie, Z. (1990) Inflation, index-linked bonds, and asset allocation. *Journal of Portfolio Management*, Volume 16, No. 2 (Winter), 48–53.

Bodie, Z. (1997) Inflation-protected retirement plans. In: M. De Cecco, L. Pecchi and G. Piga (eds), *Managing Public Debt: Index-Linked Bonds in Theory and Practice.* Cheltenham, UK: Edward Elgar, pp. 33–49.

Bohn, H. (1996) Comments on the UK debt structure. *Index-Linked Debt – Papers Presented at the Bank of England Conference September 1995*, August, pp. 45–50.

Bootle, R. (1991) *Index-Linked Gilts – A Practical Investment Guide* (2nd edn). Hemel Hempstead, UK: Woodhead-Faulkner.

Borgy, J-F. and Couzineau, G. (2001) Hedging the euro. *Risk Magazine*, Volume 14, No. 12, December.

Boschen, J.F. and Newman, J.L. (1987) The effects of expected inflation on real returns in the Argentine indexed bond market. *Economic Letters*, Volume 25, 137–142.

Branion, A. (1995) The Government of Canada bond market since 1980. *Bank of Canada Review*, Autumn, 3–21.

Brash, D.T. (1995) *Address by the Governor of the Reserve Bank of New Zealand to the New Zealand Society of Actuaries in Wellington*, 12 April.

Breedon, F.J. and Chadha, J.S. (1997) *The Information Content of the Inflation Term Structure* (Bank of England Working Paper No. 75, December).

Brown, E. (1998) The inflation risk premium – Returns on inflation-indexed and nominal British government bonds (Norwegian School of Management Master of Science Thesis – Financial Economics, 3 April).

Brown, R.H. and Schaefer, S.M. (1994) The term structure of real interest rates and the Cox, Ingersoll, and Ross model. *Journal of Financial Economics*, Volume 35, No. 1 (February), 3–42.

Bundesrepublik Deutschland–Finanzagentur GmbH (2003) *German Government Securities Newsletter*, No. 3, July.

BZW (1992) *BZW Guide to Index-linked Securities* (2nd edn, 1993). Sydney: Barclays de Zoete Wedd, Australia.

BZW (1997) *The BZW Global Inflation-Linked Bond Index* (technical documentation, October).

CADES (1999) *CADES Launches CADESi: A 1.5 Billion Euros Inflation-linked Bond Issue* (press release, 17 March).

Cairns, A.J.G. (1998) Descriptive bond-yield and forward-rate models for the British government securities' market (with discussion). *British Actuarial Journal*, Volume 4, No. 2, 265–321 and 350–383.

Campbell, J.Y. and Shiller, R.J. (1991) Yield spreads and interest rate movements: A bird's eye view. *Review of Economic Studies*, Volume 58, 495–514.

Campbell, J.Y. and Shiller, R.J. (1996) *A Scorecard for Indexed Government Debt* (Harvard Institute of Economic Research Discussion Paper, No. 1758, May).

Carmody, S. and Glover, J. (1998) CPI-linked derivatives. *The Australian Corporate Treasurer*, August, 23–25.

Central Bank of Iceland (1995) Changes in the indexation regime. *Economic Statistics Quarterly*, February, Volume 16, No. 1, 2.

Chari, V. and Weber, R. (1992) How the US Treasury should auction its debt. *Federal Reserve Bank of Minneapolis Quarterly Review*, Volume 16, No. 4.

Chatfield, C. (2003) *The Analysis of Time Series: An Introduction*. Boca Raton, FL: CRC Press, July.

Chicago Board of Trade (1997a) *CBOT Long Term Inflation-indexed US Treasury Note Futures Salient Features*, 3 March.

Chicago Board of Trade (1997b) *CBOT Medium Term Inflation-indexed US Treasury Note Futures Salient Features*, 28 May.

Chicago Board of Trade (1997c) *CBOT Launches New 5-year and 10-year Inflation-indexed Treasury Note Futures and Options Contracts*, 3 July.

(Chile) Ministry of Finance (2002) Central Bank Modifies Its Debt Administration Procedures. *Chile News*, 30 August.

Chu, Q.C., Lee, C.F. and Pittman, D.N. (1995) On the inflation risk premium. *Journal of Business, Finance and Accounting*, Volume 22, No. 6 (September), 881–892.

Côté, A., Jacob, J., Nelmes, J. and Whittingham, M. (1996) Inflation expectations and Real Return Bonds. *Bank of Canada Review*, Summer, 41–53.

Cox, J.C., Ingersoll, J.E. and Ross, S.A. (1981) A re-examination of traditional hypotheses about the term structure of interest rates. *Journal of Finance*, Volume 36, 769–799.

Cox, J.C., Ingersoll, J.E. and Ross, S.A. (1985) A theory of the term structure of interest rates. *Econometrica*, Volume 53, No. 2 (March), 385–407.

Craig, B. (2003) *Why Are TIIS Yields So High? The Case of the Missing Inflation-risk Premium* (Federal Reserve Bank of Cleveland mimeo, 15 March).

Das, S. (2001) Chapter 14: Inflation-indexed notes and related derivatives. In: *Structured Notes and Hybrid Securities – Frontiers in Finance*. Chichester, UK: John Wiley & Sons, January.

Deacon, M.P. and Andrews, B.P.A. (1996) The use and value of index-linked bonds. *The Financier: Analyses of Capital and Money Market Transactions*, Volume 3, Nos 4 and 5 (November/December).

Deacon, M.P. and Derry, A.J. (1994a) *Deriving Estimates of Inflation Expectations from the Prices of UK Government Bonds* (Bank of England Working Paper No. 23, July).

Deacon, M.P. and Derry, A.J. (1994b) *Estimating the Term Structure of Interest Rates* (Bank of England Working Paper No. 24, July).

De Beaupuy, F. (1998) France Carves Niche for Inflation-linked Bonds. *Bloomberg News*, 9 July.

Decovny, S. (1998) *Swaps* (2nd edn). Hemel Hempstead, UK: Prentice Hall Europe.

de Kock, G. (1991) Expected inflation and real interest rates based on index-linked bond prices: The UK experience. *Federal Reserve Bank of New York Quarterly Review*, Autumn, 47–60.

de Teran, N. (2003) US Exchange to Launch Inflation-linked Contract. *Financial Times*, 22 September.

Department of Finance, Canada (1998) *Standard Terms for Auctions of Government of Canada Real Return Bonds*, 14 October.

Department of Finance, Canada (2003) *Debt Management Strategy 2003–2004*, 21 March.

Department of the (Italian) Treasury (2002) *Guidelines for Public Debt Management for 2003–2004*, December.

Department of the (US) Treasury (1996a) Treasury Intends to Issue Inflation-protection Securities. *Treasury News*, 16 May.

Department of the (US) Treasury (1996b) President Clinton Announces Inflation-protection Bonds to Help Americans Save. *Press Materials*, 25 September.

Department of the (US) Treasury (1997a) *Sale and Issue of Marketable Book-entry Treasury Bills, Notes, and Bonds* (Circular, Public Debt Series No. 1–93, January).

Department of the (US) Treasury (1997b) Lawrence H. Summers, Deputy Secretary of the Treasury: Remarks on Inflation-indexed Securities. *Treasury News*, 9 June.

Department of the (US) Treasury (1998a) *Federal Register Part VII: 31 CFR Part 356 Sale and Issue of Marketable Book-entry Treasury Bills, Notes, and Bonds* (Circular, Public Debt Series No. 1–93; Final Rule, 30 June).

Department of the (US) Treasury (1998b) *New I-Bonds Go On Sale Today Will Earn 3.40 Percent Over Inflation* (News release, 1 September).

Department of the (US) Treasury (2000a) *Federal Register Part VII: 31 CFR Part 375 Marketable Treasury Securities Redemption Operations* (Final Rule, 19 January).

Department of the (US) Treasury (2000b) Treasury to Auction \$5,000 Million of $28\frac{1}{2}$-year $3\frac{7}{8}$% Inflation-indexed Bonds. *Treasury News*, 4 October.

Department of the (US) Treasury (2002a) Assistant Secretary for Financial Markets Brian C. Roseboro February 2002 Quarterly Refunding Statement. *Treasury News*, 30 January.

Department of the (US) Treasury (2002b) Treasury Announces Debt Buyback Operation. *Treasury News*, 17 April.

Department of the (US) Treasury (2002c) *Assistant Secretary for Financial Markets Brian C. Roseboro May 2002 Quarterly Refunding Statement* (Press release, 1 May).

Department of the (US) Treasury (2002d) Results of Treasury's Auction of 10-year Inflation-indexed Notes. *Public Debt News*, 10 July.

Department of the (US) Treasury (2003a) *Series I Bonds* (Information statement, 28 January).

Department of the (US) Treasury (2003b) *Monthly Statement of the Public Debt of the United States*, 31 March.

Department of the (US) Treasury (2003c) *Assistant Secretary for Financial Markets Brian C. Roseboro May 2003 Quarterly Refunding Statement* (Press release, 30 April).

Department of the (US) Treasury (2003d) *I Bonds To Earn 4.66% When Bought From May Through October 2003* (News release, 1 May).

Deutsche Bank (2003) *Economic Derivatives: Inflation Options* (Report, March/April).

Deutsche Bundesbank (1998) *The Market for German Federal Securities* (2nd edn), July.

Dudley, W., Macirowski, T., Richman, H., Strongin, S. and Youngdahl, J. (1996) *Treasury Inflation-Protection Securities: A Useful Tool, But Not a Cure-all.* New York: Goldman Sachs Investment Research/Fixed Income Research, October.

Euroweek (1997) News in brief. "Emerging Markets", 21 February.

Evans, M.D.D. (1998) Real rates, expected inflation and inflation risk premia. *Journal of Finance*, Volume 53, 187–218.

Evelyn, G.S. (1798) An account of some endeavours to ascertain a standard of weight and measure. *Philosophical Transactions of the Royal Society of London*, Volume 88, 133–182.

Fischer, S. (1975) The demand for index bonds. *Journal of Political Economy*, Volume 83, No. 3 (June), 509–534.

Fischer, S. (1983) On the non-existence of privately issued index bonds in the US capital market. In: R. Dornbusch and M.H. Simonsen (eds), *Inflation, Debt, and Indexation.* Cambridge, MA: MIT Press, pp. 247–266.

Fisher, I. (1918) Adjusting wages to the cost of living. *Monthly Labor Review*, Volume 7, November, 278–287.

Fisher, I. (1922) *The Purchasing Power of Money*. New York: Macmillan, p. 208.

Fisher, I. (1928) *The Money Illusion*. New York: Adelphi.

Fisher, W.C. (1913) The tabular standard in Massachusetts history. *Quarterly Journal of Economics*, Volume 27, May, 417–455.

Flavell, R. (2002) *Swaps and Other Derivatives*. Chichester, UK: John Wiley & Sons, April.

Foresi, S., Penati, A. and Pennacchi, G. (1997) Reducing the cost of government debt: The role of index-linked bonds. In: M. De Cecco, L. Pecchi and G. Piga (eds), *Managing Public Debt: Index-linked Bonds in Theory and Practice*. Cheltenham, UK: Edward Elgar, pp. 93–116.

Frankel, J. (1982) A technique for extracting a measure of expected inflation from the interest rate term structure. *Review of Economics and Statistics*, Volume 64, No. 1 (February), pp. 135–142.

France Trésor (1999) *Base Year Change in the Consumer Price Index: Resetting of The Base for OATi's Daily Inflation References* (News release, 24 February).

France Trésor (2000a) *French Government Indicative Financing Program for 2000* (Press release, 5 January).

France Trésor (2000b) *France Trésor's Buy Back Programme for 2000* (Press release, 25 August).

France Trésor (2000c) *Improving Debt Management, Modernising Government Action* (Press release, 6 December).

Getúlio Vargas Foundation (1976) Estatísticas básicas. *Conjuntura Econômica*, Volume 30, March, 116–117.

Gilbert, C.L. (1995) *Alternative Models for Estimating Real Interest Rates and Expected Inflation from UK Index-linked Bonds* (Queen Mary and Westfield College Draft Discussion Paper, November).

Gong, F.F. and Remolona, E.M. (1996) *Inflation Risk in the US Yield Curve: The Usefulness of Indexed Bonds* (Federal Reserve Bank of New York Research Paper No. 9637, November).

Graham, R. and Luce, E. (1997) Bank of France Attacks Bonds Plan. *Financial Times*, 5 December.

Greenspan, A. (1992) Statement before the Commerce, Consumer and Monetary Affairs Subcommittee of the Committee on Government Operations, US House of Representatives. *Federal Reserve Bulletin*, Volume 78, No. 8 (August), 603–607.

Greenwood, M. (2000) *SA Inflation-indexed Debt: An Underrated Asset Class* (Risk special report: South Africa, June).

Grieves, R.G. and Sunner, M.W. (1999) Fungible STRIPS for the US Treasury's Inflation-indexed Securities. *Journal of Fixed Income*, Volume 9, No. 1, June.

Haggerty, J. (2003) Inflation-linked market heats up. *International Financing Review (IFR)*, 22 March, 88.

Hall, R. (2001) An index-linked crisis? *Watson Wyatt Insurance and Financial Services Review*, August.

Hallsten, K. (1993) Government indexed bonds. *Sveriges Riksbank Quarterly Review*, No. 3.

Hammond, P.B. (2002) Understanding and using inflation bonds. *TIAA-CREF Institute Research Dialogue*, No. 73, September.

Hanke, S.H. and Walters, A. (1994) Greenspan Bonds. *Forbes*, 12 September.

Harper, C. (1997) US Bonds Draw Puzzled Looks. *The Wall Street Journal Europe*, 5 June.

Heath, D., Jarrow R. and Morton, A. (1992) Bond pricing and the term structure of interest rates: A new methodology for contingent claim valuation. *Econometrica*, Volume 60, 77–105.

Heenan, G. (1991) Measures of expected inflation. *Reserve Bank of Australia Bulletin*, April.

Hellenic Republic Ministry of Finance Public Debt Division (2000) *Recent Developments in Public Debt Management*, May.

Hetzel, R.L. (1992) Indexed bonds as an aid to monetary policy. *Federal Reserve Bank of Richmond Economic Review*, Volume 78, No. 1 (January/February), 13–23.

HM Treasury (1981) *Indexed Gilts* (Economic Progress Report No. 133 [May], pp. 1–2).

HM Treasury (1998) *Debt Management Report 1998–99*, 19 March.

HM Treasury (2001) *Debt and Reserves Management Report 2001–02*, 7 March.

HM Treasury (2002) *Debt and Reserves Management Report 2002–03*, 14 March.

HM Treasury (2003) *Debt and Reserves Management Report 2003–04*, 9 April.

Horrigan, B.R. (1987) The CPI futures market: The inflation hedge that won't grow. *Federal Reserve Bank of Philadelphia Business Review*, May/June, 3–14.

Housing Finance Agency plc (1983) Issue by tender of up to IR£25 million of 2% Index-linked Housing Finance Agency Stock, 2008. *Prospectus*, 17 January.

Housing Finance Agency plc (2003) *Annual Report 2002*, 30 April, 26.

Huang, H.-C. and Cairns, A.J.G. (2002) *Valuation and Hedging of LPI Liabilities* (Working paper).

Huberman, G. and Schwert, G.W. (1985) Information aggregation, inflation, and the pricing of indexed bonds. *Journal of Political Economy*, Volume 93, No. 1, 92–114.

Hull, J.C. (1993) *Options, Futures, and Other Derivative Securities*. Englewood Cliffs, NJ: Prentice-Hall.

Hungarian State Treasury (1996) *Public Offer of Government Bond 2003/F*, 27 December.

Ibbotson Associates (1996) *Stocks, Bonds, Bills and Inflation (SBBI)* (1996 yearbook). Chicago: Ibbotson Associates.

Investors Chronicle (1998) Chances are good for indexed bonds in Germany. "Viewpoint – Commerzbank's Focus on German and European Economic Issues", 27 March, p. 33.

Jarrow, R. and Yildirim, Y. (2003) Pricing Treasury Inflation Protected Securities and related derivatives using an HJM model. *Journal of Financial and Quantitative Analysis*, July.

Jevons, W.S. (1875) *Money and the Mechanism of Exchange*. New York: Appleton.

JP Morgan (2003) Greece to issue Euro inflation-linked bond. *European Fixed Income Strategy*, 12 March.

Jud, G.D. (1978) *Inflation and the Use of Indexing in Developing Countries*. New York: Praeger.

Kandel, S., Ofer, A.R. and Sarig, O. (1996) Real interest rates and inflation: An ex-ante empirical analysis. *Journal of Finance*, Volume 51, No. 1 (March), 205–225.

Kazziha, S. (1999) Interest rate models, inflation-based derivatives, trigger notes and cross-currency swaptions (PhD thesis, Imperial College of Science, Technology and Medicine, January).

Kettell, B. (1982) *Gold*. London: Graham & Trotman, pp. 201–202.

Keynes, J.M. (1927) Statement before the Committee on National Debt and Taxation. In: *Minutes of Evidence, Colwyn Committee*. London: HMSO, pp. 278 and 287.

Kitamura, Y. (1997) Indexed bonds and monetary policy: The real interest rate and the expected rate of inflation. *Bank of Japan Monetary and Economic Studies*, May.

Klemperer, P. (1999) Auction theory: A guide to the literature. *Journal of Economic Surveys*, Volume 13, No. 3, July, 227–286.

Labour Research Department (2001) *PFI – The Major Contractors* (A report on ten of the largest contractors involved in the Private Finance Initiative plus details of the sponsors of the PPP Forum: A report prepared by the Labour Research Department for the GMB, September).

Levin, E.J. and Copeland, L.S. (1993) *Reading the Message from the UK Indexed Bond Market: Real Interest Rates, Expected Inflation and the Risk Premium*. Oxford, UK: Blackwell and the Victoria University of Manchester.

Lindh, Y. and Ohlsson, K. (1992) *Indexobligationer- en samhällsekonomisk analys* (Sveriges Riksbank Working Paper No. 5, April) [in Swedish].

Litzenberger, R. and Rolfo, J. (1984) An international study of tax effects on government bonds. *Journal of Finance*, Volume 39, 1–22.

Lowe, J. (1967) *The Present State of England in Regard to Agriculture and Finance*. New York: Augustus M. Kelley, pp. 335–346 (first published in 1822).

Macquarie Research (2002) Where next the government bond market? *Australian Financial Markets Association's 2002 Australian Financial Markets Report*, 23 October.

Majoul, M. and Nehls, S. (1998) French franc inflation-indexed government bonds. *Deutsche Morgan Grenfell Fixed Income Research*, 13 March.

Marshall, A. (1886) Remedies for fluctuations of general prices. In: A.C. Pigou (ed.), *Memorials of Alfred Marshall*. New York: Augustus M. Kelley.

McCulloch, J.H. (1971) Measuring the term structure of interest rates. *Journal of Business*, Volume 44, January, 19–31.

McCulloch, J.H. (1975) The tax-adjusted yield curve. *Journal of Finance*, Volume 30, No. 3 (June), 811–830.

McCulloch, J.H. (1980) The ban on indexed bonds, 1933–77. *American Economic Review*, Volume 70, No. 5 (December), 1018–1021.

Mendoza, E.G. and Fernández, F. (1994) *Monetary Transmission and Financial Indexation: Evidence from the Chilean Economy* (IMF paper on policy analysis and assessment No. 94/17, August).

Merrill Lynch (2000) TIPS and the updated Boskin Report. *Global Inflation-linked Bond Markets Quarterly*, 17 March.

Merrill Lynch (2001) The index shift is the culprit. *Global Inflation-linked Bond Markets Quarterly*, 23 July.

Merrill Lynch (2002) UK utility supply (again!). *Global Index-linked Bond Markets Quarterly*, 17 April.

Ministère de l'Économie et des Finances (1996) *Programme Indicatif de Financement de l'état pour 1997* (Communiqué de presse, 31 December) [in French].

Ministero del Tesoro (1981) *La Difesa del Risparmio Finanziario dall'Inflazione* [The Defence of Savings from Inflation] (Report of the Baffi Commission). Rome: Istituto Poligrafico e Zecca dello Stato [in Italian].

Ministero del Tesoro (1982) *Il Sistema Creditizio e Finanziario Italiano* [The Italian Credit and Finance System] (Report on the Monti Commission). Rome: Istituto Poligrafico e Zecca dello Stato [in Italian].

Ministero del Tesoro – Direzione Generale del Debito Pubblico (1988) *Relazione del Direttore Generale alla Commissione Parlamentare di Vigilanza: Il Debito Pubblico in Italia 1861–1987* [Report of the Director General of the Parliamentary Watchdog: Public Debt in Italy 1861–1987] (Vol. 1). Rome: Ministero del Tesoro [in Italian].

Ministry of Finance, Japan (2002) *Planned Bond Issuance for FY 2003*, 24 December.

Ministry of Finance and Public Credit, Mexico (1996) *New Emission of Bonds (UDIs)* [Unidades de Inversión] (press release, 22 May).

Ministry of Finance and Public Credit, Mexico (2000) *Calendar of Government Securities' Auctions in 3Q00* (press release, 7 July).

Ministry of Finance and Public Credit, Mexico (2003) *Quarterly Report on Public Finances and Public Debt First quarter of 2003*, 2 May.

Ministry of Finance, Poland (2000) *Polish Treasury Securities* (Annual report 2000).

Mishkin, F.S. (1990) Can futures market data be used to understand the behaviour of real interest rates? *Journal of Finance*, Volume 45, No. 1 (March), 245–257.

Mitchell, B. (1996) The government of Canada's index-linked bonds: Real Return Bonds (RRBs). Presentation given at *The OECD Group of Experts on Government Debt Management*, 12–13 November.

Moss, D. and Preston, B. (1997) Inflation-linked securities: Profiting from inflation. *Asia Risk*, February.

Munnell, A.H. and Grolnic, J.B. (1986) Should the US government issue index bonds? *Federal Reserve Bank of New England Economic Review*, September/October, 3–21.

Myburgh, L. (2003) *SA Linker Update after CPI Revision* (Barclays Capital Research EMEA Note, 30 May).

National Debt Management Agency, Republic of Iceland (2001) *Treasury Bonds (Index-linked)* (Mimeo, 2 November).

National Savings and Investments (2002) *Index-linked Savings Certificates*, May.

New Zealand Debt Management Office (1995a) *Issuance of Inflation-indexed Bonds* (Media statement, 1 June).

New Zealand Debt Management Office (1995b) *Inflation Indexed Bonds* (Media release, 13 October).

New Zealand Debt Management Office (1995c) New Zealand government inflation-indexed bonds. *Prospectus*, 8 November.

OECD (2002) *Debt Management and Government Securities Markets in the 21st Century*.

Page Committee (1973) *Report of the Committee to Review National Savings* (the Page Report).

Page, S.A.B. and Trollope, S. (1974) An international survey of indexing and its effects. *National Institute Economic Review*, No. 70, November, 46–60.

Patel, N. (2003) The Fashionable Link. *Risk Magazine*, March, 59–60.

Persson, M. (1997) Index-linked bonds: The Swedish experience. In: M. De Cecco, L. Pecchi and G. Piga (eds), *Managing Public Debt: Index-linked Bonds in Theory and Practice*. Cheltenham, UK: Edward Elgar, pp. 18–32.

Pesek Jr., W. (1997) Uncle Sam's Indexed Bonds Inspire a Passel of Imitators. *Barron's Market Week*, 17 February, p. 16.

Pigou, A.C. (1929) *Industrial Fluctuations*. New York: Macmillan, pp. 262–263.

Potter, W. (1995) An overview of the money and bond markets in New Zealand. Part 1: The Crown debt market. *Reserve Bank of New Zealand Bulletin*, Volume 58, No. 3 (September), 177–192.

Price, R. (1997) *The Rationale and Design of Inflation-indexed Bonds* (International Monetary Fund working paper No. 97/12, January).

Procter, K. and Williams, H. (2003) Pension scheme inflation. *The Actuary*, May, pp. 28–29.

Prout, B., Rajendran, M., Salvadore, S. and Wyetzner, G. (1997) *Valuation Comparison of Inflation Indexed Bonds: Capital Indexed vs Interest Indexed* (Bankers Trust Inflation Linked Capital Markets Group Discussion Paper, 16 April).

Radcliffe Committee (1959) *Report of the Committee on the Working of the Monetary System* (the Radcliffe Report), August.

Ragan, C. (1995) *Deriving Agents' Inflation Forecasts from the Term Structure of Interest Rates* (Bank of Canada Working paper No. 95-1, January).

Reddell, M. and Watt, B. (1997) Some perspectives on inflation-indexed bonds. *Reserve Bank of New Zealand Bulletin*, Volume 60, No. 4, 322–331.

Republic of Poland Ministry of Finance Public Debt Department (1996) *Investor Guide to the Domestic Treasury Securities Market*, June.

Republic of Poland Ministry of Finance Public Debt Department (1997) *Public Debt Quarterly Review*, Volume 1/97, August.

Republic of South Africa Department of Finance (2000a) *Taxation of Inflation Linked Bonds* (Press release, 28 February).

Republic of South Africa Department of Finance (2000b) *Republic of South Africa Internal Registered 6.25% CPI Bond R189 Redeemable on 31 March 2013* (Terms and conditions of issue, 31 May).

Republic of South Africa Ministry of Finance (2000a) *Government to Issue Inflation-linked Bonds* (Press release, 7 March).

Republic of South Africa Ministry of Finance (2000b) *First Auction of Inflation-linked Bonds* (Press release, 15 March).

Republic of South Africa National Treasury (2002) *Republic of South Africa Internal Registered Bond R198 Redeemable on 31 March 2008* (Draft terms and conditions of issue, 18 April).

Republic of South Africa National Treasury (2003) *Holders of Inflation Linked Bonds* (Press release, 6 June).

Reuters News (1998) France to Build Yld Curve for Inflation-linked OAT, 23 November.

Reuters News (1999) French Treasury May Boost OAT*i* Programme, 12 May.

Roberts, A. (1997) *Index-linked Gilts Annual Review 1996 – Birth of a Real Global Market*. London: UBS Global Research, January.

Robertson, D. and Symons, J. (1992) *Five Weeks in the Life of the Pound: Interest Rates, Expectations and Sterling's Exit from the ERM* (Centre for Economic Forecasting, London Business School, Discussion Paper No. DP 28-92, December).

Robertson, D. and Symons, J. (1993) *Real Interest Rates and Index-Linked Gilts* (Centre for Economic Performance, LSE, Discussion Paper No. 181, November).

Royal Bank of Scotland (2001) *The Royal Bank of Scotland Completes Ground Breaking £160m LPI Bond Issue for Tesco* (Press release, 22 October).

Royal Ministry of Finance and Customs, Norway (1982) Index-linked government savings bonds Verdi-Spar '82 II. *Prospectus*, May.

Rutterford, J. (1983) Index-linked gilts. *National Westminster Bank Quarterly Review*, November.

Sack, B. (2000) Deriving inflation expectations from nominal and inflation-indexed treasury yields. *Journal of Fixed Income*, Volume 10, No. 2, 6–17.

Sack, B. and Elsasser, R. (2002) *Treasury Inflation-Indexed Debt: A Review of the US Experience* (Board of Governors of the Federal Reserve System Working paper No. 2002-32, 4 June).

Sanghera, S. (2000) South Africa: Inflation-linked bonds planned. *Financial Times*, 7 January.

Schaefer, S.M. (1981) Measuring a tax-specific term structure of interest rates in the market for British government securities. *Economic Journal*, Volume 91, June, 415–438.

Schaefer, S.M. (1996) Comments on the market structure for index-linked debt. *Index-linked Debt – Papers Presented at the Bank of England Conference September 1995, August*, pp. 103–106.

Scholtes, C. (2002) On market-based measures of inflation expectations. *Bank of England Quarterly Bulletin*, Spring.

Scrope, G.P. (1968) *Principles of Political Economy*. New York: Augustus M. Kelley, pp. 413–419 (first published in 1833).

Shen, P. (1995) Benefits and limitations of inflation indexed Treasury bonds. *Federal Reserve Bank of Kansas City Economic Review*, third quarter, 41–56.

Shen, P. and Corning, J. (2002) Can TIPS help identify long-term inflation expectations? *Federal Reserve Bank of Kansas City Economic Review*, fourth quarter, 61–87.

Shiller, R.J. (1997) *Indexed Units of Account: Theory and Assessment of Historical Experience* (Mimeo).

Shiller, R.J. (2003) The invention of inflation-indexed bonds in early America (Yale University mimeo, 5 February).

Siegel, L.B. (2002) TIPS, the double duration, and the pension plan. Presented at the *Barclays Capital Inflation-Linked Bond Conference, January 2003*, December.

Simonsen, M.H. (1983) Indexation: Current theory and the Brazilian experience. In: R. Dornbusch and M.H. Simonsen (eds), *Inflation, Debt, and Indexation*. Cambridge, MA: MIT Press, pp. 99–132.

Skorecki, A. (2003) Inflation derivatives on the rise. *Financial Times*, 2 April, p. 29.

Smith, A. (1999) A review of models for pricing caps and floors on inflation over the long term. *The Joint Institute and Faculty of Actuaries Investment Conference, Loch Lomond, May*.

Smithson, C.W., Smith Jr, C.W. and Wilford, D.S. (1995) *Managing Financial Risk*. Chicago: Irwin, pp. 27–28.

Snam Rete Gas (2002) *Report on the Second Quarter of 2002*.

Spiro, P.S. (1989) *Real Interest Rates and Investment and Borrowing Strategy*. Westport, CT: Quorum Books.

Spiro, P.S. (2003) *Evidence on Inflation Expectations from Canadian Real Return Bonds* (Ontario Ministry of Finance [Canada], mimeo, July).

Strauss-Kahn, D. (1997) Opening address. *Symposium "French Government Securities and the Euro", 3 December*.

Swedish National Debt Office (1994) *Index-linked Treasury Bonds*.

Swedish National Debt Office (1995) *Annual Report Fiscal Year 1994/95*.

Swedish National Debt Office (1996) *Terms and Conditions of Sales on a Day-to-Day Basis of Kingdom of Sweden Index-linked Treasury Bonds*, 21 February.

Swedish National Debt Office (1999a) *Changes on the Swedish Inflation-linked Bond Market* (Press release, 12 April).

Swedish National Debt Office (1999b) *Innovations on the inflation-linked bond market* (Press release, 2 December).

Swedish National Debt Office (2000) *Swedish Inflation-linked Government Bonds: A Brief Introduction*.

Swedish National Debt Office (2002a) *Government Debt Management in Sweden* (A country case study for the IMF and the World Bank Project on Guidelines for Public Debt Management, 28 February).

Swedish National Debt Office (2002b) Funding. *Central Government Borrowing: Forecast and Analysis*, Volume 2002, No. 2, 18 June.

Swedish National Debt Office (2002c) *Exact Changes of Outstanding Stock of Government Bonds* (Press release, 30 July).

Swedish National Debt Office (2002d) *Continuous Buy-backs of Inflation-linked Bond 3002* (Press release, 7 October).

Swedish National Debt Office (2002e) *Guidelines for Central Government Debt Management in 2003*, 15 November.

Swedish National Debt Office (2003a) Funding. *Central Government Borrowing: Forecast and Analysis*, Volume 2003, No. 1, 19 February.

Swedish National Debt Office (2003b) *The Swedish Central Government Debt*, 31 March 2003, No. 747.

Swedish National Debt Office (2003c) Funding. *Central Government Borrowing: Forecast and Analysis*, Volume 2003, No. 2, 18 June.

The Ambachtsheer Letter (2000) *Is "Economic Valuation" the Key to Saving the DB* [Defined Benefit] *Pension Plans?* Toronto: KPA Advisory Services Ltd, September.

Thedéen, E. (2003) The Swedish National Debt Office. *Barclays Capital Annual Inflation-linked Bond Conference (Key Biscayne 2003) Book, 26 January*.

The Treasury (Australia) (1994a) *Revised Issue Arrangements for Treasury Indexed Bonds* (Press release, 21 July).

The Treasury (Australia) (1994b) Commonwealth of Australia Treasury Indexed Bonds. *Prospectus*, 3 August.

The Treasury (Australia) (1998) *Commonwealth Debt Management 1997–98*.

The Treasury (Australia) (1999) *Commonwealth Debt Management 1998–99*.

The Treasury (Turkey) (1997) *Inflation-Indexed Government Bonds*, March.

Thomas, D. (2001) Welsh Water: Role model or special case? *Utilities Policy*, Volume 10, 99–114.

Trans-Caledon Tunnel Authority (2001) *CPI-linked Placing Document*, 3 October.

Treasury Advisory Committee of the Bond Market Association (2001) *Report to the Secretary of the Treasury*, 1 May.

Trésor (1998) *An Investor's Guide to French Government Inflation-indexed Bonds*, July/August.

UK Debt Management Office (1998) *A Proposal for the Conduct of Index-linked Gilt Auctions and the Introduction of a Specialist Index-linked Gilt-edged Market Maker List*, 10 June.

UK Debt Management Office (2000) *Response to DMO Consultation Document on "Special" Gilt Repo Operations*, 22 February.

UK Debt Management Office (2001a) *Index-linked Gilt Switch Auctions: Consultation Document*, 12 March.

UK Debt Management Office (2001b) *Index-linked Gilt Switch Auctions: Response to Consultation*, 10 May.

UK Debt Management Office (2001c) *Result of Switch Auction of Up to £500 Million Nominal of 2% Index-linked Treasury Stock 2006 into $2\frac{1}{2}$% Index-linked Treasury Stock 2016* (Press notice, 19 July).

UK Debt Management Office (2001d) *Index-linked Gilt Re-design: Consultation Document*, 7 September.

UK Debt Management Office (2001e) *DMO Annual Review 2000/2001*, 7 September.

UK Debt Management Office (2001f) *Publication of Revised Gilts Market Operational Notice* (Screen announcement, 22 November).

UK Debt Management Office (2002a) *Index-linked Gilt Re-design: Response to Consultation*, 15 January.

UK Debt Management Office (2002b) *Formulae for Calculating Gilt Prices from Yields*, 15 January.

UK Debt Management Office (2002c) *Methodology for Calculating the First Dividend Payment and Accrued Interest for 2% Index-linked Treasury Stock 2035* (Mimeo, 23 August).

UK Debt Management Office (2002d) *DMO Annual Review 2001/2002*, 7 October.

UK Debt Management Office (2003a) *Consultation Meetings with GEMMs* [Gilt Edged Market Makers] *and Gilt Investors: 20 January 2003* (Screen announcement, 21 January).

UK Debt Management Office (2003b) *Quarterly Review*, April.

United Kingdom Parliament (2003) *House of Lords Debate on Private Finance Initiatives*, 12 February, Column 663.

US General Accounting Office (2000) *Consumer Price Index: Update of Boskin Commission's Estimate of Bias* (Report to the Ranking Minority Member, Committee on Finance US Senate, GAO/GGD-00-50, February).

Wade, T. (1998) Fed's TIPS purchases raise eyebrows on Street. *Bond Week*, Volume XVIII, No. 50, 14 December.

Waggoner, D. (1997) *Spline Methods for Extracting Interest Rate Curves from Coupon Bond Prices* (Federal Reserve Bank of Atlanta Working Paper Series No. 97–10).

Weiner, S.E. (1983) Why are so few financial assets indexed to inflation? *Federal Reserve Bank of Kansas City Economic Review*, May, 3–18.

Wilcox, D. and Zervos, D. (1994) *Extracting Real Interest Rates and Inflation Expectations from the UK Gilt Market* (Federal Reserve Board mimeo, October).

Wilson Committee (1980) *Report of the Committee to Review the Functioning of Financial Institutions* (the Wilson Report), chapters 5 and 17.

Wojnilower, A.M. (1997) *Inflation-indexed Bonds: Promising the Moon*. New York: The Clipper Group, March.

Woodward, G.T. (1988) Comment: The real rate of interest: Inferences from the new UK indexed gilts. *International Economic Review*, Volume 29, No. 3 (August), 565–568.

Woodward, G.T. (1990) The real thing: A dynamic profile of the term structure of real interest rates and inflation expectations in the United Kingdom, 1982–1989. *Journal of Business*, Volume 63, No. 3, 373–398.

Wynne, M.A. and Rodriguez-Palenzuela, D. (2002) *Measurement Bias in the HICP: What Do We Know and What Do We Need to Know?* (Federal Reserve Bank of Dallas Working Paper No. 0206).

Yariv, D. (1994) *Market-based Inflationary Expectations as an Indicator for Monetary Policy: The Case of Israel* (Bank of Israel mimeo).

Yariv, D. (1997) Indexation and debt management. *Government Debt Management Workshop at the Centre for Central Banking Studies, 30 April.*

Bibliography

Bach, G.L. and Musgrave, R.A. (1941) A stable purchasing power bond. *American Economic Review*, Volume 31, December, 823–835.

Barro, R.J. (1974) Are government bonds net wealth? *Journal of Political Economy*, Volume 82, No. 6, 1095–1117.

Barro, R.J. (1979) On the determination of the public debt. *Journal of Political Economy*, Volume 87, No. 6, Part 1, 940–971.

Bohn, H. (1988) Why do we have nominal government debt? *Journal of Monetary Economics*, Volume 21, January, 127–140.

Bohn, H. (1990) A positive theory of foreign currency debt. *Journal of International Economics*, Volume 29, 273–292.

Fleetwood, W. (1707) *Chronicon Preciosum: An Account of English Money, the Price of Corn and Other Commodities for the Last Six Hundred Years.*

Friedman, M. (1974) Using escalators to help fight inflation. *Fortune*, July, 94–97 and 174–176.

Tobin, J. (1963) An essay on the principles of debt management. *Commission on Money and Credit, Fiscal and Debt Management*. Englewood Cliffs, NJ: Prentice-Hall, pp. 143–218.

Useful Websites

Country	Organisation	Website address
Australia	Australian Financial Markets Association (AFMA)	www.afma.com.au
	Australian Office of Financial Management (AOFM)	www.aofm.gov.au
	Commonwealth Treasury	www.treasury.gov.au
Bolivia	Central Bank of Bolivia	www.bcb.gov.bo
Brazil	Ministry of Finance	www.fazenda.gov.br
Canada	Bank of Canada	www.bankofcanada.ca
	Department of Finance	www.fin.gc.ca
Chile	Central Bank of Chile	www.bcentral.cl
	Ministry of Finance	www.minhda.cl
Colombia	Central Bank of Colombia	www.banrep.gov.co
	Ministry of Finance and Public Credit	www.minhacienda.gov.co
Czech Republic	Czech National Bank	www.cnb.cz
	Ministry of Finance	www.mfcr.cz
Denmark	Copenhagen Stock Exchange	www.xcse.dk
	National Bank of Denmark	www.nationalbanken.dk
Finland	Ministry of Finance	www.vm.fi
France	Agence France Trésor (AFT)	www.aft.gouv.fr
	Caisse d'Amortissement de la Dette Sociale (CADES)	www.cades.fr
Germany	German Finance Agency	www.deutsche-finanzagentur.de
Greece	Ministry of Economy of Finance	www.mof-glk.gr
Hungary	Hungarian Debt Management Agency	www.allampapir.hu
Iceland	Icelandic Bonds (hosted by the National Debt Management Agency)	www.bonds.is
	Iceland Stock Exchange	www.icex.is
	Kaupthing Bank	www.kaupthing.net
India	Reserve Bank of India	www.rbi.org.in
International	Barclays Capital	www.barcap.com
	Economic Derivatives Site	www.economicderivatives.com
	Economics Departments, Institutes and Research Centers in the World (EDIRC)	netec.mcc.ac.uk/EDIRC
	International Swaps and Derivatives Association (ISDA)	www.isda.org
	MTN-i	www.mtn-i.com
	Merrill Lynch	www.ml.com
Ireland	Housing Finance Agency	www.hfa.ie
Israel	Bank of Israel	www.bankisrael.gov.il
	Ministry of Finance	www.mof.gov.il
Italy	Department of the Treasury	www.dt.tesoro.it
Japan	Ministry of Finance	www.mof.go.jp
	Statistics Bureau	www.stat.go.jp

Kazakhstan	Ministry of Finance	www.minfin.kz
	National Bank of Kazakhstan	www.nationalbank.kz
Mexico	Ministry of Finance and Public Credit: Investor Relations Office	www.shcp.gob.mx
New Zealand	New Zealand Debt Management Office	www.treasury.govt.nz/nzdmo
	Reserve Bank of New Zealand	www.rbnz.govt.nz
Peru	Central Reserve Bank of Peru	www.bcrp.gob.pe
	COFIDE	www.cofide.com.pe
Poland	Ministry of Finance	www.mf.gov.pl
	National Bank of Poland	www.nbp.pl
South Africa	Bond Exchange of South Africa (BESA)	www.besa.za.com
	Rand Merchant Bank (RMB)	www.rmb.co.za
	National Treasury	www.treasury.gov.za
Sweden	Statistics Sweden	www.scb.se
	Swedish National Debt Office	www.rgk.se
Turkey	Central Bank of the Republic of Turkey	www.tcmb.gov.tr
UK	Bank of England	www.bankofengland.co.uk
	Glas Cymru	www.dwrcymru.com
	National Savings & Investments (NS&I)	www.nsandi.co.uk
	Office of National Statistics	www.statistics.gov.uk
	UK Debt Management Office (DMO)	www.dmo.gov.uk
	United Kingdom Parliament	www.parliament.the-stationery-office.co.uk
USA	Bureau of Labor Statistics	www.bls.gov
	Bureau of the Public Debt	www.publicdebt.treas.gov/bpd/bpdhome.htm
	Chicago Board of Trade (CBOT)	www.cbot.com
	Federal Reserve Bank of Dallas	www.dallasfed.org
	Federal Reserve Bank of New York	www.ny.frb.org
	General Accounting Office	www.gao.gov

Index

Index compiled by Annette Musker